THE
ANTHROPOLOGY
BOOK

THE
ANTHROPOLOGY
BOOK

DK LONDON

SENIOR ART EDITOR
Duncan Turner

SENIOR EDITOR
Helen Fewster

EDITORS
Tom Booth, Becky Gee,
Annie Moss, Miezan Van Zyl

ILLUSTRATIONS
James Graham

PRODUCTION EDITOR
Robert Dunn

SENIOR PRODUCTION CONTROLLER
Meskerem Berhane

MANAGING ART EDITOR
Michael Duffy

MANAGING EDITOR
Angeles Gavira Guerrero

ART DIRECTOR
Maxine Pedliham

PUBLISHING DIRECTOR
Georgina Dee

DESIGN DIRECTOR
Phil Ormerod

MANAGING DIRECTOR
Liz Gough

SANDS PUBLISHING SOLUTIONS

DESIGN PARTNER
Simon Murrell

EDITORIAL PARTNERS
David and Sylvia Tombesi-Walton

original styling by
STUDIO 8

DK DELHI

SENIOR ART EDITOR
Anjali Sachar

ART EDITOR
Debjyoti Mukherjee

SENIOR EDITOR
Anita Kakar

EDITOR
Saumya Agarwal

SENIOR MANAGING EDITOR
Rohan Sinha

MANAGING ART EDITOR
Sudakshina Basu

PICTURE RESEARCHER
Geetam Biswas

DEPUTY PICTURE RESEARCH MANAGER
Virien Chopra

PRE-PRODUCTION DESIGNER.
Anurag Trivedi

SENIOR DTP DESIGNER
Harish Aggarwal

PRE-PRODUCTION IMAGE EDITOR
Ashok Kumar

HI-RES COORDINATOR
Neeraj Bhatia

SENIOR JACKETS DESIGNER
Suhita Dharamjit

SENIOR JACKETS COORDINATOR
Priyanka Sharma Saddi

PRE-PRODUCTION COORDINATOR
Tarun Sharma

PRE-PRODUCTION MANAGER
Balwant Singh

PRODUCTION MANAGER
Pankaj Sharma

CREATIVE HEAD
Malavika Talukder

First published in Great Britain in 2025 by
Dorling Kindersley Limited
20 Vauxhall Bridge Road,
London SW1V 2SA

The authorised representative in the EEA is
Dorling Kindersley Verlag GmbH. Arnulfstr. 124,
80636 Munich, Germany

Copyright © 2025 Dorling Kindersley Limited
A Penguin Random House Company
10 9 8 7 6 5 4 3 2 1
001–337249–Sep/2025

A CIP catalogue record for this book
is available from the British Library.
ISBN: 978-0-2416-3858-3

Printed and bound in China

www.dk.com

CONTRIBUTORS

PUBLISHER'S NOTE

MIX
Paper | Supporting responsible forestry
FSC
www.fsc.org
FSC™ C018179

This book was made with Forest Stewardship Council™ certified paper – one small step in DK's commitment to a sustainable future.
Learn more at www.dk.com/uk/ information/sustainability

SUSAN PATTIE - CONSULTANT

Dr Susan Pattie is an Honorary Senior Research Associate at University College London, UK. A writer, editor, and project manager, she was co-founder and former Director of the Armenian Institute in London. Her publications include the ethnography *Faith in History: Armenians Rebuilding Community* (1996) and *The Armenian Legionnaires: Sacrifice and Betrayal in WWI* (2018).

MIRUNA ACHIM

Miruna Achim is a Professor at the Universidad Autónoma Metropolitana-Cuajimalpa, Mexico. Her research focuses on museography and the history of collection making, with a particular interest in Mesoamerican art, science, and politics. She also holds fellowships from the Beinecke Library at Yale University and the Smithsonian Institution.

PHILIPPE BLOUIN

A writer, translator, and anthropologist, Philippe Blouin is a PhD candidate at McGill University, Canada. His research interests are in traditional Kanien'kehá:ka (Mohawk) political philosophies with a view to developing a framework to understand Indigenous-led anti-development struggles. His recent publications include "Stirring the Ashes: How Mohawk Mothers Fight Against Representation" (2024).

LARA BRAFF

Lara Braff has a PhD in Comparative Human Development from the University of Chicago, US, and is a Professor of Anthropology at Grossmont College in California, US. She is a chapter author and co-editor of an open access textbook on biological anthropology: *Explorations: An open invitation to Biological Anthropology* (2019).

STACEY CAMP

Dr Stacey Camp is an Associate Professor of Anthropology and Director of the Campus Archaeology Program at Michigan State University, US. Her publications explore how different facets of migrants' identities – race, class, gender, and citizenship standing – shape their perceptions of consumerism and material culture.

PHILIP J. CARR

Philip Carr is a Professor of Anthropology and Chief Calvin McGhee Professor of Native American Studies at the University of South Alabama, US. He works closely with the Poarch Band of Creek Indians and Choctaw Nation of Oklahoma regarding the past and public archaeology.

ANA CHIRITOIU

Social anthropologist Ana Chiritoiu is a Researcher at Uppsala University, Sweden, and an editor of *Anthropology Matters Journal* for the Association of Social Anthropologists of the UK. Her research interests include kinship and politics among Roma people.

CHRISTA CRAVEN

Christa Craven is a Professor of Anthropology and Women's, Gender and Sexuality Studies at the College of Wooster, US, and co-founded the institution's Global Queer Studies minor. She is also an Editorial Board Member of the *Feminist Anthropology* journal.

ANITA DATTA

Dr Anita Datta is a Research Associate at the Guildhall School of Music and Drama, UK, investigating audience experiences of artistic performances. Her previous research while working at the University of Durham, UK, has explored knowledge production, gender, and sexuality.

LIVIA FILOTICO

Livia Filotico is a PhD candidate in anthropology at McGill University, US. Her research investigates how wild boars in Rome generate and disrupt meaning in myth, landscape, and everyday life, tracing the ways nonhumans make the world intelligible.

ALEX GOLUB

Alex Golub is an Associate Professor of Anthropology at the University of Hawai'i at Mānoa, US. His research interests are in political anthropology, particularly in mining and social change in Papua New Guinea.

EMANUELA GRAMA

An Associate Professor in the department of History at Carnegie Mellon University, US, Emanuela Grama specializes in the history of 20th century Central and Eastern Europe. Her research focuses on urban politics, memory, and cultural change in Romania.

TIM HARRIS

A writer on many subjects, including history, geography, politics, and nature, for more than 30 years, Tim Harris studied geography at university and has a particular interest in the development and evolution of colonialism.

BEN HILDRED

A Postdoctoral Research Associate at the University of Durham, UK, Ben Hildred interrogates the idea that sport can be deployed for social good. He is also the founder and director of the International Network of Sport Anthropology.

AMANDA KEARNEY

Dr Amanda Kearney is Professor of Anthropology at San Diego State University, US, and honorary Professor in Anthropology at the Australian National University. For the last 25 years she has conducted ethnographic fieldwork in Australia, Brazil, and Japan.

ROBERT L. KELLY

A Professor of Anthropology at the University of Wyoming, US, Robert Kelly is an internationally-known authority on the archaeology and ethnology of hunting and gathering societies. He was President of the Society for American Archaeology from 2001 to 2003), and the editor of the Society's flagship journal *American Antiquity* between 2015 and 2018.

JANAKA LEWIS

A professor and administrator at the University of North Carolina at Charlotte, US, Janaka Lewis is also on the board of the non-profit organization Freedom School Partners and is an Advisory Committee Member of the Women + Girls Research Alliance.

HAYLEY MACGREGOR

Hayley MacGregor is a Professor of Medical Anthropology and Global Health at the Institute of Development Studies at the University of Sussex, UK. She originally trained as a medical doctor in South Africa, where she did her fieldwork on the experience of mental disturbance in low-income urban settlements for an anthropology PhD from the University of Cambridge.

FRAN MARKOWITZ

Cultural anthropologist Fran Markowitz is Professor Emerita at Ben-Gurion University of the Negev, Israel. Her research into racialization, ethnicity, and community, and diasporas and ethnographic genres has taken her to Israel, the US, Russia, and Bosnia-Herzegovina.

OANA MATEESCU

An Assistant Professor at Babes-Bolyai University, Romania, Oana Mateescu's research looks at technology, labour, creativity, and urbanism.

JACQUELINE MESSING

Dr Jacqueline Messing is a lecturer in the Department of Anthropology at the University of Maryland-College Park, US. Her research focuses on issues of language, ideology, and racism in Mexico and the US. Her publications include "Language Acquisition, Shift, and Revitalization in Latin America and the Caribbean." (2016).

KATIE NELSON

An anthropologist and educator, Dr Katie Nelson was awarded the Minnesota State Board of Trustees Educator of the Year award in 2022. She specializes in migration in human evolution, and migration, identity, belonging, and citizenship in the contemporary US, Mexico, and Morocco.

SIBUSISIWE NXONGO

Sibusisiwe Nxongo has completed her PhD on the history of Black women in social research in South Africa in the 20th century at the University of Johannesburg. She is a Lecturer at the University of South Africa and a member of the Southern African Historical Society. Her research interests are on the transnational intellectual histories of South African Black women.

SEAN P. O'NEILL

Sean O'Neill is a Professor of Anthropology at the University of Oklahoma, US. He specializes in the Indigenous languages of the Americas and his recent publications include the *Dictionary of the Ponca People* (2019) and "Linguistic Relativity in the Age of Ontology" (2019).

NEERJA M. PATHAK

Neerja Pathak is a PhD candidate and Tutor at the University of Edinburgh, UK. Her research incorporates an ethnographic study of the first name changing practice of women post-marriage in India.

JAN KETIL SIMONSEN

Jan Ketil Simonsen is a Professor in the Department of Geography and Social Anthropology at the Norwegian University of Science and Technology. He has done extensive field research in Zambia on social and cultural change and is a former editor of the *Norwegian Journal of Anthropology*.

CHUCK STURTEVANT

Political anthropologist and documentary filmmaker Chuck Sturtevant is a Professorial Lecturer at American University in Washington DC, US. His research interests include Indigenous studies and Latin American studies.

ERICA L. WILLIAMS

Erica L. Williams is a Professor of Anthropology and Chair of the Department of Sociology and Anthropology at Spelman College, US. Her publications include *Sex Tourism in Bahia: Ambiguous Entanglements* (2013).

CONTENTS

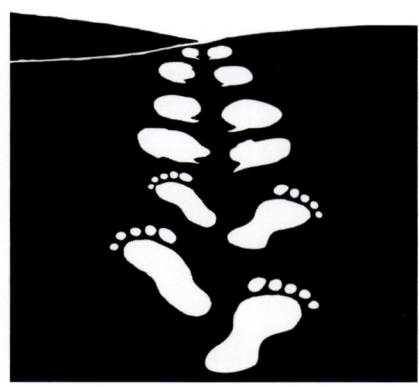
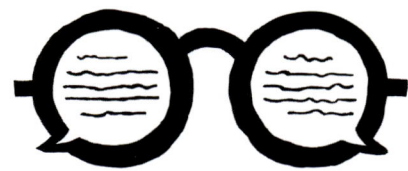

POST-WAR ANTHROPLOGY
1950–1980

CONTEMPORARY ANTHROPOLOGY
2000 ONWARDS

INTRODU

CTION

Anthropology is the study of human life from its earliest beginnings to the kaleidoscope of cultures around our contemporary world. It is holistic, exploring all aspects of what it means to be human over time and space. The field has come a long way from its early beginnings, when some anthropologists were associated with the growth of empires and colonialism, gathering data to aid their government's imperialist projects. At the same time, others used their skills to advance the causes or needs of the peoples they studied. Over the 20th century, and continuing today, anthropology has been in the vanguard of social justice, aiming to promote understanding between and about the peoples of the world.

A social science

Anthropology is a comparative social science that seeks to learn about people in their own context. It requires researchers to consider what it is like to walk in another person's shoes, whether working with contemporary people or those who came before us. It is "comparative" in the sense that anthropologists will research, for example, why people in different areas of the world take different

approaches or attitudes towards a social custom such as marriage, childcare, or economic matters. Physical, social, and economic contexts influence relationships, transactions, and beliefs, and anthropologists bring these into their overall study. The comparative aspect of anthropology is not about judging which way is better, but rather how and why people take different pathways in creating their sociocultural environments, habits, and belief systems.

Impartial attitude

The relativist approach to cultures is one of the biggest ideas in anthropology. While tolerance presents "our" way as best although others may exist, relativism sees varied ways of life and belief systems as different but neither better nor worse than one another. All are deserving of respect and dignity, a fundamental of the value of "diversity".

However, anthropology is not entirely value free. There are relatively few times and specific examples of when it is necessary to make a judgment; they are usually in times of great turmoil when ordinary life has been upended, people are endangered, and destructive actions need to

be addressed. For example, anthropologists would regard the actions of Nazi Germany as a crime against humanity. But here too, anthropologists turn to the comparative aspect of their studies to understand why and how what would be considered highly deviant behaviour becomes normalized. Generally speaking, in everyday life around the world, there are quite different approaches to common human activities, and it is helpful to think about these as possible adaptations to different histories and varied physical environments.

Alternative views

"Ethnocentrism", where other cultures are judged using one's own native frame of reference, is the opposite to a relativist approach. In our early years we learn to understand our world through the attitudes and actions of those around us but this process is often much more varied than generalizations about cultural groups would have us believe. Just as our family's genetic make-up can produce quite different – although related – members, our intellectual and spiritual approaches to life often develop quite differently to our

parents and the other people around us, while maintaining strong connections and similarities. This means that cultures – and the individuals within them around the world – are constantly evolving, changing, and adapting.

In anthropology there are no societies that are "more advanced" or "more civilized" than others. There is no social hierarchy of societies. Instead, leading early anthropologists such as Franz Boas, father of American anthropology, demonstrated that this was not a true description of cultures and cultural change. While anthropology uses comparison and context to situate its findings, it is not a judgmental comparison but one that upends and destabilizes social hierarchies, turning the lens on ourselves as well as others.

Racial issues

Anthropologists consider the concept of "race" as a social construct, not a biological fact. Race has no genetic basis – that is, no gene aligns a person with one race or another. Importantly, genetics and culture are not mapped onto each other – there is no evidence for genes predicting or being responsible for patterns in cultures. However, the popular categories of what is called race, usually based on interpretations of physical difference, have real life consequences. It is crucial to recognize that racism is real, however artificial the construct. The words "primitive" and "savage", used frequently in the early decades of anthropology were, even then, questioned by many. At the time, "primitive" was believed to be descriptive of the simplicity of life, but hid a common judgment on mental or social abilities. Boas fought against this racism – as did Bronisław Malinowski, who wrote about the complexity and skills of the so-called simple life.

Ethnography and ethnology

Ethnography combines an essential research method and a set of varied ways of writing about the culture of a people. Its most important method is participant-observation. Typically, the ethnographer lives with the people in their environment, learns their language, takes part in daily life, and where allowed, observes their interactions. Having obtained permission from the people, an ethnographer takes notes and makes recordings and videos of interviews, events, music, and other sounds around them. Often, especially in more recent years, an ethnographer will choose to focus on a particular aspect of the people's lives. This may be their religious belief systems, their foodways, their economic system, the music and sounds that are important to them, and many other possibilities.

Ethnology is an umbrella term for comparative sociocultural anthropology and its theories. Many European countries have Institutes of Ethnology or Cultural Anthropology; often they have museums that feature their nation's earlier peasant societies, and look at their own past. Ethnology and ethnography are usually combined by sociocultural anthropologists.

Fields of study

In many countries the study of anthropology focuses on contemporary sociocultural anthropology. This book takes a holistic approach, with the inclusion of biological – formerly known as physical – or evolutionary anthropology; archaeology; and linguistic anthropology. Together these broad categories provide varied perspectives that help us »

to understand life on Earth over time, and our place in the wider world. Cross-fertilization between these fields has enabled anthropology to make significant contributions to studies aimed at understanding concepts of race and racism.

Research tools

Long-term participant-observation fieldwork is usually supported by ethnographic methods such as interviews, taking life histories, open-ended questionnaires, photography, and making recordings of people, events, and the environment. The study of material objects – old photographs, books, crafts important to the people, letters, and other objects from which the anthropologist can learn about the past and present – can also add an extra dimension. Ethnographers also use kinship analysis and create kinship charts to try and understand relationships within groups.

Many of these methods are shared across the various fields of anthropology, but may be used in different ways. Some were introduced or created during the very early stages of academic anthropology and developed over time. Each area of anthropology

has a particular "tool kit", but also borrows freely from other methods of learning. Each project starts with a literature review, deep research, local language learning where needed, and making contact with others studying the people or area.

Branches of anthropology

Archaeology encompasses pre-history but extends to the present. Those who study ancient societies rely on the excavation of human artefacts, animal and human bones, pottery, and glass. Tools of all kinds – for hunting, cooking, and creating – help us to build a picture of early human life before writing began. Anthropologists can also use material remains to study more recent cultures.

Biological anthropology includes several subfields that differ broadly from each other but share methods which enable the examination of human evolution. Primatology, the study of our nearest animal relatives, uses techniques of long-term observation both in the primates' home environments and in controlled conditions. The pre-historic past is studied by paleoanthropologists who focus on human evolution using evidence found in fossil remains. Today molecular genetics adds to the

capabilities of anthropologists studying how humans and other primates have developed. Forensic anthropology also uses skeletal remains to learn about human life, often in situations connected to criminal activity, although their techniques are also used to understand historical questions.

Linguistic anthropologists use a range of methods to examine the way that culture is transmitted over generations. It is also used to demonstrate belonging to particular groups – whether social, or ethnic, or other – and, of course, to communicate with each other. Anthropologists in this field use observation, interviews, recordings, and videos, and focus on the pragmatic aspects of how language is understood in particular contexts. A symbolic system of communication, language is universal but sounds vary widely: they include clicks, particular tones, diverse accents, and many other differences. Body language, or non-verbal communication, is also a universal feature but varies widely, so both audio and visual methods are required to help understand the use of any language, as well as considering its historical, political, and social environment.

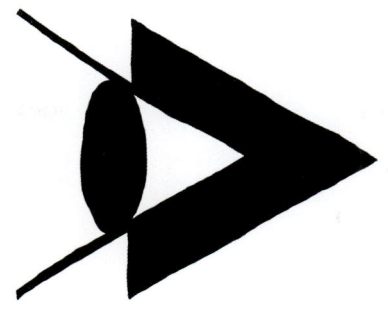

In recent decades anthropology has developed other concentrations and subdisciplines. Applied anthropology brings a practical approach in which anthropologists from all fields collaborate to find ways to improve public health, medical aid, businesses, resource management, climate change, mental health and other problems. Medical anthropology is both a theoretical and practical area that examines variables such as how different populations are affected by various diseases; how illness is understood in specific populations, and what can be learned from non-Western ways of treating illness, among other aspects of health-related treatments.

Concepts of culture

Culture has a broad meaning in anthropology. Everything is relevant, not just "high" culture such as opera or works found in a museum but all that people do, believe, and create. It is the world within which we grow, the people around us, the educational system, the sounds – both in nature and human-made – our languages, child-rearing habits, politics, economics; the list is endless. No group or people have more or less culture than others, and no culture is more or less advanced than others. While cultures have certain taboos that should not be crossed, there is great variety within those shared rules that is taken for granted as "common sense" that has been unconsciously learned. In daily practice, people everywhere stretch boundaries and make exceptions.

The diversity of human life through time and space shares some universal aspects along with generalities and particularities. Interestingly, there are few true universals but those that exist are familiar. Human babies everywhere are dependent for a long period. Human brains are complex and allow us to communicate through symbols and language, use tools, and process information. Food-sharing is also universal, and people everywhere live in groups or family units. The make-up of families and rules of behaviour within that unit vary, but one apparently universal norm, again found around the world, is that incest – sexual relations with a close relative – is prohibited; the definition of "close", however, is not the same in all cultures.

Generalities are customs or features of cultures found in many places but not everywhere. These are usually due to diffusion, the spreading of information and customs as people travel, interact, or align themselves through wars and conquests. Some new inventions appear independently, usually when physical and social conditions are similar and the people find similar solutions.

Particularities are unusual or unique aspects of culture. Here anthropologists think about where and why cultures put the most importance, investing themselves. An example is aspects of life and death: some cultures demonstrate lavish wealth at weddings while others unite a couple in a simple, private ritual. In certain cultures, death receives the highest display of wealth to honour the deceased.

Anthropology shows that culture is shared and has patterns. It is not innate, but learned from birth. It is made up of symbols and affects our perceptions and behaviour associated with biological urges and what we see as nature and "natural". It can be used creatively, and it changes over time. Cultures – and subcultures that exist within larger shared cultures – are not entirely isolated and self-contained but are adaptive and diffused, shared at different levels and ways around the world. ∎

EARLY ANTHROP

BEFORE 1918

OLOGY

Moroccan scholar Ibn Battuta **documents** his travels across the **Islamic world**.

1355

Lewis Henry Morgan suggests that **societies** pass through three **development stages** to reach **civilization**.

1877

1859

Charles Darwin articulates his ideas about **evolution** in *On the Origin of Species*.

1890

James Frazer publishes his theory on the development of **human thought**.

From the earliest times, humans have been fascinated by the customs and practices that are followed by people other than themselves. Missionaries, traders, travellers, and pilgrims – such as the 14th century Moroccan scholar, Ibn Battuta – recorded their experiences in foreign lands, and remarked on what they saw in different societies. Many of these accounts not only offer insights about the people and places observed, but often they also provide commentary that reveals something of the visitor themselves.

However, the academic discipline of anthropology is a relatively recent development. It emerged during the late 19th and early 20th centuries, and was viewed as "the science of history". In an era when scientists such as Charles Darwin began to demonstrate that natural history could be classified in particular ways and followed certain processes, it is perhaps not surprising that the anthropologists of the day – informed by superficial reports of colonial encounters – sought to identify similar laws and processes to explain the ways in which societies worked, and how civilizations developed from foraging communities into cities with organizational power structures and administrative functions. Among them were Émile Durkheim, who suggested that the shared rituals of religion – which he thought to be a universal part of the human experience – helped to hold societies together – and the linguist Ferdinand de Saussure, who looked for common elements in the structure of human languages.

Linear development
Many early writers on anthropology, including Lewis Henry Morgan and James Frazer, held ethnocentric views. They considered Western civilization to be fundamentally superior and intellectually more advanced than other systems. They also believed that "primitive" societies – such as those in the colonized places – would naturally progress towards this ideal, and move away from "savage" hunter-gatherer systems and beliefs founded in magic to become complex "civilized" societies with what they considered to be rational, scientific thought processes.

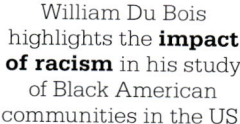

William Du Bois highlights the **impact of racism** in his study of Black American communities in the US.

Franz Boas, the father of American anthropology, promotes his vision of **cultural relativism**.

Ferdinand de Saussure's ***Course in General Linguistics*** describes structures that apply to all human languages.

1903

1911

1916

1906

1912

In a study of the **Todas** in India, William Rivers underlines the **cultural similarities** of European societies.

Émile Durkheim examines the social aspects of **religion**, and its role in creating **cohesive societies**.

The impact of this thinking – which in the 19th century was deeply embedded in Western consciousness – led to racial discrimination of the type described by W.E.B. Du Bois in *The Souls of Black Folk*, published in 1903. Du Bois challenged the notion that any one race could be biologically superior or inferior to another, and highlighted the achievements of Black people – despite the historical and social obstacles that they faced.

Du Bois was not alone in questioning the ethnocentric approach. For example, in his fieldwork with the Todas in southern India, W.H.R. Rivers noted that his research revealed similarities with Europeans, rather than their differences. However, it was the work of Franz Boas and his vision of cultural relativism that proved to be profoundly influential, and offered an alternative framework for studying different cultures.

Points of difference

Inspired by his fieldwork with Indigenous communities in Canada, Boas became convinced that every culture has ethical and social standards that reflect its own beliefs – and that these should be treated with respect. In expressing the concept of cultural relativism, Boas took the view that no culture was better than another, and that Western civilization was certainly not superior to other lifeways – it was just different. These other lifeways should not be judged by or measured against Western standards, but considered on their merits and in the context of that culture's beliefs. Rather than making comparisons with their own Western systems, Boas argued that anthropologists should first aim to understand Indigenous cultures as they understood themselves.

Often described as the "Father of anthropology", Boas became a towering figure in the field. He developed a multidisciplinary approach to the subject that embraced its cultural, biological, archaeological, and linguistic aspects, and encouraged his students – many of whom became eminent in the field themselves – to adopt his more rounded holistic approach, and reject the ethnocentric ideas of the past. ∎

TRAVELLING TURNS YOU INTO A STORYTELLER

EARLY TRAVELOGUES

IN CONTEXT

KEY WORK
Ibn Battuta, *Al Rihla*, 1355

FIELD
Pre-anthropology

BEFORE
629 CE Chinese Buddhist monk, traveller, and translator Xuanzang journeys between China and India, documenting interactions between the two countries.

1271 Venetian merchant and explorer Marco Polo begins his travels along the Silk Road. He is one of the first Europeans to visit China, where he meets the Mongol emperor Kublai Khan. His later travels take him to the Gobi Desert, Jerusalem, and Afghanistan.

AFTER
1492 Genoese navigator and colonizer Christopher Columbus sails to the Caribbean. He claims the land for Spain, and decimates the Indigenous populations.

One of the forces that has driven the development of anthropology as a field of study is an innate sense of curiosity about how different peoples live. Early anthropologists gathered the accounts of travellers, missionaries, and traders to understand the cultural diversity in other parts of the world.

An early traveller of note, Abu Abdullah Muhammad Ibn Battuta (1304–1369), was a Muslim scholar from the Moroccan city of Tangier, who travelled widely and made observations about what he saw.

The Indians address the Arabs as Saiyid, and out of respect for the Arabs the sultan also addresses them with the same title.
Ibn Battuta

A written record

Ibn Battuta intended to travel only to Mecca for the sacred pilgrimage of Hajj. However, he ended up spending 30 years journeying through the Islamic world, including parts of Europe, Africa, Southeast Asia, India, and China. When he finally returned to Morocco, the Sultan Abu Inan Faris commissioned him to document his experiences.

In the resulting travelogue *Al Rihla,* which means "travels" or "journey" in Arabic, Ibn Battuta made observations on the customs and traditions of the peoples he had encountered, describing their family structures, inheritance patterns, dress, and food, as well as political, judicial, and economic systems, education, and religious practices. His work launched a genre of Arabic travel literature that chronicled people and places, with commentary on different cultures. ∎

See also: Origins of culture 32–33 ∎ Defining ethnicity 130–31 ∎ Material culture 154–55

THEY LIVED FREE, HEALTHY, HONEST AND HAPPY LIVES
"THE NOBLE SAVAGE"

IN CONTEXT

KEY WORK
Jean-Jacques Rousseau,
Discourse on the Origins
of Inequality Among Men,
1755

FIELD
Pre-anthropology

BEFORE
1580 French philosopher
Michel de Montaigne's essay
"On Cannibals" offers a
scathing critique of Europeans
who denigrate "those ruled by
natural laws".

1651 English philosopher
Thomas Hobbes argues for a
strong government headed by
an absolute sovereign to curb
what he views as early
human's appetite for fierce
and constant competition.

AFTER
1991 Haitian anthropologist
Michel-Rolph Trouillot asserts
that anthropologists must
contest and overcome ideas
about the "noble savage".

The concept of the "noble savage" – a person who has not been corrupted by "civilization" – reflects the idea that people in rural or pre-industrialized societies live at peace with nature and each other. The figure of the "savage", noble or otherwise, has appeared in European literature since the 15th century and informed early anthropological theory. The idea is often associated with the French political philosopher, Jean-Jacques Rousseau (1712–1778), who challenged Thomas Hobbes's assumptions that early humans were fiercely competitive savages leading short, brutish lives.

A natural harmony
Rousseau described a human "state of nature" that was morally neutral and peaceful. He imagined early humans as mainly solitary and self-sufficient with an innate sense of freedom, self-preservation, and compassion for others. Rousseau insisted that there was no basis for Hobbes's view of early humans as ruthless and harsh, and

Artworks such as *Nafea Faa Ipoipo* (When will you marry?), created in Tahiti by French artist Paul Gauguin in 1892, were influenced by European ideas about pre-industrial societies.

that prior to the emergence of private property, land and resources were plentiful and available to all.

Western ideas of the "noble savage" were used to hold up racist and colonial narratives that are now subject to criticism for depicting the nuanced cultures of Indigenous societies as "savage". ∎

See also: Unilineal evolution 26–27 ▪ Culture and personality 70–73 ▪ Multilinear evolution 104–07 ▪ The ethics of anthropology 248–49

LIGHT WILL BE THROWN ON THE ORIGIN OF MAN
THE THEORY OF EVOLUTION

IN CONTEXT

KEY WORK
Charles Darwin, *On the Origin of Species*, 1859

FIELD
Biological anthropology

BEFORE
***c.*850** Arab scholar Al-Jahiz notes how animals with advantageous traits, such as effective camouflage, are more likely to survive and reproduce.

1830 Scottish geologist Charles Lyell introduces the idea of deep geological time, proposing that Earth's features form over vast periods of time.

AFTER
1942 Julian Huxley develops the "modern synthesis," which blends Darwinian evolution with Mendelian genetics.

1972 US palaeontologists Stephen Jay Gould and Niles Eldredge develop the idea of "punctuated equilibrium," which suggests that evolution can occur in sudden spurts.

Charles Darwin's theory of evolution by natural selection is one of the most influential scientific ideas of all time. Building on the work of scholars from earlier traditions, such as Arab polymath Al-Jahiz and the ancient Greek philosopher Aristotle, Darwin synthesized a theory that explained how, over generations, species adapt and change.

Darwin was born in England in 1809 into a wealthy, well-educated family. At the time, British society was deeply influenced by religious beliefs including creationism – the belief that all life was created by God – and the idea that species remained fixed and unchanging. Darwin's family, however, encouraged his scientific interests and curiosity about nature.

Journey of discovery

In 1831, aged 22, Darwin set sail on a tour of South America aboard HMS *Beagle*. As the ship's naturalist, he was tasked with studying the biology of the region and collecting specimens. Darwin's observations in places such as Brazil, Argentina, Chile, and the Galápagos Islands would later inspire his groundbreaking work on evolution.

Social Darwinism

In the late 19th century, thinkers such as British philosopher Herbert Spencer began to apply Darwin's ideas about natural selection to human societies.

Spencer, who coined the term "survival of the fittest" in his book *Principles of Biology* (1864), argued that societies – like organisms – evolve through a process of natural selection, with the strongest and most capable individuals thriving while the weak perish. This perspective echoed capitalist ideals, such as competition and individualism. According to Social Darwinists, efforts to alleviate poverty disrupted the natural order and hindered progress.

Spencer's ideas later fuelled the pseudo-scientific eugenics movement, which sought to "improve" humanity by encouraging the "fittest" members of society to have more children, and limiting reproduction among the "unfit".

See also: Unilineal evolution 26–27 ▪ The evolutionary synthesis 86–87 ▪ Origins of humanity 94–101 ▪ Multilinear evolution 104–07 ▪ Sequencing ancient DNA 290–91 ▪ Human burials 306

Darwin observed the remarkable diversity of species he encountered, noting that species living near each other often had only slight variations, while those found further apart showed more dramatic differences. In some cases, species that appeared distinct at first glance turned out to be closely related, an insight that shaped his thinking about how species evolve.

As well as studying living organisms, Darwin also collected fossils. Among his finds were fossils of extinct armadillos that he later compared with living armadillo species. The discovery of both in the same geographic region led him to question existing theories, such as catastrophism – proposed by French naturalist Georges Cuvier – which suggested that species were wiped out by sudden disasters and replaced by new ones. Instead, Darwin began to consider the possibility that species change gradually.

Darwin's encounter with the diverse fauna of the Galápagos Islands, including 13 distinct finch species, each with a uniquely

> The difference in mind between man and the higher animals, great as it is, certainly is one of degree and not of kind.
> **Charles Darwin**
> *The Descent of Man*, 1871

Comparative anatomy

can show how species are related. Darwin compared the skeletons of humans and other primates, and used similarities as evidence for common ancestry, while pointing out differences.

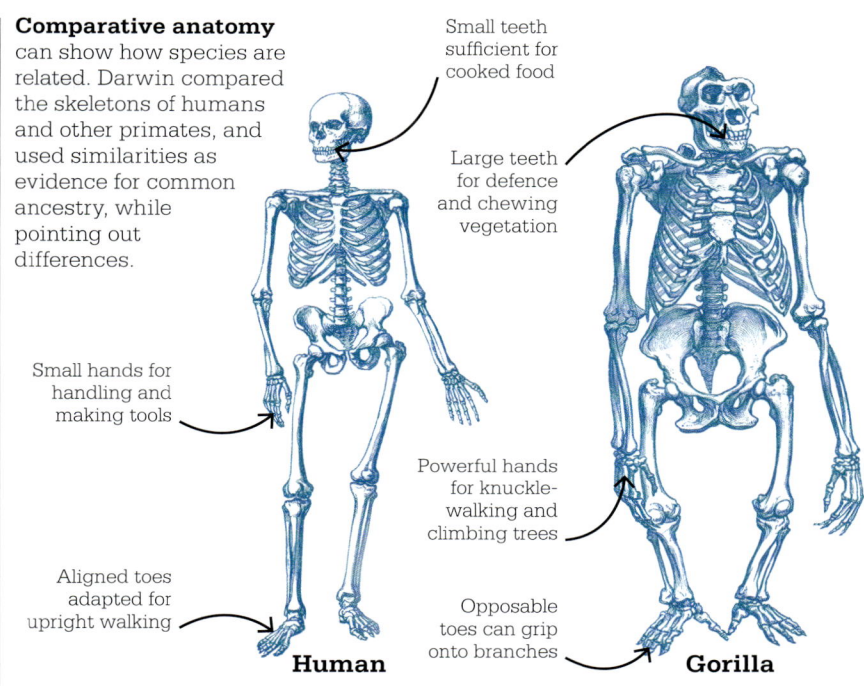

Small teeth sufficient for cooked food

Large teeth for defence and chewing vegetation

Small hands for handling and making tools

Powerful hands for knuckle-walking and climbing trees

Aligned toes adapted for upright walking

Opposable toes can grip onto branches

Human   **Gorilla**

shaped bill, sparked his curiosity about how new species form, and eventually pushed him towards a theory of natural selection.

Competing traits

After more than 20 years of research, Darwin published *On the Origin of Species* in 1859. In it, he suggested that within any population, individuals compete to survive. Each individual in the population has slightly different traits. Some traits are advantageous, in that they help the organism to survive, reproduce successfully, and pass these characteristics to their young. Individuals that have less advantageous, or disadvantageous, characteristics are more likely to die without reproducing – which means that with every passing generation, these disadvantageous traits become rarer within the population

as a whole. Conversely, as those individuals with advantageous traits continue to reproduce successfully, the presence of the advantageous traits in the population increases. Given enough time, these small changes accumulate and result in the development of a new species.

Darwin's theory of evolution had far-reaching implications. It challenged long-held religious beliefs by suggesting that humans are part of the natural world and subject to the same evolutionary processes as other species. In *The Descent of Man* (1871), Darwin applied his theory to humankind. He proposed that human evolution is also driven by natural selection. This was highly controversial, but over time it was accepted as the main evolutionary model in biology and a core perspective in biological anthropology. ■

A UNIVERSAL SEQUENCE OF SOCIAL EVOLUTION
UNILINEAL EVOLUTION

IN CONTEXT

KEY WORK
**Lewis Henry Morgan,
Ancient Society, 1877**

FIELD
Sociocultural anthropology

BEFORE
1859 Charles Darwin's book,
On the Origin of Species,
prompts speculation about
human evolution.

1864 Herbert Spencer's
Principles of Biology
introduces the phrase
"survival of the fittest".

AFTER
1884 Friedrich Engels
publishes *The Origin of the
Family, Private Property, and
the State*, which incorporates
Morgan's work into wider
Marxist theory.

1920 In *The Methods of
Ethnology*, US anthropologist
Franz Boas rejects unilineal
evolution, and advocates
understanding cultures
on their own terms.

By the mid-nineteenth century, Western scholars, influenced by colonial encounters, were increasingly aware of humanity's vast cultural diversity. Pioneering US anthropologist Lewis Henry Morgan devised a framework to categorize and comprehend this variety of societies and modes of living. Although his approach is now considered flawed, Morgan laid much of the groundwork for later anthropological thought.

Morgan was fascinated by the Haudenosaunee Confederacy, which consisted of Indigenous Iroquois nations in northeastern North America, and he wrote an influential ethnography of them in 1851. This early study sparked an interest in kinship systems – the ways in which societies organize relationships by blood, marriage, and descent. Kinship became central to Morgan's later work, as he believed it offered insights into the evolution of human institutions and social structures.

Explaining diversity

In *Ancient Society*, published in 1877, Morgan attempted to explain the reasons for cultural diversity by rationalizing the process of human development. Using insights gained from his studies, Morgan built on the existing idea that societies evolved and matured over time. Like many of his contemporaries, Morgan was ethnocentric, believing that Western civilization was inherently superior, and that the story of human history was one

Morgan recorded the minutiae of domestic life and material culture of North America's Indigenous peoples in meticulous detail – as this illustration of a Zuni water-carrier from *House-life of the American Aborigines* (1881) reveals.

See also: The theory of evolution 24–25 ▪ Origins of culture 32–33 ▪ Cultural relativism 34–41
▪ Kinship and social order 68–69 ▪ Revolutions in prehistory 74–75 ▪ Cultural materialism 124

of steady progress towards this ideal. Unlike Darwin, Morgan did not believe that humans descended from apes. Instead, he saw history as a process of moral and intellectual advancement, rather than the result of natural selection.

At the time, archaeology was still an emerging field, so scholars such as Morgan relied on the comparative method to reconstruct the past. If, as Morgan assumed, all societies followed the same path to "civilization" through specific stages of development, then contemporary "primitive" communities – being living examples of the past – could, through comparison, offer Western societies a glimpse of an earlier mode of life.

Steps to civilization

Morgan identified three key stages of development: *Savagery*, *Barbarism*, and *Civilization*, each defined by distinct modes of subsistence, technologies, kinship, and governance. He thought these stages reflected the evolution of intelligence and institutions. Technological

advancements, according to Morgan, were driven by increasing intelligence and logically built upon earlier discoveries; wagons, for example, were a development of the wheel. Similarly, institutions developed from what Morgan called "germs of thought". He argued that the earliest human societies were organized first in terms of sex, and later through kinship networks, such as lineages and clans. Eventually, as societies entered the third stage, they became centred around territory or property, developing advanced systems of governance.

Many of Morgan's ideas reflected his preconceived bias towards the superiority of European peoples and have since been proven wrong. Similarly, anthropologists no longer agree with the assumptions of the comparative method – there are no prehistoric relics, or people that time forgot. However, Morgan did leave an important legacy: he helped to establish kinship as a field of study, and posed the fundamental question of why human societies follow different historical paths. ▪

Morgan's theory of development

"SAVAGERY"
Bands of early humans hunt and forage for food, and rely on basic tools for survival.

"BARBARISM"
Communities settle, develop agriculture, domesticate animals, and forge metal tools.

"CIVILIZATION"
Complex societies emerge with written records, organized governments, and innovative technology.

Lewis Henry Morgan

Born in 1818 in New York State, US, Lewis Henry Morgan began his career as a railroad lawyer. However, his true passion lay in understanding human history and cultural diversity.

In 1843, Morgan set up an organization of white men dedicated to preserving the spirit of the Haudenosaunee Confederacy. With the help of Ely Parker, a member of the Seneca Nation, Morgan produced a full description of the Confederacy.

Morgan collected data on many Indigenous American kinship systems while he carried out

fieldwork in the western US. His writings influenced Karl Marx and Charles Darwin, and helped to establish kinship as a focus of American anthropology.

Morgan supported women's suffrage and education and left his estate to the University of Rochester to create a women's college. He died in 1881.

Other key works

1851 *The League of the Ho-dé-no-sau-nee or Iroquois*
1871 *Systems of Consanguinity and Affinity of the Human Family*

OUR RESEMBLANCES ARE MORE NUMEROUS THAN OUR DIFFERENCES
THE UNIVERSAL NATURE OF RELIGION

IN CONTEXT

KEY WORK
James Frazer, *The Golden Bough*, 1890

FIELD
Sociocultural anthropology

BEFORE
1793 German philosopher Georg W.F. Hegel publishes an essay that discusses the universal nature of religion – contrasting its objective and subjective aspects – and the principles of folk religion.

1871 British anthropologist Edward B. Tylor gathers materials from around the world, aiming to learn about human origins and processes of cultural evolution.

AFTER
1937 Based on findings from his fieldwork, British anthropologist E.E. Evans-Pritchard argues that witchcraft is a coherent and logical belief system that is similar to world religions.

In the late 19th century, British social anthropologist James Frazer was working at a time when the concept of evolution was new. It was the underlying theme of many contemporary social science studies and much scientific research, and encouraged people to rethink the meaning of life. A great collector of data, Frazer was an "armchair anthropologist". He did not conduct fieldwork and gathered much of his material by writing to missionaries, other anthropologists, and travellers around the world, questioning them about the people they encountered and observed. In this way, he was able to interpret and compare a wider range of material on religion, magic, rites, practices, and beliefs than previous anthropologists.

Evolution of thought
In *The Golden Bough: A Study in Comparative Religion*, published in 1890, Frazer explores the evolution of human beliefs in cultures over time, comparing mythologies and

Referencing J.M.W. Turner's *The Golden Bough* (1834), Frazer explored the idea that the sacrificial murder of a king or priest reflected death at harvest and rebirth in spring.

See also: The social roots of religion 42–43 ▪ Biopsychological functionalism 50–55 ▪ Local belief systems 78–79

Frazer hypothesized that human thought passes through **three** stages of development.

→

Magic involves practical attempts to **control or mimic nature** and other events.

↓

Scientific thought – based on evidence and proven by the results of experiments – **challenges religion** with its rational approach.

←

Religious ideas develop as magical methods fail. People **appeal to higher powers**, and create rituals and sacrifices to appease them.

James George Frazer

Born in Glasgow, Scotland, in 1854, Frazer studied classics and philosophy at Glasgow University. He then moved to Trinity College, Cambridge, with which he was associated for the rest of his life. He was elected four times to Trinity's Title Alpha Fellowship, and knighted in 1914. In 1921, university lectureships in social anthropology were founded in his name at the UK universities of Cambridge, Oxford, Glasgow, and Liverpool. Frazer's best-known work, *The Golden Bough*, is anchored in his efforts to understand the development of human societies and religion across the world. He introduced a far-ranging comparative method, looking for similarities around the globe, and probing for deep structures of the human mind. His later books focused on aspects of religion, such as totemism. Frazer died in 1941.

Other key works

1910 *Totemism and Exogamy*
1918 *Folklore in the Old Testament*
1936 *Aftermath: A Supplement to the Golden Bough*

describing a linear development that he believed held true across the globe. Frazer's theory was that human thought evolved through three stages: from magical, to religious, to scientific. Science, for Frazer, was the evident future, and would replace religion and magic with rational thought. Influenced by theories of evolution then current and the work of Georg Hegel, Edward Tylor, and others, Frazer opened up a new way of looking at the common ground he found among different civilizations, past and present.

Reception and influence

The Golden Bough was extremely popular when it was first published, but it was met with criticism by some anthropologists and was later dismissed by many. Frazer's theories on the evolution of religion around the world were contested by those who had done fieldwork and produced quite different findings. Edmund Leach was one of the most vocal critics, pointing out that much of the information in *The Golden Bough* was tailored to fit Frazer's preconceived ideas. Furthermore, some people resented the inclusion of the resurrection of Christ as simply another example of folklore or "pagan" religion. As a contribution to literature and folklore, however, the work was greatly appreciated. It is known to have inspired the writers T.S. Eliot, Robert Graves, and W.B. Yeats, and also the psychoanalyst Sigmund Freud. ▪

The question whether our conscious personality survives after death has been answered by almost all races of men in the affirmative.
James Frazer

EQUALITY IS NOT TO BE CONFOUNDED WITH SAMENESS

FIGHTING RACIAL SEGREGATION

IN CONTEXT

KEY WORK
W.E.B Du Bois, *The Souls of Black Folk*, 1903

FIELD
Sociocultural anthropology

BEFORE
1857 In the US, Chief Justice Roger B. Taney rules that Black people cannot be granted citizenship.

1865 The surrender of the Confederate Army brings to an end the bloody four-year American Civil War.

1896 In the case of Plessy v. Ferguson, a US Supreme Court ruling permits racial segregation in public places.

AFTER
1911 Franz Boas's *The Mind of Primitive Man* challenges racist beliefs about intelligence.

1964 The US Civil Rights Act outlaws public segregation and legal discrimination based on race, colour, religion, or sex.

In *The Souls of Black Folk*, a study of Black life in the US, W.E.B. Du Bois asserts that the experience of racial segregation, or as he termed it the "color-line", would be the key issue of the 20th century. Du Bois was primarily a sociologist, but the insights from his pioneering research into Black American communities significantly influenced other disciplines, including anthropology.

Double-consciousness

Racial discrimination was a global issue, but in the US the problem was particularly apparent in the wake of the American Civil War

Enslaved people in the Southern states **are freed** at the end of the American Civil War.

Schools, home ownership, a **banking system,** and **legal redress** are introduced for formerly enslaved Black people.

Despite such advances, **the enmity** of some white people towards Black people **increases**.

Black people are legally free, but **racial prejudice** effectively keeps them **enslaved by society**.

Prejudice cannot be removed by legislation; the problem of the 20th century is the problem of the "color-line".

See also: Cultural relativism 34–41 ▪ The fluidity of social systems 102–03 ▪ English vernacular 116–19 ▪ The role of African American Vernacular English 254–55

W.E.B. Du Bois

William Edward Burghardt Du Bois was born in Massachusetts, US, in 1868. He studied at Fisk University, Nashville, and Friedrich Wilhelm University in Berlin, Germany. In 1895 he became the first Black American to receive a PhD from Harvard University.

Du Bois became Professor of Economics and History at Atlanta University in 1897. While there, he published *The Philadelphia Negro: A Social Study* (1899), which was the first detailed sociological study of a Black American community. In 1910 Du Bois left the university and become a founding member of the National Association for the Advancement of Colored People (NAACP). He edited its magazine, *Crisis,* for 24 years. In 1934, he returned to Atlanta University as Chairman of the Department of Sociology, and remained there until 1944. Du Bois moved to Ghana in 1961 to work on the *Encyclopedia Africana*. He died in 1963.

Other key works

1920 *Darkwater: Voices from Within the Veil*
1939 *Black Folk, Then and Now*

(1861–1865) when slavery was effectively superseded by segregation. In his analysis, Du Bois powerfully describes the psychological impact of racism. He uses an image of a veil to depict the separation of the two worlds of white and Black people. The world within the veil is the Black world, which is separate and hidden. In this image, Black American people live with a "double-consciousness". Allowed no real self-consciousness, they are only able to see themselves "through the revelation of the other [white] world." For Black people, he wrote, there is always the sense of "measuring one's soul by the tape of a world that looks on in amused contempt and pity".

Dual states

Du Bois also describes a state of "twoness" caused by segregation. A Black person, he says, is simultaneously "an American, a Negro; two souls, two thoughts, two unreconciled strivings; two warring ideals in one dark body".

The history of Black Americans, he asserts, is the history of the struggle to unite these two souls into one self. Du Bois does not advocate "Africanizing" America or "bleaching" the Black soul. Rather, he says that a Black American wishes "to be both a Negro and an American, without being cursed and spit upon by his fellows, without having the doors of Opportunity closed in his face".

Du Bois's analysis was at odds with that of Booker T. Washington, an influential leader in the Black community, who recommended that Black people temporarily accept segregation in order to gain access to opportunities and develop the economic status that would earn the respect of white people.

A new narrative

In his struggle against the "color-line", Du Bois challenged ideas about the biological inferiority or superiority of certain races that were widely held in scientific and academic circles. He documented the skills and achievements of Black people and the historical and social factors that stood in their way – and found an ally in the German-American anthropologist Franz Boas, who drew on Du Bois's work in his critique of racial hierarchy. ▪

NAACP (the National Association for the Advancement of Colored People) campaigned vigorously for Black civil rights throughout the 20th century.

THE SIMILARITY OF CUSTOM
ORIGINS OF CULTURE

IN CONTEXT

KEY WORK
W.H.R. Rivers, *The Todas*, 1906

FIELD
Sociocultural anthropology

BEFORE
1871 In an example of armchair anthropology, *Primitive Culture* by E.B. Tylor draws on the written accounts of travellers to describe other cultures.

1888 Alfred Cort Haddon voyages to the Torres Strait and conducts ethnographic research among the Islanders.

AFTER
1914 Bronisław Malinowski develops participant observation fieldwork, which becomes the standard anthropological methodology.

1924 William James Perry argues that Egypt was the original site for cultural innovation, and traits diffused outward from there.

I n the late 19th century, the study of different cultures started to become less ethnocentric, as European scientists voyaged to faraway sites where they could learn about the local peoples first-hand. Renowned psychologist W.H.R. Rivers was one such scientist. In 1898, he joined the Cambridge Expedition to the Torres Strait Islands, between Australia and Papua New Guinea. Rivers collected local genealogies that revealed the social, rather than biological, basis of the Islanders' kin classification system.

Rivers then secured funding for a project among the Todas – a pastoralist, polyandrous society in India. His fieldwork culminated in *The Todas*, a book that describes all aspects of Todas life – their subsistence practices, supernatural beliefs, socialization norms, birth and death customs, and kinship and marriage rules – as well as their societal organization.

Ethnographic fieldwork among the Todas in southern India led Rivers to demonstrate the similarities between them and Europeans.

See also: Early travelogues 22 ▪ Cultural relativism 34–41 ▪ Kinship and social order 68–69

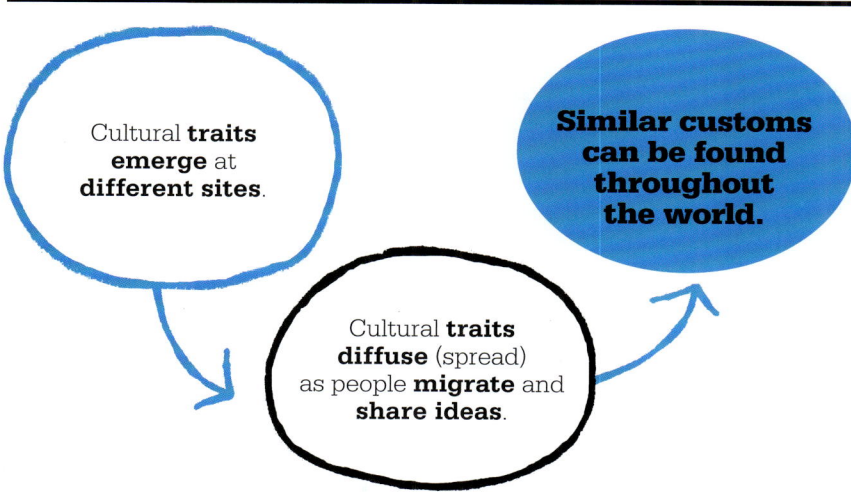

Cultural **traits emerge** at **different sites**.

Cultural **traits diffuse** (spread) as people **migrate** and **share ideas**.

Similar customs can be found throughout the world.

W.H.R. Rivers

William Halse Rivers Rivers was born in England in 1864. He trained as a doctor, surgeon, and psychiatrist and for much of his career, he was active in medical and neurological research, contributing to our understanding of the senses, the nervous system, and the effects of stimulants. He was an advocate for the humane treatment of mentally ill patients who, in the 1800s, were often physically restrained within mental asylums. From 1898, Rivers began to conduct anthropological research, first in the Torres Strait, and then India. In one of many achievements, Rivers helped to develop the genealogical method, in which the ethnographer records individual kinship diagrams in order to better understand a given society. Rivers died in 1922.

Other key works

1899 *Two new departures in anthropological method*
1914 *Kinship and Social Organization*
1923 *Medicine, Magic and Religion*

While conducting fieldwork in India, Rivers came to realize that ethnocentrism had too often led scholars to overemphasize cultural differences. To challenge such bias, Rivers conducted psychological experiments, which empirically demonstrated the profound similarities among the Todas and European peoples, specifically with respect to their sensory systems.

Moderate diffusion

According to 19th-century social evolutionists, some cultures could "progress" more quickly than others because of an innate superior innovativeness. By contrast, the early 20th-century diffusionists shifted the discussion to consider how cultural traits may be either invented or adopted. Extreme diffusionists argued that cultural traits arose in one society and spread to neighbouring groups that then adopted some of these traits. However, Rivers took a moderate approach: he argued that the ability to invent new traits could not be attributed to any one society, and suggested that traits were created in several different sites and then spread as people migrated, sharing their ways with other groups. Rivers' moderate diffusionism, along with his empirical work, contributed to an emergent scholarship on non-European cultures that emphasized similarities – not differences – and relativism, rather than ethnocentrism. ∎

There seems to be an identity of idea actuating custom in peoples very different from one another in their surroundings and conditions of life.
W.H.R. Rivers

CIVILIZATION IS NOT ABSOLUTE

CULTURAL RELATIVISM

IN CONTEXT

KEY WORK
Franz Boas, *The Mind of Primitive Man*, 1911

FIELD
Sociocultural anthropology

BEFORE
1836 German scholar Wilhelm von Humboldt writes about the connection between language and world view.

1871 British anthropologist Edward Tylor describes culture as being built around knowledge, belief, art, morals, law, and custom.

AFTER
1962 French anthropologist Claude Lévi-Strauss argues that the logic of human thought follows similar patterns across cultures.

1972 Laura Nader publishes her sardonic essay *Up the Anthropologist*, arguing that anthropologists should study the powerful as well as marginalized communities.

Dressing in traditional Inuit clothing, Boas attempted to immerse himself in the everyday life of Indigenous people.

Franz Boas is today widely regarded as one of the most influential figures in modern anthropology. His work challenged the racial and evolutionary assumptions that had shaped the discipline in the 19th century, and laid the foundation for a new approach based on rigorous fieldwork and respect for cultural differences. Boas's influence was especially strong in North America, where he trained a generation of anthropologists, but his ideas also reshaped anthropology worldwide.

The central principle of Boas's vision was cultural relativism – the idea that each culture should be understood on its own terms rather than judged by external standards. This revolutionary approach shifted the focus of anthropology from broad comparisons between societies to detailed studies of particular cultural systems. Through his support for Indigenous languages and traditions, Boas established anthropology as a discipline that was dedicated to understanding and defending the integrity of cultures in an era that was dominated by colonial expansion and "scientific" racism – the theory that sought to explain cultural and intellectual differences through biology.

Boas's cultural relativism directly countered the dominant ideologies of his era: ethnocentrism, the belief that one's own culture is superior to others; unilinear evolutionary theories, like those of Lewis Henry Morgan, which ranked societies from "primitive" to "civilized"; and

A close connection between race and personality has never been established
Franz Boas

biological determinism. His studies demonstrated that race does not determine culture and that human societies could not be ranked in terms of progress. While cultural relativism has since been debated and refined, it remains anthropology's most enduring contribution to the study of human diversity.

Journey to anthropology

Franz Boas was born in 1858 into a Jewish family in Germany, during a time when Jewish communities in Northern Europe were gaining greater social and cultural freedoms after centuries of marginalization. This period of increasing emancipation, together with global movements for equality, profoundly influenced Boas and his Jewish contemporaries, such as Albert Einstein and Sigmund Freud.

Boas's early training was in physics and geography, and he earned his doctorate in physics in 1881 in Germany. But his career took a different path after an expedition to Baffin Island in the Arctic region of Canada in 1883 to study the impact of the physical environment on the Inuit living there. For over a year Boas lived among the Inuit and immersed himself in their daily life: he learned

See also: Unilineal evolution 26–27 ▪ Biopsychological functionalism 50–55 ▪ Culture shapes behaviour 62–67 ▪ Culture and personality 70–73 ▪ Structuralism 108 ▪ Studying up 138–39 ▪ Thick description 146–53

Inuktitut to communicate effectively, meticulously mapped seasonal migration routes, and documented survival strategies for enduring the Arctic winter. He recorded oral histories, myths, and songs, paying particular attention to how storytelling reinforced communal bonds and transmitted ecological knowledge. This deep engagement with Inuit practices – far beyond mere environmental observation – marked the beginning of his lifelong commitment to ethnographic fieldwork.

A new approach

Boas's experiences among the Inuit led him to question the prevailing assumption that human behaviour was primarily shaped by geography. He observed that Inuit society was structured not just by their environment but also by systems of belief, oral traditions, and cultural knowledge. Boas argued that human life is shaped as much by ideas and imagination as by physical surroundings. Shifting his focus from geography to cultural perception, he explored how people understand their world through religious figures, mythic forces, and inherited wisdom, including the solace of music. He saw this reflected in the rich literary and oral traditions of human societies, where stories, songs, and artistic expression shape meaning.

Expanding on his work with the Inuit, Boas conducted extensive fieldwork in the 1880s and 1890s with the Kwakiutl (now known as the Kwakwaka'wakw) people of the Pacific Northwest Coast, primarily in British Columbia, Canada. Immersing himself in their society,

Ethnocentrism	Cultural relativism
Ethnocentrism relied on second-hand reports, and **rarely engaged directly** with cultures.	Anthropologists should **fully immerse themselves** in a culture, living in the community.
It believed societies progress through **the same stages of development**, with Western society at the "top".	Different societies are seen to have **radically different cultures** that shape behaviour.
Missionary work, colonial education, and governance **imposed Western values**.	**Western ideas**, such as fixed gender roles and morality, **are questioned**.
Other cultures were often considered "inferior".	**Cultures should be understood on their own terms.**

he documented their language, rituals, and social structures with meticulous detail alongside George Hunt, a cultural mediator of Tlingit and British heritage who was raised within the Kwakwaka'wakw community.

For example, Boas's study of the potlatch ceremony – a complex system of gift-giving and status negotiation that colonial authorities dismissed as "wasteful" – revealed its role in maintaining social cohesion, redistributing resources,

and preserving oral histories. By demonstrating the sophistication of Kwakwaka'wakw culture, which defied Western stereotypes of "primitive" societies, Boas challenged anthropological theories that ranked cultures hierarchically. This work reinforced the importance of understanding cultures on their own terms and formed the basis for modern ethnographic methods, prioritizing context-rich studies over broad, dehumanizing comparisons. »

This Komokwa mask is an example of the type of Kwakwaka'wakw art that Franz Boas documented – challenging Eurocentric views of Indigenous cultures as "primitive".

Over time, Boas developed a broad scientific approach to the study of humanity known as four-field anthropology. This comprises cultural anthropology, Biological anthropology, archaeology, and linguistics. Deeply interdisciplinary, it drew from the humanities – especially history, music, and language studies – while addressing nearly every aspect of human life. Boas's vision helped to establish these sub-disciplines, each contributing to a more comprehensive understanding of humankind's collective history beyond the boundaries of any single region, nation, continent, or cultural background.

Challenging racism
In the late 19th and early 20th centuries, pseudoscientific theories of race dominated academic and public discourse. Scholars measured skulls, compared facial features, and claimed these differences "proved" the superiority of white Europeans. "Scientific" racism was used to justify colonialism, segregation, and laws restricting immigration. At their core was the belief that biology determined not just physical traits but also intelligence, morality, and cultural achievement – a world view Boas began dismantling through meticulous research.

Boas rejected these claims outright. Drawing on his fieldwork among the Kwakwaka'wakw and Inuit – where he saw culture as a product of ideas, and not just the environment – he argued that race, culture, and biology were distinct. Physical differences between groups, he insisted, were superficial and had no bearing on intellectual or cultural capacity. To prove this, he turned the tools of "scientific" racism against itself. In 1911, Boas published a study analysing the head shapes of immigrants and their US-born children. He found that cranial measurements changed slightly between generations, and deduced that this was influenced by environment and nutrition. These findings undermined the idea of fixed racial "types" and showed that biology was shaped by lived experience, not heredity alone.

Boas expanded these ideas in *The Mind of Primitive Man* (1911), where he wrote: "Civilization is not something absolute, but… relative." He demonstrated that all human groups share the same capacity for innovation, although their cultural priorities might differ. For example, the intricate oral histories of Indigenous communities required memory and storytelling skills that rivalled European literacy – a direct rebuttal to claims of Indigenous "primitiveness". This work laid the foundation for modern anthropology's rejection of the belief that biology dictates human behaviour.

Putting these ideas into practice, Boas developed a range of new research methods. He used statistical analysis to expose flaws in racist research, such as biased

Franz Boas reconstructs a Kwakwaka'wakw winter initiation ritual symbolizing the transformation from wildness to communal order for a museum exhibition.

sampling or cherry-picked data. When eugenicists claimed certain groups were "naturally" less intelligent, Boas countered that such studies ignored factors such as poverty, education, and discrimination. His insistence on rigorous evidence reshaped not only anthropology but also public debates about immigration and equality. For instance, his research directly informed critiques of US immigration quotas, which targeted groups deemed "biologically inferior".

Cultural soundscapes

Boas's influence extended well beyond anthropology into the study of music and language, and he stressed their vital role as expressions of cultural identity. He argued that both are vital expressions of identity and must be understood on their own terms.

In music, Boas laid the groundwork for what later developed into ethnomusicology in the mid-20th century. He encouraged his students to transcribe and analyze song texts, focusing on their narrative and cultural significance rather than comparing them to Western traditions. This approach influenced scholars such as Hungarian-American ethnomusicologist George Herzog, whose pioneering studies of Indigenous and folk music traditions helped establish the discipline. Today, ethnomusicology still bears the unmistakable mark of the Boasian approach, with its emphasis on social context, narrative structure, linguistic analysis, and cultural relativism.

In language, Boas studied Inuit grammar, challenging the idea that it was primitive. His research contributed to the *Handbook of*

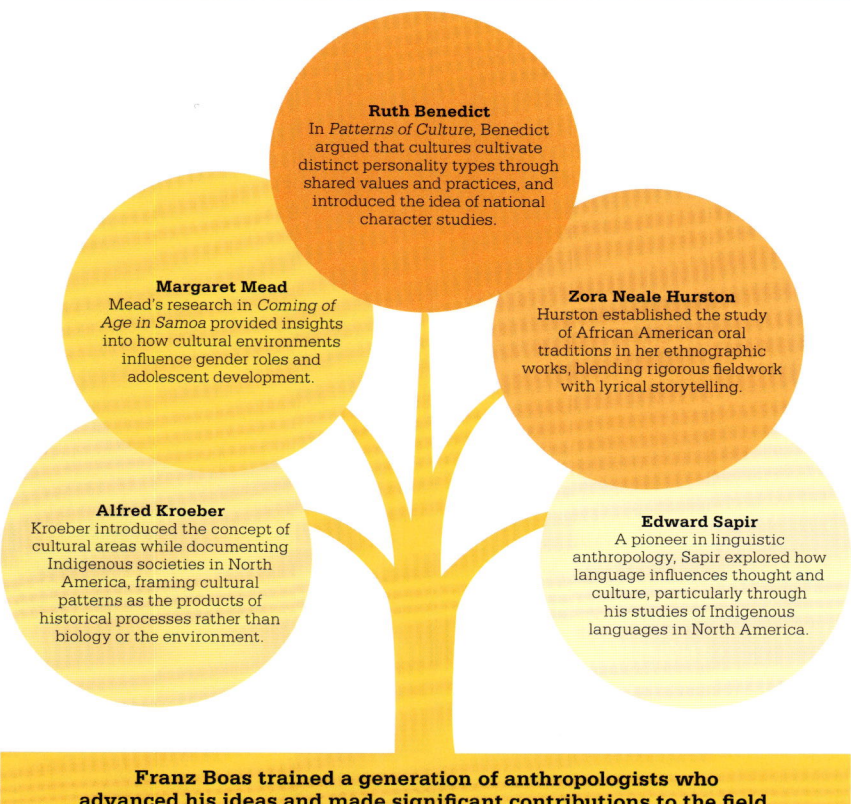

Ruth Benedict
In *Patterns of Culture*, Benedict argued that cultures cultivate distinct personality types through shared values and practices, and introduced the idea of national character studies.

Margaret Mead
Mead's research in *Coming of Age in Samoa* provided insights into how cultural environments influence gender roles and adolescent development.

Zora Neale Hurston
Hurston established the study of African American oral traditions in her ethnographic works, blending rigorous fieldwork with lyrical storytelling.

Alfred Kroeber
Kroeber introduced the concept of cultural areas while documenting Indigenous societies in North America, framing cultural patterns as the products of historical processes rather than biology or the environment.

Edward Sapir
A pioneer in linguistic anthropology, Sapir explored how language influences thought and culture, particularly through his studies of Indigenous languages in North America.

Franz Boas trained a generation of anthropologists who advanced his ideas and made significant contributions to the field.

American Indian Languages, a major effort to document Indigenous languages with scientific rigour. By integrating linguistic analysis with cultural insight, Boas and his students reinforced the importance examining languages within their own cultural frameworks.

Historical particularism

Drawing on his extensive fieldwork and his studies of language and music, Boas developed the concept of historical particularism to challenge broad generalizations about human culture. He argued that each society develops uniquely within its own historical context, regardless of external influences. Central to this perspective was a rejection of the illusion of "nominalism" – the

assumption that concepts sharing a name, such as "marriage" or "music" must be fundamentally the same across cultures. Such assumptions, Boas argued, obscure deeper, more meaningful differences in understanding.

Boas maintained that cultural elements must be understood within their full social context rather than isolated and compared superficially. For instance, he defended the diversity of Indigenous languages by meticulously documenting their sound patterns and underlying structures. Likewise, his studies of musical traditions helped to establish the idea that musical forms should be analysed on their own terms rather than judged against Western models. »

George Hunt

Born in 1854 in Fort Rupert, Canada, George Hunt was the son of a British fur trader and a Tlingit woman from Alaska. Growing up fluent in both Kwak'wala and English, he became Franz Boas's most important collaborator in documenting the culture of the Kwakwaka'wakw people.

Hunt worked closely with Franz Boas for more than 40 years, notably during the Jesup North Pacific Expedition (1897–1902), helping to record Kwakwaka'wakw language, customs, and social structures at a time of rapid change. He documented thousands of pages on Kwakwaka'wakw traditions, including potlatch ceremonies (then banned by the Canadian authorities), and played a vital role in presenting these to wider audiences. He helped to organize Kwakwaka'wakw exhibits, including the 1893 World Columbian Exposition in Chicago.

Although once overlooked in academic circles, Hunt's contributions are today recognized as essential to the study of Pacific Northwest Coast cultures.

Although he acknowledged that cultural contact and external influences occur, Boas saw each culture as a distinct system best understood through its own language and narratives. In doing so, he challenged grand, universal theories and reinforced the importance of cultural diversity.

Boas strongly argued for scientifically sound ethnography that prioritized the perspectives of the communities being studied. This ethical stance led to the development of detailed ethnographic accounts – often recorded in local languages and shaped by Indigenous viewpoints – ensuring a more accurate and respectful representation of cultural life.

The Boas school

Boas's legacy extends far beyond his own research. As a teacher and mentor, he cultivated a generation of scholars who transformed anthropology into a rigorous and socially engaged discipline. His students pioneered new methods and theories, embedding the Boasian principles – such as cultural relativism, meticulous fieldwork, and scepticism of grand theories – into the foundations of modern anthropology.

One of Boas's first doctoral students, Alfred Kroeber, founded the anthropology department at the University of California, Berkeley, which became a major centre for ethnographic research. Kroeber focused on the study of cultural patterns over time, arguing that culture operates as a collective force – what he called the "superorganic" – shaped by history and language rather than biology. His work with Indigenous Californian communities – including the last surviving member of the Yahi –

> The existence of any pure race with special endowments is a myth, as is the belief that there are races all of whose members are foredoomed to eternal inferiority
> **Franz Boas**
> *Race and Democratic Society*, 1945

helped to document and preserve their cultural practices, reflecting Boas's commitment to marginalized voices.

Another of his students, Edward Sapir, a linguist and anthropologist, revolutionized the study of Indigenous languages in North America. He demonstrated how language reflects unique cultural world views – a concept later expanded into the Sapir-Whorf hypothesis. Sapir also bridged anthropology and psychology, exploring how individual creativity interacts with cultural traditions, while his interest in music and poetry laid early foundations for ethnomusicology.

Ruth Benedict and Margaret Mead, two of Boas's most influential students, applied his ideas to the study of psychology and culture. Benedict's *Patterns of Culture* (1934) argued that societies develop distinct "personalities" through shared values, customs, and practices, while Mead's research in Samoa challenged many Western assumptions about adolescence and gender. Together, they shaped the "Culture and Personality" school, which evolved into modern psychological anthropology.

Several of Boas's students and collaborators propelled anthropology in new directions. George Hunt, for example, worked closely with Boas for decades, ensuring Kwakwaka'wakw voices contributed to the discipline. Zora Neale Hurston, one of the first Black female anthropologists and a celebrated novelist, studied under Boas at Columbia University. She documented African American folklore in the southern US states, blending academic rigour with literary artistry. Meanwhile, George Herzog pioneered the study of non-Western music through recordings and analysis of Indigenous American and African traditions.

Intellectual legacy

Boas rejected rigid theoretical frameworks, insisting that anthropology should prioritize evidence over sweeping generalizations. He distrusted dogma – even his own – and urged students to anchor ideas in fieldwork and cultural context. This emphasis on meticulous observation over abstract theory allowed his students to innovate while upholding his core principles – theory, he stressed, must grow from empirical rigour, not preconceived notions.

Even Boas's cautious approach to cross-cultural comparison had unintended consequences. Though he warned against superficial cross-cultural comparisons, students such as Alfred Kroeber and George Herzog refined comparative methods by grounding them in cultural specificity. Herzog, for instance, compared global musical traditions by first understanding their unique social meanings. This balanced methodology influenced later scholars, including Claude Lévi-Strauss, whose structuralist theories integrated Boasian attention to detail with broader comparative insights.

Throughout his long career, Boas played a major role as a public intellectual, and many of his works have had a lasting impact. His influence, and the influence of his students, extends to the present day in areas of reseach such as civil rights and the push for greater respect for neurodiversity within human communities. Despite facing backlash for his innovative contributions to modern anthropology, his work remains widely read. However, some have argued that he did not do enough to defend diversity. His critics continue to engage with his ideas and his relevance endures, carrying forward his legacy of advocating for human diversity in all its forms. ∎

What constitutes courtesy, modesty, good manners, and ethical standards is not universal
Franz Boas
Foreword to Margaret Mead's
***Coming of Age in Samoa*, 1928**

The World's Fair showcased American modernity – its gleaming "White City" masking complex debates about human progress and cultural differences.

The Chicago World's Fair

The 1893 World's Columbian Exposition in Chicago commemorated the 400th anniversary of Christopher Columbus's arrival in the Americas. It celebrated human achievements, technological progress, and presented ethnographic displays of cultures from around the world.

Franz Boas curated the fair's anthropology exhibition with George Hunt, showcasing Pacific Northwest Indigenous cultures through artefacts, reconstructed dwellings, and live performances by Kwakwaka'wakw people. Their presentation intended to emphasize the sophistication of Indigenous traditions, however some viewed the displays as reinforcing the fair's dominant narrative of Western superiority.

Boas continued to develop museum displays that showed cultural context and stressed cultural relativism. His approach revolutionized anthropological museums worldwide, although later scholars questioned if his displays truly escaped the power dynamics of colonial collection practices.

SOCIETY IS THE SOUL OF RELIGION

THE SOCIAL ROOTS OF RELIGION

IN CONTEXT

KEY WORK
Émile Durkheim, *The Elementary Forms of the Religious Life*, 1912

FIELD
Sociocultural anthropology

BEFORE
1890 British anthropologist James Frazer argues that religion evolves from magic and then develops into scientific thought.

AFTER
1937 According to British anthropologist E.E. Evans-Pritchard, religion aligns with other values and structures within a society.

1969 British anthropologist Victor Turner writes about rites of passage and their role in society.

1973 US anthropologist Clifford Geertz argues that religion must be understood within its cultural and historical contexts.

At the turn of the 20th century, social scientists began to investigate how religion shapes society. French sociologist Émile Durkheim was one of the first scholars to study the social aspects of religion rather than its supernatural features. He argued that religion was not merely a set of beliefs or rituals but a powerful force that shapes and reflects the collective life of society.

Durkheim believed that religion is a universal part of human experience, deeply intertwined with the fabric of social life. Taking a comparative approach, he studied a variety of religious practices from around the world and observed that all religions have one primary thing in common: they separate the sacred from everyday life. Sacred spaces and objects are viewed as special and fundamentally different from everyday things, which Durkheim referred to as "the profane".

A collective experience

According to Durkheim, religion originates within human social groups and functions as a collective, rather than individual, activity. He suggested that when people gather, their rituals make

This totem pole, made by a Kwakiutl artist in Canada, depicts animals and supernatural beings. Durkheim argued that a totem is a symbol of both a god and the society that made it.

them feel connected to something spiritual or greater than themselves – and they find comfort and unity in the experience. This encourages them to repeat these rituals and associate them with specific symbols – such as plants or animals – that serve as reminders of where and when they experience that spiritual feeling. These shared

See also: The universal nature of religion 28–29 ▪ Local belief systems 78–79 ▪ Structuralism 108 ▪ Purity and society 120 ▪ Thick description 146–53

Religion is a **collective experience** that originates in social groups.

→

It differentiates between the **sacred and the profane**, separating the spiritual from the everyday.

↓

Symbols or "totems" help the community to **express and reinforce** fundamental beliefs.

←

When people gather to worship, they experience a **collective feeling** and sense of community.

↓

Religion holds society together, reflecting and building on the society's beliefs.

rituals gradually form a religious system, one that each person in the group can experience individually and collectively. Eventually, the religion becomes its own entity. It evolves over time and endures even after the first practitioners are gone. It reflects the feelings and values of the society as a whole.

Serving people's needs
Durkheim saw religion as a system that adapts to meet the needs of people within a culture. It uplifts individuals and addresses their spiritual, mental, and even their physical needs. For example, certain daily tasks, such as eating, can become part of the religious tradition. When the needs of people and the community change, the purpose of the religious system also changes and adjusts to meet their new requirements.

This adaptability, Durkheim suggested, reveals how religious systems mirror the evolving feelings and beliefs of a society. However, while Durkheim viewed religion as something created by humans, this did not mean he saw it as fake or false. Instead, he looked at it in a positive way as a powerful force that promotes social cohesion and a valuable subject for scientific enquiry. The study of religion, Durkheim believed, could uncover the deep values and bonds that hold societies together. ▪

If religion has given birth to all that is essential in society, it is because the idea of society is the soul of religion.
Émile Durkheim

The anthropology of religion

Anthropologists have been interested in human religious practice since the discipline's earliest days. Although theories and perspectives on religion have changed over the past century, anthropologists remain dedicated to understanding the relationship between people's religious experiences and the broader social and cultural contexts that give rise to them.

Researchers in this field often investigate how religious beliefs address common human concerns – such as understanding the origins of humanity or its place and role in the universe. They examine the narratives that people create to answer these profound questions.

Anthropologists of religion also analyse the various ways religious beliefs and rituals appear in daily life, often in unexpected forms. Religion emerges and evolves in different forms over time and space, and many anthropologists seek to understand local meaning, context, and developments.

Mexico's Day of the Dead provides communities with a collective ritual that addresses the fundamental question of mortality.

A DIFFERENCE OF SOUND COMBINED WITH A DIFFERENCE OF IDEAS
THE STRUCTURE OF LANGUAGE

IN CONTEXT

KEY WORK
Ferdinand de Saussure, *Course in General Linguistics*, 1916

FIELD
Linguistic anthropology

BEFORE
1689 English philosopher John Locke provides an influential theory of meaning, suggesting that words pair sounds with associated ideas.

1836 German philosopher Wilhelm von Humboldt proposes an elaborate theory of linguistic relativity, alongside a quest for the principles of universal grammar.

AFTER
1921 Edward Sapir publishes a response to de Saussure with a detailed look at the vast diversity of world languages.

1947 Claude Lévi-Strauss publishes *Elementary Structures of Kinship*, inspired by de Saussure's structuralism.

A celebrated thinker of the early 20th century, Swiss linguist Ferdinand de Saussure was one of the first scholars to pursue the question of general linguistics beyond the scope of a single family of closely related languages. Instead, de Saussure followed a more abstract line of thought to consider what it was that ties all languages together.

De Saussure's brother, René, was also a linguist and may have influenced Ferdinand with his thesis (published in 1911) on word formation in Esperanto.

De Saussure's most prominent work describes the structures that define all human languages and forms the basis of his theory of signs, known as semiotics. For de Saussure, any language is a system of signs, and each sign is made of a signifier and what is signified. The signifier is not the word or sound itself, but the mental image of the word or sound. The signified is the concept we hold in our mind of what the sign represents.

Sound triggers
De Saussure characteristically fixed on two-way pairings between related aspects of linguistic structure, starting with the plane of sound, on top of which meaning is imposed. For example, the word "tree" in English suggests a plant with deep roots and a canopy of limbs. The sign from one sensory modality – such as sound – triggers a related psychological process that conjures up the idea of what a tree is. Other languages have different names for this group of life-forms, with perhaps a different sense of their interrelationships as a class of plants, but all languages are a system of relationships between the signifier and the signified.

See also: Language and cognition 88–89 ▪ Structuralism 108 ▪ The rules of language 109 ▪ English vernacular 116–19 ▪ Ritual and language 166

From there, de Saussure identified many other significant areas of parallel structure, starting with the opposition between language in the present (synchronic) and language as it changes over the course of time (diachronic). Although the structures of language may seem rigid at a given point in time, those structures clearly change over the course of history – so much so that neighbouring languages are often rendered unintelligible over a long period of time, gradually drifting from dialects into separate languages. For example, the words and grammatical rules of English in the time of Beowulf (*c*.975–1025) differ profoundly from those of modern English today, to the point where these historical texts are almost completely unintelligible to speakers now.

Pairing opposites

For de Saussure, another pairing of apparent opposites unfolds with the relationship between the signs that can be substituted for each other (paradigm) and the way the elements are ordered to convey

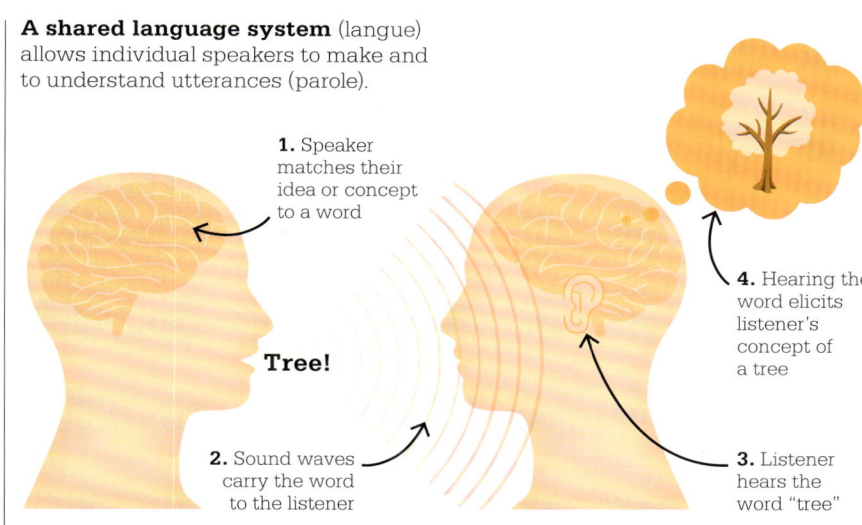

A shared language system (langue) allows individual speakers to make and to understand utterances (parole).

1. Speaker matches their idea or concept to a word

Tree!

2. Sound waves carry the word to the listener

3. Listener hears the word "tree"

4. Hearing the word elicits listener's concept of a tree

meaning (syntagm). Such an opposition can be illustrated with a simple sentence, where a noun and a verb can be paired in different ways to create a phrase with a message. A sentence such as "lions roar" joins just two words in the syntagmatic sense, creating a meaningful combination. However, this message can easily be transformed with the substitution of a single word. With the parallel construction "engines roar", there is now a metaphor in the sentence, which compares the sound of a healthy (and inanimate) machine to the sound of a living lion. Meaning is conveyed by selecting the appropriate signs and presenting them in the right order.

De Saussure's work showed that there exists a deep relationship between structure and meaning and this semiotic formula begins to explain all communication among humans. ■

Ferdinand de Saussure

Born in Switzerland in 1857, Ferdinand de Saussure became one of the giants of modern thought with his focus on the structure of language. He studied Sanskrit, Indo-European languages, and linguistics in Geneva, Paris, and Leipzig. In 1891, de Saussure returned to Switzerland to teach at the University of Geneva. He died in 1913. In 1916, the collected notes taken by students during his linguistics lectures were published posthumously as the *Course in General Linguistics*.

De Saussure's writings and teachings gave rise to contemporary linguistics and, with their focus on structural traits shared by all human languages, they inspired many developments in discourse analysis, which focuses on the messages sent by language in semiotic terms.

Other key works

1879 *Memoir on the primitive vowel system in Indo-European languages*

ANTHROP
BETWEE
WARS
1918—1950

OLOGY
N THE

Bronisław Malinowski sets out the **participant-observation** methodology.

Margaret Mead studies the **emotional development** of teenagers in different **cultural contexts**.

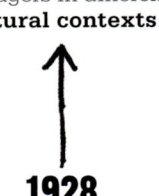

Ruth Benedict looks at the **psychological link** between **cultural norms** and individual **personality traits.**

1922

1928

1934

1925

1931

1936

Marcel Mauss examines the **social dynamics** and **rituals** at play when people **exchange gifts**.

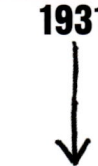

Alfred Radcliffe-Brown explores how **kinship** plays a part in maintaining **social order**.

Vere Gordon Childe argues that **changes** in **early human societies** were driven by **economics**.

The years between the two World Wars were formative ones for anthropology. During this period, the field began to define itself more clearly as a modern discipline, developing new methods, theories, and questions. While earlier anthropologists had often relied on second-hand accounts or short visits to distant places, a new generation of scholars began to take fieldwork more seriously. Many of the most influential ideas from this era emerged from long-term, immersive studies, where anthropologists lived among the communities they studied.

Immersive approach

One of the most influential figures of the time was Bronisław Malinowski, who undertook fieldwork in the Trobriand Islands during World War

I. His work set a new standard for ethnographic research. Rather than observing from a distance, Malinowski argued that anthropologists needed to live alongside the people they studied – learning the local language and joining in everyday activities. This approach, known as "participant observation", soon became central to the discipline.

From his work in the Pacific, Malinowski developed a theory known as functionalism. He argued that every part of a society – its kinship structures, religious practices, or economic exchanges – served a purpose. According to his theory of biopsychological functionalism, institutions develop in response to basic human needs, such as the need for food, shelter, and social belonging.

Other anthropologists, such as Alfred Radcliffe-Brown, developed related ideas, seeing society not in terms of individual needs but as a system that maintains social order through roles and relationships. For Radcliffe-Brown and his students, kinship – the ways in which people are related – was particularly important in shaping how societies hold together.

Boas's legacy

The interwar period also saw anthropology expanding in new directions outside Europe. In the US, the influence of Franz Boas continued to shape the discipline. His commitment to cultural relativism – the idea that each society should be understood in its own terms – laid the foundation for a series of landmark studies by his

Zora Neale Hurston uses **insights** from her **lived experience** to take **ethnography** to a new level.

Audrey Richards develops a **holistic method** for studying issues around **food** and **nutrition**.

Julian Huxley shows that **natural selection** and **genetic factors** both contribute to **evolution**.

1935

1939

1942

1937

1939

1950

Edward Evans-Pritchard explains the **rationale** behind different **world views** and **belief systems**.

Elsie Clews Parsons makes **cross-cultural comparisons** to assess patterns of **similarity** and **difference**.

Writings by Benjamin Whorf provide insights on the way that **language shapes human thought**.

---

students. Margaret Mead and Ruth Benedict, for example, explored how cultural environments shaped people's personalities and values. In Samoa, Mead's research on adolescent girls challenged American assumptions about teenage behaviour, arguing that sexual norms were not universal but culturally conditioned. Benedict, meanwhile, developed the idea that each culture has a distinct personality, shaped by its shared beliefs and values.

Another of Boas's students, Zora Neale Hurston conducted pioneering work in African American communities. Trained in anthropology but also a writer and folklorist, she used her own voice and experiences to reflect on her fieldwork – an early form of what is now known as autoethnography.

Patterns in history

During the same period, archaeology was becoming more systematic. Scholars like V. Gordon Childe combined archaeological evidence with insights from anthropology to trace long-term patterns in human history. Childe introduced concepts such as the Neolithic Revolution, which described the shift from hunting and gathering to agriculture and permanent settlements. He also helped link changes in material culture to broader social transformations.

Linguistic anthropology also developed in important ways. Building on Boas's legacy, Benjamin Whorf argued that language shapes thought – that the words and grammar of a language influence how its speakers perceive and

understand the world. This idea helped raise important questions about the relationship between language and culture.

In France, Marcel Mauss offered new insights into how societies are held together. He described how systems of reciprocity – the giving and receiving of goods, favours, or support – create lasting social bonds. Gift exchange, Mauss argued, was not simply about economics, but about building trust and obligation over time.

Across all these developments, one theme stood out – a growing recognition that societies must be understood on their own terms. Whether studying rituals, economies, languages, or daily routines, anthropologists of this period developed new ways to understand how people live. ■

HOW RULES BECOME ADAPTED TO LIFE

BIOPSYCHOLOGICAL FUNCTIONALISM

IN CONTEXT

KEY WORK
Bronisław Malinowski,
***Argonauts of the Western Pacific,* 1922**

FIELD
Sociocultural anthropology

BEFORE
1891 British anthropologist Herbert Spencer's "organic analogy" theory suggests that societies are like biological organisms.

1898 A British expedition to the Torres Strait, between Australia and New Guinea, is an early example of first-hand anthropological fieldwork.

AFTER
1957 Former colleagues of Malinowski reassess his work in the book *Man and Culture*.

1967 Malinowski's widow publishes his private diary. It reveals his ethnocentric biases and leads to scrutiny of his legacy.

Prior to the 20th century, anthropological studies were largely based upon the written accounts of explorers, missionaries, and traders. These narratives reflected their authors' ethnocentric views while focusing on specific interests – for instance, missionary reports would portray Indigenous people as "savages" in need of Christian salvation. Since so-called "armchair anthropologists" analysed these accounts without conducting any fieldwork, their studies reiterated the stereotypes espoused by their sources.

This began to change in the late 1890s, when German anthropologist Franz Boas embraced the idea of participant-observation fieldwork. Then, in the second decade of the 20th century, Bronisław Malinowski continued Boas's work to bring anthropology "off the verandah".

Participant observation

Off the eastern coast of Papua New Guinea lie the Trobriand Islands, an archipelago of 28 coral atolls. Malinowski spent extended periods of time here between 1915 and 1918, and his research resulted in several enduring

Realizing human nature in a shape very distant and foreign to us, we shall have some light shed on our own.
Bronisław Malinowski

contributions to anthropology, including the development of biopsychological functionalism.

Unlike other anthropologists of his day, Malinowski chose to immerse himself completely in the lives of the Trobrianders. He resided among them in their villages, learned their language, spoke with them, engaged in their practices, and ultimately came to appreciate their world view.

Malinowski's experiences laid the groundwork for participant-observation methodology, which involves studying a culture by

Bronisław Malinowski

Born in Kraków, Poland, in 1884, Bronisław Malinowski studied mathematics and philosophy at college, before pursuing an advanced degree in anthropology at the London School of Economics (LSE). He was inspired to become an anthropologist after reading Sir James George Frazer's book *The Golden Bough* (1890), which examines magical, religious, and scientific systems over time.

Malinowski had initially intended to study the systems of exchange among Aboriginal Australians; however, he shifted his focus to the study of the people in Melanesia, specifically the Trobriand Islanders, during his stay there in the mid-1910s.

After World War I, Malinowski taught at LSE for two decades. World War II broke out while he was on sabbatical leave in the US, which caused him to remain there until his death in 1942.

Other key works

1926 *Myth in Primitive Psychology*

See also: The theory of evolution 24–25 ▪ Unilineal evolution 26–27 ▪ Cultural relativism 34–41 ▪ Kinship and social order 68–69 ▪ Local belief systems 78–79

Armchair anthropologists **read accounts** written by **explorers**, colonists, and missionaries.

Expeditions to the Torres Strait, New Guinea, and other destinations lead anthropologists to **fieldwork**.

Surveys and **observations** made from the verandah maintain the anthropologist's **distance from the people**.

Full immersive participant-observation fieldwork reveals an insider's perspective.

immersing oneself fully within it. While participating in the daily lives of the people, the anthropologist makes detailed observations and records them as field notes. The goal is to understand the beliefs and practices of the people from their own perspective, rather than rely upon an outsider's viewpoint or second-hand accounts.

Modern ethnography

Malinowski's extensive field research in the Trobriand Islands resulted in his 1922 book *Argonauts of the Western Pacific*. Considered to be the first modern ethnography, the book has been lauded for its thorough culturally relativistic description of another society.

Argonauts begins with a detailed introduction to participant-observation methodology and the purpose of ethnography: namely, to understand another culture from the emic (insider) point of view. The book then turns to the fundamental unit of Trobriand life: the village.

Malinowski, in white, joins a group of Trobrianders in eating from a lime gourd. He believed that taking part in everyday rituals would lead to a better understanding of the local culture.

Malinowski describes how the village social structure relies upon a matrilineal kinship system and totemic clans led by ruling chiefs.

In the village, subsistence was based on small-scale gardening, with yams having special significance beyond serving as a food source. The Trobrianders would construct yam houses in the village centre; chiefs had multiple and more elaborate yam houses.

Malinowski also documented the Trobrianders' magical beliefs and practices, particularly the ways that gardening magic and fishing magic were integral to ensuring

productive outcomes, as well as the role of magic in local explanations of death and disease.

The kula ring

Several chapters of *Argonauts* are dedicated to the kula ring, a ritualized system of exchange throughout the region. Islanders would spend years building canoes in preparation for a kula ring expedition. To ensure safe passage, Trobrianders would take part in magical rituals before the voyage. Participants travelled from island to island, exchanging white shell armbands (known as *mwali*) and »

> There are no peoples, however primitive, without religion and magic.
> **Bronisław Malinowski**
> *Magic, Science, and Religion, and Other Essays*, 1925

A group of Trobrianders pose outside a dwelling hut shaded by tall palm trees. In the background is Malinowski's tent, which he pitched near the centre of the village.

red shell necklaces (*soulava*). On arrival at each island, individuals would meet their trading partner and exchange the gifts in a scripted fashion. Not everyone could participate in these exchanges: they were reserved for individuals who already had some wealth and status.

Researching the kula's cultural functions, Malinowski found that, while the armbands and necklaces had no monetary value, they had immense social value. In Western societies, the exchange of goods has an economic purpose: the accumulation of goods allows one to display personal wealth and societal position. By contrast, for the Trobrianders, exchanging the jewellery served to build and sustain social relationships in a culture where relationships – more than money – enabled people to achieve an elevated status.

A new theory of culture

Malinowski's fieldwork led him to develop a new theory of culture known as biopsychological functionalism, which differed from the two prevailing theories of the time – social evolutionism and diffusionism.

Evolutionists saw cultures as more or less "civilized" according to their inherent qualities. In this view, European societies were the tip of a developmental trajectory that "primitive" societies aspired to, with varied degrees of success. Diffusionists asserted that cultural traits only developed in privileged centres of innovation. For example, Australian anatomist Grafton Elliot Smith argued that all cultural traits evolved in Egypt and then diffused elsewhere. In Germany, geographer Friedrich Ratzel and ethnologist Fritz Graebner claimed that cultural traits arose in a small number of cultural centres, then spread via human migration. From a diffusionist viewpoint, only a few cultures were innovators, while all others adopted or adapted pre-existing traits.

This kula ring bracelet was sourced by Malinowski in the Trobriand Islands. The main overlapping ring is made from conus shell, with pendant strings of banana seeds and glass beads.

Both social evolutionism and diffusionism are diachronic theories that focus on the historical antecedents of present-day cultural forms. Both theories also express ethnocentric views about European superiority, while failing to recognize that social variations are equally valid. By contrast, participant-observation fieldwork allowed Malinowski to engage in synchronic, holistic analyses to explain how a culture functions for the individuals within it.

A two-pronged approach

Malinowski's biopsychological functionalism relied upon two key concepts: needs and institutions. Needs encompass the biological and psychological requirements that all humans share, including safety, growth, and health.

These needs are innate and universal, but the social responses to them vary by culture. For example, all humans have a biological need to eat. However, nutritional needs are not just satisfied on an individual basis. Rather, they involve a system of food acquisition, context for food consumption, political rules about food distribution, and cultural decisions about what counts as edible. For instance, while many people consider pork to be food, Jewish and Muslim cultures forbid the consumption of pigs.

The second key concept is institutions, which are forms of social organization comprising persons, a charter, a set of norms, activities, and material apparatus. Each institution – the family, education, or government – directs the social responses that fulfil individual needs.

While Malinowski's theory emphasized individual needs, another version of functionalism,

developed by his contemporary Alfred Radcliffe-Brown, focused more on societal needs. According to Radcliffe-Brown's structural-functionalism, the parts of society function to maintain the society as a whole. Individuals are interchangeable: one person's role can be fulfilled by another person, as long as the society persists.

Critique of functionalism

While functionalism offers a more culturally relativistic perspective than earlier theories, it fails to account for cultural traits that may not fulfil a need or maintain social order. Some aspects of culture might be meaningful, symbolic, or historical, but lack an identifiable purpose. Other anthropologists believe that functionalism places too much emphasis on the cohesiveness of culture, thereby overlooking social dysfunction and intercultural conflict.

Despite these criticisms, Malinowski's methodological and theoretical contributions were integral to a contemporary anthropology that was grounded in participant-observation and cultural relativism. ∎

Malinowski's students

The impact Malinowski had on anthropology can be measured by the work of his students, who built upon his theoretical and methodological contributions.

An advocate of analysing society using empirical data obtained via fieldwork, South Africa's Meyer Fortes utilized functionalist approaches to understand political systems in several African societies.

Briton Lucy Mair worked in Uganda, examining social change and development, while her compatriot E.E. Evans-Pritchard conducted extensive fieldwork among the Nuer and Azande societies in Africa. Although influenced by Malinowski, his brand of functionalism was closer to the structural functionalism of Radcliffe-Brown. Evans-Pritchard emphasized how culture sustains society as a whole, attending to collective needs, rather than to individual biological or psychological needs.

Biopsychological functionalism alleges a cultural response to a series of basic human needs. For example, the need for bodily comfort is universally satisfied by shelter; however, the way a shelter is designed, which materials are used, and other such factors are determined by culture.

Basic need	→	Social response
Metabolism	→	Food acquisition
Reproduction	→	Kinship system
Bodily comfort	→	Forms of shelter
Safety	→	Protection
Movement	→	Activities
Growth	→	Training
Health	→	Hygiene

FORGING A NATION OUT OF TWO METALS
THE INDIGENISMO MOVEMENT

IN CONTEXT

KEY WORK
Manuel Gamio, *La población del valle de Teotihuacan (The People of the Teotihuacan Valley)*, 1922

FIELD
Sociocultural anthropology

BEFORE
1585 *The Florentine Codex*, an account of the culture and history of the Indigenous peoples of Mexico, is published.

1910 The Mexican Revolution begins. It is the start of a decade-long struggle for social and political reform.

AFTER
1940 The First Inter-American Indigenous Conference takes place in Mexico to promote the spread of Indigenist ideas across Latin America.

1979 Ángel Palerm publishes *Anthropology of Marxism*, which highlights the role of class struggles in Mexican society.

In the early 20th century, the *Indigenismo* movement emerged in Latin America, campaigning for the rights and cultural recognition of Indigenous peoples. Using various methods – including literature, the visual arts, and anthropology – the movement aimed to address historical injustices faced by Indigenous communities since the arrival of the Spanish in the 1490s.

Building a nation
The Mexican Revolution of 1910 sparked a wave of nationalism that embraced *mestizaje*, the blending of Indigenous and Spanish heritage. Rejecting American and European

In order to incorporate the Indian, we must not attempt to "Europeanize" him.
Manuel Gamio

influences, Mexican intellectuals promoted a national identity grounded in this mixed heritage. This was not only reflected in artistic expression and celebrations of Indigenous culture, but also in government policies such as education programmes and land reform. Anthropologists, in particular Manuel Gamio, played a key role in shaping this ideology. They studied Indigenous communities, documenting their languages, customs, and social

Diego Rivera's murals in the National Palace, Mexico City, incorporate images from the history and folklore of Indigenous people.

See also: Cultural relativism 34–41 ▪ Local belief systems 78–79 ▪ The fluidity of social systems 102–03 ▪ Ritual and language 166 ▪ DNA politics 282–83

Indigenismo **encourages respect** for Indigenous cultures.

↓

Educational support empowers Indigenous communities while respecting their culture.

↓

Economic development allows Indigenous communities to **thrive**.

↓

Political participation gives Indigenous communities a voice in **decision making**.

↓

Indigenismo **helps to create an inclusive national identity.**

Manuel Gamio

Born in Mexico City in 1883, Manuel Gamio was a pioneering anthropologist best known for his activism and work to preserve Indigenous cultures in Mexico.

After studying archaeology in Mexico City, Gamio went on to pursue a PhD in anthropology at Columbia University under Franz Boas, where he was influenced by Boas's ideas on cultural relativism. Upon his return to Mexico, Gamio led a number of archaeological projects, including the excavations at Teotihuacán. However, from 1925 onwards, Gamio shifted his focus to promoting Indigenous rights.

In the 1930s, Gamio held positions in the Secretariat of Agriculture, and at the Institute for National Social Research. In 1942, he became director of the Inter-American Indigenous Institute, where he worked until his death in 1960.

Other key works

1916 *Forjando Patria (Forging a Fatherland)*
1931 *The Mexican Immigrant: His Life Story*
1935 *Hacia un México Nuevo (Towards a New Mexico)*

structures. Gamio also helped the government to establish institutions to help assimilate Indigenous groups into Mexican society and the country's economic life, and integrate them into the nation state.

Gamio's influence extended beyond Mexico, and set a precedent for many other Latin American countries, including Peru. Like its Mexican counterpart, the Peruvian *Indigenismo* movement sought to integrate Indigenous populations into modern society while addressing the legacy of the country's colonial past. However, Peru's government – unlike Mexico's – did not fully embrace the movement. This led intellectuals such as José Carlos Mariátegui to connect Indigenous struggles to broader class issues and argue for revolutionary change, envisioning an agrarian socialist future rooted in Inca traditions.

A paternalistic approach?

Indigenismo is often praised for creating a platform to discuss Indigenous issues, but it has also faced criticism for operating within colonial notions of racial hierarchy. Although it aimed to break down harmful stereotypes, it sometimes reinforced others. Additionally, it sometimes overlooked the autonomy of Indigenous groups and the complexities of their communities. While *Indigenismo* empowered a new, more inclusive identity, it often used paternalistic methods to do so. ■

BALANCING ACCOUNTS
THE CONCEPT OF RECIPROCITY

IN CONTEXT

KEY WORK
Marcel Mauss, *The Gift*, 1925

FIELD
Sociocultural anthropology

BEFORE
1893 French sociologist Émile Durkheim's *The Division of Labour in Society* explores the roots of social cohesion.

1902 In *Human Nature and the Social Order*, US sociologist Charles Cooley suggests that social order emerges from the individual self.

AFTER
1958 French anthropologist Claude Lévi-Strauss develops his theory of structuralism.

1986 According to French anthropologist Louis Dumont, individualism is a dominant force in modern Western society and philosophy.

I
n 1925, French anthropologist Marcel Mauss explored the universal phenomenon of giving and receiving gifts in his book *The Gift: The Form and Reason for Exchange in Archaic Societies*. Central to his investigation was the question of whether a gifted object has the power to inspire its recipient to respond in kind, and pay it back.

Mauss's inquiry went back in time to pre-capitalist societies as he considered ancient Roman, Germanic, and Indo-European laws. He also examined diverse cultural practices in the modern-day Indigenous societies of North America, Polynesia, and Melanesia

What rule of legality and self-interest ... compels the gift that has been received to be obligatorily reciprocated?
Marcel Mauss

through the ethnographic findings of contemporaries such as Bronisław Malinowski and Alfred Radcliffe-Brown. Through this vast survey, Mauss developed a view of the gift that illustrates a theory of social relationships.

In contemporary capitalist societies, people often regard an exchange in purely economic terms. When selling an item, an individual wants to receive a fair price for it, or – better yet – funds that will

The reciprocal nature of gift-giving is particularly evident at Christmas. A mutual exchange of presents is an acknowledgment of appreciation and a ritual that solidifies relationships.

augment their individual wealth. Even when giving a "free" gift, a person expects to receive a gift of equal value in the not-so-distant future. Yet whenever and wherever exchange occurs, it is seldom just an economic matter.

Mutual enrichment

In Germanic pre-market societies, people used an institution known as the *Gaben*, from the verb *geben*, meaning "to give". The *Gaben* would occur after key life events – such as baptisms and marriages – when guests would collectively repay the hosts by giving them gifts that exceeded the expenses incurred as part of the celebration. These repayments were designed to maintain social cohesion.

Germanic law also included a "pledge". Along with the sale or loan of an item, an individual

would transfer an object of little economic value but great personal significance – a life token – such as a coin, a pin, or a glove. The recipient would keep this token as a physical bond between giver and receiver that served as a reminder to fulfil their side of the contract by returning what they owed. »

Marcel Mauss

Considered the father of French ethnology, Marcel Mauss was born in the Vosges department of northeastern France in 1872. Before turning his attention to sociology and anthropology, Mauss studied philosophy at the University of Bordeaux, where he was tutored by his uncle, Émile Durkeim. Together they published a journal, *L'Année Sociologique*. They also developed a new "sociology of knowledge", which analysed the cultural context of knowledge.

Much of Mauss's career was affected by political events in Europe. An active socialist, he was a member of the French Workers' Party; then, in 1931, he became the chair of sociology at the Collège de France. His academic career, however, was cut short by Germany's invasion of France and the anti-Semitic laws that barred him, as a Jewish person, from working in academia. Mauss died in 1950.

Other key work

1902 *A General Theory of Magic*

> To refuse to give,
> to fail to invite, just
> as to refuse to accept …
> is to reject the bond of
> alliance and commonality.
> **Marcel Mauss**

Gift-giving in India also conveys reciprocity. However, according to classical Hindu law, this need not occur in the present world. For example, food or fertile land that is gifted will be returned, in augmented form, to the giver in the next life, if not within the next year. Gifting, therefore, eventually enriches both giver and receiver.

Spiritual essence

To understand how and why items exchanged create this connection, Mauss turned to the Maori concept of *hau*, which translates as "spirit" or "soul". The Maori believe that

Maori objects are thought to hold within them the *hau*, or soul, of their owners – in the case of this ornately decorated wahaika club, the spirit of a courageous warrior.

hau infuses the forest and other aspects of nature, but it can also infuse material objects. People in modern-day capitalist societies tend to view objects as soulless things with an economic value. Mauss, however, considered the possibility that objects might contain supernatural essences – the souls of their original owners to whom they yearn to return. In this way, possessions continue to "hold" their origins, so that when a person receives a gift, they also receive a piece of the giver. Since accepting something "is to accept some part of [the giver's] spiritual essence", it is imperative to give back in order to restore moral balance. When reciprocity fails to occur, it is interpreted as a total rejection – not of the gift but of the giver.

Mauss suggested that the concept of *hau* was also at play in the exchange system of the Trobriand Islands, an archipelago off the coast of Papua New Guinea. There, in the early 20th century,

Polish anthropologist Bronisław Malinowski witnessed a local institution known as the kula ring: individuals would travel by canoe across miles of open sea to exchange armbands for necklaces – or vice versa – with designated trading partners on another island. The participants were men of status, whose positions were elevated as they accumulated more pieces of jewellery. However, the objects themselves had little economic value. What they had was social value: they contained the essence (*hau*) of their former owners, which connected each recipient to every person that had previously owned them.

Competitive gifting

The Trobrianders' exchange of jewellery wove the islands together into an integrated social whole. In a culture where relationships, more than money, could enhance one's status, these connections had great significance. However, the

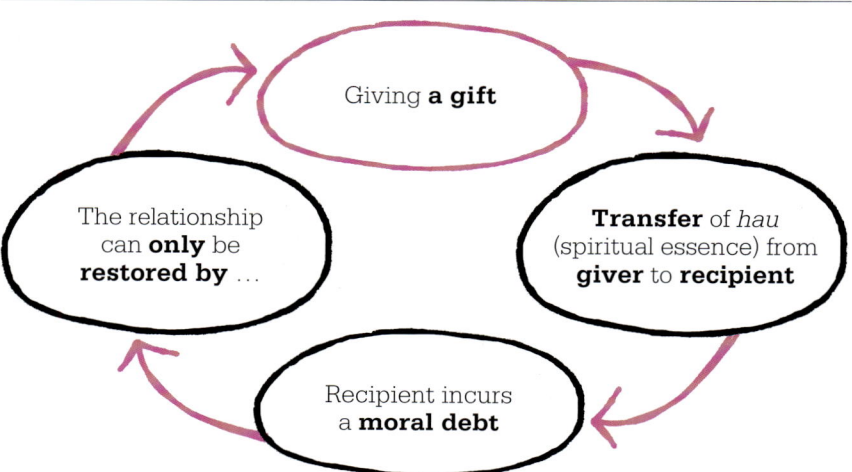

exchange of goods can also highlight inequality and discord. Mauss considered these aspects in the context of the potlatch, a gift-giving ceremony with an Indigenous American name that means "to consume".

The potlatch occurs within many cultures, including the Haida and Tlingit of America's Pacific Northwest. In these hierarchical societies, a chief has more material wealth and higher social status than the common people. This wealth is on full display at the potlatch, a large party to which the chief invites members of his own group, along with the people and chiefs of neighbouring groups. At this festival with music, dancing, and feasting, the chief gives away all his possessions. What he does not give away, he destroys, setting his things on fire in an overt display of power.

As the potlatch comes to an end, the chief declares that his generosity has brought shame upon the neighbouring group's chief, whose people have received much more from him than from their own leader. The neighbouring chief is therefore compelled to throw an even bigger potlatch, one that will take years of planning and preparation. Choosing not to reciprocate would bring dishonour upon himself and spark mistrust between the groups. So ensues an ongoing series of potlatches that can be characterized as a form of "fighting by giving" – a competition of one-upmanship – as each chief strives to give more than his group received.

A social phenomenon

Mauss looked beyond the economics of exchange, and he concluded that objects inspire cycles of giving and receiving as they move between people. It is for this reason, he argued, that gifts are not free: every gift carries the moral obligation to give back. It is by circulating things, along with their personal essences, that gifts can be considered "total social phenomena". By bringing together institutions – such as religion and the law – with an individual's personal status, honour, and prestige, gift-giving becomes a crucial mechanism by which humans create and sustain the only thing of real value: social relationships. ∎

Potlatch gifts over time
19th-century gifts
Animal hides, intricately carved wooden boxes, canoes, cedar-bark blankets, fish oil
20th-century gifts
Hudson's Bay blankets, furniture, carvings, fish oil, flour, sugar
21st-century gifts
Silver jewellery, towels and fabrics, fish oil, flour, sugar, coffee

Social capital

The rules around gift-giving identified by Mauss helped to lay the foundations for the work of French sociologist Pierre Bourdieu. Working in the 1960s, Bourdieu observed that people of the same class typically held a similar world view, as well as shared tastes and cultural values. He believed that these similarities arose from a shared disposition, or "habitus"; somehow, people had come to like and dislike the same things, and this gave them a sense of place and an awareness of how they fitted into one class or another.

In *Outline of a Theory of Practice* (1977), Bourdieu explored how social positioning helps people to adapt to the social structures they encounter. He suggested that an individual's habitus is made up of different amounts of economic, social, and cultural capital, and that the ability to control cultural and symbolic systems in ways that reproduce dominant social structures can give people the power to improve their life chances.

Young professionals lunching al fresco respond to the situation according to the accepted norms of social behaviour.

HUMAN NATURE
IS ALMOST UNBELIEVABLY MALLEABLE

CULTURE SHAPES BEHAVIOUR

IN CONTEXT

KEY WORK
Margaret Mead, *Coming of Age in Samoa*, 1928

FIELD
Sociocultural anthropology

BEFORE
1911 In *The Mind of Primitive Man*, Franz Boas questions the idea that some cultures are superior to others.

1922 A.R. Radcliffe-Brown's ethnography *The Andaman Islanders* shows how social institutions help to maintain stability and cohesion.

AFTER
1955 French anthropologist Claude Lévi-Strauss argues that human behaviour is shaped by underlying structures in culture.

1983 In *Margaret Mead and Samoa*, New Zealand anthropologist Derek Freeman rebuts Mead's conclusions and attacks her cultural relativist approach to fieldwork.

I have tried to answer the question which sent me to Samoa: Are the disturbances which vex our adolescents due to the nature of adolescence itself or to the civilization?
Margaret Mead

During the 1920s, US anthropologist Margaret Mead immersed herself in a society in American Samoa in the South Pacific for nine months. Her research transformed the way social scientists viewed adolescence and culture, and continues to resonate today. Mead revealed how behaviour and emotional development can be shaped by cultural context, and challenged the idea that biology alone drives this critical life stage. Her work offered a firm rejection of ethnocentrism – the assumption that all societies follow the same stages of development, usually based on Western norms.

Cultural debates

At the time of Mead's fieldwork in Samoa, anthropologists were engaged in fierce debate about the extent to which culture determines behaviour. Some scholars were still influenced by outdated racist theories, which Mead fiercely opposed. Others, particularly in Europe, were influenced by structural functionalist ideas that emphasized how social institutions, such as the family, religion, or political systems, met the needs of individuals and the wider cultural group. Structural functionalists, including Bronisław Malinowski and A.R. Radcliffe-Brown, focused on the ways these institutions stabilized society, preventing rapid change. Their comparative approach sought to identify social structures that were common to all societies, and they tended to highlight the similarities between cultures around the world rather than explore their differences.

In the US, Margaret Mead and her peers – under the tutelage of Franz Boas – spearheaded a new type of anthropology founded on cultural relativism. Their approach challenged the belief embedded in structural functionalism that some cultures were better than others. Instead, Boas and his followers believed that each culture should be understood on its own terms and should not be judged from the perspective of others. They rejected the idea that some cultures or features were more advanced, complex, or rational, and questioned the assumptions about the superiority of Western cultures that were typical of structural functionalist approaches. Boas and his followers were more interested in understanding cultural practices within their broader historical and social context than in looking for human universals.

Theory into practice

Mead's work would vividly illustrate this perspective. She showed that life could be experienced in vastly different ways depending on cultural norms, and her research reshaped the way anthropologists approached the study of human development.

Participant observation was central to Margaret Mead's research in Samoa. This entailed living alongside the adolescent girls she was studying and dressing like them.

See also: Cultural relativism 34–41 ▪ Biopsychological functionalism 50–55 ▪ Culture and personality 70–73 ▪ Structuralism 108 ▪ Rites of passage 126–29 ▪ Feminist anthropology 140–45

Encouraged by Boas, at the age of 23, Mead embarked on her first major fieldwork expedition in American Samoa, a US territory in the South Pacific. Her ultimate goal was to explore how culture, rather than biology or nature, shapes behaviours and world views. During the nine months in which she conducted her ethnographic research, primarily on the island of Ta'u, Mead fully immersed herself in Samoan culture. She lived in the community, participating in daily routines and social interactions to gain insight into their cultural practices – and documented everything. Mead carried out interviews with 68 Samoan girls between the ages of 9 and 20 from three villages on the island. She also spoke with other community members, including the girls' parents and village elders.

Exploring adolescence

As part of her research, Mead set out to explore perspectives on childhood, adolescence, gender roles, and sexual experiences among Samoan girls. She was particularly keen to discover whether their experiences of teenage life were as challenging, tumultuous, and anxiety-provoking as those of teenagers in the US – her broader goal being to establish whether adolescence was an equally stressful period across different cultures.

Mead concluded that adolescence for Samoan girls was a relatively carefree period – quite unlike the conflict-ridden time experienced by teenage girls in the West. The girls on the island experienced little psychological stress and maintained greater emotional balance than their US counterparts. Mead attributed this to the stability and harmony that she perceived in Samoan culture, which lacked the conflicting values and shame-inducing taboos common in the US. Her research proved, she argued, that it was cultural factors rather than biological forces that caused adolescents to experience emotional and psychological stress. »

Is adolescence **universally stressful?**

↓

Adolescence appears to be **peaceful** in Samoa.

↓

There are **open attitudes towards sexuality**.

↓

There are **flexible gender roles**.

↓

Western norms are not universal.

Margaret Mead

Born in Philadelphia, US, in 1901, Margaret Mead grew up in a family of educators and was strongly influenced by her parents' progressive views. She earned her PhD from Columbia University, studying under Franz Boas.

Mead's fieldwork in Samoa, published as *Coming of Age in Samoa* in 1928, brought her significant public attention, and she used this platform to promote progressive causes. During World War II, she contributed to the war effort, helping US policymakers to better understand allied nations. Mead later carried out fieldwork in New Guinea and Bali, where her use of film helped to establish the new discipline of visual anthropology. She held a number of prominent roles, and was president of both the American Anthropological Association and the Anthropological Film Institute. She died in 1978.

Other key works

1935 *Sex and Temperament in Three Primitive Societies*
1949 *Male and Female*
1970 *A Rap on Race*

During her fieldwork, Mead observed that gender roles were particularly flexible within Samoan society. She found that individuals of both biological sexes expressed a broader range of identities and roles than those typical in the West. Adolescence in Samoa, Mead noted, was not marked by crisis or stress, but was instead "an orderly developing of a set of slowly maturing interests and activities". The girls in Samoa faced few internal conflicts and were not troubled by existential questions or unattainable ambitions. Their aspirations, Mead believed, were "uniform and satisfying" – to have many lovers, before eventually marrying within their village, and starting families near their relatives.

Culture clash

When Mead published these findings in *Coming of Age in Samoa*, her book generated significant controversy. It was released during a time of cultural transition in the US, as traditional conservative values around the family and women's roles were being questioned. The book struck a nerve: US society as a whole seemed increasingly anxious about adolescence and shifting social and sexual mores.

Mead's research directly contradicted the prevailing belief – promoted in a study by US psychologist G. Stanley Hall – that adolescence was a life stage inherently marked by psychological turmoil. Many people were shocked by the notion that only cultural barriers prevented US society from adopting the more relaxed and permissive attitudes towards sexuality seen in Samoan communities. Even more shocking was the idea that adolescents might engage in premarital sexual relationships, and that this could potentially come to be considered

> Because our civilization is woven of so many diverse strands, the ideas which any one group accepts will be found to contain numerous contradictions.
> **Margaret Mead**

a normal part of growing up – a prospect that challenged deeply held moral norms.

Mead's fieldwork in the 1930s, firstly at sites in New Guinea, where she studied gender roles, and later in Bali, where she investigated the formation of personality, highlighted the vast variability of human behaviour. Her research at these sites further reinforced her belief in the power of culture to shape social norms.

Public campaigner

Following World War II, Mead's reputation as an academic helped to establish her as a leading public voice on issues such as gender roles, family life, and the social changes taking place in the US. By this time, her influence stretched far beyond her work in Samoa. As views on adolescence, sexuality, and cultural diversity evolved in the US during the 1950s

The rock 'n' roll era of the 1950s and 1960s brought cultural shifts. Mead's writings resonated with young people as they challenged traditional social norms, and embraced opportunities to express their sexuality more openly.

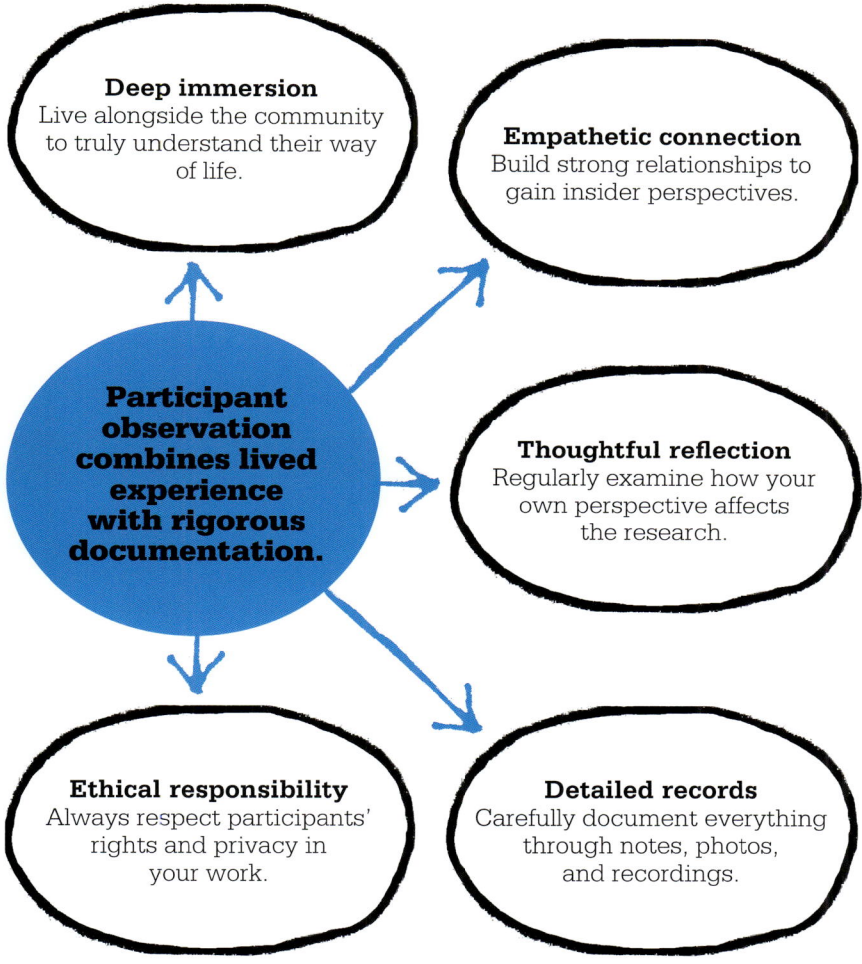

Participant observation combines lived experience with rigorous documentation.

Deep immersion
Live alongside the community to truly understand their way of life.

Empathetic connection
Build strong relationships to gain insider perspectives.

Thoughtful reflection
Regularly examine how your own perspective affects the research.

Ethical responsibility
Always respect participants' rights and privacy in your work.

Detailed records
Carefully document everything through notes, photos, and recordings.

A Rap on Race

Margaret Mead was committed to making anthropology accessible to the general public. This dedication to conveying anthropological insights in accessible language is an essential part of her legacy.

A Rap on Race (1970) is one example of Mead's enthusiasm for public-facing anthropology. The book was based on her tape-recorded conversation with the US writer and activist James Baldwin, who was widely known for his autobiographical novel *Go Tell It on the Mountain* (1953) and his works addressing race, politics, and sexuality. Their wide-ranging discussion touched on social injustice, civil rights, racism, and the importance of cultural diversity in the US. Baldwin offered personal reflections on these issues, while Mead contributed cross-cultural perspectives. Their goal was to use their dialogue to bridge cultural divides and foster greater understanding.

Civil rights activist James Baldwin's writings challenged Americans to confront issues of racism and inequality.

---

and 1960s, Mead's insights from *Coming of Age in Samoa* resonated with a new audience.

However, her work continued to attract criticism. Conservatives expressed concerns about the influence it might have on changing social values, while other academics questioned her research methods. Chief among them was New Zealand anthropologist Derek Freeman, who in the 1980s argued that Mead had misrepresented Samoan culture and misinterpreted her data.

Despite such critiques, *Coming of Age in Samoa* remains one of the key ethnographies in anthropology, particularly in the study of adolescence, culture, and human development. It continues to shape debate on how culture informs identity.

Throughout her career, Mead consistently challenged ethnocentrism and emphasized the importance of viewing cultures on their own terms. Her writings helped to establish anthropology as a vital tool for addressing societal challenges. Mead's work continues to inspire a broader appreciation for cultural diversity and the complexities of human societies. ■

A COMPLEX NETWORK OF SOCIAL RELATIONS
KINSHIP AND SOCIAL ORDER

IN CONTEXT

KEY WORK
A.R. Radcliffe-Brown,
The Social Organisation
***of Australian Tribes*, 1931**

FIELD
Sociocultural anthropology

BEFORE
1895 French sociologist Émile Durkheim publishes *The Rules of Sociological Method*, arguing that social facts should be treated as things.

AFTER
1949 Claude Lévi-Strauss publishes *Les Structures élémentaires de la parenté* (translated to *The Elementary Structures of Kinship* in 1969). He states that incest is a universal taboo that helps to underpin social structures.

2024 Kamilaroi Nation sociologist Jamie Sorby publishes "Kinship and Cultural Strengths". It places kinship at the core of First Nations peoples' culture.

British anthropologist Alfred Reginald Radcliffe-Brown aimed to create a field called "comparative sociology" based on empirical observation, and hoped to establish the general "laws" on which societies function. His emphasis on empirical observation – information based on direct experience – was shared by other anthropologists such as Franz Boas and Bronisław Malinowski, and his approach

Ngarrindjeri senior leader Major Sumner performs a smoking ceremony at WugulOra – meaning "one mob". "Mob" is a First Nations kinship term denoting a family or community.

was rigorous and systemic. He studied the kinship structures of First Nations peoples in Western Australia, believing that society could be understood through comparison with natural organisms – both are complete entities formed of many related parts.

Different terminology
Kinship was a central focus for anthropologists, many of whom believed that in the absence of formal policing or government regulation, kinship roles and obligations maintained peace. Previous observers of First Nations Australian and Torres Strait Islander people had noticed that kinship terminologies differed from Western terminology, with some peoples calling the father's brother "father". This practice was perceived as promiscuous and implied that First Nations people did not recognize nuclear families.

Radcliffe-Brown dismissed these speculations, using field material to show that First Nations people did recognize the nuclear family. He also showed that certain kinship terms were used to classify relatives from one side of the family or the other. This use of kinship

See also: The fluidity of social systems 102–03 ▪ Stages of social organization 160–61 ▪ Kinship studies 192 ▪ Kinship ideologies 218–19

terminology – which later became known as a form of "prescriptive terminology" – indicated how one should behave towards relatives and outlined their rights and obligations. Radcliffe-Brown reasoned that for nomadic populations such as these, who travelled across deserts, it was crucial to establish relations when encountering other groups, and that these relations were organized into a classification system.

Social prescriptions

Drawing on detailed data from his own and other travellers' observations, Radcliffe-Brown created a broad typology of First Nations kinship systems, concentrating on two prototypes – Kariera and Arrernte – named after the population groups that used them. He focused on marriage prescription and on how lines of descent were coded inside these groups, as well as on language, land possession, and cosmology. Radcliffe-Brown analysed numerous prescriptions in detail: who a

> Society has certain **accepted ways** of **doing** and **being**.

> Those who deviate from these **social norms** are **excluded**, **shamed**, or **punished**.

> Individuals follow social norms in order to **preserve** their **close relationships**.

> **Kinship systems maintain social order.**

person was supposed to marry; how one would address relatives on either side of the family; and what one could expect from cousins, nephews, or grandchildren. In doing so, he showed that these prescriptions regulated systems of solidarity not just within the family, but also within the wider group, the Nation, and beyond.

Lasting impact

Today, anthropologists reason that societies are not as similar to natural organisms as Radcliffe-Brown believed, nor are their functions as mechanistic as he thought. Despite this, many of his other ideas were crucial in opposing the dominant approaches in anthropology at the time, particularly evolutionism and diffusionism, which viewed non-Western societies as primitive. Radcliffe-Brown argued that this entailed a moral evaluation that had no place in a rigorous science of society, and he sought to counter historical speculation about the origins of social practices. ∎

Complex societies

The societies of First Nations Australian and Torres Strait Islander people were historically considered by Western anthropologists to be among the simplest societies on Earth. This misconception was largely based on the Western prioritization of material culture. These First Nations people did not appear to have many physical possessions – which is typical for nomadic peoples – and therefore their societies were perceived to be simple. However, this view did not take into account the intricate social organization of First Nations communities and the detailed understanding of sciences, including cosmology and aerodynamics, that First Nations people had held for tens of thousands of years.

Today, anthropologists are able to make more informed and nuanced observations of First Nations practices that recognize the complexities and sophistication of such long-standing societies.

First Nations Australian peoples used boomerangs for thousands of years. Although visually simple, the tool is aerodynamic and thought to be the world's first flying machine.

A CONSISTENT PATTERN OF THOUGHT AND ACTION

CULTURE AND PERSONALITY

IN CONTEXT

KEY WORK
Ruth Benedict, *Patterns of Culture*, 1934

FIELD
Sociocultural anthropology

BEFORE
1872 In *The Birth of Tragedy*, German philosopher Friedrich Nietzsche discusses two contrasting artistic impulses: Apollonian and Dionysian.

1901 Sigmund Freud profoundly influences the understanding of individual personality in *Psychopathology of Everyday Life*.

AFTER
1939 US psychiatrist Abram Kardiner argues that a "basic personality structure" can be identified in people from the same culture.

1940 Benedict repudiates the racial stereotyping of cultures in *Race: Science and Politics*.

An individual's "personality" can be thought of as a unique cluster of traits – their style of thinking, feeling, and acting – that sets them apart from others. In some cases, people living in the same social group share not only similar lifestyles, but also similar tastes, attitudes, and even personality traits. During the 1930s, US anthropologist Ruth Benedict began to explore the links between individual personality and culture.

The concept of personality first entered mainstream US and European thought in the early 20th century. At that time, many people were reading the works of Austrian psychologist Sigmund Freud, whose

See also: Cultural relativism 34–41 ▪ Culture shapes behaviour 62–67 ▪ Language and cognition 88–89

According to Freud, the human mind can be likened to an iceberg, most of which is submerged under water. The small part above water represents the conscious mind, and the underwater bulk is the unconscious.

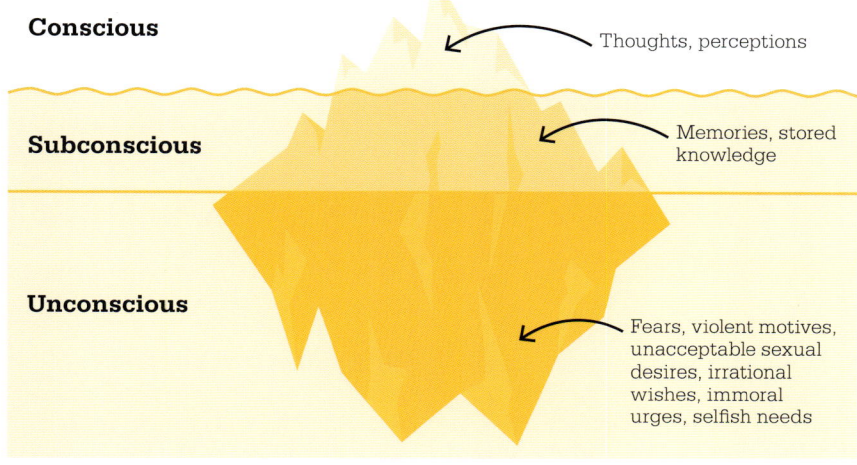

Conscious — Thoughts, perceptions

Subconscious — Memories, stored knowledge

Unconscious — Fears, violent motives, unacceptable sexual desires, irrational wishes, immoral urges, selfish needs

theories changed perceptions of how the human mind operates, as well as ideas about human behaviour and development.

Freud's contribution

According to Freud, the human mind is mostly made up of the unconscious. The deep-seated urges, wishes, and fears that shape the conscious mind are within the unconscious mind. However, the unconscious remains inaccessible to us except through dreams, hypnosis, and Freud's novel technique of psychoanalysis. Freud proposed that, as a child develops, it learns how to harness unconscious urges and instincts, and progresses through a series of time-sensitive psychosexual stages. Failure to progress can result in the child being stuck in one of these stages. This can affect the individual's personality well into adulthood.

Amid growing interest in Freudian psychology, some anthropologists began to question whether the Austrian doctor's theories could be applied outside of white European and North American societies. They wanted to know if children developed differently in other cultures and, if so, if they would mature into adults with »

The lenses through which any nation looks at life are not the ones another nation uses.
Ruth Benedict

Ruth Benedict

Born in New York in 1887, Ruth Benedict studied literature at the city's Vassar College and became a published poet. Later, she pursued a degree in anthropology, studying first under Elsie Clews Parsons and then under Franz Boas at New York's Columbia University, where she earned her PhD in 1923.

Benedict's lifelong interest in literature shaped her anthropological work, which drew upon literary tropes and mythology. In 1924, she taught her first anthropology course at Columbia University. Her students included Margaret Mead, who became a good friend of Benedict's and an influential anthropologist.

From 1925 to 1940, Benedict edited the *Journal of American Folklore* and later became president of the American Anthropological Association, just months before her sudden death in 1948.

Other key works

1935 *Zuni Mythology*
1946 *The Chrysanthemum and the Sword: Patterns of Japanese Culture*

distinctive personality traits. These questions spawned the "school of culture and personality", which was spearheaded by Ruth Benedict.

Culture and personality

Benedict was profoundly influenced by her university professor Franz Boas – the "father of American anthropology" – who stressed the importance of conducting first-hand fieldwork to support his views about cultural relativism and the idea that no culture is better or worse than another.

Like many other US-based anthropologists in the early decades of the 20th century, Benedict was drawn to the Indigenous peoples who lived nearby, yet appeared distinct from mainstream US society. Initially, Benedict's research focused on the folklore and religion of the Indigenous populations, but her interest eventually shifted towards psychological issues as she began to explore the possible connection between culture and personality.

In her best-selling book *Patterns of Culture*, Benedict expanded on a concept already expressed by Nietzsche in *The Birth of Tragedy* and drew upon Greek mythology to develop two basic cultural

> I have the faith of a scientist that behaviour … is understandable if the problem … can be answered by investigation.
> **Ruth Benedict**
> **Speech given in 1946**

types – "Apollonian" and "Dionysian" – each encapsulating the characteristics of that god.

Apollo – the god of the Sun, the arts, and truth – was associated with calm restraint, so Benedict argued that people living in an Apollonian culture would be rational, orderly, and self-controlled. By contrast, Dionysus – the god of wine, festivity, and religious ecstasy – was associated with wild abandon and uncontrolled behaviour; Benedict suggested that people living in a Dionysian culture would be exuberant and passionate.

With these contrasting cultural types in mind, Benedict studied three cultures: the Zuni, Kwakiutl, and Dobu. The Zuni, one of several Pueblo peoples of the southwestern US, were farmers whose ethos centred on the cycles of nature, which sustained them materially and spiritually. According to Benedict, the Zuni seldom expressed strong emotions, such as anger or jealousy, and they avoided conflict even when it was merited. Their dances and ceremonies were structured, reflecting the sense of order that permeated their lives. For Benedict, the Zuni exemplified the Apollonian cultural type.

Dionysian variations

Benedict then considered the Kwakiutl – fishers and hunters living along Canada's Pacific Northwest coast. For this case study, Benedict relied on accounts written by Boas; her mentor had worked with this group for more than 30 years and described many of their customs, including a ritual called the potlatch.

The potlatch was initiated by a chief, who would spend years, or decades, accumulating a store of goods. He would then invite the people of his own and neighbouring

Apollonian cultural traits		Dionysian cultural traits	
Self-control	Strong emotions are not expressed, and rational behaviour is the norm.	**Chaos**	Conflict, rather than consensus, is usual and may be settled with violence rather than discourse.
Moderation	Behaviour is neither excessive nor destructive; rituals are not exuberant.	**Excess**	Frenzied, unrestrained behaviour and indulgence in food, festivities, and sex.
Individualism	There is a focus on personal restraint, discipline, and balance.	**Passion**	Strong emotions are expressed; rituals are exuberant and fuelled by intoxicating substances.
Order	Rules are important, routine is encouraged, and everything has its place.	**Disorder**	Society has few rules or routines.

Potlatch ceremonies held in America's Pacific Northwest involved the redistribution of property in an overt display of generosity to reinforce hierarchical relations.

groups to a grand festival in which he would give away or destroy all his possessions. The excessiveness of this ritual defied mainstream US economic logics, which valued the accumulation, not loss, of material goods. Boas, however, discovered that the potlatch served a social purpose: it was through the act of giving that the chief elevated his status and earned prestige. Moreover, his generous gift-giving would pressure neighbouring chiefs, compelling them to throw even bigger potlatches, resulting in an endless cycle of gifting. For Benedict, the excess and drama of the potlatch ceremony exemplified a kind of Dionysian frenzy.

Given the vast number of cultures worldwide, Benedict was aware that she was unlikely to find the same version of Apollonian or Dionysian cultural types – and when she turned to the Dobu people of Papua New Guinea, that proved to be the case. A belief in magic and witchcraft permeated all aspects of Dobuan lives, to the degree that Benedict believed they were paranoid and suspicious, and that their interpersonal relationships were tainted by a lack of trust. The

fearfulness of the Dobuans led her to characterize them as Dionysian, albeit in ways distinct from the alleged wildness of Kwakiutl culture.

Cultural patterns

Based on these case studies, Benedict claimed that each culture selects, from myriad possibilities, a set of personality traits to idealize and to impress upon their children. These traits characterize the people and are projected outwardly on to their culture, shaping rituals, world views, and institutions. The ideal personality is thus intertwined with culture in a socially valued pattern.

Benedict's broader argument was that culture and personality reflect one another: culture is personality "writ large" and personality is culture "writ small." If a culture idealizes calm, then its people will learn to control strong emotions; its politicians will opt for consensus over argument; and its gods will be benevolent. In these ways, the idealized personality is internalized by individuals and externalized in social life.

Critics pointed out that *Patterns of Culture* overlooked variations within a culture and perpetuated

stereotypes. Furthermore, a culture could appear either calm or wild, depending on the person studying it, and the area of life on which they chose to focus. Indeed, Benedict emphasized the calmer aspects of Zuni life – such as farming rituals – while examining the exuberance of the Kwakiutl potlatch ceremonies; had she studied other aspects, she may have reached a different conclusion. Critics also cast doubt on the notion that the vast range of cultural diversity could be reduced to just two polarized types.

Despite evident shortcomings, Benedict's work made two particularly significant contributions. She helped to establish the theory of "configurationism" – that is, the notion that cultural elements interact with one another, meaning that a culture is more than the sum of its parts. Secondly, her work supported cultural relativism by showing how each culture produces distinctive individuals, well suited for their particular context. ■

No man ever looks at the world with pristine eyes. He sees it edited by a definite set of customs and institutions and ways of thinking.
Ruth Benedict

THE CULMINATION OF A PROGRESSIVE CHANGE
REVOLUTIONS IN PREHISTORY

In the early 20th century, archaeologists struggled to piece together human prehistory. Techniques such as radiocarbon dating were not yet available, making it difficult to determine the precise age of sites or artefacts. As a result, most archaeologists focused their studies on individual sites or specific regions. Australian archaeologist V. Gordon Childe, however, took a different approach. He sought to connect these isolated findings to build a broader picture of early human history.

The settlement of Skara Brae, in Scotland, was viewed by Childe as evidence that complex social structures existed within Neolithic communities.

As a lifelong socialist, Childe saw revolutionary changes described in the writings of Karl Marx reflected in prehistory. According to Marx, history is shaped by material conditions, with economic forces determining social structures, such as political systems or class hierarchies. Childe recognized that migration and the diffusion of new ideas played a big role in social change, but like Marx, he believed that economics was the driving force behind societal evolution.

Defining moments
Childe was influenced by British historian Arnold Toynbee's analysis of the Industrial Revolution and Friedrich Engels' writings on early societies. Drawing on their

See also: Unilineal evolution 26–27 ▪ The fluidity of social systems 102–03 ▪ Processual archaeology 136–37 ▪ Global capitalism 186–87 ▪ Structure and agency 196–99

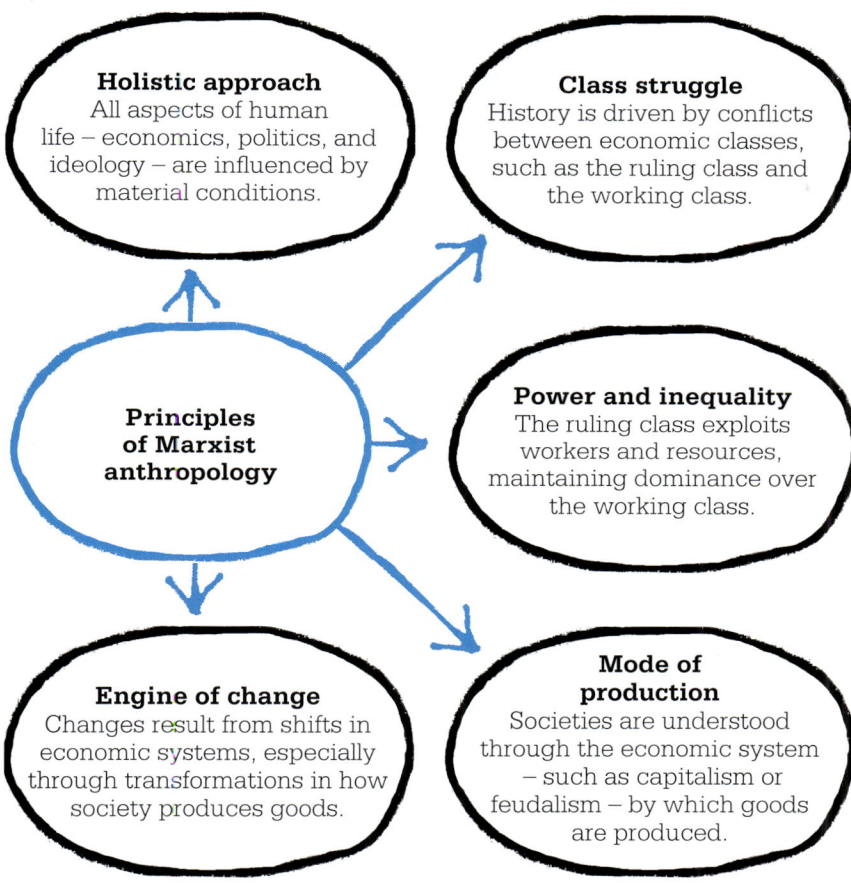

Holistic approach
All aspects of human life – economics, politics, and ideology – are influenced by material conditions.

Class struggle
History is driven by conflicts between economic classes, such as the ruling class and the working class.

Principles of Marxist anthropology

Power and inequality
The ruling class exploits workers and resources, maintaining dominance over the working class.

Engine of change
Changes result from shifts in economic systems, especially through transformations in how society produces goods.

Mode of production
Societies are understood through the economic system – such as capitalism or feudalism – by which goods are produced.

V. Gordon Childe

Born in Sydney, Australia, in 1892, V. Gordon Childe became a socialist at an early age and held these beliefs for the rest of his life. After studying archaeology at Oxford, he worked at the University of Edinburgh. In 1947, Childe became director of the Institute of Archaeology in London.

Childe is best-known for the excavation at Skara Brae on the Orkney Islands, Scotland. He used his discoveries to support his Marxist understanding of historical change. Childe also pioneered the synthesis of European and West Asian archaeology, creating a more cohesive understanding of prehistoric developments in these regions.

Through several books, Childe made prehistory accessible to the public, focusing on the origins of plant and animal domestication, and the rise of state societies. He died in 1957.

Other key works

1922 *The Most Ancient East*
1925 *The Dawn of European Civilization*
1942 *What Happened in History*

---

ideas, Childe coined the terms "Neolithic Revolution" and "Urban Revolution" to describe two key points in human history – the domestication of animals and the rise of cities. Both of these revolutionary events, he argued, brought profound social changes, as predicted by Marx. The Neolithic Revolution introduced new social structures, as people related to one another in new ways. For example, family lineages and land ownership became increasingly important. Consequences of the Urban Revolution included the development of markets, craft specialization, writing, and money, but also growing social inequality.

A non-violent revolution
Childe rejected the racist ideas associated with unilinear evolution, the intellectual model of his day. Instead, he believed that the driving factor behind change was a society's mode of production. Although class struggle was key to Marxist philosophy, it played little part in Childe's interpretation of history. In his view, social change was revolutionary, but non-violent. ■

EVERY MAN'S SPICE-BOX SEASONS HIS OWN FOOD

AUTOETHNOGRAPHY

IN CONTEXT

KEY WORK
Zora Neale Hurston, *Mules and Men*, 1935

FIELD
Sociocultural anthropology

BEFORE
1887 Franz Boas asserts that cultural practices should be understood within their context. This theory becomes known as cultural relativism.

1903 W.E.B. Du Bois studies the issues of racism and racial segregation experienced by his own community.

AFTER
1945 Qualitative research – the study of non-data sources such as personal accounts and stories – is established by Paul Felix Lazersfield.

2012 The term Collaborative Autoethnography (CAE), in which several researchers interpret autoethnographic studies on the same theme, is popularized.

As a prolific writer and collector of folklore, US anthropologist Zora Neale Hurston created a form of self-reflective anthropological research which incorporated her own experiences and also the folklore of African American communities to form a broad social commentary. Her work was an early example of what is now known as "autoethnography", although the term was not in use until 1975. Autoethnography is now understood as the connecting of an anthropologist's personal experiences to larger cultural practices and it has since become widely recognized in the field of anthropology as a method of qualitative research.

Renaissance influences

Hurston's mentor, the eminent German-American anthropologist Franz Boas, encouraged her interest in the anthropological study of folklore. She undertook fieldwork for Boas in the Harlem

The Cotton Club was a bustling venue for musicians and performers that celebrated the talents of Black people during the Harlem Renaissance.

See also: Cultural relativism 34–41 ▪ Reflexive ethnography 162–65 ▪ Anthropology at home 170–71 ▪ Critical ethnography 270–71

Ethnography	Autoethnography
The researcher studies a **separate cultural group** to understand their beliefs and practices.	The researcher sets out to understand **broad cultural themes** by analysing their **own experiences**.

They participate in **cultural events**, hold **interviews**, and **make observations** based on what they uncover.	They create **personal accounts**, often in a narrative style, to explore their **own perspectives**.

The researcher aims to make an **objective analysis** of their findings.	The researcher aims to **critique** their **own understanding** and interpretation of cultural themes.

Ethnography studies the society of others.	Autoethnography studies the self within society.

district of New York City, where the Harlem Renaissance – a vibrant cultural movement celebrating Black culture – had developed between the 1910s and the mid-1930s. The movement saw Black identities and history explored through art, performance, music, and writing. A key writer within the movement, Hurston both studied and contributed to the literary and artistic expressions of identities of race, gender, and sexuality during the period, and enriched her work with insights from her own experiences.

Studying the familiar

Hurston later returned to her hometown of Eatonville, Florida – the first incorporated Black township in the US – to continue her research into folklore. There she built upon her experiences and the extensive oral folklore of African American peoples to create an insightful treatise on African American culture in the southern US. The resulting title, *Mules and Men*, was also the first collection of African American folklore by an African American writer. ▪

Zora Neale Hurston

Born in the US town of Nosatulga, Alabama, in 1891, Zora Neale Hurston was an anthropologist, writer, and a significant figure in the Harlem Renaissance movement of the early 20th century. She studied at Howard University between 1918 and 1924 before moving to New York City in 1925. There she achieved success as a writer, and attended Barnard College, from which she graduated in 1928. Alongside her ethnographic work, Hurston wrote several novels, musical productions, and plays. In 1939 she received an honorary doctorate from Morgan State College. Between 1947 and 1948 Hurston travelled to Honduras to study Black communities in Central America. However, towards the end of her life she wrote less and worked instead as a maid, librarian, reporter, and substitute teacher until her death in 1960.

Other key works

1934 *Jonah's Gourd Vine*
1937 *Their Eyes Were Watching God*
1938 *Tell My Horse*

WITCHCRAFT HAS ITS OWN LOGIC

LOCAL BELIEF SYSTEMS

IN CONTEXT

KEY WORK
**E.E. Evans-Pritchard,
*Witchcraft, Oracles,
and Magic Among the
Azande*, 1937**

FIELD
Sociocultural anthropology

BEFORE
1909 British ethnologist Robert
Ranulph Marett proposes a
trajectory of "mana", or natural
energy, magic, and religion.

1922 During fieldwork among
the Trobrianders, Bronisław
Malinowski observes that the
islanders use magic to cope
with uncertainty.

AFTER
1970 In *The Kababish Arabs*,
Saudi anthropologist Talal
Asad examines the politics of
a group of Sudanese nomads.

1976 Indian sociologist
M.N. Srinivas publishes
The Remembered Village,
a study of India's social
structure and caste system.

During the late 1920s,
British anthropologist
Sir Edward Evan Evans-
Pritchard conducted fieldwork
among the Azande people in
Africa. Their territory, Zandeland,
encompassed parts of three modern
countries: the Central African
Republic, the Democratic Republic
of Congo, and South Sudan.

The Azande people were a
distinct social group with their
own political chiefdoms, ethnic
identity, and cultural traditions.
In a book drawn from his research,
Witchcraft, Oracles, and Magic

Witchcraft has ... its own rules
of thought, and these do not
exclude natural causation.
Belief in witchcraft is quite
consistent with ... a rational
appreciation of nature.
E.E. Evans-Pritchard

Among the Azande, Evans-
Pritchard explained the rationale
behind their seemingly illogical
witchcraft-based belief system.

Azande magic
Zandeland fell under the control
of three different colonial
administrations – Belgian, French,
and Anglo-Egyptian – during the
19th century. Despite encounters
with colonizers and missionaries,
and their subsequent widespread
conversion to Christianity, many
Azande people also maintained
their traditional way of life,
including a belief in "mangu",
or witchcraft.

The Azande see magic and
witchcraft everywhere. They
believe this manifests itself inside
a witch's abdomen in the form of a
black substance that passes from
parent to child; an individual might
carry this substance inside them
without knowing it, so everyone
is seen as a potential witch.

Signs of magic are revealed
through unfortunate events, such as
injury or death. The Azande build
elevated wooden structures that
store grain and provide shade for
people who gather underneath on
a hot day. However, in Zandeland's

See also: Cultural relativism 34–41 ▪ The social roots of religion 42–43 ▪ Biopsychological functionalism 50–55 ▪ Religion and secular power 188–89

humid climate, wooden materials are at risk of rot – which attracts insects – and these granaries occasionally collapse, injuring or killing the people below. The most logical explanation for such an event is cause-and-effect: termites prevalent in warm environments chew through the wood and cause the structure to collapse.

For the Azande, however, all misfortune has both a logical cause and a supernatural cause. They believe that the termite scenario offers only a partial explanation: it does not account for why the granary collapsed on that day, at that time, and on that particular person. The injured person was not just the victim of termites (a logic-based explanation); they were also the victim of witchcraft (a supernatural explanation).

A two-pronged approach

For Westerners in the early to mid-20th century, the magical belief systems found among peoples living across Africa and elsewhere were indicative of "primitive" forms

Witchdoctors are central figures in the Azande community. It is believed that they can predict disasters and counteract evil spells using a range of medicines and charms.

of cognition that they believed to be less sophisticated than rational "modern" thought. Evans-Pritchard's fieldwork proved that the Azande were fully capable of rational thought; however, they considered logic to be just one of several elements at play, with supernatural forces also an important factor.

The longer Evans-Pritchard remained in Zandeland, the more he came to understand that Azande witchcraft was a coherent belief system that made as much sense to its practitioners as any other religion to its devotees. Ultimately, Evans-Pritchard's work challenged ethnocentric assumptions about the existence of "primitive" and "civilized" minds, as he extended the principle of cultural relativism to encompass different world views. ▪

This 1920s British poster reflects colonial attitudes towards the Indigenous people of East Africa by showing locals in subservient roles.

British colonialism and anthropology

Although Evans-Pritchard espoused cultural relativism in his scholarship, he was criticized for his cooperation with the colonial powers that had carved up Africa – a charge that he vehemently denied.

In the early 1930s, while Evans-Pritchard was conducting fieldwork in Sudan, he was approached by the country's Anglo-Egyptian administration. The governing forces had an issue with the Nuer people, who were actively resisting colonial rule. The administration knew little about this group or how to subdue them, so they asked Evans-Pritchard to carry out a study, which he agreed to "after hesitation and with misgivings".

While his work increased general understanding of the Nuer people, Evans-Pritchard did not align himself with colonial efforts. However, he was not critical of them either, saying little about the negative effects that foreign occupation had on local populations.

ALTERNATION BETWEEN HUNGER AND PLENTY

SOCIAL AND CULTURAL DIMENSIONS OF NUTRITION

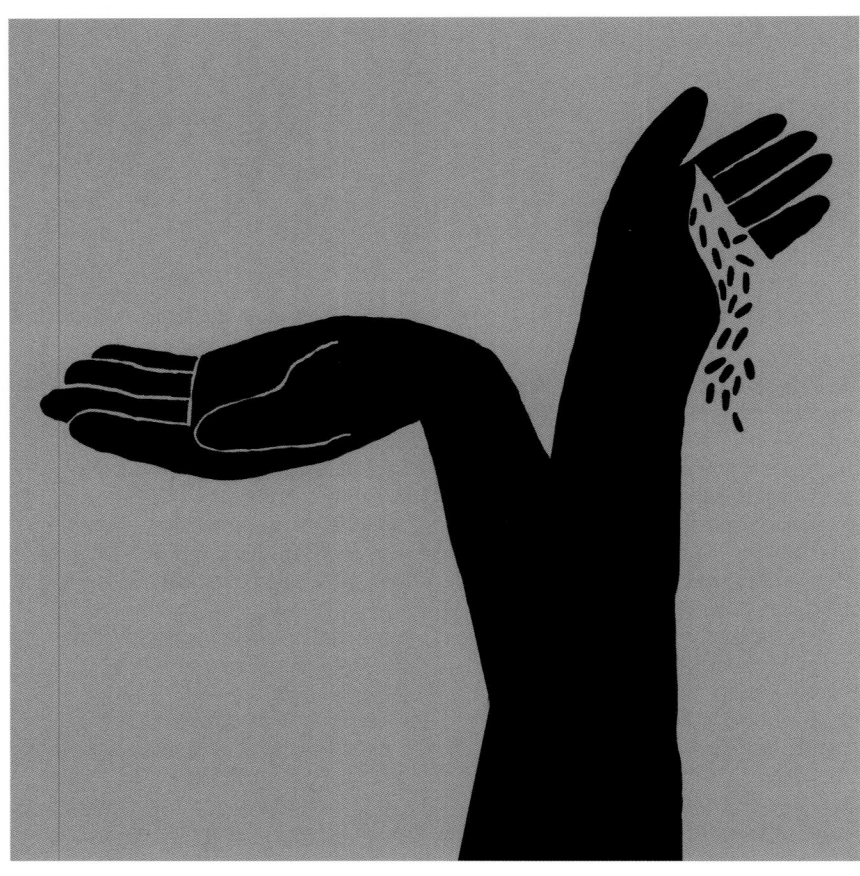

IN CONTEXT

KEY WORK
Audrey Richards, _Land, Labour and Diet in Northern Rhodesia_, 1939

FIELD
Sociocultural anthropology

BEFORE
1888 In "Manners and Meals", US ethnologist Garrick Mallery looks at the social and symbolic significance of meals.

1920 US anthropologist Frank Hamilton Cushing's _Zuñi Breadstuff_ explores the role of bread in everyday life.

AFTER
1985 _Sweetness and Power_, by Sidney Mintz, links rising sugar consumption to the expansion of Europe's colonial powers.

2017 British anthropologist Stanley Ulijaszek and colleagues examine changing diets in _Evolving Human Nutrition_.

In the late 1920s, when Audrey Richards studied anthropology at the London School of Economics (LSE), the dominant perspective was functionalism – founded by Bronisław Malinowski. A core concern was examining how human communities developed social institutions to meet their basic needs, and Richards prepared a thesis on the social and cultural dimensions of nutrition.

In _Hunger and Work in a Savage Tribe_, Richards asserted that, historically, psychologists and sociologists had been too narrow in their views on nutrition. She argued that psychological approaches were limited because

See also: Biopsychological functionalism 50–55 ▪ The anthropology of food 200–05 ▪ Nutrition and human evolution 280

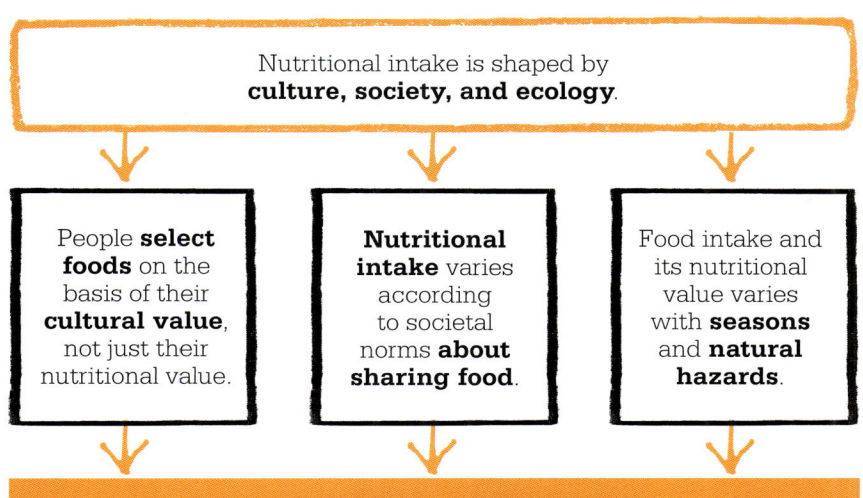

Nutritional intake is shaped by **culture, society, and ecology**.

People **select foods** on the basis of their **cultural value**, not just their nutritional value.

Nutritional intake varies according to societal norms **about sharing food**.

Food intake and its nutritional value varies with **seasons** and **natural hazards**.

Food is about more than nutrition.

they regarded the acquisition of food as an inherited instinct and a biological drive. However, Richards noted that sociological approaches tended to consider the production and distribution of food in strictly economic terms, isolated from biological needs and the effects of nutrition on growth, health, and labour.

Fundamental needs

By taking a more holistic approach that incorporated biological, social, cultural, political, economic, and ecological factors – and assessing the relationships between them – Richards established a probing tool to study issues of nutrition. At the start of her thesis, Richards reflected on the relative significance given to nutritional needs, as opposed to sex, in the making of society. The functions of sex beyond biological reproduction had already received much attention in psychology and sociology, but nutrition had largely been neglected.

Sex was seen as a potentially disruptive force in society – as in cases of marital infidelity – and it was analysed in terms of norms and social control. Richards regarded satisfying hunger as a daily necessity rather than a disruptive drive. Humanity cannot survive without sexual reproduction; an individual can, however, live without sexual gratification but cannot survive without food – their impulse is to satisfy their hunger every day.

Children are completely dependent on others for food, while adults tend to cooperate in its production, preparation, and consumption. In traditional societies, this cooperation is regulated by institutions of marriage, kinship, and the political organization of the village.

Richards also asserted that cultural beliefs affect nutrition. Humans are omnivorous and able to adapt to different environments. A wide range of foods is usually available, but people do not »

Audrey Richards

Born in London, UK, in 1899, Audrey Richards grew up in India. In the early 1920s, she spent two years in Germany, as a relief worker; witnessing post-war experiences of extreme deprivation and hunger shaped her interest in nutrition.

After studying for a degree in natural sciences at Cambridge, in 1931 Richards obtained a PhD in social anthropology from the London School of Economics (LSE), where Bronisław Malinowski was her supervisor.

Between 1930 and 1956, Richards divided her time between fieldwork – in Zambia (then Northern Rhodesia), South Africa, and Uganda – and academia, lecturing at LSE and the University of Witwatersrand, Johannesburg.

After returning to England in 1956, Richards was made a fellow of her alma mater, Newnham College in Cambridge. She died in 1984.

Other key works

1932 *Hunger and Work in a Savage Tribe*

The Bemba constantly talk about "hunger months" … At the end of the rainy season, they expect a shortage.
Audrey Richards

necessarily choose to consume those with the highest nutritional value. Preferences for different foods – and their selection – are mediated through cultural values that are internalized during our upbringing. Food that is taboo in one society may be a dietary staple in another.

People may also produce more food than they actually require for sustenance because, according to Richards, it can serve other purposes. Malinowski, for example, had shown that Trobriand islanders grew more yams than they needed and stocked them outside their houses to symbolize wealth and prosperity.

Fieldwork in Africa

Richards based her thesis on ethnographic records of Bantu-speaking people in Southern Africa. After its completion, she travelled to Zambia (then Northern Rhodesia) to test her theories empirically among the Bemba.

In 1936, Richards and British dietitian Elsie Widdowson co-published an investigation into the nutritional value of the diet in five Bemba villages. Richards estimated how much food of various

> [The Bemba diet] has deteriorated in contact with white civilization rather than the reverse.
> **Audrey Richards**

types the villagers consumed over a six-month period, and recorded the impact of cultural rules on sharing food according to family obligations and traditions of hospitality. Samples of foodstuffs were sent to the UK for chemical and nutritional analysis. The villagers' food intake – and its nutritional value – varied due to fluctuating seasonal availability and environmental hazards such as drought and locust plagues. During the months leading up to the April harvest, for example, when stocks from the previous year were depleted, the people struggled to feed themselves adequately.

Three years later, with the publication of *Land, Labour and Diet* (1939), Richards showed that her perspective had shifted away from studying how nutrition, as a basic biological need, formed social institutions. Instead, she now focused on how social relationships and institutions affected the diet.

The book explored Bemba cultural views on diet, land tenure, and the social relations linked to the cultivation, preparation, and distribution of food. The Bemba produced their main source of carbohydrate – finger millet – following the practice of slash-and-burn agriculture, or shifting cultivation. Trees were lopped and burned to fertilize the poor tropical soil. Women generally looked after the crop and were the principal cultivators, sowing, weeding, and harvesting. Men were responsible for fishing and hunting, but they also lopped trees, fenced fields against animals, and helped the women with the heavy work of tilling.

The family was the basic unit of production, cultivating crops to satisfy its own nutritional needs. At times, a family might also cooperate with relatives and other villagers, helping one another in the field and sharing food if needed.

Colonial impacts

The expansion of Zambia's copper-mining industry at the hands of the colonial powers meant that many men had to leave their villages to work in the mines. This migration was driven by forceful recruitment policies and a need for cash to pay taxes imposed by the colonial authorities, whose

African women beat their finger-millet harvest after it has been dried, to separate the husk and grain. The grain is then used to produce flour.

Workers in the copper mines often subsisted on foods lacking nutritional value. This led to reduced performance and accusations of laziness.

labour policies were based on an assumption that men would work as temporary contractors in the mining towns, and that rural farming communities could provide a constant supply of labour.

However, Richards questioned the capacity of slash-and-burn agriculture to sustain families and provide future workers for the mines. She also showed that the nutritional value of the Bemba diet deteriorated as a result of the colonial encounter. The extraction of male labour from the villages placed heavier physical burdens on the women, who then had less time to spend on harvesting and food preparation. As a result, cultivation yields suffered. This, in turn, led to breakdowns in food-sharing systems between relatives, which was an essential safeguard against starvation. Meanwhile, in the mining towns, the staple millet was replaced with less nutritional alternatives, such as white flour and polished rice.

By showing how factors such as ecology, social organization, and colonization negatively affected the Bemba diet, Richards was able to counter the long-standing European prejudice that starvation and inefficient work in Africa were due to "laziness".

An influential approach

Richards's holistic method has become the model for nutritional anthropology and the anthropology of food in general. Researchers in her wake have regularly combined cultural approaches to food with a focus on health, or investigated diet in relation to issues such as gender politics, class, and ethnicity. Concerns about globalization, sustainability, and food security have also come under scrutiny.

British anthropologist Jack Goody's 1982 book *Cooking, Cuisine, and Class* expanded the scope of Richards's approach to include culinary practices in hierarchical societies. He concluded that the more complex a society is, the more diverse its cuisine, and that in class-based societies, cuisine both reflects and reinforces inequalities.

In 1994, Henrietta L. Moore and Megan Vaughan published *Cutting Down Trees*, a historical study of agricultural development in the Northern Province of Zambia, where Richards had conducted her fieldwork. They investigated the long-term effects of colonization, post-independence development programmes, and changing gender roles. The historical study disclosed that the women cultivators and village communities had been able to cope with the problems of change and nutrition. ∎

The chisungu ritual

Chisungu is a rite of passage held for an individual Bemba girl at the onset of menarche – or first menstruation – a stage that indicates the arrival of sexual maturity. Richards witnessed chisungu as part of a long marriage ritual.

In the final sequence of the ritual, the groom-to-be joins the young girl, or novice, as senior women impart advice about married life. This includes explaining the division of labour between husband and wife, which is the foundation of slash-and-burn agriculture, and the ritual knowledge about the role of women as cultivators, mothers, and wives.

The chisungu ritual tests the novice's ability to take on a central position in Bemba society as a food provider. However, she will already have participated in everyday women's tasks from a young age. Consequently, the teaching in the initiation process reiterates values and norms that urge the novice to undertake her responsibilities with a renewed sense of commitment.

The child-bearing potential of a novice is a key concern of chisungu. Richards drew parallels between this ritual and the agricultural cycle.

A RIGOROUSLY EMPIRICAL APPROACH

COMPARATIVE ETHNOGRAPHY

IN CONTEXT

KEY WORK
Elsie Clews Parsons,
***Pueblo Indian Religion*,**
1939

FIELD
Sociocultural anthropology

BEFORE
1934 US anthropologist Ruth Benedict – a student of Clews Parsons – publishes *Patterns of Culture* in which she draws comparisons between the Indigenous Zuni, Kwakiutl, and Dobu people of North America.

AFTER
1940 Franz Boas publishes *Race, Language, and Culture*, a collection of essays that use cultural relativism to show the importance of context when studying a group.

1963 US anthropologist and linguist Gladys Reichard publishes *Navajo Religion*, a study of the symbols used in the rituals and mythologies of Diné people.

Perhaps more widely known at the time for her sociological work on feminism, pacifism, and social roles, US anthropologist Elsie Clews Parsons was inspired by Franz Boas to explore the cultures of Pueblo peoples in the southwestern US. For 25 years Clews Parsons studied and analysed the religious beliefs, practices, and ceremonies of the Indigenous Pueblo peoples of Arizona and New Mexico. The resulting text became her most detailed ethnographic work and her

The Turtle Dance – a mural at the Indian Pueblo Center in Albuquerque, New Mexico – depicts Pueblo people performing a ceremonial dance to bring the blessing of rain.

critical approach led to the new methodology of comparative ethnography, in which comparisons are drawn between multiple subjects to identify patterns of similarities or differences.

Observing change
In her analysis, Clews Parsons compared different Pueblo groups including Hopi, Zuni, and Tiwa peoples to each other while noting differences among their social and religious structures. She also detailed forms of cultural change including resistance, acculturation, and invention. She observed that the Pueblo peoples were not static and unchanging, but a dynamic cultural group influenced by history and possessing the agency to make changes in their own social world. She also compared Pueblo groups to different Indigenous peoples across the western US and northern Mexico, including Nahua peoples and the Indigenous peoples of the Great Plains. Furthermore, her research considered the influence of colonization – something that other researchers often noted but omitted in their final published works. Her form of research analysis emphasized the use

See also: Origins of culture 32–33 ▪ Autoethnography 76–77 ▪ Local belief systems 78–79 ▪ Critical ethnography 270–71

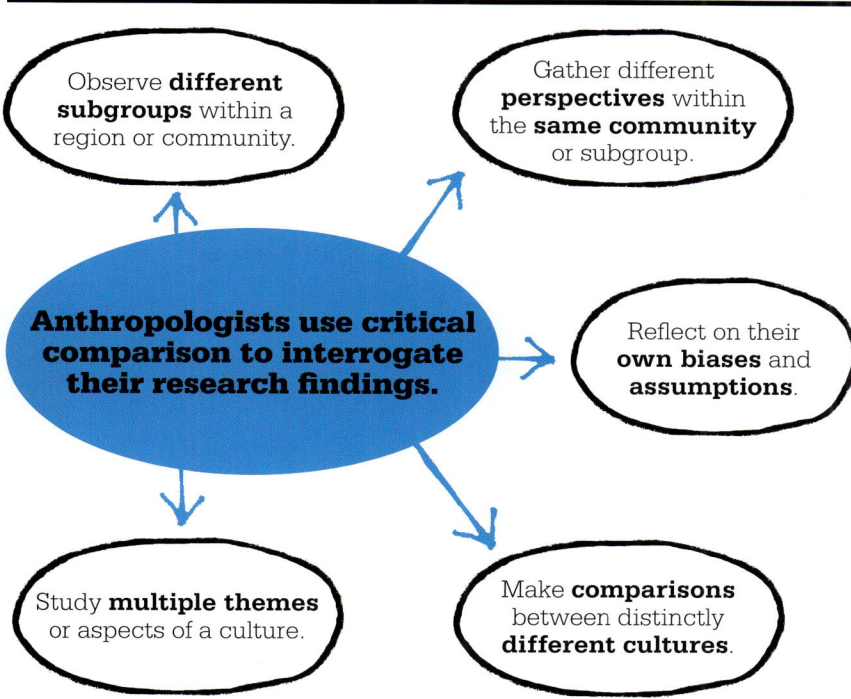

Observe **different subgroups** within a region or community.

Gather different **perspectives** within the **same community** or subgroup.

Anthropologists use critical comparison to interrogate their research findings.

Reflect on their **own biases** and **assumptions**.

Study **multiple themes** or aspects of a culture.

Make **comparisons** between distinctly **different cultures**.

of cultural relativism as a methodological tool, and demonstrated that it was necessary in cross-cultural research.

Critical approach

Throughout her anthropological work, Clews Parsons emphasized the importance of having accurate and contextualized information and not making generalizations about any particular group. She repeatedly changed and republished information to maintain accuracy and the trust of the reader. Clews Parsons also stressed the importance of understanding all aspects of a culture, including language, before coming to any conclusions. In this way she recognized how language itself carried cultural meaning and influenced thought.

Although Clews Parsons's ethnographic work was among the most comprehensive and detailed surveys of Pueblo peoples at the time, she remained critical of her own work, even leaving a 60-page appendix at the end of *Pueblo Indian Religion* listing what she considered to be its limitations, and questions that merited future study.

Nevertheless, Clews Parsons's meticulous research made important contributions to anthropology and encouraged people to apply a comparative approach not just to the study of other cultures but also to their own by interrogating social roles, structures, and the cultural values that underpin them. In this way, her work set the standard for high quality in-depth comparative ethnographic research. ▪

Elsie Clews Parsons

Elsie Clews Parsons was born in New York City, US in 1875. She was an anthropologist, sociologist, and feminist known for critically unpacking gender roles among different groups. She graduated from Barnard College in 1896 and in 1899 she gained a PhD from Columbia University. She lectured in sociology at Barnard College from 1902 to 1905. Her work was viewed as so radical and subversive that in 1913 she published two books under the pseudonym John Main to protect her husband's political career. Clews Parsons became the Associate Editor of the *Journal of American Folklore* from 1918, and served as the president of the American Ethnological Society from 1923 to 1925. She was also selected to be the first female president of the American Anthropological Association, but died before she could take office in 1941.

Other key works

1906 *The Family*
1913 *The Old Fashioned Woman*
1936 *Mitla: Town of the Souls*

WE ARE PRODUCTS AND ACTIVE AGENTS
THE EVOLUTIONARY SYNTHESIS

During the 1940s, British biologist Julian Huxley, alongside other scientists including Ukrainian geneticist Theodosius Dobzhansky and German biologist Ernst Mayr, played a huge role in advancing the understanding of how evolution works. Together, they developed the evolutionary synthesis (also known as the "modern synthesis"), which unified Charles Darwin's theory of natural selection with emerging insights from genetics. This comprehensive framework demonstrated that evolution occurs not only through natural selection, but through other mechanisms, such as mutation, genetic drift, and sexual selection. Importantly, they noted that these changes occur at the population level, accumulating over generations rather than within individual organisms.

Understanding inheritance

When Charles Darwin published *On the Origin of Species*, he was unable to explain how inherited traits were passed from parents to offspring.

According to Mendel's concept of dominant and recessive genes, two parent plants that each have one dominant purple gene (B) and one recessive white gene (b) are three times more likely to produce offspring with purple flowers than white.

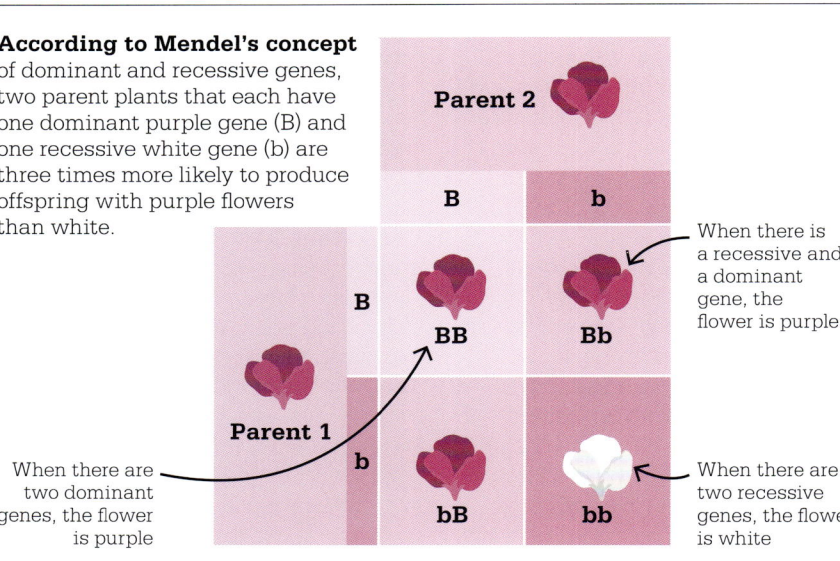

When there is a recessive and a dominant gene, the flower is purple

When there are two dominant genes, the flower is purple

When there are two recessive genes, the flower is white

See also: The theory of evolution 24–25 ▪ Unilineal evolution 26–27 ▪ Origins of humanity 94–101 ▪ Multilinear evolution 104–07 ▪ Bioarchaeology 167 ▪ Sequencing ancient DNA 290–91

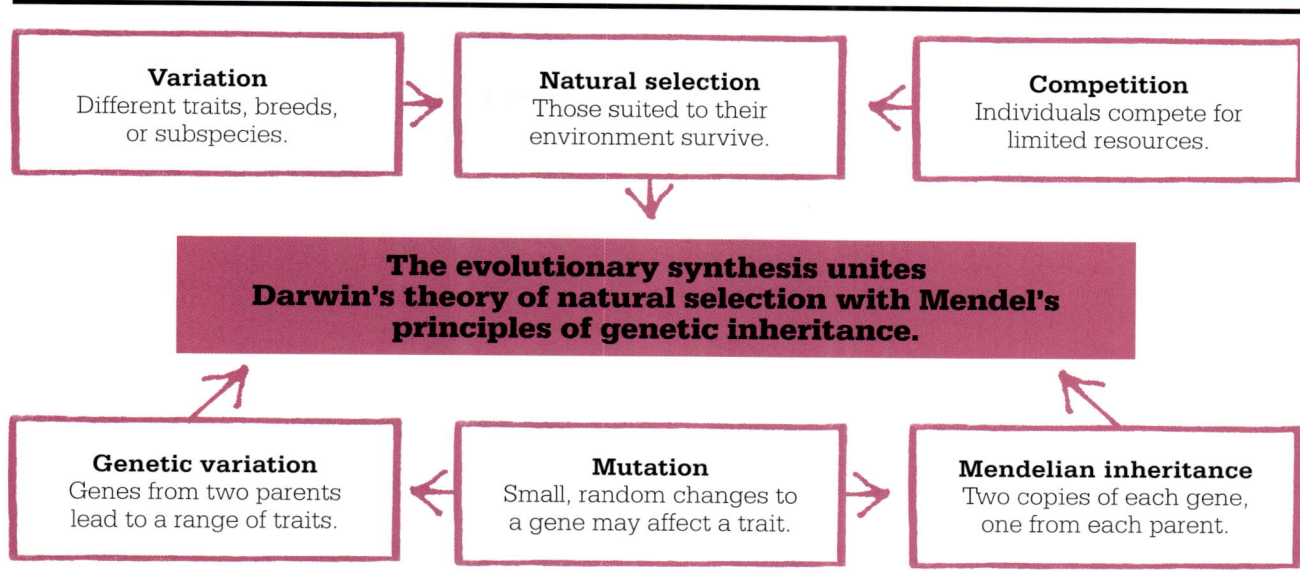

Variation
Different traits, breeds, or subspecies.

Natural selection
Those suited to their environment survive.

Competition
Individuals compete for limited resources.

The evolutionary synthesis unites Darwin's theory of natural selection with Mendel's principles of genetic inheritance.

Genetic variation
Genes from two parents lead to a range of traits.

Mutation
Small, random changes to a gene may affect a trait.

Mendelian inheritance
Two copies of each gene, one from each parent.

One discredited idea came from Jean-Baptiste Lamarck, who in 1809 suggested that organisms could inherit traits developed during their parents' lifetimes. However, a more accurate explanation of inheritance came from Austrian monk Gregor Mendel in the 1860s. Mendel discovered the basic laws of inheritance, identifying how traits are transmitted from one generation to the next. His research laid the foundation of what is today called genetics.

While Darwin described large-scale evolutionary changes, Mendel's work on genetic inheritance revealed the small-scale mechanics of inheritance. Mendel accomplished this through a series of detailed experiments with pea plants – over the course of eight years, he bred more than 10,000 of them. The results showed that genes come in pairs, with one inherited from each parent, and that traits are passed down as dominant or recessive in predictable patterns.

During the 1930s, scientists including Huxley, Dobzhansky, and Mayr sought to unify the ideas of natural selection and Mendelian genetics. Their work led to the evolutionary synthesis, which recognized that genetic mutations, inherited randomly, are the primary source of variation, and are passed on via sexual reproduction. They redefined evolution as the gradual change

Evolution … is the most powerful and the most comprehensive idea that has ever arisen on earth.
Julian Huxley
Essays of a Humanist, 1964

in the frequency of genes within populations over generations. This groundbreaking framework united two key ideas: Mendel's principles of how traits are inherited across generations and Darwin's theory of how species evolve over longer periods of time. The combined theories explained both short-term genetic changes within populations and the long-term emergence of new species.

Roots of humanity
The evolutionary synthesis has also proved to be an indispensable tool for understanding human evolution. As significant new fossil discoveries emerged in the decades following its formulation, the synthesis provided anthropologists with a robust framework for exploring the genetic underpinnings of human traits. Today, the synthesis continues to serve as the cornerstone of biological anthropology, guiding ongoing research and discoveries. ∎

A DEFINING FRAMEWORK FOR EXPERIENCE

LANGUAGE AND COGNITION

IN CONTEXT

KEY WORK
Benjamin Whorf, *An American Indian Model of the Universe*, 1950

FIELD
Linguistic anthropology

BEFORE
1836 In a work published posthumously, German philosopher Wilhelm von Humboldt proposes a theory of universal grammar, alongside a related concept of linguistic relativity.

AFTER
1966 US linguist Dell Hymes identifies two types of linguistic relativity, one based in existing grammatical structures, and another based on emerging social changes within a speech community.

1992 US linguist John Lucy publishes *Language Diversity and Thought*, which provides scientific support for Whorf's linguistic relativity.

The notion that language shapes thought has attracted a great deal of attention, particularly in relation to the idea that our entire sense of reality is profoundly influenced by the structures of our language. The concept is an ancient one, expressed throughout history by scholars, scribes, and religious specialists whose work it was to preserve wisdom with attention to the grammatical patterns of everyday speech.

In the 1950s, the posthumously published writings of Benjamin Whorf offered insights into this overarching influence of language on human life – how it shapes not only the flow of thought, but also affects related perceptions and subsequent actions. Whorf saw language as a powerful catalyst in the formation of shared thoughts, perceptions, and actions – leading to shared understandings but also shared misperceptions out of step with reality.

Differences in science

Whorf formally took up the study of linguistics during the 1930s under the direction of Edward Sapir, the preeminent linguist of the time,

The events depicted in this Hopi wall hanging – used for remembrance or storytelling – are shown as occurring, rather than presented in the context of a dated historical moment.

and a specialist in the structures of Indigenous American languages. In his subsequent work on Indigenous American languages, Whorf came to consider alternative models of science – or ways of knowing – as a pan-human preoccupation that was reflected in the grammars and vocabularies of every human language. For example, Whorf came to realize that Indigenous languages provided a relativistic sense of space and time. Unlike English – in which the concept of time is often expressed in a linear

See also: The structure of language 44–45 ▪ Structuralism 108 ▪ The rules of language 109 ▪ Ritual and language 166

English semantics	Hopi semantics
"He is running" puts an **action** in the **present tense**.	"Wari" – meaning running – is a **statement of fact**.
"He ran" puts the **same action** in the **past**.	The same word is used when the **action** is occurring in **the present** or occurred in **the past**.
English language **emphasizes** the **time** that actions or events occur.	Hopi language **emphasizes** the **action or event** rather than the time it occurs.

Semantic structures such as tenses, or the lack of tenses, shape the perception of time in different cultures.

Benjamin Whorf

Born in 1897, Benjamin Lee Whorf graduated from the Massachusetts Institute of Technology with a degree in chemistry and worked as a respected fire prevention engineer even as he pursued other interests. His passion for languages led him to study linguistics at Yale under Edward Sapir. Whorf died in 1941, leaving behind a series of unfinished works that were eventually published by his alma mater, MIT Press, in the 1940s and 1950s. Although Whorf's writings were barely known during his lifetime, his ideas have been studied by subsequent generations of scholars, especially in anthropology, linguistics, and cognitive science.

Other key works

1940 "Science and linguistics"
1944 "The Relation of Habitual Thought and Behavior to Language"
1956 Selected Essays: Language, Thought, and Reality

fashion, by recording the annual progression of years – Whorf noted that speakers of other tongues, such as the Hopi language in Arizona, US, often frame time in a more cyclical fashion that focuses on the periodic return of the days, weeks, months, and seasons.

Reality of language

Alongside his pursuit of science, Whorf also examined mysticism, and the way in which linguistic structures of grammar and vocabulary were used to capture and catalogue the wisdom of earlier generations that had been passed down by word of mouth. His work highlighted the power of structure, not only in everyday language, but throughout society, as the rules that govern us all.

According to Whorf, how we see the world in part reflects the views of our neighbours – the people with whom we share a language – who shape our thoughts with their deeds and words, especially as expressed in the grammar and vocabulary of everyday life. Whorf also noted that grammar and vocabulary are shaped by culture, and therefore evolve in response to changing needs within the culture.

Whorf's writings have encouraged scholars to explore the relationship between language and thought, particularly regarding the perception of reality and the power of speech in human consciousness. Today, beyond the fields of anthropology or linguistics, neuroscience appears to be verifying ideas put forth by early 20th-century anthropologists, such as Whorf, by showing that brain activity related to language influences a person's thinking and perception. The language one speaks, as Whorf pointed out, has an influence on how one perceives the world. ∎

POST-W

ANTHROP

1950–1980

R
OLOGY

Louis Leakey claims that **fossils** found in Tanzania's Olduvai Gorge show **humans evolved in Africa**.

1953

Claude Lévi-Strauss uses **structuralist principles** to understand **patterns** in **different cultures**.

1955

William Labov notes that **differences in pronunciation** and the use of language can be linked to **social class**.

1964

1955

Julian Steward's theory of **multilinear evolution** suggests that **societies** in **similar environments evolve** in similar ways.

1962

Lewis Binford calls for **archaeologists** to adopt a more **rigorous scientific approach** to analysing their finds.

1969

Victor Turner examines how rituals in **rites of passage** help to **maintain social order**.

The decades following World War II were a time of dramatic change – not only in politics and technology, but in how anthropologists studied human societies. As places that had been colonized gained independence and global connections grew, anthropology moved toward dynamic, interdisciplinary approaches. This period saw three major shifts: a new scientific rigour in archaeology, a deeper focus on meaning and power in culture, and |a growing awareness that anthropologists themselves – their biases and perspectives – shaped what they observed.

New approaches

At the heart of these changes were new ways of thinking about human societies. French anthropologist Claude Lévi-Strauss argued that beneath the surface of cultural diversity, universal patterns of thought – such as those found in myths or kinship systems – shaped how people understood the world. This approach, called structuralism, influenced many others, including British anthropologist Mary Douglas, who showed how symbols of purity and pollution reinforced social boundaries.

However, not everyone agreed that culture could be reduced to mental structures. Some, such as Julian Steward and Marvin Harris, insisted that material conditions – climate, food production, or economic needs – were the drivers of cultural change. Steward's idea of multilinear evolution explained why societies developed differently depending on their environment, while Harris's cultural materialism framed everything from religion to warfare as practical adaptations.

Yet for cultural anthropologist Clifford Geertz, these grand theories missed the point. Culture, he argued, was not a puzzle to solve but a web of meanings to interpret. His method of thick description – decoding rituals, art, or everyday interactions – revealed how people made sense of their own lives. Similarly, British anthropologist Victor Turner studied rites of passage, showing how rituals temporarily dissolved social hierarchies, creating moments of unity and transformation.

Rethinking the past

While cultural anthropologists debated symbolism and structure, archaeology was undergoing its

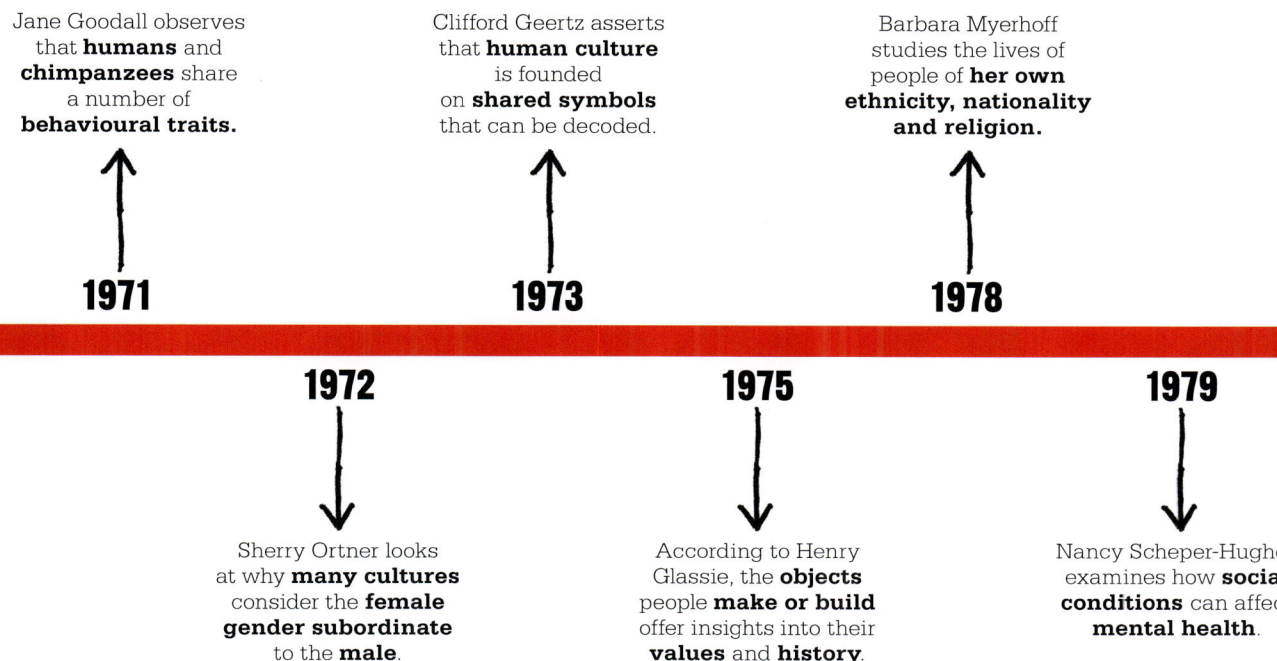

Jane Goodall observes that **humans** and **chimpanzees** share a number of **behavioural traits.**

1971

Clifford Geertz asserts that **human culture** is founded on **shared symbols** that can be decoded.

1973

Barbara Myerhoff studies the lives of people of **her own ethnicity, nationality and religion.**

1978

1972

Sherry Ortner looks at why **many cultures** consider the **female gender subordinate** to the **male**.

1975

According to Henry Glassie, the **objects** people **make or build** offer insights into their **values** and **history**.

1979

Nancy Scheper-Hughes examines how **social conditions** can affect **mental health**.

own revolution. Lewis Binford and his followers rejected old-fashioned artefact cataloguing in favour of the New Archaeology (or processual archaeology), which treated the past as a scientific laboratory. They tested hypotheses about ancient economies, migrations, and ecological adaptations, using methods borrowed from biology and physics. Meanwhile, field discoveries reshaped the understanding of human origins. Paleoanthropologists Louis and Mary Leakey's excavations at Olduvai Gorge in Tanzania uncovered fossils that pushed back the timeline of human evolution, while archaeologists Kent Flannery and Patty Jo Watson applied systems theory to study how early communities interacted with their environments.

Power, ethics, and gender

By the 1960s and 1970s, anthropology's scope widened further. Feminist scholars such as Sherry Ortner and Karen Sacks challenged the discipline's male-dominated narratives, asking why women were so often sidelined in studies of politics or economics. At the same time, anthropologists grew more self-aware about their role in research. Paul Rabinow and Barbara Myerhoff pioneered reflexive ethnography, openly discussing how their own backgrounds shaped their work, while Nancy Scheper-Hughes confronted ethical dilemmas in medical anthropology, particularly when studying power and suffering.

New methods also emerged. Linguists like William Labov documented how dialects reflected social class, and Fredrik Barth

demonstrated that ethnicity was not fixed but constantly negotiated. Advances in science transformed archaeology – Jane Buikstra's bioarchaeology extracted life stories from ancient skeletons, while L.L. Cavalli-Sforza used genetics to trace human migrations. Anthropologist Laura Nader urged scholars to "study up" – turning her attention to governments and corporations instead of marginalized communities.

By 1980, anthropology had reinvented itself. It was more rigorous, more critical, and more willing to ask uncomfortable questions about gender, power, and even its own methods. The discoveries of this era gave scholars the tools to understand humanity in a rapidly changing world. ■

WE'RE ALL REALLY FROM AFRICA

ORIGINS OF HUMANITY

IN CONTEXT

KEY WORK
Louis Leakey, *Adam's Ancestors*, 1953

FIELD
Archaeology; biological anthropology

BEFORE
1871 Charles Darwin publishes *The Descent of Man*, hypothesizing that humans and African apes share a common ancestor.

AFTER
1988 Palaeoanthropologist Rick Potts publishes *Early Hominid Activities at Olduvai*, which uses stone tools and animal bones found at Olduvai Gorge, Tanzania to explore the behaviour of hominids.

2013 Archaeologist Lawrence Barham argues that human dependency on tools dates back to 3 million years ago in *From Hand to Handle*.

Africa was formerly inhabited by extinct apes closely allied to the gorilla and chimpanzee; and… it is somewhat more probable that our early progenitors lived on the African continent.
Charles Darwin
The Descent of Man, 1871

Louis and Mary Leakey examine the upper jaw of a hominin skull found in Tanzania in 1959, and estimated to be around 600,000 years old.

The scientific community today widely supports the view that humans evolved in Africa and then dispersed in a series of migration flows, first across Europe and Asia, and later across the world. However, before the mid-19th century, the predominant explanation in the Western world for humanity's origins was based on a literal interpretation of the Bible. When research findings presented perplexing data that did not align with this interpretation, early biologists began to propose alternative explanations as to where humans originated.

In 1871, Charles Darwin published *The Descent of Man*, in which he suggested that humans are a type of primate that originated in Africa. It was a theory that proved controversial at the time, even among scientists. German biologist Ernst Haeckel, for instance, rejected Darwin's Out-of-Africa hypothesis, arguing instead

that humans were more closely related to the primates of Southeast Asia. Gradually, over the years and decades that followed, scientific evidence grew to support Darwin's ideas, the most convincing of which came from the evidence unearthed by Louis and Mary Leakey in the 1950s and 1960s.

Louis Leakey, a Kenyan-British palaeoanthropologist, had long been a strong supporter of Darwin's theory that the origins of humanity lay in Africa. Together with his wife and fellow palaeoanthropologist Mary, Leakey set out to accumulate physical evidence to support the hypothesis in East Africa, and found a collection of revelatory fossils, including the remains of the earliest known ancestor of modern humans – *Homo habilis*.

See also: The theory of evolution 24–25 ▪ Population genetics 121 ▪ Chimpanzee behaviours 132–135 ▪ Nutrition and human evolution 280 ▪ Sequencing ancient DNA 290–91 ▪ Human burials 306 ▪ Early human wood technology 317

The Asia theory

The first known fossil of an early human was found by two miners in a cave in the Neander valley in Germany in 1856. It had robust features including a large brow ridge and an elongated skull, and scientists of the time did not fully know what to make of it. It was later recognized as a new human species and named *Homo neanderthalensis,* or Neanderthal, by geologist William King. Similar fossils were found in Europe and Asia in the decades that followed, including a fossilized skull cap and femur found in Java, nicknamed the Java Man. Because of these finds and some other early primate fossils found in Asia, many scientists began to hypothesize that humans may have evolved in Asia from an earlier species that left Africa.

One of Louis Leakey's professors even warned a young Leakey that if he wanted to spend his life studying human origins, that he should look to Asia, not Africa. The debate remained heated for many years until a wave of important fossil finds were made in Africa and significant DNA evidence strengthened the Out-of-Africa hypothesis.

African finds

In 1924, Australian anthropologist Raymond Dart analyzed a fossil skull found by workers in a limestone quarry in Taung, South Africa. Named the Taung Child, the fossil was unique in that it was a very young hominin of about 3 or 4 years of age. It appeared to have many more primitive features than the Neanderthal fossils, yet the location of its

> I looked to see whether Darwin was right – and he was right.
> **Louis Leakey**
> **9in interview with the *Leakey Foundation*, 1969**

foramen magnum – the hole at the bottom of the skull through which the spinal cord enters – indicated that it could definitely walk on two feet, an ability known as bipedalism. Scientists were excited by the possibility that it represented a transitional species between apes and humans. However, it took many palaeoanthropologists until the late 1940s to accept that Taung Child was indeed likely to be an ancestral species of human and a member of the species *Australopithecus africanus* – by which time the Leakeys had already made significant discoveries about early tool use in Africa.

In 1931, the Leakeys were working at Olduvai Gorge in Tanzania, a steep ravine that forms a part of the Great Rift Valley that spans swathes of East Africa. Formed by two tectonic plates pulling away from each other – the Somali plate from the Nubian plate – the area has historically been active with volcanoes, and fossils are preserved remarkably well

there. Here, the Leakeys uncovered crude stone tools some 2.6 million years old, known as Oldowan tools. The earliest known tools at the time, they included stones used for hammering and cutting. This discovery was ground-breaking evidence of the time period that tool-using human ancestors may have lived in the area.

In 1942, the Leakeys also found a large collection of ancient stone handaxes and tools that had been flaked on two sides (called bifacial tools) at a site in Olorgesailie near Nairobi, Kenya. The quantity of handaxes found in the area was highly unusual and has since been studied to understand more about how human ancestors may have lived, how they made the tools, and how they responded to their changing environment.

Locating other species

Following these discoveries, many researchers became interested in searching for hominin fossils in Africa. In particular, Robert Broom, a Scottish medical doctor and palaeontologist, made several »

Remains of *Homo habilis* – including this well-preserved skull – were found in Tanzania. *H. habilis* lived approximately 1.75 million years ago.

important discoveries in South African caves. In 1936, he discovered the first known adult *A. africanus* while excavating in Sterkfontein cave, and in 1938, he found more fossil remains of *A. africanus* and other early hominins in Kromdraai cave, near Johannesburg. Some of these fossils were very robust, with larger, thicker, and more prominent bones.

Broom named the species *Paranthropus robustus*, which is now recognized as a form of *Australopithecus*. Significantly, these robust hominins also had a sagittal crest – or ridge of bone – across the top of the skull. Sagittal crests provide support for thick jaw muscle attachments. This skeletal feature, along with their large wide teeth suggested *P. robustus* had exceptionally strong jaw muscles and probably ate tough food such as roots and other rough vegetation.

While sagittal crests are common among large apes today, they are not present among humans nor had they been found before among hominin remains. This strongly indicated that multiple species of hominins evolved at the same time and that there existed a wide variation among them. The

discovery provided strong evidence that human evolution took place over several millions of years and that Africa was the most likely origin of humanity.

Building support

In 1948, at a site on Rusinga Island in Lake Victoria, Kenya, Mary Leakey found the perfectly preserved skull of a hominoid ape relative from about 16 million years ago, recognized as a *Proconsul*. This was a significant discovery supporting Darwin's Out-of-Africa hypothesis because *Proconsul* was thought to be a link between tree-dwelling apes and early human ancestors. This skull provided for the first time a cranium of the genus, which revealed that it had a comparatively large brain.

Returning to Olduvai Gorge, the Leakeys continued to search for evidence of human origins in Africa. In 1959, Mary Leakey discovered a particularly well-persevered fossil of a new group of hominin – *Paranthropus boisei*. The fossils were dated to about 1.8 million years ago, meaning that *P. boisei* was the earliest known hominin at the time. The discovery was not only

> The more we do know, the more we realize that early interpretations were completely wrong.
> **Mary Leakey**
> in interview with *Scientific American*, 1994

revolutionary in finding a new species, it also added more weight to the growing body of evidence backing Darwin's Out-of-Africa hypothesis.

Finding *Homo habilis*

Although all these finds provided compelling evidence of hominin evolution, none of the fossils belonged to the same genus – *Homo* – as modern humans. The first fossils of the genus *Homo* to be found were discovered in the Olduvai Gorge in Tanzania by Mary and Louis Leakey.

In 1960, the Leakeys' son Jonathan found a jaw bone that resembled a human's. Upon further investigation, the Leakeys found more fossil remains in the area including parts of a cranium, hands, and feet. Importantly, the fossils were found close to where Mary and Louis Leakey had previously found Oldowan stone tools, which suggested that this hominin might be the toolmaker.

The remains showed that this species had smaller teeth and larger brains than the Australopithecines. In addition, the hand anatomy indicated that this species was capable of a

Hand anatomy dictates the types of grip a hand is able to form. In a power grip, all fingers wrap around the object in a strong hold. For a precision grip, the object is pinched between the thumb and index finger.

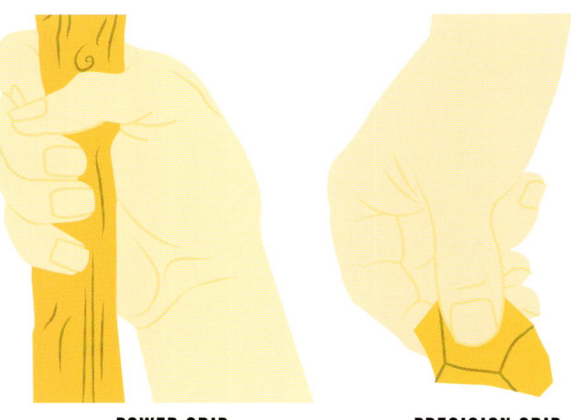

POWER GRIP   **PRECISION GRIP**

precision grip. As the hand anatomy of non-human primates and their ancestors is too long for precision grip, and humans are capable of both a power and precision grip, these fossil remains had to be from a human ancestor of the *Homo* genus. Based on these findings, Louis Leakey and his colleagues Phillip Tobias and John Napier gave the species the name *Homo habilis*, which means "handy man". The discovery was a turning point in the understanding of human evolution: not only did it uncover a new species and the earliest human ancestor to create and use tools, but it also provided the most compelling evidence that human ancestors had lived in Africa, confirming Darwin's hypothesis. A once controversial theory was now widely accepted within the scientific community.

Discovery of Lucy
In the decades that followed, many more searches for evidence of human origins were undertaken in Africa. One of the most remarkable fossil finds following the discovery of *H. habilis* was of an *Australopithecus afarensis* fossil that was nearly 40 per cent complete. The most complete fossil of this species, it was discovered by US palaeoanthropologist Donald Johanson in 1974 in Ethiopia, and he named the female fossil Lucy. The remains showed that she would have stood a little over 1 m (3 ½ ft) tall, had a relatively slender body, and shared many features in common with humans, with the exception of her brain case, which was much smaller. The discovery of such a complete skeleton helped to confirm the idea that evolution occurred over millions of years.

Identifying footprints
Around the same time as Lucy's discovery, Mary Leakey was researching fossilized animal tracks in Laetoli, Tanzania. In 1978, Leakey and chemist Paul Abell discovered a trail of 70 humanlike footprints – now »

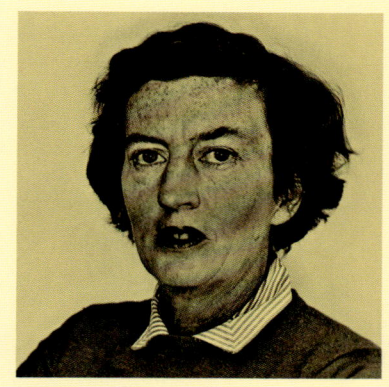

Mary Leakey

Born in London, UK in 1913 as Mary Nicol, Leakey spent much of her childhood in France. She began working on archaeological expeditions at only 17 years old, when she attended the Hembury Dig in Devon, UK, led by eminent archaeologist Dorothy Liddell. Her role on the dig was to create scientific illustrations of the tools that were found at the site. Although Leakey did not receive a formal university education, she frequently attended lectures on archaeology, geology, and prehistory at University College London and the British Museum, which nurtured her interest in the subjects. In 1934, Leakey was asked to illustrate Louis Leakey's *Adam's Ancestors*. They married in 1936 and moved to East Africa where they began their long and prolific palaeoanthropology careers conducting research in Kenya and Tanzania. Mary Leaky made many important discoveries but she considered the most significant to be the finding of the Laetoli footprints in 1978. She died in Nairobi, Kenya in 1996.

Crude tools made of stone are found at Olduvai Gorge, Tanzania.

The tools require a **precision grip**, but are older than the earliest known human ancestor with this **capacity**.

Fragments of hands and feet of *Homo habilis* are found. The **hand components** suggest *H. habilis* was capable of precision grip.

Homo habilis is identified as the earliest human ancestor to use tools.

Timeline of the presence of human ancestors and relatives

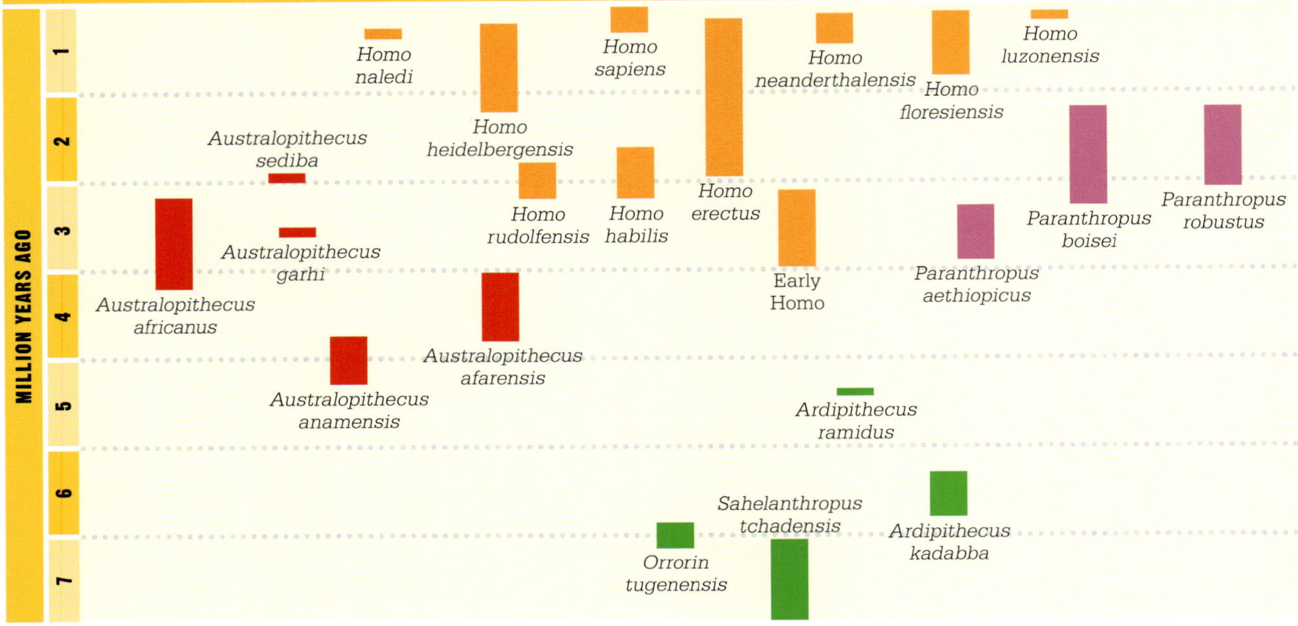

MILLION YEARS AGO

- Homo naledi
- Homo sapiens
- Homo neanderthalensis
- Homo luzonensis
- Homo floresiensis
- Australopithecus sediba
- Homo heidelbergensis
- Australopithecus garhi
- Homo rudolfensis
- Homo habilis
- Homo erectus
- Paranthropus boisei
- Paranthropus robustus
- Australopithecus africanus
- Early Homo
- Paranthropus aethiopicus
- Australopithecus anamensis
- Australopithecus afarensis
- Ardipithecus ramidus
- Sahelanthropus tchadensis
- Ardipithecus kadabba
- Orrorin tugenensis

known as the Laetoli footprints. Thought to be 3.6 million years old, the footprints were preserved in volcanic ash, and had deep impressions in the heel and toe suggesting that their maker had a similar way of walking to modern

> The past shows clearly that we all have a common origin and that our differences in race, colour, and creed are only superficial
> **Louis Leakey**

humans with the heel pressing into the ground at the start of the step and the toes being used to push off from the step. The prints also showed a toe shape that was more similar to the shaping of human toes than those of other primates. The combined evidence provided the first unequivocal proof that bipedalism was possible for human ancestors at that time.

It is widely accepted that the footprints were made by at least three individuals, and it is also thought that the footsteps may have belonged to at least two hominin species – including *A. afarensis* – who walked across the same volcanic ash just hours apart. The footprints add weight to the idea that multiple species of hominin lived alongside each other in Africa before they spread across the world, and eventually died out to leave only *H. sapiens*.

Missing links

Although the Leakeys and their contemporaries provided a wealth of evidence for the African origin of humans, there are still many unknowns about human ancestors. In recent decades, a number of fossil discoveries have been made in Africa that have come to both fill in the gaps in the human evolutionary tree, but also complicate our understanding of it.

In 2009, palaeoanthropologist Tim White discovered a 4.4 million year old fossil in Ethiopia of a very early hominin, *Ardipithecus ramidus*. It possessed a number of intermediate features – the structure of its pelvis and skull show that it was bipedal, but it had long arms and feet that had retained a grasping ability despite being adapted to walking. This suggested that *A. ramidus* spent a considerable amount of time in

Footprints of *Australopithecus afarensis*, known as the Laetoli footprints, were found by Mary Leakey in volcanic beds called tuffs.

trees, contradicting the general hypothesis that human bipedalism evolved as an adaptation to walking long distances in savanna.

In another curious discovery, palaeoanthropologist Lee Berger found in 2010 two partial skeletons of a new species; *Australopithecus sediba*. This species lived 1.9 million years ago in South Africa, and Berger and his colleagues suggested that it may be a direct descendant of *A. africanus*. If correct, this would fill in an important gap in evolution between the Australopithecines and the genus *Homo*.

Berger also made headlines in 2015 for the discovery of *Homo naledi* fossils which were found in two chambers of the Rising Star cave system near Johannesburg. The team recovered more than 1,500 fossil bones that represented at least 15 different individuals. This suggested that the bones may have been deposited intentionally, perhaps as a burial ritual. The fossils also demonstrated that this species had an unexpected combination of modern and ancient traits. For instance, it was fully bipedal and had dexterous hands like modern humans, but it also had features that suggest it spent time in the trees. In 2017 the team announced they had dated the fossils to between 335,000 and 236,000 years ago – a shockingly recent date for a species with such hybrid traits. It means that the species lived at same time as *H. sapiens*, and in the same region.

Lasting significance

Palaeoanthropology remains a fast-changing area of anthropology. Each year new fossil discoveries and new analysis promise to reshape our understanding of human evolution. However, what remains clear is that due to the discoveries of Louis and Mary Leakey, and their colleagues, the long human evolutionary journey is known to have started in Africa. ∎

Hominins, including *Homo sapiens*, **evolve in Africa**.

Homo sapiens **travel across Asia** and **Europe**. They later reach Australia, and North and South America.

Other hominin species eventually **die out**, but *Homo sapiens* **survive**.

All humans today are descended from *Homo sapiens* that evolved in Africa.

No biological races

Scientists today overwhelmingly agree that humans originated in Africa at least 300,000 years ago and there are no longer any other species or subspecies of humans alive today. Indeed humans are among the most genetically homogeneous species on earth.

The idea of "race" was created in an attempt to justify the privilege of some and the disadvantage others, and was based on arbitrary physical characteristics. However, scientific evidence does not support the existence of human biological races. We now know that human traits are inherited independently of one another – traits such as intelligence or athletic ability are the result of complex interrelationships between one's genes and one's environment. Genetic diversity is also greater within each so-called race than it is between different races. Although race does not exist in a biological sense, the concept continues to shape society and people's lives.

EVERY REAL SOCIETY IS A PROCESS IN TIME
THE FLUIDITY OF SOCIAL SYSTEMS

IN CONTEXT

KEY WORK
Edmund Leach, *Political Systems of Highland Burma*, 1954

FIELD
Sociocultural anthropology

BEFORE
1895 Émile Durkheim formulates the idea of "social facts" – concepts and institutions that can exercise social control. His work greatly influences British social anthropology.

1922 Bronisław Malinowski and A.R. Radcliffe-Brown publish key works that set precedents for social anthropological analysis and ethnographic writing.

AFTER
1969 Fredrik Barth argues that it is the boundary, and the work done to maintain it, that separates one ethnic group from another, rather than language, religion, or dress.

In the 1950s, most social anthropologists assumed that societies naturally exist in a stable state of equilibrium. British anthropologist Edmund Leach challenged this view, using his fieldwork in colonial Burma (present-day Myanmar) to show that social systems are constantly shifting.

Unlike other anthropologists, who preferred to focus on one small village cluster or "tribe", Leach carried out fieldwork over a wide area, to include some of the many linguistically distinct groups living in the Kachin Hills of northern Myanmar. This broad reach was necessary, he argued, because the villagers here could hold a defined place in several different social systems at the same time.

Immersed in the region

Leach spent five years in northern Myanmar during World War II, learning local languages and engaging with its cultures. He used census data and government reports to trace the area's long history of shifting cultural patterns and social structures, shaped by both local dynamics and British colonialism.

Dressed as bird-human figures from Shan legend, two dancers perform a Bird Dance. Customs may suggest fixed ethnic identities, but Leach revealed that social groups are much more fluid.

See also: The social roots of religion 42–43 ▪ Local belief systems 78–79 ▪ Structuralism 108 ▪ Defining ethnicity 130–31

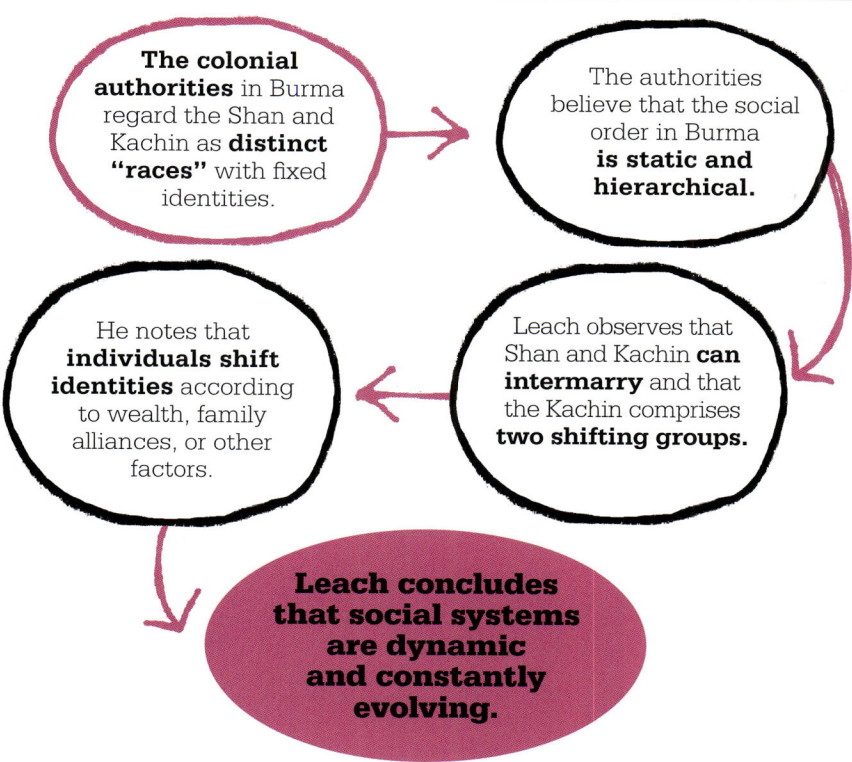

The colonial authorities in Burma regard the Shan and Kachin as **distinct "races"** with fixed identities.

The authorities believe that the social order in Burma **is static and hierarchical.**

He notes that **individuals shift identities** according to wealth, family alliances, or other factors.

Leach observes that Shan and Kachin **can intermarry** and that the Kachin comprises **two shifting groups.**

Leach concludes that social systems are dynamic and constantly evolving.

Edmund Leach

Born in Lancashire, UK, in 1910, Edmund Leach attended the London School of Economics (LSE), where he studied under pioneering anthropologists Bronisław Malinowski and Raymond Firth.

Leach began his fieldwork in the north of what was then known as Burma in August 1939. When World War II broke out, he joined the Burma Army, which allowed him to travel, learn the Kachin language, and gain a deep understanding of Kachin and Shan society.

After the war, Leach completed his doctorate at LSE and conducted a survey of the peoples of Sarawak (now part of Indonesia) for the British government. In 1953, he was appointed lecturer at Cambridge University.

Leach published several influential books and scores of academic articles, ranging from ethnographies to more pointedly theoretical work on kinship, language, and myth. He died in 1989.

Other key works

1961 *Pul Eliya, a Village in Ceylon*
1976 *Culture and Communication*

Despite the region's linguistic and cultural diversity, 19th-century Burmese and British officials had grouped its inhabitants into two categories: the literate, Buddhist Shan, who lived in permanent settlements with state-like structures, and the illiterate Kachin, who practised shifting agriculture in mobile, family-based villages. The Shan were seen as "civilized", while the Kachin were labelled "savages".

Societies in flux

Leach observed that the social system here was, in reality, much more complex, with individuals often identifying as both Shan and Kachin. He also established that there were two types of Kachin: the *gumlao* Kachin, characterized by egalitarian principles, and the *gumsa* Kachin, who maintained a hierarchical structure with chiefs. Leach noted that Kachin villages shifted between *gumlao* and *gumsa* systems, with some *gumsa* Kachin even becoming Shan by marrying into princely families and accepting Buddhism. Leach argued that the Kachin were continually shifting between the *gumlao* and *gumsa* systems, moving back and forth in response to social, economic, and political pressures.

Leach's work in Myanmar revolutionized social anthropology: it challenged traditional views of societies as static entities, and provided a framework for understanding complex societies and structural change. ∎

A QUEST FOR CULTURAL REGULARITIES OR LAWS

MULTILINEAR EVOLUTION

Julian Steward was among the first US anthropologists to develop a theory of culture change – that is, an explanation of the processes that drive cultural, social, and behavioural shifts. Grounded in cultural ecology, or the study of the reciprocal links between environment and culture, Steward's theory came to be known as multilinear evolution.

Steward was following in the footsteps of renowned US anthropologists Alfred Kroeber and Franz Boas, who were committed to demonstrating that the theory of unilinear evolution was incorrect. Supporters of this theory assumed that all people moved along the

See also: Cultural relativism 34–41 ▪ The New Archaeology 110–15
▪ Reflexive ethnography 162–65

While it is true that cultures
are rooted in nature …
they are no more produced
by that nature than a plant.
Alfred Kroeber
*Cultural and Natural Areas
of Native North America*, 1939

same, predetermined, evolutionary
path, with Western culture as the
endpoint; they equated this path
with progress, an upward movement
of greater intelligence and higher
morality. Unilinear evolutionists
believed that differences among the
world's peoples were due either to
harsh environments that thwarted
the population's efforts to make
progress, or to biological or genetic
factors, such as a lower intelligence.

As part of their efforts to debunk
unilinear evolution, Boas and his
students argued that environment
played only a minor role in creating
variation in world cultures –
for example, by virtue of their
barren surrounds, Arctic societies
cannot be based on agriculture.
They also rejected the search for
regularities among societies.
Instead, they focused on the
histories of individual communities,
investigating how various cultural
traits were either developed
independently or borrowed
from neighbouring groups.

Analysing patterns

As more ethnographic data became
available, it was difficult for
anthropologists such as Steward to
ignore the patterns that emerged.
He therefore rejected a key element
of Boasian anthropology – what »

Steward's excavations in Utah
uncovered finely crafted moccasins
from the 13th century, along with
other evidence of a thriving population
of Indigenous American hunters.

Julian Steward

Born in Washington, DC, in
1902, Julian Steward attended
school in rural California,
where he was required to work
the land. As a result, he came
to know some of the local
Paiute people. After receiving
a BSc in zoology from Cornell
University, Steward studied
anthropology under Alfred
Kroeber at the University of
California, Berkeley, obtaining
a doctorate in 1929.

Steward went on to create
the University of Michigan's
anthropology department,
and he taught at several
universities, including New
York's Columbia University,
where his students included
Eric Wolf, Elman Service,
and Sidney Mintz.

A prolific writer, Steward
contributed numerous articles
to anthropology journals,
promoting his theories of
cultural ecology and the
development of civilizations.
He died in 1972.

Other key works

1938 *Basin-Plateau Aboriginal
Sociopolitical Groups*
1959 *Handbook of South
American Indians*
1967 *Contemporary Change
in Traditional Cultures*

he called the "fruitless assumption that culture comes from culture". In order to identify causes of cultural change, Steward combined Boas's focus on the histories of individual societies with the patterns he observed among those who lived in similar environments.

In Steward's opinion, the world's peoples do not all move along the same path to European civilization, but they follow myriad routes, largely dictated by human responses to the environment. However, these routes are not completely unique to each society. Communities may have different cultural ideas and practices, but Steward thought that the structures of the different pathways – for example, the development of social inequality – exhibited a number of similarities.

Cultural ecology
Steward developed his theory of cultural ecology during the 1930s, initially focusing on hunter-gatherer societies. He examined the

> There are no theories unless based upon fact, but facts exist only within the context of a theory.
> **Julian Steward**
> Quoted in *Scenes from the High Desert*, Virginia Kerns, 2009

environment and the technology used to extract food and other resources from that environment, as well as the pattern of work that those two factors created.

Like Kroeber, Steward believed that the environment, technology, social organization, and religion were all linked; however, the two anthropologists disagreed over the direction and strength of those connections, with Kroeber favouring what he called "value culture" – that is, art, myth, rituals, and other unique expressions of a society. Steward, on the other hand, believed that the main factors were the environment – especially those aspects that provided food – and technology. In his opinion, these two factors conditioned all other aspects of a human society and formed a "cultural core" on which other elements could be built.

Bands of hunters
Steward argued that a common cultural core of hunter-gatherer societies was the patrilineal band. This consisted of several families who traced their descent through related men. A residential group, for example, might consist of an older man and his wife, their sons, and their sons' wives and children, with the men and their offspring belonging to the same patrilineage. These groups were also exogamous, meaning that the men married women from a different patrilineage who then came to live in the same territory as their husbands, a practice known as patrilocality. Other aspects of these societies – such as religion, art, and mythology, which Steward called secondary features – could be variable and affected by the diffusion of ideas from neighbouring groups.

Believing that the patrilineal band resulted from the hunting of large, non-migratory herd animals using bows or spears, Steward suggested that related men remained together to hunt communally – especially brothers, since they knew one another and the territory where they grew up. Steward pointed out that this

---

A community's **subsistence strategy** is determined by the combination of **natural resources** and **available technology**.

The **behaviour of individuals** changes to fit the **subsistence strategy**.

Similar **social patterns emerge** from subsistence strategies in different places with similar or **comparable resources**.

Cultures develop according to the needs of their environment.

Steward investigated how technological change in agrarian communities in Puerto Rico – including mechanization, chemical spraying, and irrigation – drove cultural change.

pattern of behaviour did not result from the diffusion of ideas from neighbours, because it appeared in many different places in the world, even where neighbours did not have patrilineal bands. Nor did he think the pattern was simply a legacy from an earlier stage of human evolution, as unilinear theorists thought, since it was found only in certain hunter-gatherer societies, rather than all of them. This suggested that the pattern was a behavioural adaptation.

The role of the environment

From the mid-1950s, Steward shifted his attention to other forms of society, studying the effects of irrigation agriculture and conducting a comparative study of modernization in 11 traditional societies, including Puerto Rico. He sought to understand how different initial conditions – notably environment and technology – created different cultural cores that led societies to different paths of change.

This was not a sterile exercise in scholarship, but one that Steward saw as critical to assisting other cultures in their own social

development. Understanding the causal relations between environment and technology was crucial to knowing which path would lead to the beneficial result sought by all involved.

A unified approach

Steward's approach had a serious limitation, in that there was no clear and consistent method for defining the cultural core. One researcher even pointed out that in hunter-gatherer societies, the entire society constitutes the

cultural core, which is not helpful. Much more is known about hunter-gatherer societies today, and some of Steward's predictions have not held up. In fact, Steward never reached the level of explanation that he hoped to achieve – one that would permit modern agencies to use his research to direct social development.

However, Steward's work on cultural ecology was the foundation and inspiration for another approach: that of human behavioural ecology. This united cultural ecology with evolutionary theory, and looked at the material conditions of life: environment, technology, subsistence, and population density. Although it focuses on hunter-gatherer societies, since the 1980s it has proved to be remarkably useful in helping to understand variation in human behaviour across many kinds of societies. ∎

Circumscription theory

Early cultural evolutionists saw state-based societies as an inevitable end product of human evolution. However, this idea was not universally accepted, and in 1970 US anthropologist Robert Carneiro proposed a theory that linked environmental factors with technology and population density.

Carneiro noticed that agricultural land is spread over wide areas in Amazonia, which had not experienced a series of state societies. In northern Peru – which had – agriculture is constrained in narrow river valleys. As a population grows, Carneiro reasoned, it reaches carrying capacity. If it is not possible to migrate, the people must invest in technology to increase production. This augments the carrying capacity, but eventually the population will exceed it. The solution may then be to take the land of an adjacent valley. This requires warfare and a bureaucracy to subjugate the conquered peoples; with this bureaucracy in place, a state is born.

MYTHS OPERATE IN MEN'S MINDS WITHOUT THEIR BEING AWARE
STRUCTURALISM

IN CONTEXT

KEY WORK
**Claude Lévi-Strauss,
Tristes Tropiques, 1955**

FIELD
Linguistic anthropology

BEFORE
1916 Swiss linguist Ferdinand de Saussure offers a plan for studying the foundations of human languages in the posthumously published *Course in General Linguistics*.

AFTER
1967 French-Algerian philosopher Jacques Derrida publishes *Of Grammatology*, which challenges the dualistic nature of structuralism, and leads to post-structuralism.

1981 The post-structuralist writings of Russian philosopher Mikhail Bakhtin are published posthumously in *The Dialogic Imagination*. It shows that deep layers of truth can emerge from conversations with opposing points of view.

French anthropologist Claude Lévi-Strauss applied the principles of structuralism – the theory that elements gain meaning by their relationship to other elements – to anthropology in order to understand patterns within cultures. He considered these patterns to act as an unconscious infrastructure that applied to all cultures.

For example, he explored the idea of mythology as a language with laws and principles that create narratives. People then use these narratives to provide guidance and share wisdom across multiple generations. Similarly, he considered the importance of music in human life, studying its role in kinship, ceremony, and religion, where the rhythm and melody of song can easily pass from one generation to the next.

Creating meaning

Far from reducing human life to a series of simple, predictable rules with his structuralist theory, Lévi-Strauss explored the philosophical principles of semiotics – the relationship between language and meaning. He concluded that meaning is derived from the reflections of simple binary principles. In many myths, for example, agriculture and hunting represent the opposing binaries of life and death, and this meaning is understood across cultures. He concluded that such structures were universal in human minds. ∎

Claude Lévi-Strauss conducted fieldwork among Indigenous peoples in the Amazonian rainforest during the 1930s, whilst a teacher of sociology at the University of São Paulo, Brazil.

See also: Ritual and language 166 ▪ The agricultural theory of language diffusion 210–11

LANGUAGE IS A HUMAN POSSESSION
THE RULES OF LANGUAGE

IN CONTEXT

KEY WORK
Noam Chomsky, *Syntactic Structures*, **1957**

FIELD
Linguistic anthropology

BEFORE
1641 French philosopher René Descartes publishes *Meditations on First Philosophy*, where he proposes that a set of innate ideas, including language, are shared equally by all humans.

AFTER
1979 Psychology professor Herbert Terrace publishes *Nim*, documenting an experiment in teaching human language to a chimpanzee named "Nim Chimpsky" after Noam Chomsky.

1997 US neuroanthropologist Terrence Deacon publishes *The Symbolic Species*, which claims that innate structural tendencies only go so far in explaining language.

L ike many working in his field before him, US linguist Noam Chomsky wanted to understand the universal presence of grammar across languages. Chomsky sought to describe the systems of rules that speakers follow without conscious awareness. Hypothesising that all people have the capacity for language, he hoped to understand the basic design principles of sound and the rules around the formation of words and phrases, which he claimed are shared by all humans, regardless of language.

Innate ability

Chomsky pursued the idea of a universal capacity for language by studying the rules of syntax – the arrangement of words in order to create a sentence – and phonology – the sounds made by speech – as they might apply to all human languages. He argued that children learn grammar rules with ease because of an innate human ability to acquire language.

A language is not just words. It's a culture, a tradition, a unification of a community.
Noam Chomsky
in the documentary film
***We Still Live Here*, 2010**

In later years, Chomsky began to recognize the importance of culture and identity when it comes to expressing oneself in a given language. This brought him full circle in his theories on the deeper expression of linguistics across cultures throughout history. Looking at both the universals and relativity of human thought, Chomsky came to understand that universal language structures can express infinite meanings. ■

See also: The structure of language 44–45 ▪ Language and cognition 88–89 ▪ Accents, dialects, and code-switching 244–45

THE ENTIRE SPAN OF CULTURAL HISTORY AS OUR LABORATORY

THE NEW ARCHAEOLOGY

IN CONTEXT

KEY WORK
**Lewis Binford,
*Archaeology as
Anthropology*, 1962**

FIELD
Archaeology

BEFORE
1935 Arthur Tansley coins the
term "ecosystem", presenting
nature as comprising
interconnected systems.

1942 Julian Huxley's
"New Synthesis" unites
Darwinian evolution and
Mendelian genetics.

AFTER
1968 Ludwig von Bertalanffy
shows how complex systems –
biological, ecological, and
social – work by the same
fundamental rules.

1980s Ian Hodder publishes
a series of papers and books
that challenge the New
Archaeology, emphasizing
the role of human agency.

Archaeologists study past societies by examining the material traces they left behind. But how they do this – and what they aim to learn from it – has changed over time. In the 1960s, US archaeologist Lewis Binford transformed the field by arguing that archaeology should adopt scientific methods to understand human behaviour and cultural change.

In 1962, Binford, then a young scholar at the University of Chicago, published one of the most influential papers in archaeology. *Archaeology as Anthropology* called for a fundamental change in how archaeologists understood their purpose and conducted their research. Over the following years, Binford expanded on these ideas, shaping what was first known as the "New Archaeology" and later "Processual Archaeology". Binford argued that archaeology was failing to contribute meaningfully to anthropology. To change this, he believed it should adopt a scientific approach, and treat artefacts as reflections of human behaviour; analyse societies as systems; use quantitative methods, such as statistical analysis; and understand human behaviour as an adaptation to the environment.

Scientific foundations

Binford's new theory built on the foundations of earlier scientific advancements. In the first half of the 20th century, scientists combined the theory of evolution with genetics to create a "new synthesis", one that unified large-scale evolutionary trends with the fine details of genetic inheritance.

> Archaeologists should be among the best qualified to study and directly test hypotheses concerning the process of evolutionary change…
> **Lewis Binford**

Lewis Binford

Born in 1931 in Norfolk, Virginia, US, Lewis Binford studied forestry and wildlife biology at Virginia Polytechnic Institute. A visit to Japan during the Korean War sparked his interest in human cultures, and he completed an anthropology PhD at the University of Michigan in 1964. Influenced by US anthropologists Leslie White and Julian Steward, he specialized in hunter-gatherer societies.

An engaging teacher and lecturer, Binford taught at the Universities of Chicago, California (Los Angeles), New Mexico, and Southern Methodist University, and published widely. As a leading figure in the development of processual archaeology he emphasized the importance of scientific methods in archaeological research. He also helped to establish the fields of ethnoarchaeology and taphonomy. He died in 2011.

Other key works

1981 *Bones: Ancient Men and Modern Myths*
1983 *In Pursuit of the Past*
2001 *Constructing Frames of Reference*

See also: Unilineal evolution 26–27 ▪ Cultural relativism 34–41 ▪ The evolutionary synthesis 86–87 ▪ Systems theory 125 ▪ Processual archaeology 136–37 ▪ Post-processual archaeology 190–91

Archaeologists carefully excavate a site, using systematic methods to uncover artefacts. The New Archaeology emphasized scientific analysis to interpret past behaviour.

This led to a deeper understanding of Charles Darwin's idea of evolution through natural selection, or adaptation. At the same time, the development of systems theory – particularly the idea of ecosystems – demonstrated that species could not be understood in isolation but as part of the web of life in which they evolved. These concepts of adaptation and ecosystems would become key to studying the past.

Binford, like all archaeologists in the US, received his training in the field of anthropology. Archaeology was a subfield of anthropology in the US, unlike in Europe and the UK, where it was associated with geology, palaeontology, or art history. This American framework was pioneered by Franz Boas, who was strongly opposed to the racist theories of unilinear evolution. Boas proposed a different approach, rejecting the idea that living cultures, such as the Indigenous societies of North America, were remnants of an earlier era or had been forgotten by time. Instead, he argued, they were complex products of their unique circumstances and histories.

In this way, archaeological sites came to be seen as primary sources of historical understanding for North America's Indigenous populations, standing in stark contrast to European approaches.

Bridging the gap

In 1962, however, Binford realized that there was a disconnect between what anthropologists and archaeologists did. Anthropologists typically studied kinship and social organization, political systems, myths, cosmology, and language. Out of necessity, archaeologists studied material culture – pottery shards, stone projectile points, and the remains of dwellings. Binford believed that despite their different sources of data, archaeologists and anthropologists could study the same subjects. Yet in practice, they rarely did. At that time, archaeologists focused on categorizing artefacts into specific types or styles. Pottery, for instance, might be classified based on its painting style, while projectile points could be identified by features such as side-notches or a teardrop shape. By carrying out excavations, archaeologists could see that different artefact styles were replaced over time. For example, unpainted ceramics might be succeeded by painted pottery.

To understand such changes, archaeologists interpreted artefacts as reflections of cultural templates – ideas of what the "proper" pot or projectile point should look like. They explained changes in artefact styles over time as resulting from either migration – the arrival of new people, bringing with them new skills – or the diffusion and adoption of new ideas from one region to a neighbouring one.

Binford, however, argued that these were not true scientific explanations – they failed to ask *why* changes occurred. For »

	Culture-historical Archaeology	New Archaeology
Main focus	Describing and categorizing cultures based on artefacts	Explaining how and why cultures change over time
Method	Collecting and organizing artefacts by location and type	Using the scientific method to test hypotheses about cultures
View of cultures	Static, seen as fixed in time	Dynamic, changing through processes and adaptation
Theory	Emphasis on chronology and cultural evolution	Emphasis on systems theory and environmental factors

Reconstructing copper tools from the Great Lakes region has helped archaeologist Michelle Bebber to gain insights into their use. Binford believed that copper tools had transitioned from a functional to symbolic role.

example, why did people choose to adopt certain designs but not others? Why did they develop a new type of pottery or a new way of building houses? He criticized archaeologists for treating artefacts merely as "traits", ignoring their functional purpose, and for interpreting them without a solid theoretical framework. Change was too often vaguely attributed to "cultural blending" or influences from other traditions, rather than to specific, identifiable causes.

Binford contended that not only were archaeology's methods ill-suited to its goals, but that its goals themselves needed rethinking. Influenced by contemporary systems theory, Binford argued that archaeologists should attempt to reconstruct behavioural sub-systems – distinct but interconnected activities such as tool-making, food-gathering, or shelter-building

– that together formed a culture's adaptive strategy. Borrowing from his mentor, Leslie White, he understood culture as humanity's way of adapting to its physical and social environments.

Artefacts and behaviour

Crucial to Binford's argument was the idea that artefacts were not merely "traits" that reflected a culture's template for a "proper" pot, arrowhead, and so on. Instead, artefacts were reflections of human behaviour. With proper analysis, Binford argued, archaeologists could create "a systematic and understandable picture of the total extinct cultural system". He identified three major classes of artefacts that provided insights into different sub-systems.

Technomic artefacts, such as arrowheads, represented behaviour that directly interacted with the physical environment, such as hunting animals. Socio-technic artefacts, such as a king's crown or badges of political office, reflected behaviour in the social realm, such as a coronation or a social feast. Ideotechnic artefacts,

such as religious figurines, reflected behaviour in a society's ideological realm, such as religious rituals. Although these terms are not used by archaeologists today, they highlighted archaeology's growing desire to reconstruct the behaviour of ancient societies.

Reinterpreting the past

Binford's innovative perspective reshaped the understanding of how copper was used in ancient times in the Great Lakes region of the US. These tools, first produced several thousand years ago from raw, unsmelted copper, initially served as functional implements, such as adzes (woodworking tools) and axes. However, about 2000 years ago, copper was increasingly used for symbolic or ceremonial objects, such as plaques and ornaments, rather than for functional tools. In the 1950s, scholars working within the evolutionary thinking of the day, interpreted this shift as "technological devolution" – a decline in technical skills. Binford, however, saw things differently.

Copper tools, he argued, were more costly to mine and manufacture than comparable

… with the entire span of culture history as our "laboratory", [archaeologists] cannot afford to keep our theoretical heads buried in the sand.
Lewis Binford

Artefacts reflect how societies interact with their environment, organize socially, and express beliefs.

Technomic artefacts are used to interact with the **physical environment**.

Socio-technic artefacts communicate **social status, authority, or group identity**.

Ideotechnic artefacts convey **symbolic or religious** meaning within a culture.

---

stone tools. Furthermore, stone tools were just as effective, if not more so, at cutting and adzing wood. Copper artefacts were rarely discarded in waste dumps, but instead carefully placed in burials, often far from their mining sites.

Based on these patterns, Binford suggested that copper tools were both technomic *and* socio-technic. These tools had a practical use and expressed a social relationship. They offered archaeologists deep insights into the social and political sub-systems of the past.

Binford interpreted the shift in the use of copper from functional tools to ornaments as evidence of a transition from an egalitarian society to a ranked one. In an egalitarian society, individuals achieve status through their skills in daily activities, with functional tools such as axes and adzes marking this status. In contrast, a ranked society assigns status at birth, with items such as copper ornaments symbolically representing this hierarchy. Binford reframed the discussion of copper tools to one in which artefacts reflect changes in sociopolitical organization. This in turn opened the door to questions about why the sociopolitical system changed.

A rigorous approach

Binford argued that archaeologists should regard themselves as scientists testing anthropological hypotheses. For example, two of his students used archaeology to test whether ancient Puebloan peoples had matrilineal kinship, where descent is traced through a female line. Binford also argued that a scientific approach required quantitative methods, such as the use of statistics and rigorous sampling procedures. His approach was widely adopted among the new generation of archaeologists, aided in part by the radical changes occurring in American society during the 1960s.

The New Archaeology, with its focus on the process of change in cultural systems, soon became known as "processual archaeology". Binford's approach emphasized behaviour, often at the expense of cultural aspects. It downplayed the significance of migration and the diffusion of ideas, both of which were important factors. Instead, archaeologists concentrated on the environment, climate, and population density. Binford's method was eventually challenged by archaeologists such as Ian Hodder, who introduced a new approach known as "post-processual archaeology". ■

Interpreting bones

While studying Neanderthal sites in France in the 1960s, Lewis Binford realized he needed better ways to link archaeological remains with human behaviour. He turned to studying living people, and in 1969, began research with Alaska's Nunamiut Inuit people.

Binford demonstrated that Nunamiut hunters butchered caribou differently depending on season, distance from the camp, or whether the meat would be stored. Nunamiut hunters left some bones at the kill site and took others home, creating different bone patterns depending on the conditions.

In addition, Binford investigated wolf dens and kills, seeking patterns in bone assemblages that separated human from carnivore kills. His research advanced the field of taphonomy, the study of how bones enter the archaeological record, and asked whether early humans were hunters or scavengers of game.

PEOPLE HEAR SPEECH THROUGH A SCREEN OF STEREOTYPES

ENGLISH VERNACULAR

IN CONTEXT

KEY WORK
William Labov, *The Social Stratification of English in New York City*, 1964

FIELD
Linguistic anthropology

BEFORE
1913 *Pygmalion* by Irish playwright George Bernard Shaw premieres in Austria. The play highlights the social stigmas associated with speaking Cockney, a non-standard English dialect.

AFTER
1974 In *Foundations in Sociolinguistics*, US linguist Dell Hymes explores the place of Indigenous languages in the modern world.

2019 Linguists Susan Gal and Judith Irvine publish *Signs of Difference*, which examines the social meanings of linguistic differences.

Sociolinguist William Labov grew up in New Jersey, US, in a region that is known for its vast linguistic diversity. He came to be a keen observer of how dialects assert social identity in everyday interactions – and exploring the links between language and social background became a key aspect of his work.

Linguistic variations

In his early research Labov examined the sociolinguistic differences in New York City – a multilingual speech community with many different accents marked by neighbourhood,

See also: Accents, dialects, and code-switching 244–45 ▪ The role of African American Vernacular English 254–55

WILLIAM LABOV'S 4TH FLOOR STUDY

Individuals were asked a **question engineered** to get them to give the **same specific response**: **"4th floor"**.

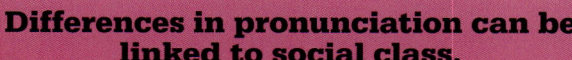

"Fou**r**th floo**r**"	"F**au**th fla**w**"
Pronounce "r"	Do not pronounce "r"
High social class	**Low social class**

Differences in pronunciation can be linked to social class.

ethnicity, and social class. He used a highly innovative methodology to study the speech of employees working in three department stores that catered for different demographics: Saks Fifth Avenue, which was expensive and high end; Macy's, an average price, mid-range store; and S. Klein, which suited a working-class budget.

Posing as a customer to elicit a natural response, at each store Labov asked employees a question to which the answer was "fourth floor". He did this knowing that the loss of the "r" sound in the words "fourth" and "floor" was a potent indicator of lower social class. The data he collected revealed that 62 per cent of employees with higher socioeconomic status – the group working in Saks – pronounced the "r", but only 20 per cent of those with lower socioeconomic status who worked at S. Klein did so. Labov also found that this simple linguistic feature made all the

difference in terms of social stereotyping, revealing that the forms without the "r" sound were more heavily stigmatized.

Social status
In *Sociolinguistic Patterns*, first published in 1972, Labov documented his study of the »

I have resisted the term sociolinguistics for many years, since it implies that there can be a successful linguistic theory or practice which is not social.
William Labov

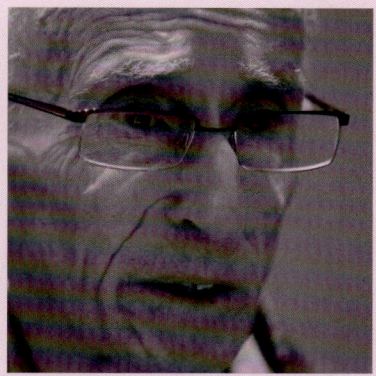

William Labov

Born in New Jersey in 1927, William Labov attended Harvard University, where his early studies included philosophy, science, and the humanities. After graduating in 1948, he took up a position in his family business, working as a chemist. When he returned to graduate school at Columbia University in 1961, Labov combined his scientific acumen with his interest in the humanities. This synthesis came to define his many contributions to linguistics, and key research areas included the science of humanity and deconstructing racism on scientific terms. Labov was also well respected for his contributions to theories of language change. He remained an active figure in the field of linguistics until he retired in 2015. He died in 2024 at the age of 97.

Other key works

1969 *The Study of Non-Standard English*
1972 *Language in the Inner City*
1972 *Sociolinguistic Patterns*
1994 *Principles of Linguistic Change*

Immigrant Portuguese fishermen were part of Labov's study on vowel sounds. Unlike local-born fishermen, the older men were less likely to use centralized pronunciation.

sociolinguistic dialects heard on the island of Martha's Vineyard, Massachusetts. There, he found a sharp contrast between the long-term members of the community and the so-called "summer people" who were there only for a season. The permanent population of Martha's Vineyard included those who lived in the towns, known as down-islanders, and up-islanders who lived in rural areas. It also included several generations of people who had emigrated from Portugal. By analysing data from recorded interviews with the islanders – in which he asked them to speak freely of childhood experiences or island life – Labov found that a number of individuals spoke with a more centralized pronunciation of vowel sounds, with words like "sound" and "bout" sounding more like "seund" and "beut". These "older" vowel sounds were particularly prevalent among middle-aged up-islanders. By contrast, among the residents with

Style and class stratification of language are actually independent.
William Labov
A Study of Non-Standard English, 1969

Portuguese heritage, Labov found that the younger generations were most likely to use centralized pronunciation, possibly because they had more involvement in the wider community than their elders. Importantly, the use of this linguistic variation set the permanent residents of Martha's Vineyard apart from the summer people, and subtly marked their social status as true islanders.

Solving the paradox

Like many linguists, Labov sought to resolve one of the fundamental puzzles in the history of linguistics – the Saussurean paradox. Broadly speaking, the paradox is that to understand the language of individual speakers, you need to study the language of the whole community; but to understand the language of the community, you need to look at individual speakers.

The paradox exists because – as Swiss linguist Ferdinand de Saussure explained – language is both an individual form of expression, and a social construct, or system. De Saussure explored the notion that each so-called "speech community" shares a

common set of rules that relate to the basic structures of grammar and vocabulary. Essentially, to speak a given tongue, community members must share a basic sense of the meaning of the language that they use. This includes everything from individual words, to the rules for forming phrases and sentences. All the parts of a given construction must, therefore, work together to make sense. Any departure from the rules can potentially cause a breakdown in understanding.

Labov brought interdisciplinary skills to his consideration of the Saussurean paradox, with his background in statistics and a sensibility for the humanities. He sampled speech based on demographics, and included every sound – however small – in his analyses, which also linked linguistic structures to non-linguistic factors such as time.

On the strength of this information, Labov examined the ways in which words acquire different meanings in order to solve the Saussurean paradox. The definition of the word "cool", for example, gradually changed from "not hot" to "something that is admirable". Today, this shift in meaning is recognized across the English-speaking world – but this modern usage would be completely nonsensical to the people who spoke English in the late 19th and early 20th centuries.

Similarly, since the end of the 20th century, the use of "they" to refer to a single person – regardless of gender – has become a common feature of the English language. In fact, the singular use of "they" has existed since at least 1375, but in recent generations it was most commonly used to refer to two or more people, leading many to mistakenly believe that the singular usage was incorrect. This illustrates how changes in meaning and popular usage can and do evolve over time, and across generations.

Black English

Labov applied the same rigorous scientific approach to a study of African American Vernacular English (AAVE), documented in his 1972 work *Language in the Inner City: Studies in Black English Vernacular*. In his exploration of what

Sound changes

Labov used statistical analysis to study subtle sound changes that can occur within dialects. He paid close attention to the way in which a speaker would shift between accents at particular moments – for example, when identifying with one of their social peers, or addressing clients or colleagues. As part of his research, Labov asked participants to speak about poignant moments from their past, as a way to unconsciously invoke their accents. This innovative technique prompted spontaneous shifts in accent – and the resulting data could be assessed for linguistic patterns, and used to identify the causes of significant sound changes. He was also able to compare sound changes from speakers across different social classes, situations, and generations to produce a nuanced understanding of the social contexts that affected sound change.

he referred to as "Black English", Labov defended its legitimacy as an independent dialect on strict scientific grounds. From interviews with young Black people in cities including New York City and Philadelphia, and states such as Georgia and South Carolina, Labov found that the language had well-established, consistent rules of pronunciation across the different locations. He also found that AAVE had a grammatical system that was the equal of other languages, including formal "Standard" English. The consequences of these findings were significant: previous researchers had concluded that Black children who struggled to read and write in Standard English were deprived. Labov's work challenged this assumption – he argued that teachers mistakenly identified the rules of AAVE to be errors, and that this explained why Black children appeared to fall behind. ∎

Saussurean Paradox

The Saussurean paradox acknowledges the social aspects of language. In order to fully understand the meaning of words, sociolinguists must look not only at the formal definition, but also the social context in which the word is used. Labov noted that meanings can change significantly in different contexts.

Word	Social context	Subtext	Meaning
"Cool"	Used in a weather report	Negative	Cold
	Used to describe clothing	Positive	Fashionable
	Used to describe a person	Negative	Unfeeling
		Positive	Attractive

An important aspect of the current situation is the strong social reaction against suggestions that the home language of African American children be used in the first steps of learning to read and write.
William Labov

WHERE THERE IS DIRT THERE IS SYSTEM
PURITY AND SOCIETY

IN CONTEXT

KEY WORK
Mary Douglas, *Purity and Danger*, 1966

FIELD
Sociocultural anthropology

BEFORE
1912 French sociologist Émile Durkheim argues that symbols are distinguished as either sacred or profane.

1951 British anthropologist Edmund Leach explores themes of religion and kinship in his essay "The Structural Implications of Matrilateral Cross-Cousin Marriage", and proposes new theories about social structures.

AFTER
1966 Louis Dumont studies ideas of purity in the hierarchy of the Indian caste system.

1970 Mary Douglas publishes *Natural Symbols: Explorations in Cosmology*, which explores the social meaning of symbols.

There is a familiar saying that "God made dirt and dirt don't hurt." While dirt itself may not cause injury, people typically perceive it to be unclean, even impure. All societies draw a line between dirty and clean things – the impure and the pure – but where that line is drawn can vary considerably.

In a survey of ideas about impurity and pollution, British social anthropologist Mary Douglas examines how these ideas vary across cultures and over time. For example, she considers food taboos: why are Christians allowed to eat pork, but Jews are not? The answer lies in the *Book of Leviticus*, which establishes an animal classification system. This states that animals with cloven hooves that chew cud, such as sheep and cows, may be eaten but cloven-hoofed animals that do not chew cud, such as pigs, cannot. By not chewing cud like other cloven-hoofed animals, pigs defy the expected natural order. Pigs are out of place and therefore are considered unclean and taboo.

Douglas summarizes that through these rules of clean and unclean animals "holiness was given a physical expression in every encounter with the animal kingdom and at every meal".

Creating order
Every culture classifies objects and symbols in specific ways with the aim of establishing order out of potential chaos. Things that do not fit neatly into this system disrupt the order and are thereby deemed out of place, like dirt itself. ■

Purity is the enemy of change, of ambiguity and compromise.
Mary Douglas

See also: The universal nature of religion 28–29 ■ The social roots of religion 42–43 ■ Caste systems 122–23

WHY NOT TRACE HUMANITY'S SPREAD ACROSS THE PLANET?

POPULATION GENETICS

IN CONTEXT

KEY WORK
L.L. Cavalli-Sforza, "Population structure and human evolution", 1966

FIELD
Biological anthropology

BEFORE
1924 British geneticist J.B.S. Haldane introduces the theory of the chemical origins of life.

1931 US geneticist Sewall Wright pioneers methods that compute the distribution of gene frequencies among a given population. This enables a greater understanding of the mechanisms of evolution.

AFTER
2006 Research increases into the structural variation within population genomes. Structural variations are large-scale changes that impact the appearance and function of organisms and may have contributed to human evolution.

I talian physician Luigi Luca Cavalli-Sforza was among the first to use genetics to track early human migration patterns. His blend of anthropology and genetics led to a new discipline called population genetics, and his interest in what – genetically – separated groups of people throughout the world led to research on the representation of A, B, and O blood types across populations.

As technology improved, Cavalli-Sforza examined genetic changes in the Y chromosome in various human populations. He traced the male lineage of all living male humans back to a single male ancestor, coined "Adam", who lived roughly 70,000 to 100,000 years ago in sub-Saharan Africa.

Dismantling race
Cavalli-Sforza's genetic work contributed to dismantling the idea that human races have a biological basis. He found that individuals from the same population are just as genetically diverse as people from two different groups, which demonstrated that at the genetic level, there is no such thing as race among humans. He called for analysis of the world's populations in finer genetic detail. Learning about the past through DNA is an active area of research today. ■

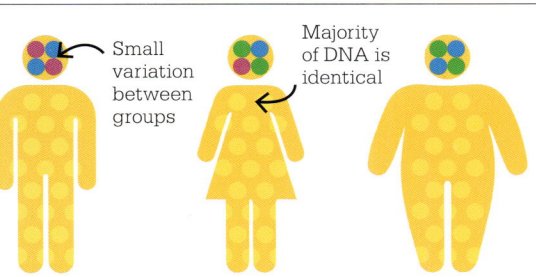

Small variation between groups

Majority of DNA is identical

Population 1 **Population 2** **Population 3**

Despite diverse appearances, 99.9 per cent of their DNA is common to all. Cavalli-Sforza's analysis of the genetic makeup of different populations revealed that only tiny variations were present across individuals and communities.

See also: Origins of humanity 94–101 ▪ Multilinear evolution 104–07 ▪ Defining ethnicity 130–31 ▪ Sequencing ancient DNA 290–91

HIERARCHY IS A FUNDAMENTAL SOCIAL PRINCIPLE
CASE SYSTEMS

IN CONTEXT

KEY WORK
Louis Dumont, *Homo Hierarchicus*, 1966

FIELD
Sociocultural anthropology

BEFORE
1762 Swiss philosopher Jean-Jacques Rousseau sees equality as following from the notion of man as an individual entity.

1937 US sociologist Talcott Parsons proposes that individuals perform social roles that make up the collective social system.

AFTER
1977 Indian anthropologist Veena Das uses Sanskrit texts to study Hindu caste groups in her book *Structure and Cognition*.

1980 Dumont's student Jean-Claude Galey studies how low-ranking castes in the eastern Himalayas live in perpetual debt to landlords.

Although several countries have caste-based systems, India's is arguably the best known. Indian society has thousands of sub-castes, which are grouped into four broad categories, each associated with specific occupations, traditions, and lifestyles. From highest to lowest rank, these categories are Brahmins, Kshatriyas, Vaishyas, and Shudras. Below these are the Dalits, or "untouchables", who are viewed as impure and therefore innately well suited to perform the most degrading of tasks.

The rigidity of the caste system in many parts of India means that someone born into one caste can perform only their caste-specific tasks and must marry within the same caste. The system derives from Hindu socio-religious logics about purity and impurity.

A hierarchical structure
One of the foremost scholars of Indian society, Louis Dumont argued that the caste system is a unique ideology and set of values. In his book *Homo Hierarchicus: The Caste System and Its Implications*,

India's caste system classifies people at birth, defining their position in society, what employment they can take, and who they can marry.

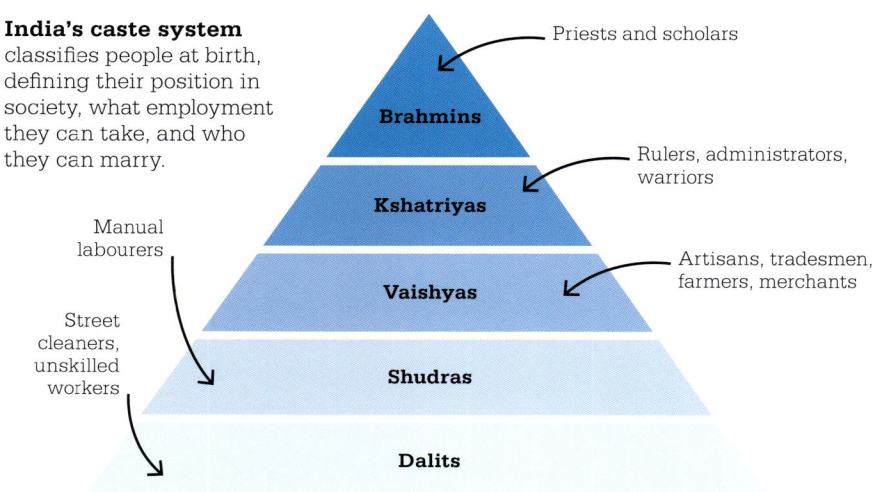

Priests and scholars — Brahmins

Rulers, administrators, warriors — Kshatriyas

Artisans, tradesmen, farmers, merchants — Vaishyas

Manual labourers — Shudras

Street cleaners, unskilled workers — Dalits

See also: The concept of reciprocity 58–61 ▪ Structuralism 108 ▪ Stages of social organization 160–61 ▪ Socialization of gender roles 258–59

The principle of equality and the principle of hierarchy are facts, indeed they are among the most constraining facts, of political and social life.
Louis Dumont

Dumont drew a distinction between India and the West. He argued that the caste ideology is based upon the principle of hierarchy, whereby groups of people are ranked as superior or inferior to one another and separated from one another in all aspects of life.

According to Dumont, relationships in India – whether between individuals or castes – are comprehensible only in the context of the entire hierarchical social structure. By contrast, social structures in the West are founded on the principle of egalitarianism; this means individuals stand alone as independent entities in society and can move between ranks.

Binary oppositions

More broadly, Dumont alleged that "traditional" cultures view the individual within society, whereas "modern" cultures emphasize the independence of the individual. Hierarchical societies reflect a kind of social consensus in which "hierarchy encompasses social agents and social categories". Utilizing structuralist theory in his analysis, Dumont suggested that social structures are based upon binary oppositions – such as individual versus society, hierarchy versus egalitarianism, and East versus West – that are fundamental to human thought.

Ultimately, Dumont argued that "India is one" – a unified society founded on Sanskritic culture. However, other anthropologists have challenged this portrayal of

The Dalit people, previously known as "untouchables", are an oppressed Indian caste. They are now starting to fight for their basic human rights.

ideological cohesion, pointing out that the country exhibits a multiplicity of identities, cultural diversity, and societal conflicts.

Just as problematic is Dumont's interpretation of the "West" as a monolith, overlooking its obvious heterogeneity. Contemporary scholars emphasize the nuances within cultural regions, rather than seeing societies as either communal or individualistic, and either "traditional" or "modern". ▪

Louis Dumont

Born in 1911 in Thessaloniki (then part of the Ottoman Empire, now Greece), Louis Dumont trained as a sociologist at the Institut d'Éthnologie in Paris under Marcel Mauss. During World War II, while a prisoner of war in Germany, Dumont learned Sanskrit and several Indian languages.

On his return to France, Dumont continued his earlier research while maintaining a keen interest in India. From 1949 to 1950, he conducted fieldwork in southern India, where he became fascinated by the caste system. Later, he focused on kinship and marriage, political movements, and individualism.

In the 1950s, Dumont taught at the Institute of Social and Cultural Anthropology at Oxford University, UK, and later became the director of the École des Hautes Études en Sciences Sociales in Paris. He died in the French capital in 1998.

Other key works

1977 *Homo Aequalis*

Our first aim is to come to understand the ideology of the caste system. This ideology is directly contradicted by the egalitarian theory which we hold.
Louis Dumont

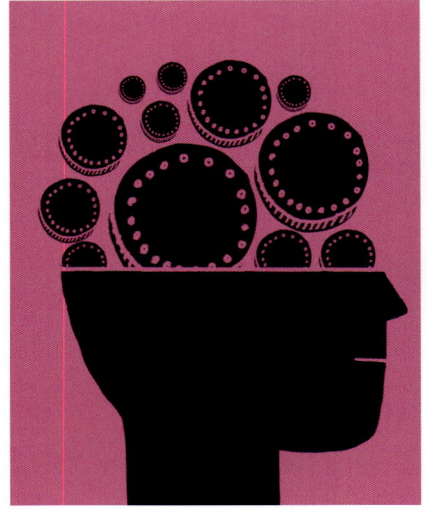

BELIEFS ARE SHAPED BY MATERIAL CONDITIONS
CULTURAL MATERIALISM

IN CONTEXT

KEY WORK
Marvin Harris, *The Rise of Anthropological Theory*, 1968

FIELD
Sociocultural anthropology

BEFORE
1845 Karl Marx and Friedrich Engels use historical materialism to show that societal developments are driven by changes in material conditions, such as technology and production methods.

1887 Franz Boas argues that a society's history and environment shape its unique cultural traits and should be understood on its own terms. These ideas become known as historical particularism and cultural relativism.

1955 Julian Steward develops his theory of cultural ecology – the idea that interactions with the environment can shape human behaviour.

The theory of cultural materialism was developed by US anthropologist Marvin Harris as a reaction to ideas of cultural relativism and historical particularism. Harris suggested that cultural practices are the result of people's economic or material conditions.

One of his most famous examples was built around the prohibition of cattle butchering in India. Harris argued that this practice arose not because of Hindu ideology, but because it was more economically viable to use cattle for work than for food. Harris also suggested that the religious rituals of the Aztec included cannibalism due to a lack of protein in their diet.

Controversial theory
Harris's critics often argue that his use of cultural materialism oversimplified complex cultural phenomena and ignored other important social, political, and ideological influences. His work has also been criticized for underestimating human agency, or the capacity of individuals to shape their own cultural practices and worlds. Nevertheless, the concept of cultural materialism was influential and offered new ways for cultural practices and systems to be interpreted and analysed. ∎

The sanctity of cows and bulls in India is strengthened by depictions of Hindu god Shiva's bull mount Nandi. Here Nandi rests at the feet of Shiva.

See also: Origins of culture 32–33 ▪ Cultural relativism 34–41 ▪ The fluidity of social systems 102–03 ▪ Multilinear evolution 104–07

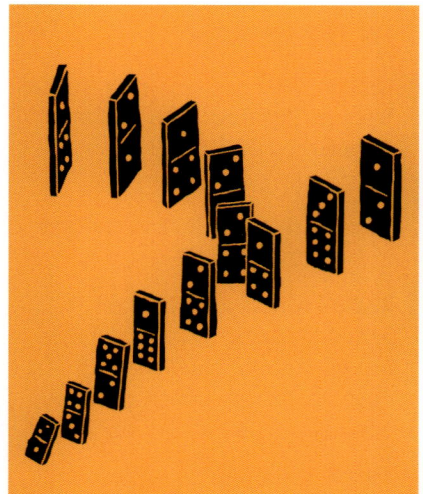

SMALL DEVIATIONS INTO LARGE DIFFERENCES
SYSTEMS THEORY

IN CONTEXT

KEY WORK
**Kent Flannery,
*Archaeological Systems
Theory and Early
Mesoamerica*, 1968**

FIELD
**Environmental
anthropology**

BEFORE
1935 British botanist Arthur
Tansley proposes the concept
of an "ecosystem".

1960 US archaeologist Robert
Braidwood argues that
agriculture was the inevitable
result of cultural specialization.

AFTER
1984 US archaeologist David
Rindos claims that agriculture
is a co-evolutionary process
between human foraging and
plant genetics.

1999 US botanist John
Doebley shows that a few
genetic mutations convert the
wild grass teosinte into maize.

Before 1960, archaeologists saw agriculture as a sign of increasing intellectual sophistication. However, in 1968 Kent Flannery began to explore the development of agriculture using systems theory – the idea that changes are caused by a process of negative and positive feedback.

System cycles

The food system of ancient Mexico provided Flannery with material for his case study. He realized that it was composed of several sub-systems, including agave, deer, and wild grass. Each sub-system was seasonal and had to be scheduled, which gave negative or positive feedback. If deer, for example, are over-hunted, hunting ends, the deer population then rebounds, and hunting begins again.

Similarly, maize comes from a wild grass, teosinte, that produces only a few, hard-shelled kernels per seedhead. However, through selective use of the seeds, starting 9,000 years ago, ancient peoples began to grow grasses with ever larger seedheads, and kernels without the hard shells. Eventually, teosinte became so productive that when its planting and harvesting seasons conflicted with other less-productive foods, people shifted to maize agriculture.

Flannery therefore argued that agriculture originated not from a singular push for sophistication, but from hunter-gatherers surviving and, in an example of positive feedback, becoming farmers. ■

I compare agriculture to bipedalism and fire; it changed completely the way we interact with the environment.
Hugo Oliveira
quoted by John Carey in "Unearthing the orgins of agriculture", 2023

See also: Social and cultural dimensions of nutrition 80–83 ■ Multilinear evolution 104–07 ■ The anthropology of food 200–05

RITUALS CREATE SOCIETY

RITES OF PASSAGE

IN CONTEXT

KEY WORK
Victor Turner, *The Ritual Process*, 1969

FIELD
Sociocultural anthropology

BEFORE
1893 French social scientist Émile Durkheim lays the basis for structural functionalism, arguing that different parts of society are interdependent.

1909 Arnold van Gennep, a French anthropologist, coins the phrase "rites of passage".

AFTER
1983 US anthropologist Nelson Graburn suggests that tourism is a form of modern ritual because it temporarily takes individuals outside their everyday routines. When they return, they resume their usual routines but with the added experience of their travels.

Renowned for his work on religious rituals, British cultural anthropologist Victor Turner was especially interested in the roles that symbols and rites of passage play within societies. In 1969, he published *The Ritual Process: Structure and Anti-Structure*, which was based on his ethnographic work in parts of south-central Africa, particularly among the Ndembu people of Zambia.

Turner built on the work of Arnold van Gennep, who had suggested that rites of passage allowed participants to temporarily step away from their social status into a state that was neither here nor there; it was liminal, or transitional.

See also: The social roots of religion 42–43 ▪ Kinship and social order 68–69 ▪ Transitology 234–39

Accordingly, Van Gennep identified three stages in rites of passage – separation, transition or liminality, and reincorporation – with the intermediate stage allowing people to experiment with new social roles, arrangements, and statuses.

Transitional state

Turner described in greater detail how, in the separation stage of a rite of passage, the participant is removed from their current status or social position. This separation can be physical, symbolic, or both. It marks the beginning of the transition and often involves rituals or actions that signify leaving behind the previous identity or role. The process of separation may involve specific symbols such as clothing or personal objects that symbolically represent the detachment from the earlier status.

The second stage – liminality – was for Turner the most interesting part of a rite of passage. In the

Society … is a process in which any … human group alternates between fixed and, to borrow from our Japanese friends, "floating worlds".
Victor Turner

liminal stage, the participant is in an ambiguous state: no longer in their old role or status but not yet fully transitioned into the new one. They are in an in-between state that is often marked by intensive rituals, teachings, or experiences intended to engender growth, transformation, or learning. Liminality also often »

Victor Turner

Born in Scotland in 1920, Victor Turner studied poetry and classics at University College London (UCL), earning a BA in English literature in 1941. As a pacifist and conscientious objector, he served in a noncombatant role in World War II, often performing dangerous work such as disarming bombs.

After the war, Turner returned to UCL, where he completed a BA in social anthropology, then earned a PhD in social anthropology at Manchester University in 1955. While at Manchester, he studied the social organization of the Ndembu of Northern Rhodesia (now Zambia) and developed insights into the functions of rites of passage. Turner's work is often referred to as symbolic or interpretive anthropology, although its foundation was in structural functionalism.

In 1961, Turner began teaching at several universities in the US, including Stanford University, California, and Cornell University, New York. He died in 1983.

Other key work

1970 *The Forest of Symbols*

South African Xhosa boys, smeared in grey clay and wearing only a blanket as clothing, prepare to spend several weeks in bushland. Following this compulsory rite of passage, they are circumcised and declared men.

involves challenges, tests, or symbolic actions that prepare the individual for the phase of reintegration. In this final stage, the participant is reincorporated into society with a new status and is now expected to behave according to the cultural norms that define their new role.

Ritual significance

Turner built much of his theory on his experiences among the Ndembu people, which he used to support his ideas. For example, he studied the Ndembu rite of passage for newly selected kings, in which the crown-elect is subjected to ritual humiliation, stripped of his royal status and given a lowly position before being exalted as king. This humiliation is intended as a reminder that the role of king is meant to serve the people and their common needs rather than his own personal interests.

Turner believed that rituals like this, which supported the existing social order, were often controlled by those with a vested interest in maintaining it. These authorities attempt to regulate rites of passage to reinforce existing social roles

> Each individual's life experience contains alternating exposure to structure and communitas, and to states and transitions.
> **Victor Turner**

and identities, especially during times of crisis that might challenge the status quo. In such cases, the subversive and innovative potential of rituals is often restricted, and traditional cultural values are emphasized instead. According to Turner, rites of passage always have some purpose in society.

Christian marriage

Anthropologists argue that for a cultural experience to be considered a rite of passage, it must include a marked moment in which an individual is no longer in their old identity and has obtained a new one. For example, simply advancing through the teenage years cannot be considered a rite of passage because there is no ceremony or specific moment that marks the individual's new identity as an adult. Instead, each individual becomes respected as an independent adult gradually as their age progresses and as they achieve various cultural milestones.

Using Turner's theory, a traditional Western Christian wedding provides an example of a rite of passage. The first step, separation, is both symbolic and physical. On the day of the wedding, it is common for the bride and groom to prepare separately, and they are discouraged from viewing each other until the start of the ceremony.

The wedding ceremony itself represents a liminal phase, where the couple are between statuses – no longer single but not yet married. During this stage, the couple may walk down an aisle surrounded by friends and family. They then face the celebrant or priest, and during this time are in a state of transition, undergoing rituals that represent

The quinceañera

A *quinceañera* ceremony is a rite of passage that marks a girl's transition from childhood to womanhood at the age of 15. Celebrated across Mexico, Latin America, the Caribbean, and by Latino communities in the US, it serves as a significant milestone in the life of a young woman, emphasizing her new social role within her family.

The ceremony begins with a religious mass to symbolize the girl's acceptance of new responsibilities as she moves towards adulthood. Following the mass, a grand reception includes a choreographed dance, which acts as a public display of her new social status.

Symbolic actions are central to the *quinceañera*. They include the presentation of a doll to a younger sister to signify the girl's separation from childhood, and the placing of heeled shoes on her feet, to mark her introduction into a new identity as a woman. Through its rich symbolism and rituals, the *quinceañera* embodies transition and celebrates a girl's journey into womanhood.

A Mexican *quinceañera*, dressed in white, celebrates with her "court" of *damas* (maids of honour). Together, they perform a waltz-type dance.

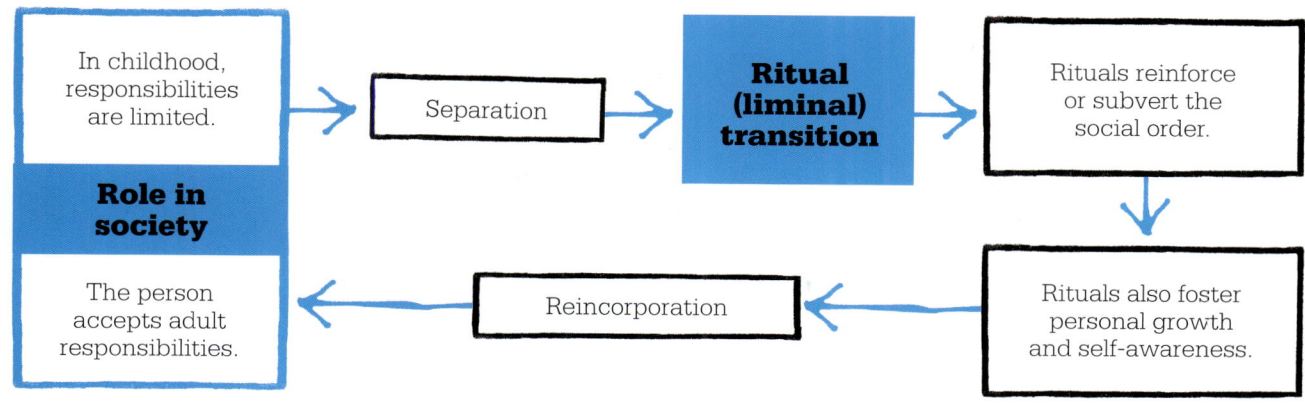

In childhood, responsibilities are limited.

Role in society

The person accepts adult responsibilities.

Separation

Ritual (liminal) transition

Rituals reinforce or subvert the social order.

Rituals also foster personal growth and self-awareness.

Reincorporation

their new roles and responsibilities. These rituals, such as an exchange of rings and spoken vows, each symbolize certain values that the couple are expected to comply with during their marriage.

The final, reincorporation stage involves the couple facing their audience, reintroduced into society as a married unit. They now occupy a new social role as a married couple, with new responsibilities and expectations. This stage is often marked by celebrations such as a wedding reception, where family and friends acknowledge and celebrate the couple's new status.

In parts of the Western Christian world, this type of ceremony is a requirement for the couple to be considered married. Regardless of how long a couple has resided together, neither partner is granted the role or status of a spouse until after the marriage has taken place. Unlike the gradual transition from childhood to adulthood, the marriage ceremony is a cultural event with certain ritualized stages through which

Rumspringa is a rite of passage in some Amish communities, where youths of 16 or over are allowed to explore otherwise forbidden behaviours before they commit to the church.

the participants' new identities are forged, and there is a single defined moment at which a new identity is assumed and understood.

Symbolism and identity

Victor Turner's work on rites of passage and the concept of liminality has profoundly influenced our understanding of how individuals and societies navigate transitions and transformations. By examining rituals through the lens of symbolic and interpretive anthropology, Turner highlighted the power of rituals in shaping social structures and identities. His exploration of the liminal phase,

where individuals exist in a state of ambiguity and potential, reveals the dynamic nature of social roles and the possibilities for innovation and change within societies.

Turner's insights, rooted in his study of the Ndembu and extended to broader cultural practices such as Western marriage ceremonies, underscore the relevance of rites of passage in maintaining and challenging social order. His work continues to be a cornerstone in anthropology, offering a framework for analysing how societies manage transitions, reinforce cultural norms, and allow for the possibility of new social configurations. ∎

A PRODUCT OF SELF AND GROUP IDENTITY
DEFINING ETHNICITY

IN CONTEXT

KEY WORK
Fredrik Barth, *Ethnic Groups and Boundaries*, 1969

FIELD
Sociocultural anthropology

BEFORE
1954 In *Political Systems of Highland Burma*, Edmund R. Leach notes that an individual may be part of several social systems at the same time and may move between them.

1965 In his article about the Lue people of Thailand, US ethnographer Michael Moerman states ethnicity should be self-defined and seen as a native category of belonging.

AFTER
1974 In *Urban Ethnicity*, Iraqi anthropologist Abner Cohen notes that cultural symbolism helps to explain power relations when ethnicity emerges as a distinctive feature of group identity.

After its publication in 1969, Fredrik Barth's introduction to *Ethnic Groups and Boundaries* became one of the most widely referenced articles on ethnicity. Previous works by other anthropologists had focused on ethnic groups as fixed entities, listing particular cultural traits that were seen to define each one, such as language, religion, and rituals. Barth proposed that studies of ethnic groups should focus instead on the boundaries groups draw between each other. He believed that these boundaries are often contingent on people's social or political needs, and that they can be porous and fluid, allowing a person of different ethnicity to participate in some situations and not others.

Earlier portrayals of cultures often described them as isolated and static, but Barth noted that ethnic groups often share aspects of culture with other groups nearby – even "enemies" – and changes in values, inter-relationships, and contact occur regularly within and between groups. Barth focused his work on the interactions between neighbouring groups, shared commonalities, and the differences that can be masked or that may emerge into hostility, depending on the sociopolitical context.

Pashtun leaders from Pakistan and Afghanistan attend a meeting with Afghan president Hamid Karzai in 2010, looking for peaceful solutions to the longstanding border conflict.

Negotiating identity
Barth wrote that distinct ethnic groups are not formed because they are isolated or because they lack

See also: The fluidity of social systems 102–03 ▪ Thick description 146–53 ▪ Kinship studies 192 ▪ DNA politics 282–83

Approaches to ethnicity

 **Primordialism** The belief that personal identity is natural and fixed at birth emerged in ancient times. People were thought to share common language, traditions, and traits.

 **Constructivism** People's identities are shaped by social interactions, influenced by changing social norms. Members of an ethnic group may share some traditions but not others.

 **Instrumentalism** Social movements are organized according to a constructed shared ethnicity. People within an ethnic group may mobilize and influence political policy.

information about other ways of life. Social exclusion is practised and separation is maintained in spite of the many individuals who may take part in the economic, political, or social actions of neighbouring groups. This fluidity is central to the idea that identity is negotiated and often situational. Ethnicity is likely to be one of a number of identities juggled by an individual, but certain situations, such as threats of danger to a group, may reinforce a collective identity, making it more rigid and specific. The ability to partially reinvent or reaffirm a collective identity to adjust to rapid changes in society is not confined to ethnic groups.

Conflict and harmony

After World War II, researchers expected a new internationalism to grow. They thought that attachment to – and scholarly interest in – ethnicity would wane, but instead its importance rapidly increased, with both harmonious and deeply destructive examples. Many of the conflicts of the late 20th and early 21st centuries have been between neighbouring ethnic groups, including some within the same country. In his work *Small Places, Large Issues*, first published in 1995, Norwegian anthropologist Thomas Hylland Eriksen notes that ethnic identities are relative and so may change in different contexts and situations. Certainly, conflicts reflect this reality, but ethnic relations in relatively peaceful conditions may also include competition for resources alongside a bewildering rush to adjust to quickly changing social and physical conditions. ▪

Ethnicity is a social and cultural product which anthropologists contribute to creating.
Thomas H. Eriksen
Ethnicity and Nationalism, **1993**

Thomas Fredrik Weybye Barth

Norwegian sociocultural anthropologist Fredrik Barth was born in Germany in 1928. He studied at the London School of Economics and at Cambridge, later founding the social anthropology department at the University of Bergen and teaching at the universities of Oslo, Harvard, Emory, and Boston. Barth's ground-breaking work on ethnicity was informed by ethnographic fieldwork with different groups, such as the Basseri of South Persia and the Baktaman of New Guinea, which focused on individual creativity and the mechanisms of change. Well-known for his studies on micro-economics and entrepreneurship in Darfur, Sudan, Barth contributed to economic anthropology and was deeply committed to public anthropology and intellectual growth. He died in 2016.

Other key works

1961 *Nomads of South Persia*
1975 *Ritual and Knowledge Among the Baktaman*
1987 *Cosmologies in the Making*

WHEN YOU MEET CHIMPS YOU MEET INDIVIDUAL PERSONALITIES

CHIMPANZEE BEHAVIOURS

IN CONTEXT

KEY WORK
Jane Goodall, *In the Shadow of Man*, 1971

FIELD
Biological anthropology

BEFORE
1925 US primatologist Robert Yerkes observes the social behaviour of chimpanzees in a laboratory setting.

1931 US comparative psychologist Henry Nissen conducts a naturalistic study of chimpanzees.

AFTER
1986 Following 15 years of fieldwork in Indonesian Borneo, Biruté Galdikas founds the charity Orangutan Foundation International.

2013 *Time* magazine names chimpanzee David Greybeard one of the 15 most influential animals that ever lived.

B ritish primatologist Jane Goodall is renowned for her research into wild chimpanzee populations in Tanzania. During years of extensive fieldwork, Goodall observed that chimpanzees displayed a number of behaviours that had been thought to be exclusive to humans. This added to a body of data suggesting that we inherited similar behaviours from a shared ancestor some 7–8 million years ago.

Family connections
Before the 1960s, little was known about the behaviour of wild apes or their social structures. This

See also: The theory of evolution 24–25 ▪ Origins of humanity 94–101
▪ The capacity for communication 182

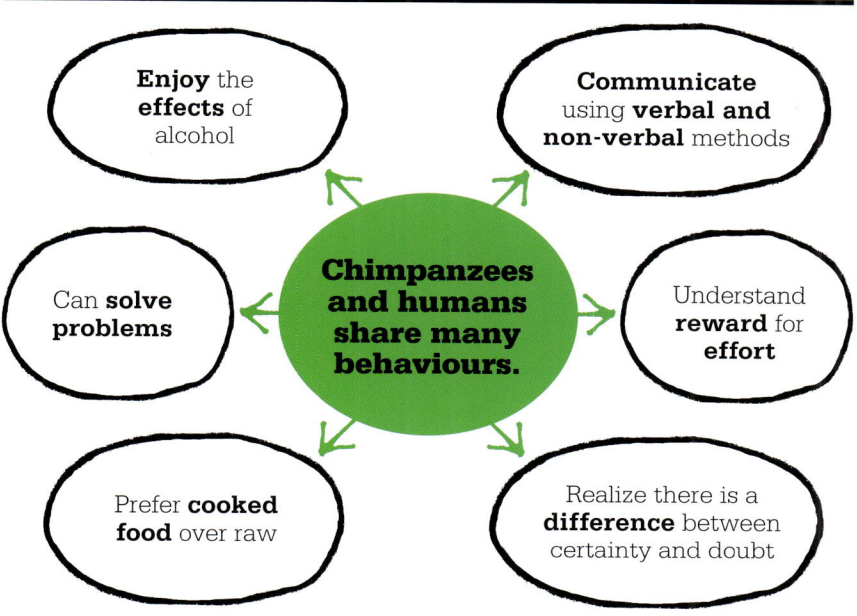

Enjoy the **effects** of alcohol

Communicate using **verbal and non-verbal** methods

Can **solve problems**

Chimpanzees and humans share many behaviours.

Understand **reward** for **effort**

Prefer **cooked food** over raw

Realize there is a **difference** between certainty and doubt

Jane Goodall

Born in Bournemouth, UK, in 1934, Jane Goodall developed a passion for animals at a young age. In 1957, during a holiday in Kenya, she met Louis Leakey. Initially, Leakey offered Goodall a job at the local natural history museum. Impressed by her knowledge, attention to detail, and drive, he then invited her to join a project he was setting up: to study primate behaviour in the wild. Leakey believed that Goodall's lack of formal academic training would be an advantage, because her research would not be biased by traditional thinking.

Goodall completed her doctoral degree at Cambridge University in 1966, and the following year she published her first book, *My Friends the Wild Chimpanzees*. In 1986, Goodall moved away from active fieldwork to campaign as a conservationist. After witnessing the devastating effects of deforestation on primates, she has worked tirelessly to preserve the habitat of the chimpanzees.

Other key works

1990 *Through a Window*
2021 *The Book of Hope*

changed in 1960, when British paleoanthropologists Louis and Mary Leakey uncovered the remains of *Homo habilis* at the Olduvai Gorge in Tanzania. Louis Leakey realized that by studying our close living relatives – wild apes such as chimpanzees, gorillas, and orangutans, all of which shared a recent common ancestor with our own species – he might gain insights into the lives of early humans. Having secured funds for a project to study primate behaviour in the wild, Leakey recruited Jane Goodall, US primatologist Dian Fossey, and Canadian anthropologist Biruté Galdikas, who became collectively known as the Trimates. Each researcher was to focus on one member of the hominid family: Goodall on chimpanzees, Fossey on gorillas in Congo and later in Rwanda, and Galdikas on orangutans in Borneo.

The first few weeks of Goodall's research experience in Tanzania's Gombe Stream National Park were challenging. Although she learned to navigate difficult terrain and thick vegetation, she had little luck finding chimpanzees. When she managed to locate a group, she »

You cannot share your life with a dog … or a cat and not know perfectly well that animals have personalities and minds and feelings.
Jane Goodall
The Observer newspaper, 2010

found that she could not get closer than about 450 m (500 yards) before the chimpanzees fled.

Eventually, Goodall changed her strategy. Instead of showing up unannounced in the chimpanzees' territory, she let the chimps slowly become accustomed to her presence and approach her when they were comfortable. To accomplish this, she used a technique that she called "Banana Club". Every day, Goodall consistently turned up at an elevated area that she knew to be a common feeding ground. She remained patient and still, and generally took care to exhibit non-threatening behaviours. She learned to imitate many of the chimps' actions, spent time in the trees and even ate the same foods as they did. She often brought bananas to the feeding area to encourage the group to think of her as a positive presence rather than a menacing one.

Social acceptance

Slowly, Goodall's persistence and patience began to pay off: the chimpanzees came to tolerate her presence, and within a year, many allowed her to move close to them when feeding in that area.

Goodall's acceptance by a high-ranking member of the group that she called David Greybeard proved something of a breakthrough. Once he accepted her, other chimpanzees quickly became comfortable around her, allowing her to stay in their presence and interacting with her. Decades later, David Greybeard remained Goodall's favourite. While chimpanzees are known for being emotionally volatile and at times violent, Goodall found David Greybeard to be tolerant, generous, and kind, even during stressful moments when others grew aggressive. Goodall stated that without David Greybeard's helpful introductions, she may not have been able to meet the other Gombe chimpanzees.

Food for thought

After the majority of the group grew accustomed to Goodall's presence, she was able to observe the chimpanzee community more closely and for longer periods. The conclusions that she drew from her research shook the world of primatology and upended existing assumptions about the things that differentiated humans from apes.

> **The least I can do is speak out for the hundreds of chimpanzees … without hope, staring out with dead eyes from their metal prisons.**
> **Jane Goodall**
> Quoted by Jennifer Lindsey in
> *40 Years at Gombe*, 1999

One of Goodall's early insights was that chimpanzees are capable of making and using tools. Previously, it was thought that only humans had the complex cognitive abilities to do this. David Greybeard was the first to demonstrate this behaviour. He selected a thick reed that he then repeatedly and systematically dipped into a termite mound, before licking and eating the termites that stuck to it. Goodall also observed that the chimps would modify the reed to better fit into the mound holes, and they would also use a stick like a spoon to eat the termites more efficiently.

Goodall discovered, too, that chimpanzees are not herbivores; they have an omnivorous diet. She watched them hunt, catch, and eat insects, birds, and other small animals in the tree canopy. When she telegraphed Louis Leakey about her groundbreaking observations, her adviser famously

Goodall sits with chimpanzees on the jungle floor. Her hands-on, almost familial approach meant that initially her research was considered less objective by the scientific community.

wrote back, "Now we must redefine 'tool', redefine 'man', or accept chimpanzees as humans".

Communication systems

Goodall unveiled a complex social hierarchy that includes ritualized behaviours and communication methods. She identified more than 20 separate sounds associated with meanings. For example, pant-hoots, grunts, and barks all function as alerts to other chimpanzees that a food source has been located. Each individual also has its own vocalization, which allows them to be identified by others.

Additionally, Goodall observed several forms of non-verbal communication that included mutual grooming, and dominance displays such as charging, slapping hands, stomping feet, throwing rocks, and dragging branches. Such displays are common among males, who attempt to intimidate higher-ranking males by making themselves look dangerous while falling short of engaging in a physical fight. These actions also demonstrate to other chimpanzees the chimp's aspirations within the social order.

As species evolved and adapted to suit their environment and conditions, some ancestors have become extinct. Humans and chimpanzees shared an ancestor that died out comparatively recently, around 7–8 million years ago, and they remain close genetic relatives.

Key

○ Extinct common ancestor

Orangutan Gorilla Chimpanzee Bonobo Human

Present day

3 million years ago

7 million years ago
8 million years ago

Extinct common ancestor of chimpanzees, bonobos, and humans

13 million years ago

Chimpanzees express anger by standing on two feet, screeching loudly while scowling, and throwing rocks and branches. To show their submission, chimps adopt a crouching stance to approach others, holding out a hand while pant-grunting, or displaying their rump.

Naming practices

When Goodall began her research, giving study subjects a name was not considered good scientific practice; most primatologists took what they thought was a more objective approach and only assigned a number to each animal. Goodall was unaware of this convention and named all of the chimpanzees that she studied. Believing that she had personalized them too much and that she had incorrectly related their behaviour to that of humans, some researchers initially discounted her work. In the years that followed, however, attitudes changed, and Goodall's approach is now the norm. ∎

Cooperation and reconciliation

While studying chimpanzees and bonobos during the 1970s, Dutch-American primatologist Frans de Waal began to observe social dynamics that involved empathy, cooperation, and conflict resolution. These characteristics were not previously known to exist in such complexity among non-human primates.

De Waal's work focused on how social conflicts among primates are resolved. He noted that, following conflicts, apes often embraced, groomed, or engaged in other peaceful interactions, all of which underscored the existence and importance of mechanisms for repairing social bonds after disputes.

Drawing parallels with human societies, De Waal argued that behaviours like cooperation and reconciliation probably provided evolutionary advantages to the ancestors we share with living apes and that they were retained by both ape and human evolutionary lines after they diverged.

Grooming is one of several social interactions that primates use to maintain cohesion within the group, especially after conflict.

A MORE EFFECTIVE WAY OF SPEAKING ABOUT THE PAST

PROCESSUAL ARCHAEOLOGY

IN CONTEXT

KEY WORK
Patty Jo Watson, Steven LeBlanc, and Charles Redman, *Explanation in Archaeology*, 1971

FIELD
Archaeology

BEFORE
1958 US archaeologists Gordon Willey and Philip Phillips demand that archaeology answer scientific questions, rather than simply catalogue finds and create timelines.

1968 US archaeologist Kent Flannery proposes using systems theory, which views societies as being made up of interconnected components, to understand culture.

AFTER
1984 British archaeologist Ian Hodder challenges the processual approach in archaeology. He emphasizes that archaeology is subjective.

During the 1960s, a group of US archaeologists associated with Lewis Binford broke with many of the traditional approaches of their field and began to develop a more scientific approach to archaeology. Until then, archaeology had focused on cataloguing artefacts, tracing cultural histories, and ranking societies based on their perceived level of development. These scholars, however, sought to answer broader questions about how and why societies change over time. This movement, known as processual archaeology, built on Binford's ideas,

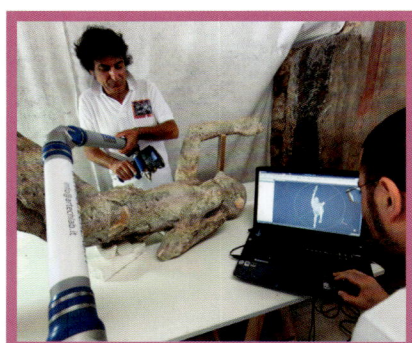

Specialized tools such as laser scanners help archaeologists to analyse and interpret their finds. This approach is rooted in the emphasis on scientific precision in processual archaeology.

emphasizing the importance of scientific methods, hypothesis testing, and the study of ecological systems to archaeological research.

Culture as a process
One early supporter of this approach was US archaeologist Patty Jo Watson. Together with fellow archaeologists Steven LeBlanc and Charles Redman, she outlined her thinking in *Explanation in Archaeology: An Explicitly Scientific Approach*. In the book – which became a foundational text of processual archaeology – Watson argued that cultures were processes rather than fixed "types" or snapshots in time.

Instead of merely accumulating data and descriptions, Watson suggested that research should focus on specific questions, with archaeological finds assessed by how well they support the hypotheses. Research should be judged on its methodological rigour, not the researcher's reputation.

In order to do this, Watson took an interdisciplinary approach. Rather than confine herself to traditional archaeological cataloguing or strictly historical approaches, she integrated a range

See also: Revolutions in prehistory 74–75 ▪ Multilinear evolution 104–07 ▪ The New Archaeology 110–15 ▪ Systems theory 125 ▪ Symbolism in cave art 262–65

Archaeobotany
Analysing ancient plant remains provides evidence about farming and domestication.

Zooarchaeology
Studying ancient animal remains provides evidence about hunting and pastoralism.

Geoarchaeology
Studying local geography provides evidence about the environment of the past.

Processual archaeology brings together different scientific methods to reveal the past.

Ethnoarchaeology
Studying modern societies can help archaeologists to understand past societies.

Experimental archaeology
Recreating ancient skills helps archaeologists to test hypotheses.

of scientific techniques into her fieldwork. Her research broke new ground by drawing on disciplines, such as ecology, archaeobotany, zooarchaeology, and geoarchaeology to demonstrate how cultures functioned as evolving systems shaped by their environments.

One of the techniques that Watson applied to her work was ethnoarchaeology, which uses studies of modern communities to better understand those of the past. For example, by observing contemporary farming practices in West Asia, such as crop processing and tool use, Watson was able to develop analogies for understanding prehistoric subsistence farming. This approach provided insights into how early humans might have lived and worked, and opened up new avenues for understanding the interplay between human societies and their environments.

Team-based methods
This shift towards interdisciplinary collaboration marked a significant departure from traditional archaeology, which had typically been conducted by a lone archaeologist, or an archaeologist working with a team of labourers. The interdisciplinary approach developed by processual archaeologists such as Watson emphasized the value of a cooperative team effort, with multiple specialists from diverse fields working together to address complex research questions, and it remains an essential component of modern archaeology. ▪

Mammoth Cave

Located in Kentucky, US, Mammoth Cave is the world's longest known cave system. In the 1960s and 1970s, Patty Jo Watson studied the lives of the late Archaic and early Woodland Indigenous people that once lived in the region and used the caves. Watson uncovered evidence of human activity dating back at least 5,000 years and pioneered the use of scientific methods to analyse the diets of the people whose remains were found there. This allowed her to trace the shift from hunter-gatherer lifestyles to early agriculture with precision.

Watson applied innovative techniques, including recreating ancient activities, such as food preparation and the use of textiles. She pioneered the use of flotation technology – a method that involves washing soil with water so that seeds and plant fragments float to the surface for easier study. Her committed archaeology helped to make Mammoth Cave one of the most thoroughly studied cave sites in North America.

Excavations at Mammoth Cave continue; in 2022, a dig near the cave entrance revealed evidence of its use in the 19th century.

BEHIND THE FACELESSNESS OF A BUREAUCRATIC SOCIETY

STUDYING UP

IN CONTEXT

KEY WORK
Laura Nader, *Up the Anthropologist*, 1972

FIELD
Sociocultural anthropology

BEFORE
1949 US sociologist Edwin Sutherland researches "white-collar crime", defining it as non-violent crime committed by individuals of high social status in their occupations.

1970 US anthropologist James Spradley studies homeless and alcoholic men in Seattle, terming them "urban nomads".

AFTER
1989 US anthropologist Emily Martin explores how women's reproduction is presented in US culture. Through interviews and medical texts, Martin finds a common metaphor of female bodies as industrial systems, and explores how this idea shapes womens' self-image.

Historically, anthropologists tended to study small-scale groups and non-industrialized societies, but during the 1970s, they began to turn their attention to industrial and post-industrial nations such as the US and European countries, often studying underrepresented or disenfranchised groups within these large societies.

The study of powerful institutions, such as the UK's House of Lords, can reveal how power operates as well as how social hierarchies shape and impact society.

As US anthropologist Laura Nader observed in her 1972 essay *Up the Anthropologist: Perspectives Gained from Studying Up*, anthropologists "prefer the underdog", and tend to study disempowered "down" groups. However, this creates a notable imbalance between the ethnographers and their subjects, and can result in anthropologists failing to fully understand the scale, logic, and logistics behind power itself.

Nader proposed that anthropologists should study the "middle" and "upper" ends of social power structures, not just the "lower"

See also: Feminist anthropology 140–45 ▪ Thick description 146–53 ▪ Gender, sexuality, and power 158–59 ▪ Global capitalism 186–87

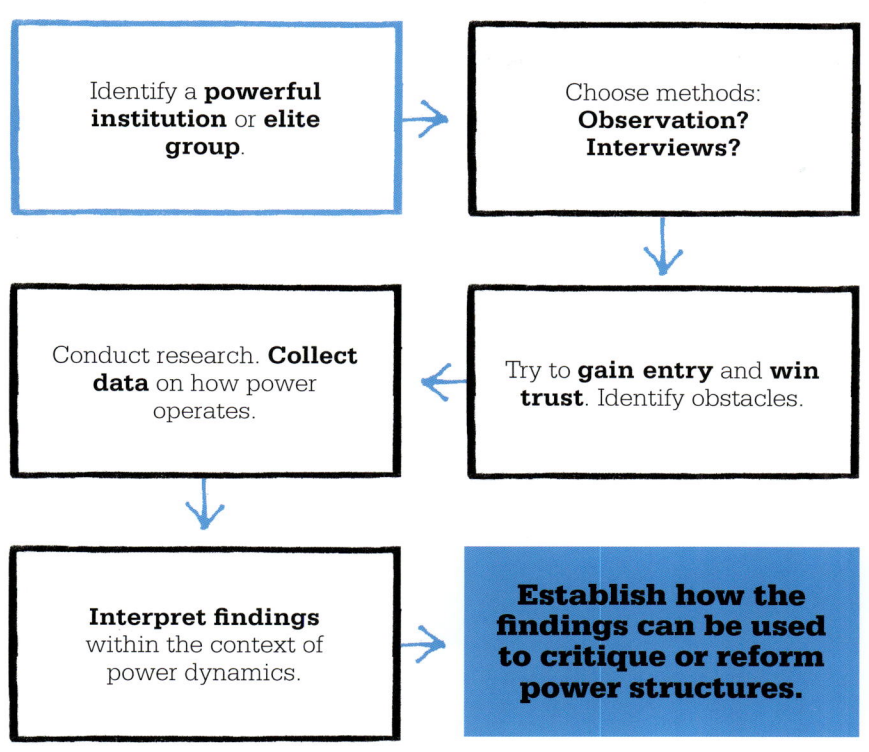

Identify a **powerful institution** or **elite group**.

Choose methods: **Observation? Interviews?**

Conduct research. **Collect data** on how power operates.

Try to **gain entry** and **win trust**. Identify obstacles.

Interpret findings within the context of power dynamics.

Establish how the findings can be used to critique or reform power structures.

Power in the 21st century

Laura Nader's call to study up was remarkably successful. Today, it is common to study people who are powerful or wealthy. However, many of the theoretical frameworks and ethical norms of anthropology were devised for studying those with little power.

Cultural anthropologist Daniel Souleles has addressed some of these challenges. He emphasizes the need to develop clear theories that explain how and why the powerful act and what their actions mean. Souleles recommends establishing connections with people – such as personal assistants and domestic workers – who have insider knowledge about the wealthy and powerful. He also suggests identifying places, such as galas or conferences, where the rich and powerful can be observed and studied. According to Souleles, these strategies enhance ethnographic methods for research among the powerful.

Never before have so few, by their actions and inactions, had the power of life and death over so many members of the species.
Laura Nader

end. She argued that focusing only on "exotic" or "primitive" – or "down" – cultures in non-Western societies perpetuates stereotypes and marginalizes the voices of those communities.

How power works

By "studying up", Nader suggested that anthropologists can also critically examine powerful people, corporations, governments, and institutions. Ethnographies of such people and institutions are needed, she argued, because they help us to understand how power operates and shapes societies at various levels. These ethnographies can also reveal the often invisible ways that exploitation and inequality affect both local and global communities.

Nader outlines three primary reasons for studying up. Firstly, it engages anthropology students in ways that traditional ethnography does not, which enables them to explore powerful institutional forces that shape their own lives and the lives of others. Secondly, studying up offers insights into the mechanics of power, and allows scholars to examine significant institutions and better understand how these entities influence the less powerful communities traditionally studied by anthropologists. Finally, studying up has significant democratic relevance, because it gives anthropologists a tool with which they can align the aims of social sciences to pressing large-scale social concerns. ▪

WOMAN IS NOT CLOSER TO NATURE THAN MAN

FEMINIST ANTHROPOLOGY

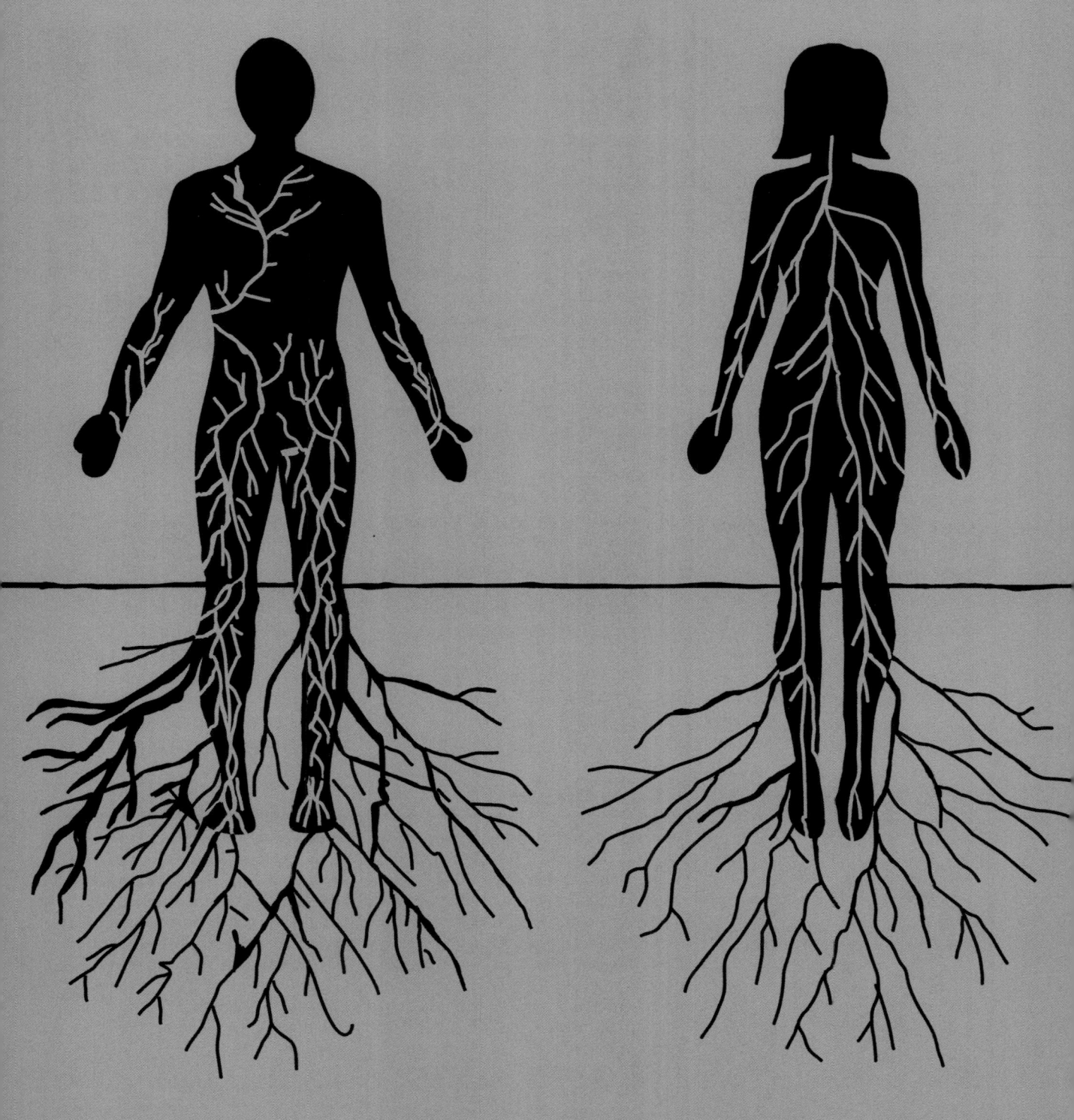

IN CONTEXT

KEY WORK
Sherry Ortner, "Is Female to Male as Nature Is to Culture?", 1972

FIELD
Sociocultural anthropology

BEFORE
1949 Claude Lévi-Strauss articulates structuralism, which focuses on universal binary thought processes.

AFTER
1973 US anthropologist Clifford Geertz argues that cultures are made up of symbols to be interpreted.

1993 Palestinian-American anthropologist Lila Abu-Lughod begins to write about women in the Islamic world and challenges Western opinions about gender inequality.

1996 Ortner's *Making Gender: The Politics and Erotics of Culture* contemplates the future of feminist anthropology.

At its inception, the discipline of anthropology was spearheaded by Judeo-Christian white men from Europe and the US. Their personal backgrounds influenced the topics that they chose to study, such as politics, religion, kinship, and language. However, the experiences of women – and indeed the very concept of gender – were largely omitted from this early scholarship.

This began to change at the beginning of the 20th century, as more women trained as anthropologists. Some of them questioned the exclusion of women from the ethnographic record, and they found evidence that gender identities are culturally constructed in many different ways.

During the 1960s and 1970s, as the second-wave feminist movement gained momentum in the US and Europe, anthropologists started to explicitly investigate the reasons for gender inequality in their own and other societies. US anthropologist Sherry Ortner's essay, "Is Female to Male as Nature Is to Culture?" is one example. Ortner sought to explain the

US women march along New York's Fifth Avenue in August 1970 demanding equal rights. Their lived experiences informed Ortner's views of women's position in most societies.

seemingly universal fact that women everywhere appear to be devalued relative to men.

Traditional gender roles

For anthropologists, a cultural universal – such as gender inequality – is rare; most human universals are based in biology, not culture. However, while female subordination appears to be widespread, Ortner did not believe

Sherry Ortner

Born in Newark, New Jersey, US, in 1941, Sherry Ortner studied anthropology under Clifford Geertz at the University of Chicago. For her PhD, obtained in 1970, she conducted fieldwork among the Sherpas, an ethnic group from the Himalayas of Nepal, focusing on their rituals, religion, and politics.

Ortner is renowned for her work on class, gender, and popular culture. In particular, she helped to advance feminist theory in anthropology by critiquing male biases in ethnographic writing,

which prioritized the study of men's needs and values over women's. She also contributed to practice theory, examining the relationship between social structure and individual agency.

Awarded a MacArthur Genius Grant in 1990, Ortner has since become a fellow of the American Academy of Arts and Sciences.

Other key works

1996 *Making Gender*

See also: Comparative ethnography 84–85 ▪ Structuralism 108 ▪ Women and the political economy 156–57 ▪ Emotional control 216–17 ▪ Gender equality 266 ▪ Challenging systemic oppression 294–95

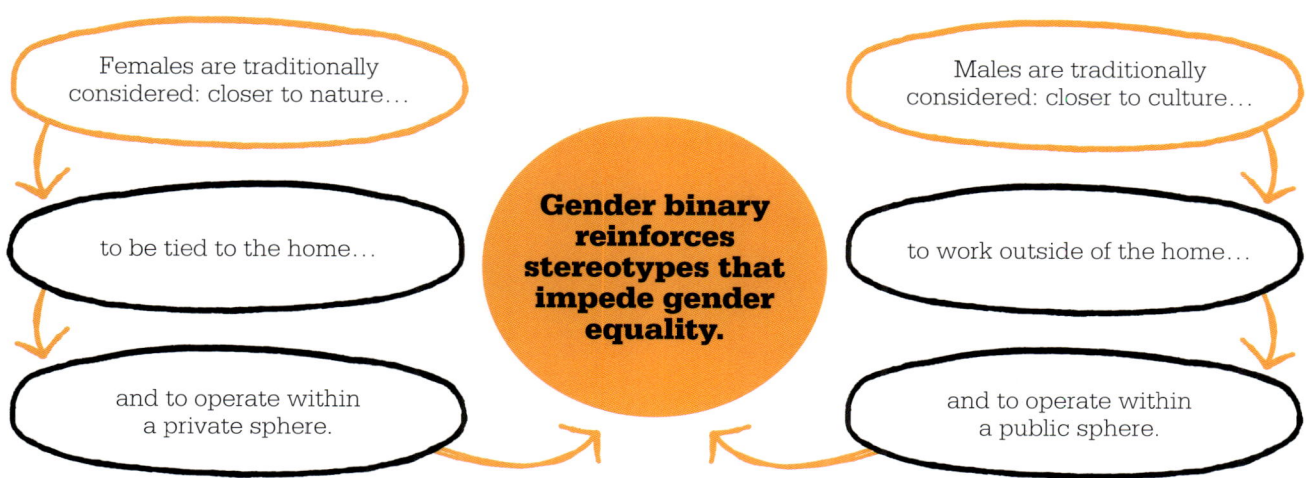

Females are traditionally considered: closer to nature…

to be tied to the home…

and to operate within a private sphere.

Gender binary reinforces stereotypes that impede gender equality.

Males are traditionally considered: closer to culture…

to work outside of the home…

and to operate within a public sphere.

the reason to be biological. She therefore set out to investigate the cultural conditions that helped to give rise to this gender "asymmetry".

Ortner observes that "feminine" symbols and structures are generally associated with nature, whereas "masculine" symbols and structures are associated with culture – the values, ideas, concepts, and rules shared by a particular society. These associations are problematic, she argues, because the prevailing view is that nature is inferior to culture. Often, the aim of culture is to subjugate nature: to take raw natural materials and convert them into cultural objects that people can use. In this way, it can be argued that culture (men) transcends nature (women).

Ortner questions why the association of men with culture and women with nature exists in the first place. According to her, it is partly based on the physiological differences between men and women – specifically, that women's bodies allow them to bear children and lactate. These activities seem

to consign women to the private (domestic) sphere. In contrast, men do not perform these roles, so they are able to occupy the public sphere and therefore take on expanded leadership roles in politics and religion.

Binary approach

Ortner's use of binary opposites – male or female, nature or culture, private or public – evokes the work

Much of the creativity of anthropology derives from the tension between two sets of demands: that we explain human universals, and that we explain cultural particulars.
Sherry Ortner

of French structural anthropologist Claude Lévi-Strauss. He argued that, everywhere, the human mind tried to make sense of the observable world by using binary contrasts to categorize a wide range of things. For Ortner, opposites such as nature or culture, and private or public, map on to female or male and are valued differentially in ways that reinforce gender inequality.

However, Ortner is also quick to point out that these dichotomies are not as rigid as they first appear. After all, there is no denying that women are also fully cultural human beings. Although women's bodies place them comparatively closer to nature than men, she argues that women represent "something intermediate between culture and nature". This intermediary position is apparent, for example, in the act of childrearing, in which women primarily transform pre-cultural infants into fully human – and cultural – agents. In so doing, women generate a kind of symbolic ambiguity: they move between » the poles of nature and culture and, in doing so, appear to be out of place. Ortner claims that men try to control this ambiguity by restricting women's roles, relegating them to the home, and denigrating their activities as "natural".

Mothers and children

Just as women's bodies are naturalized, so too are their psyches. Drawing on the work of US sociologist Nancy Chodorow, Ortner examines the idea that female thought processes tend to be more subjective and concrete, while male cognition tends to be objective and abstract. This pattern is not biologically determined; rather, it is produced through familial systems that render mothers as the primary socializers of children. For boys, an eventual shift is made as they come to identify with the father and enter the world of cultural abstractions. For girls, continued identification with the mother results in feminine personality traits that are, like nature, direct and unmediated.

Male is, as I am suggesting, everywhere (unconsciously) associated with culture, and female seems closer to nature.
Sherry Ortner

Consequently, boys and girls learn to acquire either masculine or feminine personalities.

In these ways, women's bodies, roles, and psyches are depicted as closer to nature, while men are depicted as closer to culture. The more these associations are entrenched in societies, the more difficult it becomes to achieve gender equality. However, Ortner claims that the path forward to gender equality involves recognizing that gender inequality is a social construction, not a

biological fact. The "secondary status" of women is a product of cultural ideologies that are reaffirmed by societal structures that further constrain their choices and activities. Ortner states that the "implications for social change are … circular: a different cultural view can only grow out of a different social actuality", which, in turn, "can only grow out of a different cultural view". In other words, gender symmetry requires both cultural and social changes. For example, feminine symbols and social roles must be upheld rather than disparaged.

Critiques and alternatives

Ortner's essay contributed to a new type of feminist anthropology that went beyond just adding women's experiences to the ethnographic record; it also decried male bias within anthropological scholarship. Yet some people – academics and otherwise – criticized her for generalizations that oversimplify the position of women in society. Despite her own stated aim to the contrary, Ortner seems to fall back on biological determinism by claiming that a woman's body – and specifically its reproductive functions – consigns her to the domestic sphere. Ortner also fails to consider the way in which men oscillate between the poles of nature and culture, since their natural bodily functions also have an impact on their social lives.

Some anthropologists point out that Ortner's essay was written from a distinctly Western Judeo-Christian perspective that does

Sumatra's Minangkabau people have a matriarchal culture. Property, land, and family names are passed from mothers to daughters, and women make key community decisions.

not attend to the range of gendered experiences found in other parts of the world. They argue that in some societies men and women are equally valued despite, or even because of, enacting different social roles. The people of Vanatinai (Tagula), a remote island in Papua New Guinea, provide one example. In this matrilineal and egalitarian society, both men and women are socialized to be relatively assertive and autonomous. Further, women are esteemed as "life-givers" due to their ability to bear children.

Even in the West, the structure of some societies challenges Ortner's view. In Iceland, Finland, and Norway, for example, women have achieved near-equal rates of educational attainment with men, and more women than men hold political office in Iceland. Such cross-cultural examples from Oceania and northern Europe undermine the universal assumption that biology underpins gender aysmmetry.

Intersectionality

In the decades following the publication of Ortner's essay, the focus of feminist anthropology

The concept of intersectionality explains that individuals are the sum of their parts, and difficult to categorize in any simplistic, one-size-fits-all way. As a result, any discrimination that individuals face may be multiplied according to the various aspects of their being – from gender and race, to social class.

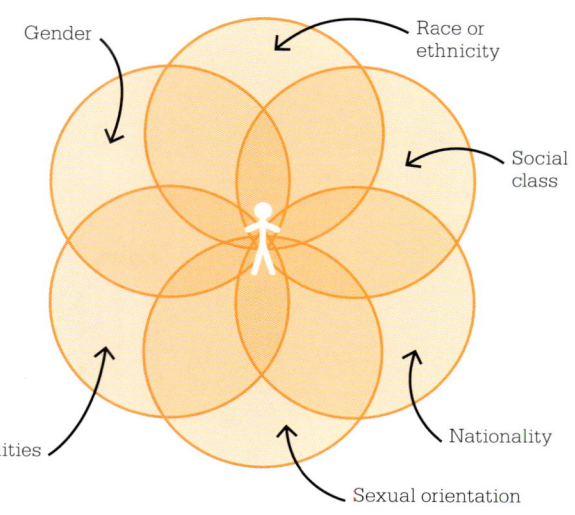

Gender

Race or ethnicity

Social class

Nationality

Sexual orientation

Capabilities

shifted away from investigating gender universals and gender inequality towards examining the differences among women. Much of this work is influenced by the concept of "intersectionality" as presented by US critical race theorist and legal scholar Kimberlé Crenshaw, among others.

Intersectionality implies that individuals do not have singular identities: a person is not just a woman, a man, or non-binary. Rather, individuals are made up of multiple identities, including class, race, ethnicity, sexuality, and religion. By virtue of these identities, people may be subjected to overlapping systems of oppression, such as sexism, classism, racism, and homophobia. An intersectional analysis, therefore, emphasizes that individuals cannot be reduced to their gender alone, because social and political conditions shape their multiple identities, roles, and lived experiences. ∎

A 1947 US advertisement for Hotpoint cookers targets women, who were assumed to be the main users of domestic products.

The Second Sex

French philosopher and activist Simone de Beauvoir's most famous and controversial book – *The Second Sex* – was published in 1949. Women in France had received full political and voting rights five years earlier, yet they continued to be disadvantaged in society relative to men.

The book focused on several aspects of a woman's physical, emotional, and social existence in order to explain the causes of female inequality. Beauvoir looked at how women are constructed as "other" in relation to men; how they are relegated to physical tasks such as housework and reproduction; and how they are socialized to fulfil a "feminine" existence characterized by male oppression. Importantly, Beauvoir argued that these conditions could be changed if societies recognized that, although men and women are different, they are essentially equal.

Beauvoir's highly influential title was the inspiration for the second wave of feminism that swept across France during the 1960s.

MAN IS SUSPENDED IN WEBS OF SIGNIFICANCE HE HIMSELF HAS SPUN

THICK DESCRIPTION

IN CONTEXT

KEY WORK
Clifford Geertz,
Interpretation of Cultures,
1973

FIELD
Sociocultural anthropology

BEFORE
1905 Max Weber argues that differences between Catholics and Protestants stem from rival interpretations of core symbols and texts.

1911 Franz Boas emphasizes cognitive similarities across human societies, based on shared symbols in language and culture.

AFTER
1972 Laura Nader urges scholars to study the cultures of dominant societies, not only those affected by colonialism.

1983 Talal Asad argues that cultural experiences can transcend symbolic interpretation.

Javanese shadow theatre dramatizes myth and morality, embodying layered symbols and performance. It is a "text" to be read, not merely watched.

Behind every gesture, ritual, or social interaction lies a web of meanings – shaped by history, power, and shared symbols – waiting to be decoded. A simple wink might be a conspiratorial signal, a nervous twitch, or an ironic gesture. To grasp these nuances, anthropologists need a method that goes beyond surface observation.

Clifford Geertz, one of the 20th century's most influential anthropologists, answered this need with his concept of "thick description": a way of interpreting human behaviour by unpacking the hidden layers of context – cultural, historical, and personal – that give actions meaning. Unlike mere observation, thick description asks why a wink is significant: is it a

Clifford Geertz

Born in San Francisco, USA, in 1926, Clifford Geertz was one of the most influential figures in anthropology. His work focused on cultural interpretation by analyzing the symbols of everyday life.

After studying literature and philiosophy at Antioch College, Ohio, Geertz earned a PhD in Anthropology at Harvard in 1956. His fieldwork in Indonesia established him as both an anthropologist and an authority on religion, particularly Islam in Southeast Asia. After teaching at the University of Chicago and UC

Berkeley, he joined Princeton's Institute for Advanced Study, where he held a leadership role and produced his most influential writings.

Geertz's concept of "thick description" remains one of the cornerstones of interpretive anthropology.

Other key works

1960 *The Religion of Java*
1968 *Islam Observed*
1981 *Negara: The Theatre State in Nineteenth-Century Bali*
1983 *Local Knowledge*

See also: Cultural relativism 34–41 ▪ Biopsychological functionalism 50–55 ▪ Structuralism 108 ▪ Rites of passage 126–29 ▪ Feminist anthropology 140–45 ▪ Religion and secular power 188–89 ▪ Kinship studies 192

private joke? A rehearsed gesture? The difference lies in the webs of interpretation people themselves spin. Geertz applied this method to diverse contexts: in Java, his analysis of shadow puppetry revealed how leather figures can convey moral and cosmological truths, while in Bali, his observations of cockfights offered insight into status competition and ideals of manhood.

Geertz, a lifelong humanist, saw understanding other cultures as a path to understanding what it means to be human. By decoding the symbolism woven into everyday life, he sought to find common ground across cultures. For him, anthropology was not just about documenting the past but engaging with present debates, using cultural diversity to deepen understanding of human life.

Layered meanings

Geertz helped to establish what is known as "symbolic" or "interpretive" anthropology, an approach that remains influential today. Although his writings could be complex and sometimes difficult to decipher, Geertz's central argument was straightforward: culture, especially among humans, is founded on a tapestry of shared symbols. It is not fixed but is rather constantly shaped by interpretation, with meanings that shift depending on the observer's perspective and experience.

Building on this idea, Geertz drew inspiration from philosophy, particularly British philosopher Gilbert Ryle, who had introduced the concept of "thick description" to explain how meaning is layered within symbolic encounters. It was

Ryle who first used the example of a wink to illustrate this: an identical movement of the eye could be interpreted as a conspiratorial signal of shared understanding or as an involuntary twitch with no meaning at all. At first glance, it would be hard to tell the difference between the two, at least without looking into

the minds of the speakers, or understanding the full context in which it took place.

In Geertz's view, ethnography should study how people create and interpret meaning – and it should begin by understanding how individuals explain their own thoughts, feelings, and actions. Geertz's approach was semiotic, »

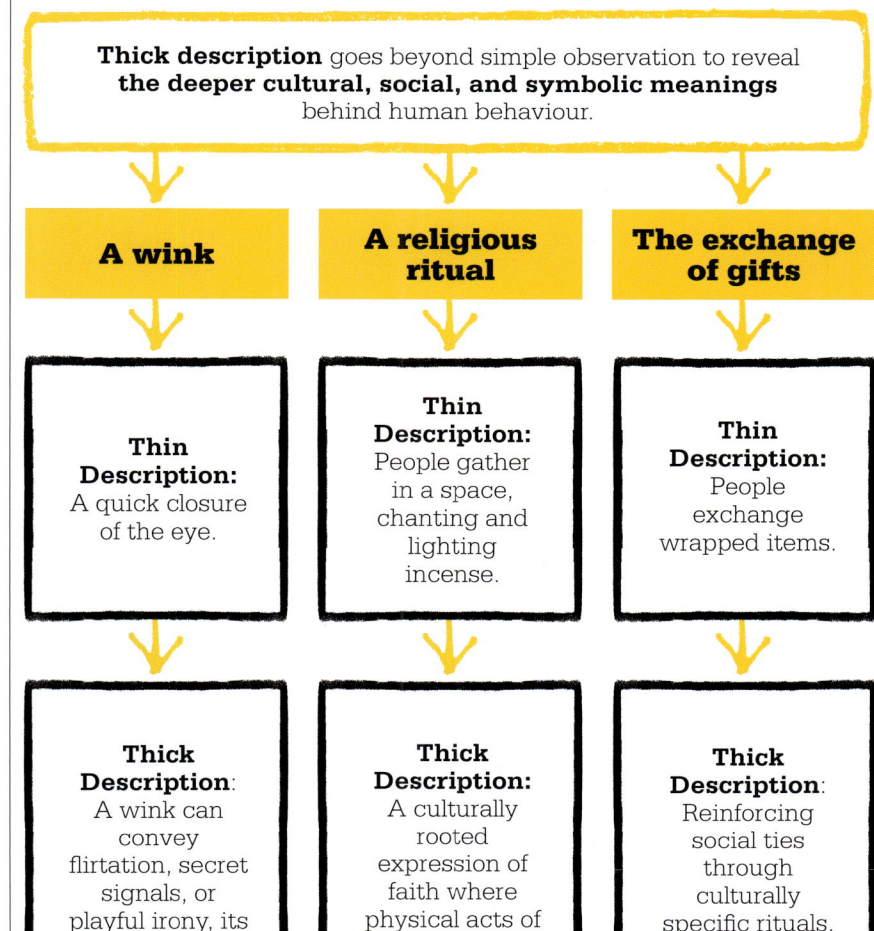

Thick description goes beyond simple observation to reveal **the deeper cultural, social, and symbolic meanings** behind human behaviour.

A wink

Thin Description: A quick closure of the eye.

Thick Description: A wink can convey flirtation, secret signals, or playful irony, its meaning shaped by social context.

A religious ritual

Thin Description: People gather in a space, chanting and lighting incense.

Thick Description: A culturally rooted expression of faith where physical acts of worship embody deep symbolism.

The exchange of gifts

Thin Description: People exchange wrapped items.

Thick Description: Reinforcing social ties through culturally specific rituals, such as wrapping and timing.

emphasizing the role symbols and signs play in generating meaning. This method helps to distinguish between a nervous twitch from a meaningful wink – or between a conspiratorial wink and an ironic gesture mocking the practice itself.

The layers of meaning are endless, and the interpretations perhaps never completely capture every possible layer of meaning for each participant. This complexity becomes even more pronounced when exploring unfamiliar cultures. Drawing on Ryle's philosophy, Geertz argued that human behaviour is riddled with intention, and successful communication depends on the continuous assessment of these intentions.

Culture as text

Geertz approached the study of culture by viewing it as a complex system of public symbols that require interpretation. These symbols come into play when people encounter new situations, and individuals often manipulate them to achieve immediate effects. This manipulation is not solely based on the symbols' traditional meanings but also on personal motives and the ongoing reactions of others around them. In this sense, culture is fluid and ever-changing – people are not automatons, nor do they fit neatly into predefined personality types or cultural profiles.

Drawing inspiration from the German sociologist Max Weber, Geertz elaborated on this idea, stating that humans are "suspended in a web of signification" that they themselves have spun. This metaphor highlights the intricate and self-created nature of cultural meanings that individuals navigate in their daily lives. His thick description of Balinese cockfighting illustrates this approach. What might appear as mere gambling and sport to outsiders revealed itself as a complex drama of status, masculinity, and social relationships. Through careful interpretation, Geertz showed how the cockfight encoded important aspects of Balinese society – from social hierarchy to concepts of self and community.

> What we call our data are really our own constructions of other people's constructions of what they and their compatriots are up to.
> **Clifford Geertz**

Geertz likened culture to a dynamic, evolving story – shaped by its author, influenced by its audience, and subject to countless ongoing interpretations that defy summarization. He illustrated this with a vivid metaphor: an Indian myth about infinite regression – the philosophical idea where every explanation demands another explanation, creating an endless chain. In the myth, the world rests on the back of a giant turtle. When someone asks what supports the world turtle, the response is: "It's turtles all the way down."

This interpretive approach marked a sharp departure from many of the dominant theoretical frameworks that had been prominent in anthropology's earlier history. Before Geertz, scholars often relied on a one-size-fits-all model to analyze human societies, imposing external blueprints on diverse cultures. For example, cultural evolutionists believed that

Geertz saw the Balinese cockfight as a public spectacle and cultural performance – where status, identity, and values play out through ritual, rivalry, and high-stakes betting.

history naturally progressed toward Western ideals, placing modern capitalist societies at the top. This ethnocentric perspective implied that all cultures should strive to meet Western standards.

Other theorists, such as the US anthropologist Marvin Harris, argued that culture was a mere byproduct (or epiphenomenon) of deeper material forces. For example, Harris argued that the avoidance of pork in the Middle East arose from the fear of diseases spread by pigs.

Geertz rejected these approaches, asserting that it was a mistake to interpret human behaviour through a universal framework without fully taking local perspectives into account. Central to his work was the belief that anthropology should deepen our understanding of human cultures, fostering richer and more meaningful cross-cultural dialogue.

The role of ideology

Geertz was one of the first American anthropologists to recognize the value of studying ideology – the system of ideas, values, and beliefs that shapes how individuals or groups interpret and engage with the world. He saw ideology as more than "political propaganda"; he saw it as a cultural tool kit that people use to make sense of their world and justify their actions. Breaking with some contemporaries, Geertz championed this broader understanding of ideology, seeing it as a shared framework of meaning that helps people navigate their social environments.

Geertz was a severe critic of the structuralist approach of French anthropologist Claude Lévi-Strauss, which sought to identify universal patterns in human thought and culture.

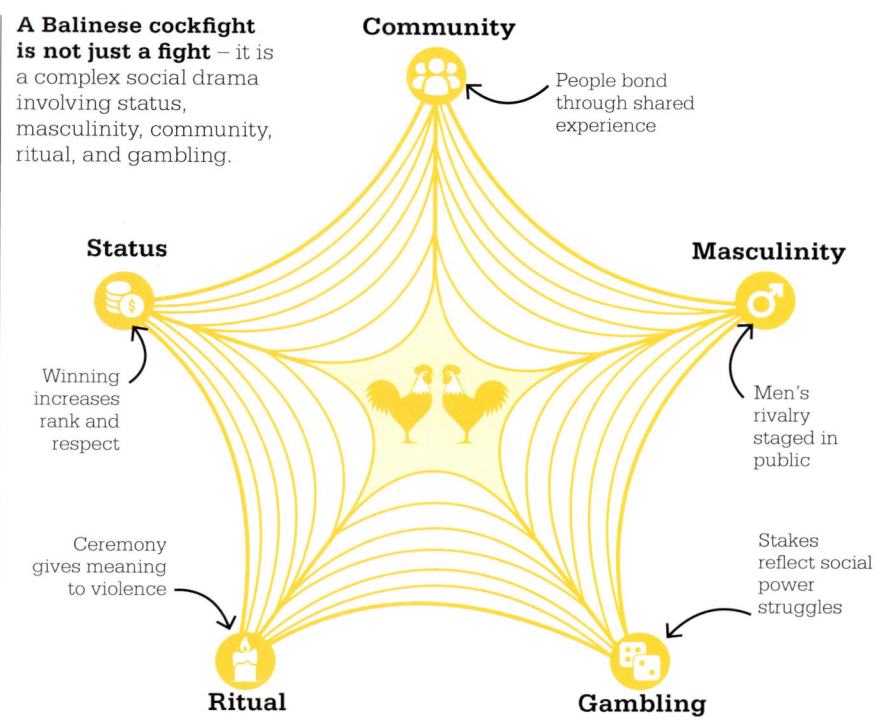

A Balinese cockfight is not just a fight – it is a complex social drama involving status, masculinity, community, ritual, and gambling.

Community
People bond through shared experience

Masculinity
Men's rivalry staged in public

Status
Winning increases rank and respect

Ritual
Ceremony gives meaning to violence

Gambling
Stakes reflect social power struggles

While he admired some aspects of Lévi-Strauss's work, Geertz disagreed with the focus on these universal patterns. For Geertz, structure is only one part of the equation, as people constantly manipulate symbols in their everyday interactions with other people who participate in these shared cultural practices.

Geertz felt that Lévi-Strauss had reduced human experiences to abstract concepts, losing touch with the nuances of genuine human interaction. By focusing too heavily on theoretical structures, Lévi-Strauss, in Geertz's view, overlooked the lived realities of how people engage with one another. Geertz claimed that he would not presume to know what someone thought without talking to them, in stark contrast to Lévi-Strauss, who often claimed to discern the structure of thought, not merely in one culture, but all societies.

Interpreting religion

Geertz's focus on symbols makes his approach especially well suited to the study of religion. Religious symbols may be material, such as icons, which are invested with meaning through collective practice, or they can be linguistic, such as sacred texts or prayers, which convey profound spiritual messages. His approach helps to explain how religions adapt and how symbolic meanings can be mobilized to stir powerful responses, particularly when believers see themselves as defending the very fabric of the cosmos.

An example of this is Geertz's use of thick description to reveal the deeper social meanings behind religious symbols and rituals in Java. To an outsider, these might appear as simple prayer rituals, but Geertz revealed the complex hierarchies at play. In Java, there are three main styles of religious »

> Understanding a people's culture exposes their normalness without reducing their particularity... It renders them accessible.
> **Clifford Geertz**

expression: *abangan*, peasant animist traditions; *santri*, Islamic orthodoxy; and *priyayi*, Hindu-influenced mysticism.

By interpreting these practices through thick description, Geertz showed how these religious variations reflected and reinforced broader social divisions. The same religious gesture or ritual could carry entirely different meanings: for a *santri* merchant, it demonstrated pious devotion; for a *priyayi* aristocrat, it expressed refined spirituality; and for an *abangan* farmer, it connected to ancestral traditions.

Grounded relativism

In a time when much of mainstream anthropology was focused on identifying broad human universals, Geertz stood out as a strong advocate for relativism – the view that different societies

Geertz's work on Balinese religion examined how temples, ceremonies, and offerings create a symbolic system that reinforces cultural values and collective identity.

may hold distinct, internally coherent ways of thinking that should be understood on their own terms. He sought a return to the more grounded roots of anthropological knowledge: careful engagement with the lives of others. Cultural practices, he argued, should not be forced to fit within Western value systems, as reflections of supposed universals, nor dismissed as less than human – or, perhaps more seriously, exoticized as strange. His was a soft, situational relativism, not the radical relativism associated with figures such as Benjamin Lee Whorf.

In this sense, Geertz echoed Franz Boas, sometimes insisting on relativism as a method, but more often expressing scepticism towards grand abstractions or universals. Like Boas, Geertz was very sceptical of universals, but, more importantly, he believed they were intellectually sloppy. Supposed universals, such as religion, were often vague and lacked real substance, he argued.

Above all, Geertz is known for his lucid and provocative writing style, which reached audiences well

beyond the academy. He is remembered not only for his theoretical work, but also for his many vivid ethnographic sketches. Alongside his celebrated account of cockfighting in Bali, Geertz wrote with insight about funeral rituals in Java and about haggling in Moroccan marketplaces – settings he presented as sites of social interaction and cultural performance. While many of his contemporaries were turning to increasingly theoretical schools, from the structuralism of Claude Lévi-Strauss to the materialism of Marvin Harris, Geertz consistently stressed the humanistic side of the discipline: the importance of empathizing with others and seeing the world from their point of view, without objectifying them or reducing their experiences to theoretical models.

For Geertz, theory was only valuable if it remained grounded in lived experience. He criticized both vague abstractions and simplistic models that ignored the richness of actual social life – charges he often levelled at structuralism in particular. His

In his study of a Moroccan souk, Geertz explored how trade is shaped by cultural meanings, personal networks, and local understandings of risk and trust.

work insisted that meaning must be sought in context, not imposed from above.

Although his writings could be philosophically dense and difficult to understand, Geertz's lasting influence lies in how he reshaped the practice of anthropology. He modelled a way of thinking that was analytical yet attuned to nuance, showing that meaning must be interpreted in context and never taken for granted.

Lasting legacy

Geertz engaged himself deeply in the humanities – from philosophy to art and comparative literature. This engagement helps to explain why his ideas spread far beyond anthropology. They found eager audiences in sociology, philosophy, and other fields devoted to human nature and cultural diversity, and his works have had an enormous

impact in these fields. In time, Geertz emerged as one of anthropology's most influential public intellectuals, not only in the academy, but in the wider world.

Geertz's students helped to shape postmodern anthropology, a movement that similarly rejected universal explanations in favour of cultural particularism, and built on his interpretive approach. This development coincided with a broader return to philosophical foundations in the social sciences. The most striking development came in ontological anthropology, the study of how different societies conceptualize existence itself, which reinvigorated the tradition associated with Boas and Geertz of rigorous cultural relativism.

While Geertz's work faced criticism – notably from the British-Pakistanvi anthropologist Talal Asad, who argued it overlooked power dynamics – these debates underscore the enduring relevance of his core insight: that cultural meaning is layered, contested, and embedded in symbolic systems. ∎

Memory and anthropology

Anthropologists have long explored how communities remember. Rather than viewing memory as a purely individual or psychological process, ethnographers such as US anthropologist Jonathan Boyarin approach it as a social and cultural practice. In his 1991 work, *Polish Jews in Paris*, Boyarin examines how Jewish immigrants in Paris recall and transmit their past, showing how memory is woven into everyday life.

Working within Geertz's interpretive tradition, Boyarin treats memory as a cultural practice shaped by language and relationships. His fluency in Yiddish and immersion in the community positioned him as both an ethnographer and cultural heir, revealing how stories and rituals sustain identity. Like Geertz's thick description, Boyarin's work reveals memory is experienced, narrated, and sustained – connecting identity, history, and belonging through layers of shared meaning.

We all begin with the natural equipment to live a thousand kinds of life but end having lived only one.
Clifford Geertz

AN EXPRESSION OF ITS MAKER'S MIND
MATERIAL CULTURE

IN CONTEXT

KEY WORK
Henry Glassie, *Folk Housing in Middle Virginia*, 1975

FIELD
Sociocultural anthropology

BEFORE
1916 Ferdinand de Saussure's *Course in General Linguistics* outlines a method for analysing language to interpret culture, and sets the stage for the emergence of structural anthropology.

1962 In *Archaeology as Anthropology*, Lewis Binford introduces a new, more scientific approach to archaeology that becomes known as "processualism".

AFTER
1977 US anthropologist James Deetz publishes *In Small Things Forgotten*, one of the founding texts of the then-emerging field of historical archaeology.

Broad and interdisciplinary, material culture studies focus on the "things" that surround people in their everyday lives and what they reveal about their users. One of the first and most prominent scholars of material culture is US ethnologist Henry Glassie, whose 1975 book *Folk Housing in Middle Virginia* began

Techniques used in the ancient craft of carpet making in Türkiye have been refined by generations of weavers, with processes influenced by the different dyes and yarns available.

his 60 years of publishing on how architecture and the objects people use give extraordinary insight into the past, reflecting cultural and societal values.

History of things
According to Glassie, "Material culture records human intrusion in the environment". He believes that the key to understanding past and contemporary cultures is through their material creations, such as the rugs people weave and the buildings they construct. His work is rooted not only in the search for common characteristics among objects and architecture, but also in the desire to understand how and why people build and craft. Rather than studying the people themselves, Glassie is more interested in "what they choose to present as emblems of their being". Using detailed ethnographic research, his unique approach has helped him form a more nuanced understanding of the material things that constitute people's worlds.

Glassie is particularly preoccupied with the narratives told by historians, who use documents – letters, work orders, receipts, books, and diaries – to reconstruct and

See also: The structure of language 44–45 ▪ Structuralism 108 ▪ The New Archaeology 110–15 ▪ Post-processual archaeology 190–91

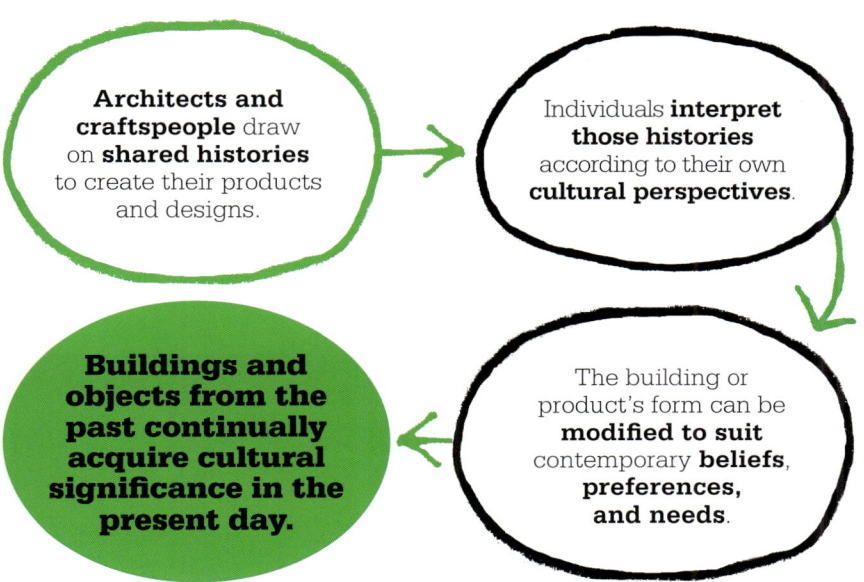

Architects and **craftspeople** draw on **shared histories** to create their products and designs.

Individuals **interpret those histories** according to their own **cultural perspectives**.

The building or product's form can be **modified to suit** contemporary **beliefs, preferences, and needs**.

Buildings and objects from the past continually acquire cultural significance in the present day.

Henry Glassie

Born in 1941 in Washington, D.C., Glassie received a BA from Tulane University in 1964, an MA from the State University of New York at Oneonta in 1965, and a PhD from the University of Pennsylvania in 1969. He was the first-ever state folklorist in Pennsylvania from 1967 to 1969, and has held many academic appointments, including professorships in folklore, ethnomusicology, American studies, and anthropology at Indiana University and the University of Pennsylvania. Glassie's curiosity about global patterns in material culture and architecture has involved fieldwork in various US states, and also in Ireland, Sweden, Türkiye, Bangladesh, Brazil, Nigeria, and many other countries. Through a shared interest in structuralism and the histories of ordinary people's daily lives, Glassie became close friends with US anthropologist James Deetz.

Other key works

1982 *Passing the Time in Ballymenone*
1999 *Material Culture*
2000 *Vernacular Architecture*

explain historical events and behaviour. However, some societies do not have written histories – and as Glassie writes in the 1990s, most people in the past were illiterate, and many remain so in the modern world. For this reason, Glassie and the scholars who followed in his footsteps believe that historians fail to capture the totality of the human experience. Despite his criticisms of history, Glassie does not believe we should ignore its findings. Rather, he wants historians to see "potsherds, old houses, and the like" as valid and important points of entry to history.

Drawing on structuralism

Much of Glassie's work involving material culture draws upon a theoretical framework known as structuralism, in which language is seen as a complex system of interrelated parts – rather than individual words – that can be analysed to interpret culture,

change, and innovation. Equating material culture with language, Glassie argues in *Folk Housing* that political upheaval during the American War of Independence and in the colonies in the 18th century led to changes in household design and layout: "Communal obligations were replaced by individual land and labor; from then on man became increasingly separated from man." House designs transformed from simplistic open one or two room layouts, where space was shared and communal and neighbours were welcome, to homes with multiple private rooms intended for individuals.

Today, material culture scholars, may examine the evolution of objects such as skateboards and cell phones. Stickers and markings on a skateboard may reveal the owner's political beliefs or hobbies, while the make and model of a cell phone may indicate the owner's social status. ∎

AN ORGANIZATIONAL BASIS FOR A SEXUAL DIVIDE-AND-RULE POLICY

WOMEN AND THE POLITICAL ECONOMY

IN CONTEXT

KEY WORK
Karen Sacks, "Engels Revisited", 1975

FIELD
Sociocultural anthropology

BEFORE
1877 US anthropologist Lewis Henry Morgan writes in *Ancient Societies* that human communities "evolved" from matrilineality to patrilineality.

1971 In "The Origin of the Family", British anthropologist Kathleen Gough examines the biological and economic factors that underpin the emergence of modern family life.

AFTER
1975 US anthropologist Gayle Rubin's "The Traffic in Women" investigates sex and gender from a political-economic perspective.

1988 Karen Sacks explores race and gender in the context of healthcare in her book *Caring by the Hour*.

In her critical re-evaluation of *The Origin of the Family, Private Property, and the State* (1884) by German philosopher Friedrich Engels, US anthropologist Karen Sacks explores the status of women within society.

Women and capitalism
Engels's book, written in response to the theories expressed by Lewis Henry Morgan in *Ancient Societies*, examined how the rise of private property and capitalism shaped the family structure and the status of women. Engels argued that gender equality was more prevalent in non-class-based societies than in class-based societies. This is because class-based societies were formed in the context of capitalism, with an emphasis on productive labour that is largely performed by men.

Under the capitalist system, reproductive tasks usually carried out by women in the domestic arena were deemed less valuable than work – by men – that took place in the public sphere and generated wealth. According to Engels, the subordination of women and the decline in

Men have an **active engagement** in the **public sphere**.

This allows them to generate wealth through **productive labour** outside the home.

Men have more public power than women.

Women tend to have **more involvement** in the **private sphere**.

They have an **active and essential** role in **reproduction** in the home.

Women wield less power than men in the public realm.

This 1926 advertisement for a vacuum cleaner confirms gender roles, squarely positioning the woman in the domestic environment while the man goes to work in the public sphere.

when considering several African societies – each with distinct modes of subsistence, politics, and economy – Sacks discovers that, contrary to Engels's claim, women can be both "social adults" and "wifely wards". Therefore, a woman's position within the family does not always determine her status outside of the home.

Property and labour

Engels placed emphasis on the ownership of private property as key to male power. Sacks, however, argues that it is not lack of property that leads to female subordination but, rather, the exclusion of women from public labour, which is integral to adult social status and public power. Female status consequently declines as women are consigned to the private domestic sphere.

Private property transformed the relations between men and women ... only because it also radically changes the political and economic relations in the larger society.
Karen Sacks

In essence, capitalism, rooted in the production and accumulation of wealth, results in the elevation of public work and private property. Within this context, the unpaid and private work of women has rendered them "wards" of men. However, Sacks believes that this can change when the work of men and women is considered of equal importance, and the family is recognized as the base of society. ▪

their social position were side effects of capitalism and the way it prioritized public labour and new forms of private property.

Dual status

In "Engels Revisited", Sacks adds ethnographic clarity to the German philosopher's central argument. For instance, she finds examples of gender inequality even in non-class-based societies. In addition,

---

The OvaHimba people

Around the world, patrilineal systems – in which inheritance and status pass through the male line – are the norm, but some matrilineal systems do exist. Additionally, there are societies that defy neat categorization or are in a state of transition from one kinship system to another.

In northern Namibia, the OvaHimba are an ethnic group that has a bilateral, or double-descent, kinship system. Each individual is considered to be a member of both their mother's and father's clan, but they inherit different things from each side. For example, status comes from the male family line, while cattle, which represent wealth, are inherited matrilineally. In the polygamous OvaHimba society, cattle are also the main form of bridewealth – that is, a dowry paid by a man to the family of his wife-to-be.

Recent shifts towards more patrilineal inheritance have resulted in social change that has affected OvaHimba attitudes towards the autonomy of women.

The hairstyles of OvaHimba women reflect their age and status, with thick braids – shaped using a buttery red paste – an indicator of fertility.

THE SOUL IS THE PRISON OF THE BODY
GENDER, SEXUALITY, AND POWER

IN CONTEXT

KEY WORK
Michel Foucault, *Discipline and Punish*, 1975

FIELD
Sociocultural anthropology

BEFORE
1781 German philosopher Immanuel Kant publishes his *Critique of Pure Reason*. An inquiry into the limits of knowledge and reason, it influences Foucault's scepticism towards universal systems of thought.

1945 French philosopher Maurice Merleau-Ponty writes about how our embodied experience and perception shape the understanding of reality.

AFTER
1993 Anthropologist Talal Asad applies Foucault's approach to analyse how religious discourses and practices were formed and transformed.

The work of French philosopher Michel Foucault on power, sexuality, and the construction of knowledge has had a huge influence on cultural anthropology and the other social sciences.

In his book *Discipline and Punish*, published in 1975, Foucault describes how modern European culture emerged through specific governmental practices. One of his key insights is how power has changed over time in European societies. In premodern times, power was a repressive force wielded by centralized authorities using law, censorship, and taboo to maintain control. These societies often relied on public displays of physical punishment to regulate behaviour. From the 17th century, however, governments moved from exerting absolute control to what Foucault called "biopower" – an altogether more subtle way of regulating and managing people's lives.

Power and surveillance
In order to maintain a compliant and productive population, governments began to regulate birth, death, disease, sexual relations, and other aspects of peoples' lives. An important element within biopower was what Foucault termed "disciplinary power," which involved placing people under surveillance. Initially confined to institutions such as prisons and schools, this form of power gradually spread throughout society. Over time, individuals began to regulate their own behaviour, even without surveillance. This kind of self-discipline became a central feature of modern societies.

Foucault later extended his ideas of biopower to sexuality and, by extension, gender. In *The History of Sexuality* (1976), he describes how governments – through the application of biopower – began

Surveillance is permanent in its effects, even if it is discontinuous in its action.
Michel Foucault

See also: Structuralism 108 ▪ Studying up 138–39 ▪ Thick description 146–53 ▪ Religion and secular power 188–89 ▪ Structure and agency 196–99 ▪ Kinship ideologies 218–19

Examinations Assessments categorize and rank individuals.	**Institutions** Schools, prisons, and churches enforce discipline.	**Self-regulation** Individuals modify their behaviour to what is "normal".

Disciplinary power

Surveillance Constant observation enforces conformity.	**Timetables and routines** Schedules regulate people's time.

to define what was considered normal and healthy, and what was considered abnormal, unhealthy, and deviant.

Setting the standard
In the modern world, Foucault argues, governments control gendered bodies and sexual behaviour by establishing standards for what is "normal" and "abnormal"; these standards

A panopticon prison exemplifies Foucault's ideas about surveillance. The central tower allows unseen guards to monitor the inmates, and fosters a persistent sense of being observed.

are used in healthcare, criminology, and psychology, as well as in other areas.

Significantly, people actively participate in their own self-regulation as they become invested in these standards of sex and gender, and view them as "normal". As a result, governments no longer need to repress or monitor their populations. Instead, they achieve and maintain control by relying on individuals to self-regulate and conform to normalized standards. These regimes of power, Foucault explains, function to create people who are at once objects of power and vehicles of that same power.

Foucault's insights into power, discipline, and self-regulation have become essential tools in anthropology for understanding how social norms shape individual lives. His work challenges anthropologists to examine the subtle ways in which power operates within cultures, influencing everything from personal identity to collective beliefs. ∎

Sexuality and society

Published in 1976, Michel Foucault's *The History of Sexuality* examines how discourses and practices surrounding sexuality have evolved through history.

Foucault argues that sexuality is not simply a biological condition, but something that is culturally constructed and shaped by the institutions of power. He traces how society changed from being concerned with sexual acts and behaviours, to defining or labelling people as homosexual or heterosexual, for example, and ultimately came to pathologize certain forms of sexuality. Foucault critiques the idea that sexuality is fixed; instead, he suggests that sexual identities are historical products influenced by changing discourses and power structures.

THE EVOLUTION OF CULTURE IS AN ADAPTIVE PROCESS
STAGES OF SOCIAL ORGANIZATION

IN CONTEXT

KEY WORK
Elman Service, *Origins of the State and Civilization*, 1975

FIELD
Sociocultural anthropology

BEFORE
1867 In *Das Kapital*, Karl Marx critiques and analyses economic, social, and political systems throughout history.

1955 In *Theory of Culture Change: The Methodology of Multilinear Evolution*, US anthropologist Julian Steward outlines a framework that emphasizes the environment's role in shaping cultural practices and social structures.

AFTER
1981 Italian geneticist Luigi Cavalli-Sforza and Australian biologist Marcus Feldman publish their theory of cultural evolution, inspired in part by Service's work.

Anthropologists often classify human societies based on their social and economic patterns. In the mid-20th century, US anthropologist Elman Service developed a typology – a system of classification – that linked forms of sociopolitical organization to different types of human economies, dividing societies into four categories. Once influential, Service's typology is now seen as overly rigid, as it does not fully account for the complexity and adaptability of human societies.

Inuit hunters demonstrate how Indigenous people have adapted their lives to the modern world, highlighting the limitations of rigid classifications such as Elman Service's typology.

Four types of society

Service's first category, the "band", is a small social structure typically composed of 30 to 100 people. Bands are usually hunter-gatherers, and often territorial. They are formed of extended family members, with spouses selected from outside of the group. Political organization is informal with little specialization.

The "tribe", Service's next level of organization, is usually larger than a band, and often has a horticultural economy with some foraging. Tribal societies place greater emphasis on social cohesion and group identity, with decision-making achieved by consensus. Rituals and communal activities reinforce group identity.

See also: Unilineal evolution 26–27 ▪ Cultural relativism 34–41 ▪ Multilinear evolution 104–07 ▪ Structuralism 108 ▪ Cultural materialism 124 ▪ Structure and agency 196–99

Elman Service

Elman Service was born in Tecumseh, Michigan, US, in 1915 and grew up in poverty during the Great Depression – a background uncommon among early anthropologists. These experiences fuelled his passion for the social sciences and for social justice. He served in both the Spanish Civil War and World War II, and later earned a PhD in anthropology from Columbia University in 1950.

Service went on to teach at Columbia, the University of Michigan, and the University of California, where he eventually

retired. In 1962, he published *Primitive Social Organization*, one of his most influential works, in which he outlined his typology of social organization. Service had a long and accomplished career; he died in Santa Barbara, California, in 1996, at the age of 81.

Other key works

1960 *Evolution and Culture* (with Marshall Sahlins)
1962 *Primitive Social Organization*
1963 *Profiles in Ethnology*
1966 *The Hunters*

The third category, the "chiefdom", often relies on raising livestock and small-scale agriculture. Chiefdoms have a higher degree of economic specialization and complexity. The population is significantly larger, even reaching several thousand. There are also strong social hierarchies, each with privileges and obligations.

The final level of organization is the "state", a system characterized by intensive agriculture and cities with complex social systems. States are the most stratified form of social organization, with specialization, formal institutions, and legally defined groups.

Legacy and limitations

Service's typology emphasizes the links between the economic system and a group's sociopolitical organization, which suggests that social features are adaptations to material conditions. His model implies an evolutionary progression in social organization, a view largely set aside in contemporary anthropology. Many anthropologists now believe that these types of

organizations are more flexible than Service proposed. In *The Dawn of Everything* (2023), US anthropologist David Graeber and British archaeologist David Wengrow challenged the idea that human societies evolve from simpler to

more complex forms, noting that throughout history societies have experimented with various forms of organization, complexity, and hierarchy, and that simpler societies were often not transitional stages to more complex ones. ■

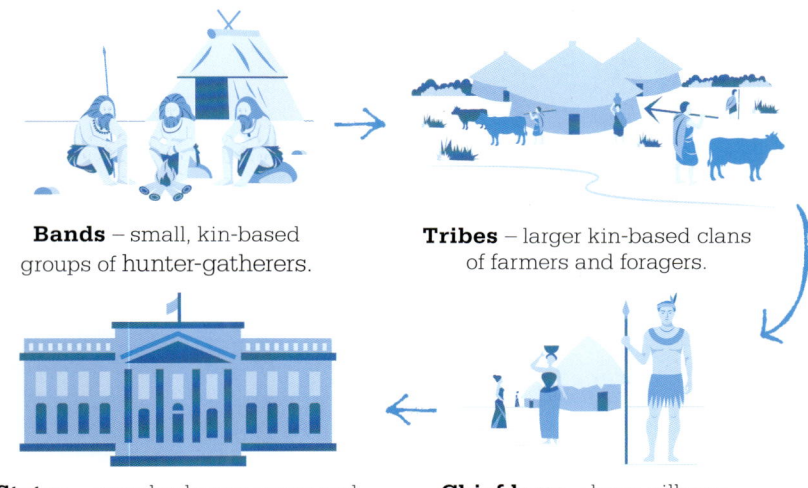

Four stages of social organization

Bands – small, kin-based groups of hunter-gatherers.

Tribes – larger kin-based clans of farmers and foragers.

States – complex bureaucracy and institutionalized leadership.

Chiefdoms – large villages led by a chief.

CULTURE IS INTERPRETATION

REFLEXIVE ETHNOGRAPHY

IN CONTEXT

KEY WORK
Paul Rabinow, *Reflections on Fieldwork in Morocco*, 1977

FIELD
Sociocultural anthropology

BEFORE
1807 In *The Phenomenology of Spirit*, German philosopher Wilhelm Friedrich Hegel analyses the evolution of self-awareness.

1928 Austrian-German philosopher Edmund Husserl's *The Phenomenology of Internal Time-Consciousness* explores individuals' lived experience.

AFTER
1986 US anthropologists James Clifford and George E. Marcus call for greater reflexive experimentation with writing strategies in anthropology such as dialogue, pastiche, and memoir.

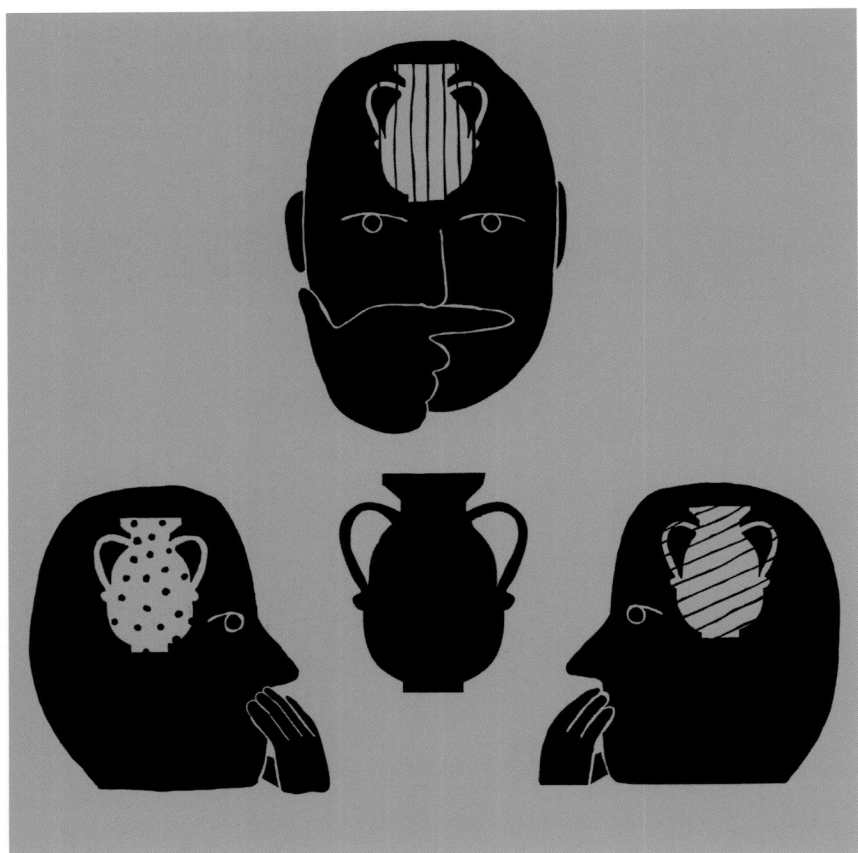

Ethnography – the practice of conducting extensive in-person fieldwork – is a core tool used by sociocultural anthropologists when carrying out research. It is also a term that is used to describe a written account of such research. In many ways, ethnography – as both research method and the product of research – is at the heart of sociocultural anthropology, even defining the field as a whole. However, before about 1970, ethnographic fieldwork had never been critically examined. Anthropology students were not commonly taught how to conduct ethnographic research, and

See also: Studying up 138–39 ▪ Thick description 146–53 ▪ Structure and agency 196–99

Early ethnographers present their findings as **authoritative**, but their research processes and results are **rarely scrutinized**.

→

Ethnographers such as Rabinow **engage more** with their **subjects** and **reflect** on their own position as **observers**.

→

Anthropologists increasingly subject ethnographic **fieldwork** to **critical examination**.

↓

Ethnographic fieldwork is a relationship between the observer and the observed.

---

ethnographies tended to reveal little about how the research was gathered and interpreted.

This situation began to change during the 1970s, when some anthropologists began to publish ethnographies that not only incorporated their own perspectives and experiences, but also recorded how those perspectives influenced their interpretation of the findings. US anthropologist Paul Rabinow was a trailblazer in this new form of ethnographic framing, which came to be known as reflexive ethnography. In his 1977 monograph *Reflections on Fieldwork in Morocco*, Rabinow wrote as much about his own experience conducting research as he did of his subjects' perspectives. He provided a deeply personal account of his successes and frustrations as a novice anthropologist and illustrated key theoretical themes about the nature of fieldwork.

The Moroccan city of Sefrou provided a traditional North African backdrop to Rabinow's fieldwork with his subject Ali, who was treated as an outsider in his own home village.

Ethnographic tension

One of Rabinow's themes relates to the way in which ethnographic research is inherently subjective and an act of dual interpretation between researchers and their subjects. Rabinow defined ethnography as consisting of participant observation, but he also appreciated that there was tension between participation and observation. Anthropologists must, of course, be observers of cultural situations, but to get the most accurate observations of cultural worlds, they must participate in them to the greatest possible extent. However, no matter how much anthropologists participate, they inevitably always remain cultural outsiders. Rabinow argues that this tension between "the poles of observation and participation" changes the anthropologist, leading to new observation, which "changes how he participates". »

Insider or outsider?

Rabinow explored the insider–outsider theme in various ways throughout *Reflections*. One of his key informants, Ali, was both an outsider and an insider of sorts. Rabinow met Ali in the city of Sefrou but later went to live in his home village, Sidi Lahcen Lyussi. Ali was an engaging and energetic informant, but he was surrounded by a form of social stigma. He was a married man with children, yet he also had a girlfriend and was fairly open about the relationship. In addition, he engaged in some economic activities – such as running a prostitution ring – that attracted social condemnation. Ali was not fully accepted in his native village because most of its residents considered his activities to be immoral. Ali further antagonized the villagers by poking fun at their simple and unworldly lifestyle.

Despite these drawbacks, Rabinow considered Ali to be an especially strong informant. In fact,

The "facts" [that] the anthropologist has gone to the field to find are already themselves interpretations.
Paul Rabinow

Rabinow argued that Ali's marginal position in society was precisely what made him so effective.

Self-awareness

Ali was not an average villager, and he was far from the solid-citizen stereotype in Sefrou. Because of this, he was more self-reflective – about society at large and his place in it – than most Moroccans known to Rabinow. Ali had rejected

village life and was paying the social price of that choice. He had to justify and explain his decisions, both to himself and to his critics. Additionally, he had crafted his own way of living in Sefrou. Already ostracized by much of the community, he would mock social norms by flaunting his freedom.

While Ali was undeniably a cultural insider, having been born and raised in the village, his rejection by the community and its members' critiques of him gave him an outsider status. The duality of being both insider and outsider, together with his keen awareness of his place in society, made Ali one of Rabinow's most valuable research subjects.

Social facts

Alongside his detailed reflections about the process of fieldwork and the complex relationships that he developed with his informants, Rabinow made other important points that extended beyond simply exploring how ethnography is carried out and encapsulated ideas at the heart of anthropology. One example was Rabinow's treatment of social facts and the possibility of cross-cultural understanding. He explained that social facts are things that social scientists often treat as existing externally from cultural interpretation. For instance, a social fact could be that one of his informants owned 20 hectares (50 acres) of land. This cannot easily be disputed. However, the interpretation of what this means changes and is shaped by the researcher–informant relationship.

Mirrors placed at different angles reveal how both the observer – the ethnographer – and the observed have multiple facets that may affect how they interpret what they see.

As an example of this complex relationship, Rabinow cited another Moroccan informant, Malik, who saw himself as a down-trodden man whose life was hard. When Rabinow began an exercise with Malik in which he documented on paper all of Malik's properties and financial resources, the results stood in contrast to how Malik saw himself. The findings did not compute with how Malik – or others in his village – evaluated his status.

Rabinow discovered that, in Morocco, economic poverty does not carry the same social stigma as it does in a society like the US, for example. Instead, social and familial relationships are key to a person's self-image of well-being. This means that a person could be financially well-off but still considered poor if they did not have the right kind of family or social relationships. As Rabinow and Malik worked together to construct a social fact – Malik's financial resources – Malik began to realize that, economically, he was actually relatively prosperous. This prompted Malik to reflect further on the issue. Ultimately, Malik concluded that he was not doing

Ethnographers unconsciously hold certain biases that will affect their studies. The basic tenet of reflexivity is that before ethnographers can understand their research subject, they have to be aware of their own prejudices.

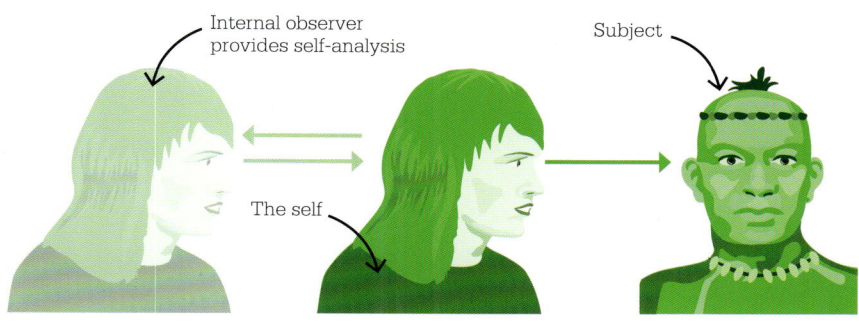

Internal observer provides self-analysis

The self

Subject

well because, although he had many landholdings, his father was dead, his son was sickly, his mother needed support, his brothers were unmarried, and his uncle was out to steal his land.

A new reality

The conflicting interpretations of well-being by Malik and Rabinow caused them to see things in a different light and together form a new reality. Rabinow pointed out that "what seemed to my naive consciousness to 'speak for itself' proved to be the most in need of interpretation". In this situation, the economic conditions of Malik's town could only be understood when the history of the religious, political, ecological, psychodynamic, and social factors came into play.

Rabinow used Malik's example to emphasize the point that anthropological facts are cross-cultural in nature, because they are made across cultural boundaries. They do not exist outside of lived experience and a shared and negotiated reality. They are made into facts in the interactions between the ethnographer and the informant – a dynamic process in which all parties engage. ∎

A fresh approach

Before the 1990s, most cultural anthropologists conducted ethnographic research in a way that clearly differentiated the people being studied from the researcher. The researcher's task was to observe and participate in the lives of their informants while maintaining an emotional and interpersonal separation from them.

In 1996, Cuban-American anthropologist Ruth Behar published *The Vulnerable Observer*, which engaged with the evolving anthropological movement of reflexive ethnography. Her work offered a new approach to ethnography that explored the relationship between the observer and the observed with greater nuance. Behar reflected on her own life as a part of the ethnographic process, describing her experiences conducting research in Spain, Mexico, and Cuba, and reflecting on her personal struggles. She proposed an anthropology that is lived and written in a personal voice, rather than an objective one.

The streets of Havana, in Cuba, provided a vibrant location for much of Behar's fieldwork. She advocated removing the divide between researchers and the observed.

CREATING THE WORLD THROUGH LANGUAGE
RITUAL AND LANGUAGE

After years of living among the Diné (Navajo people) in the Southwest US, Gary Witherspoon argued that for the Diné, language held a creative force in rituals that constructed their reality of the world. Witherspoon lived on Navajo Nation (Diné Bikéyah) lands in the 1960s as a Mormon missionary, but later became involved with education there and married into a Diné family. What he learned came from research and his immersion in the culture: he participated in rituals and customs, talked with Diné thinkers, and he also engaged in an analytical study of the language.

Create, control, classify

Witherspoon suggested that a culture's reality is an imaginative construct based on assumptions about the nature of language, myth, and ritual. He observed that Diné language was the foundation for creating, controlling, and classifying the world. In the language, Witherspoon noted that an opposition between static and active phenomena lay behind many grammatical and semantic structures. He records prefixes that mark circular, repeated action and others that symbolize linear movement. For the Diné, language created, rather than reflected, their understanding of the universe. Witherspoon argued that the emphasis on values of harmony, control, order, and creativity – what he termed "living in beauty" – were fundamental to Diné culture, and visible in rituals and art forms. ∎

> In mythology things came into being or happened as people thought or talked about them.
> **Gary Witherspoon**

See also: The social roots of religion 42–43 ∎ The structure of language 44–45 ∎ Language and cognition 88–89

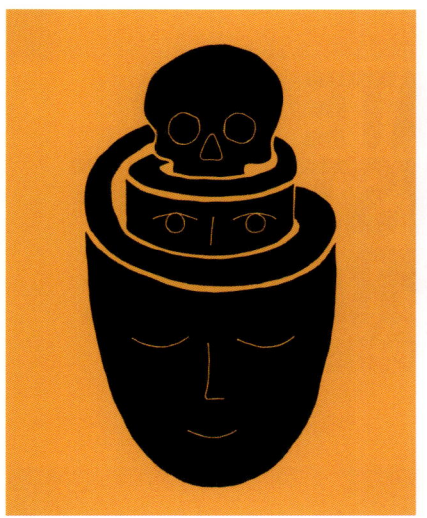

IDENTITIES ARE EMBODIED IN THE HUMAN SKELETON
BIOARCHAEOLOGY

In the late 1970s, archaeologist Jane Buikstra called on her colleagues to recognize a new form of archaeology, which she called bioarchaeology. The term had been used some years before in a different sense but Buikstra provided a new definition: the use of tools, theories, and methods from the disciplines of both biological anthropology and archaeology to study human remains. She argued that human remains are especially valuable to archaeologists as they can provide information about the health, living conditions, diet, and mortality of people of the past.

Bioarchaeology now
The field of bioarchaeology has since expanded and diversified to include research into pollen grains and other ancient plant material as well as bacteria and DNA. Recent bioarchaeological research has uncovered the first evidence of familial embalming, aiding the study of medieval embalming. And bioarchaeology is also being used in research into migration, climate change, warfare, famine, and the effects of disease. Buikstra encourages the media and medical fields to examine bioarchaeology data and insights, but emphasizes that this should be done carefully and ethically so as not to mislead the public. ∎

Buikstra extracts pathogen DNA from human remains at archaeological sites to study the evolutionary history of ancient tuberculosis in the US.

See also: Biopsychological functionalism 50–55 ∎ The New Archaeology 110–15 ∎ Mental health and society 172–75 ∎ Post-processual archaeology 190–91

AN ELABORATE AND ORDERED SYSTEM OF IDEAS AND PRACTICE

MEDICINE AND HEALING PRACTICES

IN CONTEXT

KEY WORK
Harriet Ngubane,
Body and Mind in
***Zulu Medicine*, 1977**

FIELD
Medical anthropology

BEFORE
1936 Eileen Jensen Krige, one
of a trio of important female
social anthropologists working
in South Africa – the others
being Hilda Kuper and Monica
Wilson – publishes *The Social
System of the Zulus*.

1962 In *Zulu Transformations*,
South African anthropologist
Absolom Vilakazi focuses on
the role of Christianity to
explore subjects such as
kinship and cultural and
psychological integration.

AFTER
1988 Rhodes University
professor Felicity Souter
Edwards leads research into
spirit possession among the
Xhosa in the Eastern Cape.

In the middle of the 20th century, South Africa was experiencing significant political and social upheaval. Carrying out fieldwork there in the 1960s and 1970s, social anthropologist Harriet Ngubane began to explore the anthropology of health and illness – a rapidly emerging area of research – within a wider social context. In her seminal work *Body and Mind in Zulu Medicine: An Ethnography of Health and Disease in the Nyuswa-Zulu Thought and Practice,* Ngubane illuminates how Zulu conceptions of bodily health in mid-20th-century South Africa are closely related to psychological, relational, and spiritual wellbeing. She provides insights into traditional and contemporary Zulu healing practices and how these are intrinsically linked to a person's ecological and cosmological environment.

Insider ethnography

Ngubane's research was informed by her status as a South African Zulu woman: "In most aspects of daily life, outlook and habits, I am Zulu in spite of my mission background." As such, she was able to establish a rapport with the

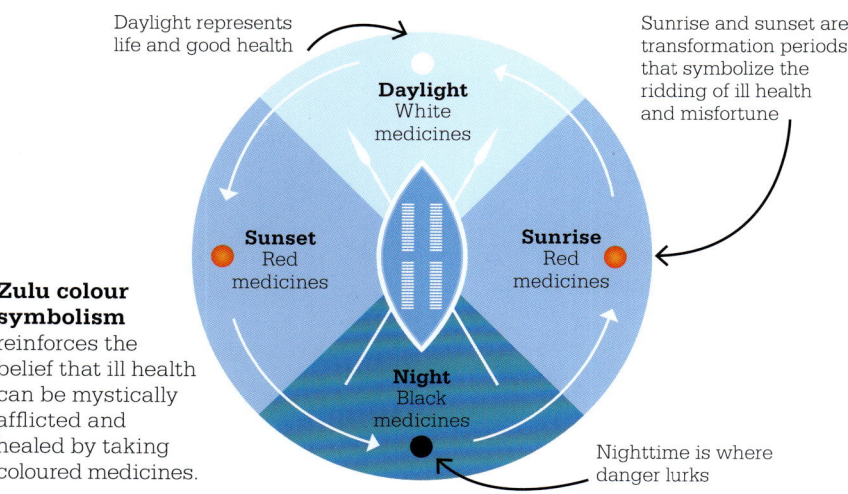

Daylight represents
life and good health

Daylight
White
medicines

Sunrise and sunset are
transformation periods
that symbolize the
ridding of ill health
and misfortune

Sunset
Red
medicines

Sunrise
Red
medicines

**Zulu colour
symbolism**
reinforces the
belief that ill health
can be mystically
afflicted and
healed by taking
coloured medicines.

Night
Black
medicines

Nighttime is where
danger lurks

See also: Local belief systems 78–79 ▪ Purity and society 120 ▪ Mental health and society 172–75

people she was studying, and was accepted at intimate Zulu family gatherings and social interactions. During her research, Ngubane spoke mostly to women, because the men were often away working in the cities. She engaged them in casual conversations in their homes, on buses, in hospitals, and during the ceremonies and rituals she observed.

Symbols and colour

Among many insights in *Body and Mind,* Ngubane highlights the importance of colour symbolism in Zulu medicine. She describes how Zulu society emphasizes that a person must be in balance with their environment and how symbols are used to direct ritual healing practices. More than this, she shows how colour symbolism in medicines and rituals is linked to Zulu ideas concerning social organization and Zulu beliefs about life and death. She explains that "primary" colours – black (*mnyama*), red (*bomvu*), and white (*mhlophe*) – are used serially in ritual healing.

> If I could help it, I would be a social scientist and nothing more. But the South African situation is such that any social aspect is also a political aspect.
> **Harriet Ngubane**
> **Letter to Meyer Fortes, 1973**

Harriet Ngubane

Born in 1929 and raised in a Roman Catholic mission in Natal, South Africa, Ngubane trained as a teacher at St Francis College in Mariannhill before obtaining her bachelor's degree in 1957 at the University of Natal. In 1963, she began her fieldwork under Eileen Jensen Krige among the Nyuswa-Zulu society in Botha's Hill, Natal. Ngubane then left South Africa to study at Cambridge University in 1969, where she became the first Zulu woman to receive a doctorate. In the 1980s, Ngubane returned to South Africa, where she joined the Inkatha Freedom Party and sat on its land committee during South Africa's transition to democracy in the early 1990s. Ngubane became Member of Parliament for Inkatha in 1994. She died in 2007.

Other key works

1960 *Urban Bantu Housing*
1976 "Some aspects of treatment among the Zulu"
1986 *Zulus of Southern Africa*

They are directly related to the cosmic order of day and night and also to bodily functions, such as intake and expulsion.

Associated with darkness, black medicines or symbols – including those with dark shades such as green – are used to expel ill health or misfortune during the night, when it is necessary to withdraw and rest to become strong again. They are always followed by white medicines, which are associated with the light, and bring good health and fortune. In practical terms, tasks should be completed in the light during the day, because in the darkness of night misfortune may occur. Red symbolizes the twilight, and hence the transition between day and night, between health (light) and illness (darkness). Red medicines are also always followed by white ones. The symbolic meanings of these colours are further used in ritual performances related to birth, death, marriage, and other life events where women's bodies play a central role.

A highly significant contribution to the study of health and illness, *Body and Mind* describes an "elaborate and ordered system of ideas and practice" that enables the Zulu people to "perceive and cope, conceptually and practically, with the problems of health and disease as they present themselves". ▪

In Zulu societies during the 20th century, the diviner, or *isangoma*, was often a woman. She used her special connection with ancestral spirits to diagnose illnesses and decide on cures.

WHY DON'T YOU STUDY YOUR OWN KIND?

ANTHROPOLOGY AT HOME

IN CONTEXT

KEY WORK
Barbara Myerhoff, *Number Our Days*, **1978**

FIELD
Sociocultural anthropology

BEFORE
1937 In *Their Eyes Were Watching God,* anthropologist Zora Neale Hurston focuses on the lives of black women in the American South.

1974 US anthropologist Sherry Ortner looks at the roles of women around the world in her article "Is female to male as nature is to culture?".

AFTER
1988 In *Persistence and Flexibility,* German-born Walter P. Zenner examines the interactions between the "native" anthropologist and the people being studied.

2001 US anthropologist John L. Jackson explores Harlem and finds it is more varied and complex than he expected.

With the publication of *Number Our Days* in 1978, US anthropologist and filmmaker Barbara Myerhoff prompted a rethinking of ethnographic research and writing by focusing on her own backyard. The number of anthropologists working "at home" had been on the increase since the early 1970s – for example, in her 1972 article "Up the anthropologist:Perspectives gained from studying up", US professor of anthropology Laura Nader wrote that more work should be done to understand people's own systems and structures of power. However, in the late 1970s,

Collaborative ethnography

An anthropologist asks to **work with a group** of people to **learn about them**.

Together, they **discuss the purpose of the work** and what the **end product(s)** will be.

The anthropologist and group **plan** how to carry out **fieldwork and interviews together**.

The anthropologist **teaches** the group the **skills that they need** to conduct fieldwork.

They conceive and **create material together**, with diverse audiences in mind.

End products may be poetry, songs, texts, or artworks.

See also: Autoethnography 76–77 ▪ Feminist anthropology 140–45 ▪ Medicine and healing practices 168–69 ▪ White privilege 214

it was still an unusual step for Myerhoff, an American Jewish woman, to choose to study a Californian cultural centre for elderly Jews.

Familiar ground

Myerhoff and her colleagues at the University of Southern California were part of a new wave of anthropologists working in gerontology – the sociocultural, biological, and political processes by which we grow old. After conducting fieldwork in Mexico in the 1960s, Myerhoff began to study age and ethnicity, intending to work with Chicano people. However, her first encounters were far from encouraging, because the elderly Mexican Americans questioned why she was working with them and not with her "own kind". Myerhoff then began to explore the lives of people of her own ethnicity, nationality, and religion. As she explains in *Number Our Days*, she was initially unsure whether this would be considered "real" anthropology and worried about questions of objectivity. Many anthropologists believed that in working on familiar ground with familiar people, much would be taken for granted, overlooked, or under-questioned.

Inside scoop

Myerhoff's early concerns abated as she became aware that her own experiences of being Jewish were in fact limited by time, place, and education. The elderly people she worked with at the cultural centre made it clear that they were also conscious of these limitations. They were primarily multilingual, many were survivors of the

Jewish women engaged in crafting activities at a Community Centre in Denver, Colorado, have an opportunity to share their experiences of culture and community.

Holocaust, and most were struggling just above the poverty line. Politically, they were passionate about a range of issues, but they were generally socialist, communist, or left wing in their ways. Raised in poverty in Eastern Europe, they had seen their children educated and become professionals in diverse fields, living utterly different, quite separate lives from their own. US anthropologist Jonathan Boyarin describes a similar situation in his 1991 book *Polish Jews in Paris*.

Myerhoff's compelling narrative ethnography asks: "What really counts?" Those at the Jewish centre replied that successful educated children were most important, but Myerhoff's project spotlights the rituals, storytelling, and songs that connect people and protect them from the loneliness and invisibility that they most fear. She notes that Yiddish – "the beloved mama-losen [mother tongue] of their childhood" – helps to tie these people together, despite their underlying differences. ▪

Native anthropology

In a 1993 article "How native is a 'native' anthropologist?", Indian-born anthropologist Kirin Narayan questions the term "native anthropologist" – then used to describe someone who works in their own country or region of birth – and asks whether the outsider/insider dichotomy is properly framed. For example, an anthropologist trained in questioning the world and reporting their findings in a particular professional dialect is already different and apart from others. Narayan explains that cultures themselves are not uniform anywhere, and so each "native anthropologist" will have a different set of dynamics. Each person has a hybrid identity that combines professional, gendered, and personal aspects, and they know their society from a particular perspective. Narayan notes that there will inevitably be some aspects of the self that connect anthropologists to the people they study and other elements that highlight fundamental differences.

The best lives and stories are made up of minute particulars that somehow are also universal.
Barbara Myerhoff

A MANIFESTATION OF DIS-EASE

MENTAL HEALTH AND SOCIETY

In 1974, US anthropologist Nancy Scheper-Hughes set off for a village that she called Ballybran (a pseudonym) in rural southwest Ireland. At that time, Ballybran was a cluster of cottages and farms, with a population of fewer than 500 people. Within the picturesque setting and seemingly close-knit community, she found a traditional agrarian economy with a village-based way of life that was in decline as marriage and birth rates plummeted. Most strikingly, she found high rates of schizophrenia, a severe mental illness characterized by distorted patterns of thought, feelings, and behaviours. The majority of those

See also: Caste systems 122–23 ▪ Medicine and healing practices 168–69
▪ Sequencing ancient DNA 290–91

> During periods of rapid change and cultural distortion, many individuals will tend to become disorganized internally.
> **Nancy Scheper-Hughes**

affected were single men aged 25 to 40 years old who had spent time in psychiatric hospitals.

Mental-health pressures

Scheper-Hughes wanted to know why this part of rural Ireland was experiencing such high rates of mental illness and specifically why young men were affected. In search of answers, she used a combination of psychological and anthropological methodologies, including participant observation, interviews, demographic data, hospitalization rates, and psychological tests. She also drew on ethno-historical techniques, analysing folk tales, proverbs, and superstitions. She published her findings in *Saints, Scholars and Schizophrenics: Mental Illness in Rural Ireland*.

To provide context for her conclusions, Scheper-Hughes opens her study with a description of the

As farming in Ireland drifted into decline in the aftermath of World War II, many rural communities saw increased rates of psychiatric illness, especially among young men.

social and economic conditions that had affected village life in Ireland. Following World War II, the rise of industrial capitalism had drawn many young men and women away from their family farms and rural villages to take up residence and find employment in cities.

According to Scheper-Hughes, the country-to-city migration left a significant gap in the social fabric of rural villages, creating a dilemma for older adults who continued to subsist on their farms. Once their daughters and first-born sons had left, parents exerted pressure, through scapegoating and guilt, to keep their youngest sons at home. Often told they were not bright enough to succeed in the cities, these sons had low expectations for themselves. They were, however, told that they were good farmers who were needed to maintain the family farm and care for aging relatives. Raised with a puritanical version of Irish Catholicism, the boys were taught self-denial and sexual repression, such that, as men, they seldom married and rarely had children of their own. »

Nancy Scheper-Hughes

Born in New York City, US, in 1944, Nancy Scheper-Hughes worked as a Peace Corps volunteer in Brazil in her early 20s, focusing on the rights of rural workers and street children. That experience shaped her views as she subsequently pursued a PhD in anthropology at the University of California at Berkeley. She later became a professor there and co-founded a PhD programme in critical medical anthropology.

Having worked in a range of countries – including Brazil, South Africa, the Philippines, and Israel – Scheper-Hughes has continued to focus on social justice and social inequality in relation to the body, health, and healthcare. The impact of violence and social marginalization on the lives of poor people has been a common theme throughout her career.

Other key works

1992 *Death without Weeping: The Violence of Everyday Life in Brazil*

They became isolated and even hostile towards the opposite sex. These young bachelor farmers found themselves trapped in the rural setting. They were caught in a double bind – both loved and unloved by their parents – and as a result, they eventually succumbed to mental illness.

Critical opinions

Although economic and social change had undoubtedly disrupted rural life in Ireland in the post-war era, many villagers believed their portrayal in Scheper-Hughes's book to be inaccurate and overly negative; others claimed that she placed too much emphasis on how social conditions shape mental disorder. In response to her critics, Scheper-Hughes argued that "schizophrenia is one of the many expressions of the human condition" and that it is "the translation of social ills into private troubles". While exacerbated by "social ills", schizophrenia, like other psychological disorders, has biological underpinnings – a fact that Scheper-Hughes seems to overlook. Nevertheless, her book remains an enduring example of

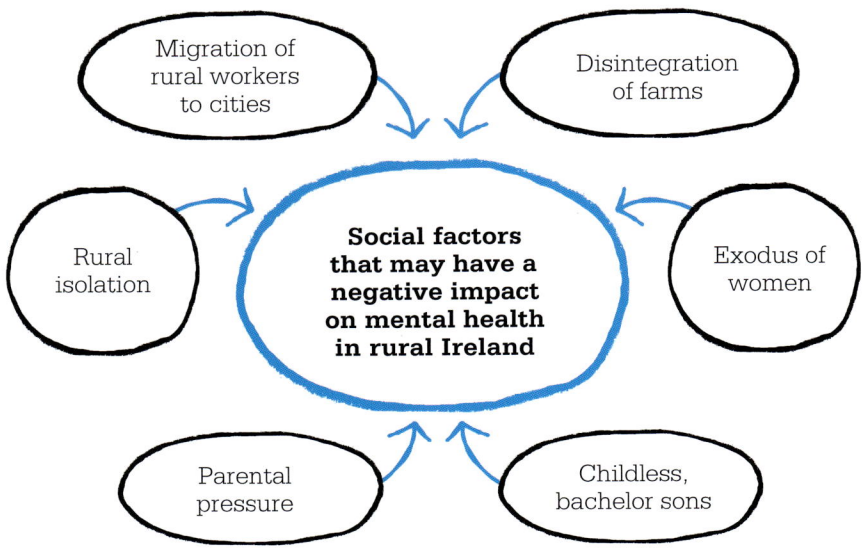

Migration of rural workers to cities

Disintegration of farms

Rural isolation

Social factors that may have a negative impact on mental health in rural Ireland

Exodus of women

Parental pressure

Childless, bachelor sons

how anthropological analyses can explain how cultural factors affect mental health.

Attitudes to mortality

In the 1980s, Scheper-Hughes took up another epidemiological puzzle, this time in Brazil, where, at the time of her study, about one million children under five years old died each year, half of them in the poor northeast of the country. It was feared that these staggeringly high figures were likely to be underestimates, due to unreliable reporting. The deaths were not evenly distributed, but there were "two contradictory epidemiological profiles, one for the rich and middle classes and the other for the poor".

To understand these contrasting profiles of child mortality, Scheper-Hughes considered the history of the region. Beginning in the mid-16th century, northern Brazil was the site of vast, productive sugar

Medical anthropology

The basic premise of medical anthropology – which examines how culture shapes the human body, health, and medicine – is that the body is affected by its socio-cultural context, as well as by biology. Medical anthropologists use cultural, biological, and linguistic anthropology to move beyond purely physical explanations of human behaviour. They favour a broader social understanding of topics such as the prevention of illness, as well as views on

health risk and vulnerability, healing and treatment processes, and the globalization of medical technologies. Contemporary anthropologists focus on how socio-political forces – such as structural violence, poverty, war, and racism – influence the distribution of disease and people's experiences of illness.

Another area of interest is the culture of medicine. This is the idea that biomedical knowledge and therapeutic practices do not stand outside of culture but are also produced by social, political, and economic conditions.

People in refugee camps have faced traumatic events that may lead to mental illness. Cramped living conditions often exacerbate this.

Brazilian *favelas*, or shantytowns, like this one in Rio de Janeiro, experience such high rates of child mortality that the expectation of loss has redefined maternal bonds.

plantations. However, by the 19th century, sugar exports had waned and the economy shifted, leading rural squatters and tenant farmers to seek work as low-paid wage labourers and domestic servants. The lingering feudal class system gave rise to socioeconomic disparities that Scheper-Hughes found to be relevant at her study site: the market town of Bom Jesus da Mata and, specifically, its shantytown area Alto do Cruzeiro (both pseudonyms).

Social context

Life in Alto was plagued by extreme poverty. The residents had limited access to clean water and faced chronic hunger, which resulted in physical and psychological effects. People spoke of being afflicted by *nervos* – a folk illness category related to anxiety – and "hunger madness" brought about by the emotional toll of starving and watching others starve. In this context, women experienced high rates of fertility along with very high rates of infant mortality. Babies commonly died from starvation, malnutrition, infectious disease, dehydration, or lack of medical care.

What surprised Scheper-Hughes most was that women appeared to be indifferent when their infants died. However, she soon learned that, in this environment, desperately poor women had to "triage" their limited resources (both material and emotional) by investing only in infants that showed a "thirst for life" at the expense of those that were listless and weak. Never knowing which

infant would survive, women withheld emotional attachment – and even refrained from naming their child – until it showed some fortitude. When an infant died, as too often occurred, the women did not grieve, instead claiming that their "angel baby" had found solace.

Coping strategy

Scheper-Hughes argued that maternal love is not a biological given but a luxury that these

Ideally, anthropology should try to liberate truth from its Western cultural presumptions.
Nancy Scheper-Hughes
Death without Weeping: The Violence of Everyday Life in Brazil, **1992**

mothers could not afford. She wrote that "mother-love as defined in the psychological, social-historical, and sociological literature is far from universal or innate". Instead, she added, it represents an "ideological, symbolic representation grounded in the basic material conditions that define women's reproductive lives".

In the shantytown, material circumstances led the women to protect themselves by withholding maternal love and supporting only those children that might live beyond their most vulnerable years. Rather than criticize these mothers, Scheper-Hughes argued that they have adapted to survive amid social injustice and structural violence.

Context matters

Whether considering mental or physical health, life or death, Scheper-Hughes's work shows the importance of the anthropological approach. While illness and disease do have biological underpinnings, they are also influenced by the cultural context, which shapes how people diagnose, interpret, and treat malaise. ∎

MODERN ANTHROP

1980–2000

OLOGY

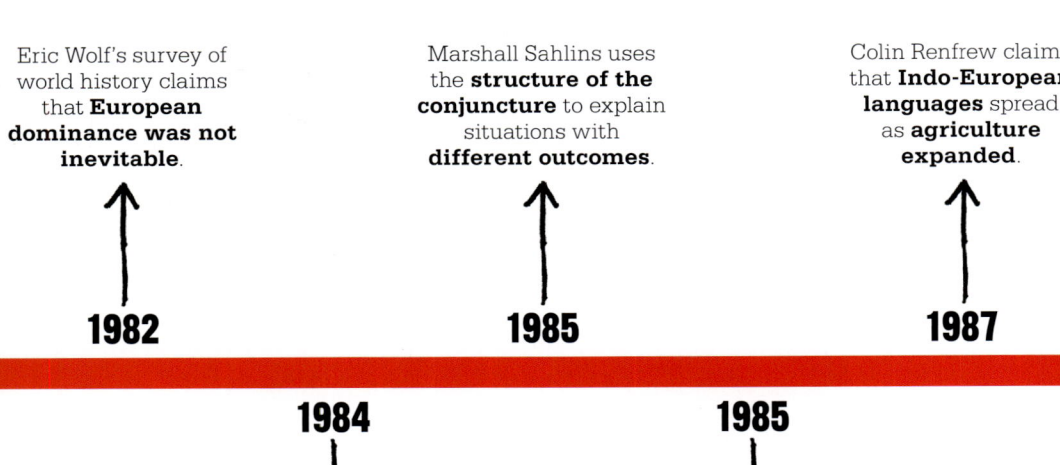

Eric Wolf's survey of world history claims that **European dominance was not inevitable**.

Marshall Sahlins uses the **structure of the conjuncture** to explain situations with **different outcomes**.

Colin Renfrew claims that **Indo-European languages** spread as **agriculture expanded**.

1982

1985

1987

1984

1985

1991

Ian Hodder looks for **cultural explanations** for past events, and introduces the concept of **post-processual archaeology**.

Sidney Mintz investigates the **social impact** of the **global sugar trade**.

Kath Weston examines ideas around **kinship** and **chosen families** in the **gay community**.

The final decades of the 20th century were marked by rapid globalization and profound social change. Anthropology, too, underwent a transformation. Scholars began to question long-held assumptions – about objectivity, power, and even what it means to be "human". During this era, archaeologists declared that an artefact can tell multiple stories, cultural anthropologists confronted the forces of global capitalism, and the discipline itself reckoned with its colonial roots. New voices – feminist, postmodern, and Indigenous – challenged anthropology to become more self-critical and inclusive.

Archaeology in this period moved beyond rigid scientific approaches, embracing more nuanced ways of understanding the past. Ian Hodder developed "post-processual archaeology", arguing that artefacts could not be understood without considering the beliefs and biases of the people who made them. For Hodder, a Bronze Age pot was not just a tool but a symbol – shaped by ritual, identity, or power. Colin Renfrew, meanwhile, argued that languages could disperse peacefully through migration and agricultural diffusion. Archaeology became less concerned with uncovering singular "objective" truths and more focused on interpreting the past as a mosaic of human experiences.

Global perspectives

The rise of global capitalism became a central focus for many anthropologists. Eric Wolf argued that colonialism and trade networks had long intertwined the world's economies, and he dismissed the myth of "isolated" cultures. Sidney Mintz traced the story of sugar – from Caribbean plantations to European tea cups – to show how everyday objects and food carried legacies of exploitation and resistance. Arjun Appadurai explored how objects, people, and cultural forms move across borders, arguing that as goods circulate, they acquire new meanings and values shaped by local contexts.

Alongside these global perspectives came deeper attention to power, voice, and representation. Talal Asad and Lila Abu-Lughod questioned the role of anthropology in producing "knowledge" about others, asking whose voices are heard and whose are silenced.

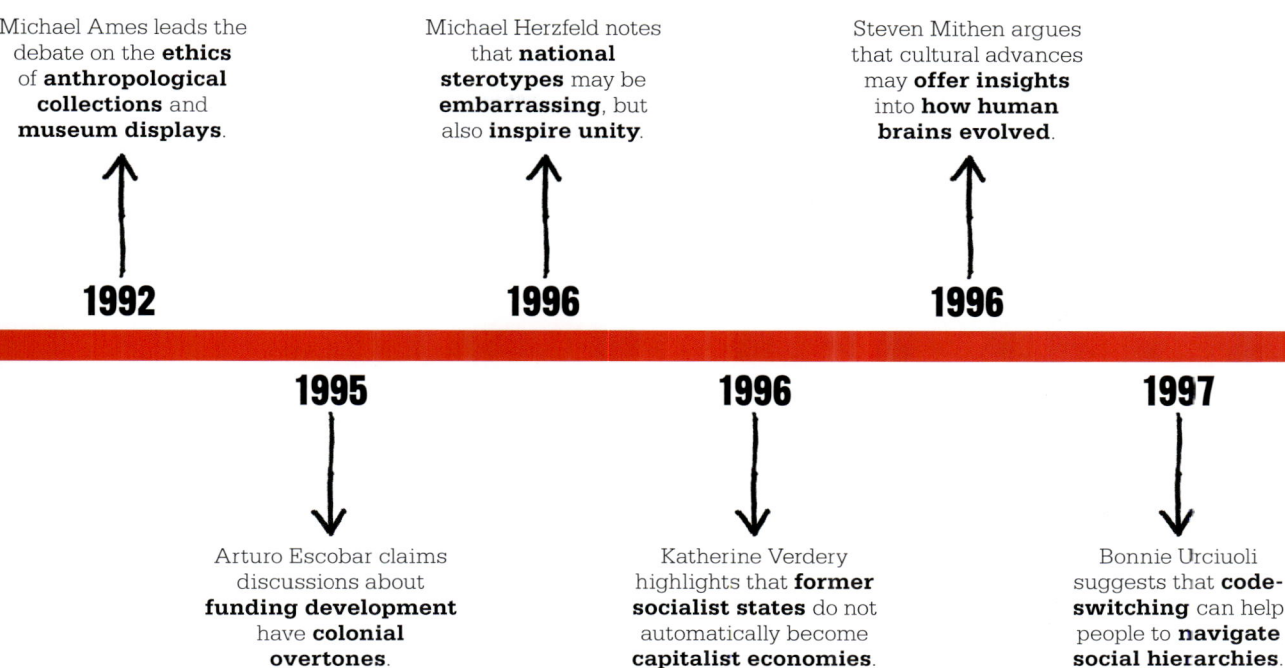

Michael Ames leads the debate on the **ethics** of **anthropological collections** and **museum displays**.

1992

Michael Herzfeld notes that **national sterotypes** may be **embarrassing**, but also **inspire unity**.

1996

Steven Mithen argues that cultural advances may **offer insights** into **how human brains evolved**.

1996

1995

Arturo Escobar claims discussions about **funding development** have **colonial overtones**.

1996

Katherine Verdery highlights that **former socialist states** do not automatically become **capitalist economies**.

1997

Bonnie Urciuoli suggests that **code-switching** can help people to **navigate social hierarchies**.

Others, such as Michael Herzfeld, turned the lens back on Europe, showing how nationalism and bureaucracy shape modern life.

Feminist anthropology flourished, dismantling stereotypes about gender and family. Sylvia Junko Yanagisako reexamined kinship, showing how ideas of "blood" and marriage were shaped by power, not biology. Philosopher Judith Butler, although not an anthropologist, profoundly influenced the field with their idea that gender is enacted through rituals, speech, and daily life. Scholars such as Kath Weston documented gay and lesbian communities, proving that kinship could be chosen, not just inherited.

New methods and questions emerged. Donna Haraway's multispecies ethnography asked humans to share the stage with animals, plants, and even microbes. Arturo Escobar criticized Western-led "development," showing how it often perpetuated colonial power.

Revisiting old questions

Anthropologists also returned to long-standing questions with new methods and theories. Marshall Sahlins reignited debates about human agency – the ability of individuals to make choices and shape their own lives. He argued that people could act creatively within cultural systems and were not merely shaped by economic forces. Archaeologist Steven Mithen explored the evolution of human thought and creativity, proposing that early humans drew on overlapping domains – such as music, art, and technology – through what he termed cognitive fluidity.

Meanwhile, museums and archives came under critical scrutiny. Anthropologist Michael Ames encouraged institutions to question their own authority and to collaborate more closely with the communities whose heritage they held. New approaches in museum anthropology explored how objects are displayed, interpreted, and valued across cultures.

By 2000, anthropology had become more self-critical, yet also more ambitious. It grappled with its past complicity in colonialism while embracing new tools – such as DNA analysis and collaborations with Indigenous scholars. The work of this era laid the groundwork for today's urgent questions: climate change, digital worlds, and global inequality. ∎

WHAT IS BUSINESS GOOD FOR?

COMMODITY FETISHISM

IN CONTEXT

KEY WORK
Michael Taussig, *The Devil and Commodity Fetishism in South America*, 1980

FIELD
Sociocultural anthropology

BEFORE
1949 French philosopher Georges Bataille develops new economic theories based on ideas of excess in *La Part Maudite*.

1923 The Frankfurt School is founded by Carl Grünberg. The school develops critical theory, which builds upon a Marxist appraisal of modernity, capitalism, and mass culture.

AFTER
2005 In *Friction: An Ethnography of Global Connection* Chinese-American anthropologist Anna Tsing examines the tensions in Indonesia between capitalists and environmentalists.

Informed by Karl Marx's theories on commodification, during the 1970s, Australian anthropologist Michael Taussig studied the folk stories of South American communities who were engaged in producing commodities. He found that workers on Colombian sugar plantations and in Bolivian tin mines often told stories relating to evil and the devil, and in the account of his fieldwork among sugar plantation workers in Colombia's Cauca Valley, Taussig includes the story of a devil-pact.

The story goes that when a man makes a pact with the devil to become more productive he will earn more money – but it will be

Cultural beliefs are informed by **society, heritage, and religion**.

The views of a **society** and its **people** may evolve in response to **economic changes**.

Objects **gain or lose significance** and value as **views change**.

The value of an object is governed by cultural, societal, and economic factors.

See also: Cultural materialism 124 ▪ Material culture 154–55 ▪ The value of objects 206–07 ▪ Documenting the undocumented 296–303

Representations of the devil – such as this antique devil mask worn at a festival in Bolivia – are a conspicuous feature of South American folklore about morality.

"barren" money that can only be used to buy luxury goods. It cannot be invested, and any land bought with it will be infertile. Ultimately, the man will die an early, painful death amongst his newly acquired things. His fleeting wealth comes at the cost of a shortened life.

Modern tales

Taussig found that while the devil trope appeared in South American stories about the Spanish conquest, it became prominent in the region's modern folklore, amid social and economic change in rural and Indigenous communities.

These transformations were spurred by the global spread of a capitalist system that prioritized production and profit, and replaced traditional exchange systems that had fostered social relationships. In the case of Colombia, many rural people had been self-sufficient workers of their own land, with strong social ties to one another. However, as they were recruited to work on newly established sugar plantations controlled by capitalist owners, they were transformed into the "proletariat". This term comes from Marx's critique of capitalism which asserts that the bourgeois –

profit-driven business owners – exploit the workers – the proletariat. Marx argued that the fundamental inequality between these groups will eventually lead to the downfall of capitalism.

New ways

Taussig observed how rural and Indigenous people throughout South America were experiencing the transition from self-sufficient life to a new capitalist order. As they witnessed fundamental changes to their communities, some South Americans came to view capitalism as a threat to their lifestyles and perceptions of moral order. Under capitalism, vices like greed became valued, and individual self-interest replaced community. The move from a pre-capitalist system to a capitalist one invoked for these people a kind of moral degradation that led the workers to speak of the devil. ▪

Instead of man being the aim of production, production is the aim of man and wealth the aim of production.
Michael Taussig

Mimesis and alterity

In the 1993 title *Mimesis and Alterity*, Taussig developed a compelling theory of the cultural processes of colonialization that link what seem to be two contradictory processes. These are mimesis – the imitation of, or desire to be like, the other – and alterity – the distancing from or denial of commonalities with the other. Mimesis and alterity shaped how societies perceived and interacted with one another. According to Taussig, colonizers portrayed non-Western peoples as "others" who were allegedly inferior because of their difference. This was furthered by anthropological work that depicted Indigenous peoples as distinctly non-Western. Both anthropology and colonialism, he critiqued, were integral to the politics of representation and the construction of difference.

Wooden dolls used for medicinal purposes by Panama's Cuna people gained European aesthetics in an example of colonial mimesis.

SHE UNDERSTOOD SIGNS HAD POWER
THE CAPACITY FOR COMMUNICATION

IN CONTEXT

KEY WORK
Francine Patterson and Eugene Linden, *The Education of Koko*, 1980

FIELD
Biological anthropology

BEFORE
1967 Beatrix and Allen Gardner set out to teach a young chimpanzee named Washoe to use American Sign Language.

1971 Primatologist Jane Goodall publishes *In the Shadow of Man*, which recounts her early field research into chimpanzee behaviour at Gombe Stream National Park in Tanzania.

AFTER
2006 Psychologist and primatologist Sue Savage-Rumbaugh claims that a bonobo named Kanzi at a research facility in Iowa can understand 3,000 words of spoken English.

U ntil the late 1960s, little was known about the cognition of non-human primates and their methods of communication. Primatologists were eager to learn if primates could be taught to understand and reproduce human language. The first experiments to teach great apes human speech failed, in large part because apes and humans have different vocal anatomy. Nevertheless, researchers learned that apes can understand spoken language and reproduce it in the form of symbols and sign language.

Learning signs

Perhaps the most famous ape to learn a form of human language was Koko, a female lowland gorilla. Researchers Francine Patterson and Eugene Linden taught Koko to use American Sign Language (ASL) to communicate. Patterson and Linden claimed that Koko knew more than 1,000 signs and that she could understand 2,000 words of spoken English. They also found that Koko could combine

Koko the gorilla practised signs with Francine Patterson and eventually learned how to use them to communicate about types of food, moods, actions, and types of animals.

words to express emotion and use language with subtlety – learning to rhyme, lie, and even joke.

Despite complaints about a lack of scientific rigour to the research, Koko came to represent the great intelligence of non-human primates and the research provided remarkable glimpses into ape cognition, including their curiosity, humour, and empathy. ∎

See also: Chimpanzee behaviours 132–35 ▪ Relating to non-human beings 284–89

CONCRETE PROCEDURES IN THE FACE OF DEATH
BURIAL RITUALS

IN CONTEXT

KEY WORK
Loring M. Danforth, *The Death Rituals of Rural Greece*, 1982

FIELD
Sociocultural anthropology

BEFORE
1909 Arnold van Gennep's *The Rites of Passage* proposes that rituals have three stages – separation, liminality, and reincorporation – and inspires ethnographers to explore ritual as a universal experience.

AFTER
1993 Nancy Scheper-Hughes's *Death without Weeping* shows that grief and mourning are less likely to be expressed by women living in poverty.

2021 Archaeologist and ethnographer Shannon Lee Dawdy documents the changing landscape of approaches to death rituals in the US in her book *American Afterlives*.

Death is one of the few experiences universal to humankind. All cultures have rituals to cope with loss, but these practices vary across time and place. Rituals tend to follow a pattern that can be applied to the study of human responses towards death. Rituals allow people to exert control over the uncontrollable, and to find stability in a chaotic and unpredictable world.

US anthropologist Loring M. Danforth studied a unique death ritual in Potamia, a small village in Greece, where he conducted ethnographic fieldwork in the 1970s. Mourning the deceased in Potamia requires an extended time-period, that starts with the individual's burial. After burial, a female relative of the deceased begins a five-year period of mourning. During this time, the female relative is expected to wear black clothing, make daily visits to the deceased's grave, and must avoid singing or dancing within her home. Once the five years have passed, mourning ceases.

The deceased's bones are exhumed and placed in the village ossuary, to mark the individual's transition from the mortal world into the afterlife.

Maintaining a connection
Danforth posits that by performing rituals around death and mourning, societies mediate between life and death by making death a part of life. Through these practices the living are able to cope with the inevitability of death and continue a relationship with the dead. ∎

This study of the dead can yield profound insights into the nature of human life itself.
Loring M. Danforth

See also: Rites of passage 126–29 ▪ Ritual and language 166 ▪ Mental health and society 172–75 ▪ Human burials 306

BIRDS ARE VOICES IN THE FOREST
THE ANTHROPOLOGY OF SOUND

IN CONTEXT

KEY WORK
Steven Feld, *Sound and Sentiment*, 1982

FIELD
Sociocultural anthropology

BEFORE
1950s Anthropologist Colin Turnbull records the Mbuti people for the Smithsonian Institution and brings sound to the forefront of ethnography.

1977 Canadian composer R. Murray Schafer introduces the concept of the "soundscape" to describe music that captures sounds from any environment.

AFTER
1992 British ethnomusicologist Martin Stokes explores debates about music-making in the context of Turkish state politics, education, and technology.

2012 A first of its kind, the anthology *Ethnomusicology in East Africa* brings together those studying the music of Uganda and its neighbours.

The exploration of the "anthropology of sound" emerged from the 19th-century interest in collecting music of the people and from a parallel strand of musicology focused on context – that is, the people making the music and their environment. Early musicologists initially concentrated on traditional music in their own countries, but interest soon expanded to music around the world, and opened up a debate as to whether "ethnomusicology" should focus solely on non-Western music.

Sounds as voices
From the late 1960s, US sound artist and anthropologist Steven Feld engaged with recording sound as part of his anthropological studies. He also encouraged fellow researchers

Feld explored the different genres of Kaluli ceremonial singing, some of which are accompanied by the *sologa* (seedpod rattle), *degegado* (crayfish claw rattle), or *sob* (mussel shell rattle).

See also: Culture shapes behaviour 62–67 ■ Material culture 154–55 ■ Ritual and language 166 ■ Commodity fetishism 180–81 ■ The power of photography 292–93

Ethnomusicology

The term "ethnomusicology" was coined in the mid-20th century to describe the comparative study of musical systems and cultures. Professor and chairman of anthropology at Indiana University, US, Alan P. Merriam soon broadened the scope of ethnomusicology, looking beyond the collection and analysis of music and sound alone. His fieldwork – with Indigenous groups in Montana, US, during the 1950s, and later with the Songye, Bashi, and Burundi peoples in central Africa – led Merriam to explore how music is pivotal in human nature. He proposed that the goals of ethnomusicology should be to appreciate the music of other cultures, to understand transformation in such music, and to learn how people use music to communicate. Later, Merriam suggested three key research areas for the study of music in culture: behaviour in relation to music, conceptualizing music, and the analysis of musical sounds.

Music teacher Frances Densmore recorded and preserved the voices and music of Indigenous people in the US in the early 20th century.

to take sound seriously, listening to the full range of sounds that we hear and sensing the relationships between them. In the 1970s, Feld began his fieldwork, conducting research with the Kaluli people in Papua New Guinea. Feld recorded everything *in situ* – from seances, *gisalo* (poetic) songs, stories, and conversations, to the sounds of the forest and the birds in particular – in his exploration of how relationships are created through sound.

Feld's teacher, Jubi, however, observed that Feld was on the wrong path to understanding Kaluli natural and cultural history, explaining to him that, "To you they are birds. To me, they are voices in the forest." This led Feld to the realization that the Kaluli people think differently about birds, acknowledging their existence primarily through sound and believing them to be the spirit reflections of deceased men

and women. In 1982, Feld published his *Sound and Sentiment*, which describes how his exploration and analysis of sounds informed his understanding of Kaluli society.

New terms

Linking acoustics and epistemology (theory of knowledge), in the early 1990s Feld coined the word "acoustemology" to create an analytic tool for understanding the interrelationships of humans, animals, and their surroundings. Acoustemology depends on bringing in sensory perceptions to convey the complexity of these relationships, rather than relying solely on words.

Sound recordings retain a certain relationship to the people and places where they originate, but they also provide opportunities for recontextualization – especially with the emergence of technologies that offer new ways to present and even reinvent sounds. In 1996, Feld coined the phrase "schizophonic

memesis" to describe the gateway to understanding how recordings that are separated from their source – as part of the circulation process, for example – can both "stimulate and license renegotiations of identity". He went on to advocate for a more sophisticated use of sound technologies in ethnography, arguing that until that happens "the anthropology of sound will continue to be mostly about words". ■

Things have a visible and invisible aspect ... sounds and behaviours have an outside, an inside, and an underneath.
Steven Feld

THERE ARE NO PEOPLE WITHOUT HISTORY
GLOBAL CAPITALISM

IN CONTEXT

KEY WORK
Eric Wolf, *Europe and the People Without History*, 1982

FIELD
Sociocultural anthropology

BEFORE
1939 In *The Civilizing Process*, German sociologist Norbert Elias analyses the consolidation of power.

1974 US sociologist Immanuel Wallerstein's world system theory categorizes countries based on their roles within the global capitalist system.

AFTER
1985 *Sweetness and Power*, by US anthropologist Sidney Mintz, examines Western history through the lens of the commodification of sugar.

1997 In his book *Guns, Germs, and Steel*, US scientist Jared Diamond depicts geography as an influential factor in Eurasian dominance.

In the Western world, historical narratives have long excluded the experiences of non-European people. Instead, these populations became the subjects of anthropological studies. Such works assumed that, prior to the European expansion of the 1400s and industrialization, these people were living as if "frozen in time" in remote locales.

Europe and the People Without History set out to revise this view. In a survey spanning 600 years of world history, Eric Wolf presented a more nuanced narrative that

Most of the societies studied by anthropologists are an outgrowth of the expansion of Europe and not the pristine precipitates of past evolutionary stages.
Eric Wolf

challenged traditional Western perspectives and undermined assumptions that had previously been made about the inevitability of European ascendency.

Wolf contended that this "timeless pre-contact" vision was not an accurate representation of the situation. Non-European groups around the world interacted with one another – conquering smaller adjacent societies and consolidating their power – long before the Age of Exploration and subsequent wave of European colonialism. For example, after the fall of Rome in 476 CE, a series of Islamic caliphates created an empire stretching from Arabia to the Indian subcontinent; similarly, it was Muslim armies from North Africa that seized control of the Iberian Peninsula starting in 711 CE. At that time, Wolf noted, Europe was not a major player in world affairs.

European expansion
The onset of the Little Ice Age in the 1300s ushered in a period of climate changes that disrupted harvests and destabilized food supplies. This was exacerbated by the limitations of the era's technology. Wolf theorized that

See also: Multilinear evolution 104–07 ▪ Studying up 138–39 ▪ Stages of social organization 160–61 ▪ Structure and agency 196–99 ▪ The anthropology of food 200–05 ▪ The ethics of anthropology 248–49

Peasants work the fields for a feudal landlord. Wolf argued that the medieval tribute system led to the creation of an economically dominant class that had military resources and political power.

this agricultural crisis led Europeans to search further afield for new, more reliable resources.

European agricultural centres began to expand significantly around 1400. This was a necessary pre-condition for the rise of large state-based societies. Within this context, Wolf alleged, tribute-taking landlords amassed food surpluses, consolidated their control, and became the dominant social class. These resources were then used to provision armies capable of conquering neighbouring groups.

The colonial encounter

After the 16th century, Europe's largely agrarian societies started to develop an interest in trade. As these economies shifted towards commercialization and large-scale production, their need for labour increased. With colonial expansion, workers were sourced from far-flung regions, outside of Europe's newly formed manufacturing hubs.

These workers – usually enslaved people and peasants – formed a new social category: "ethnic groups" that had left their home countries, often forcefully, to be placed into the emergent capitalist system as underpaid, low-skilled workers, part of the developing proletariat.

Wolf stressed that before European expansion, these Indigenous populations had distinctive histories and active networks of their own, which were often overlooked by both European conquerors and early anthropologists. However, they were crucial players in the construction of a new world order that would solidify Europe's dominant role both in the future and in its own version of the past. ▪

Eric Wolf

Born in Austria in 1923, Eric Wolf grew up in several European countries. His family eventually fled to the United States because, as Jews, they were unsafe during the rise of Nazism.

After serving with the US army during World War II, Wolf pursued a doctoral degree in anthropology at New York's Columbia University. His dissertation research, on the people of Puerto Rico, was conducted under the tutelage of Julian Steward.

From 1971, Wolf taught at the City University of New York, which became a hub for Marxist anthropology. In his research, Wolf used a Marxist lens to analyse the capitalist basis of societal and world development. He was also critical of the way in which academic writing can reinforce social inequalities. Wolf died in 1999.

Other key works

1969 *Peasant Wars of the Twentieth Century*
2001 *Pathways of Power*

European expansion everywhere encountered human societies and cultures characterized by long and complex histories.
Eric Wolf

POWER ASSUMES A RELIGIOUS FORM

RELIGION AND SECULAR POWER

IN CONTEXT

KEY WORK
Talal Asad, *Anthropological Conceptions of Religion: Reflections on Geertz*, 1983

FIELD
Sociocultural anthropology

BEFORE
1624 Lord Herbert's *De Veritate* proposes one of the first universal definitions of religion as a combination of beliefs, practices, and ethics existing in all societies.

1973 Clifford Geertz publishes *The Interpretation of Cultures*, describing religion as a system of cultural patterns working as a model for and of reality.

AFTER
1986 Asad questions traditional anthropological methods by analysing colonial power relations at play in ethnographic writing.

1996 Michael Gilsenan looks at the relationship between power and violence in Lebanon.

D rawing on Marxist theories to interpret Western images of colonized peoples, Saudi anthropologist Talal Asad pointed out the role of anthropology in creating tools that allowed European empires to understand and control

During the Spanish Inquisition, auto-da-fé were ceremonies in which the Inquisition's sentences were carried out. They were a show of the combined power of the Church and State.

them. Asad questioned the claims that Indigenous peoples' behaviours are determined by unconscious structures that anthropologists could uncover. Conversely, Asad examined how this power relation shapes the anthropology of religion and how Europe's religious history subliminally influences the perceptions of anthropologists.

Many interpreted Asad's text as rejecting religion, or as dismissing the concept as a European invention.

See also: The universal nature of religion 28–29 ▪ The social roots of religion 42–43 ▪ Local belief systems 78–79

Europeans use religion to **hold on to power** by convincing the poor that things **will be better in the hereafter**.

The **Indigenous poor** take **comfort** in **moral teachings** in the belief that they will be **rewarded for suffering**.

Religion has a **stabilizing effect** on society and **upholds the status quo**.

Power creates religion.

Rather than addressing religion as a reality or term, Asad addresses it as a historically situated concept that took on a specific meaning in Europe before it was applied universally. His question is not what religion is, but how it is constructed.

Struggles of power
Asad recounts how early Christian theologians such as St Augustine of Hippo acknowledged that religious truth is the object of power struggles, because, at the time, the medieval Church exerted control over the authorization and authentication of religious discourses and practices, and subjected them to its rule. Only with the inception of Europe's "modern project" in the 17th century did an essential, universal idea of religion emerge among Enlightenment philosophers such as John Locke and Immanuel Kant.

This occurred alongside the rise of natural science, which became the backdrop against which all religions would be compared.

For Asad, this universal concept of religion prevailed when religious observance became more distinct from – and regulated by – the secular space carved out by the modern state. Europe's colonial expansion then drew on the anthropology of religion to isolate the worldviews of colonized peoples into digestible knowledge that could be used politically.

Asad challenged the notion of symbolism – which had dominated the field since the 1960s – that regarded Indigenous rituals as texts to be decoded to gain insights into sociocultural patterns. Instead of a system with universal symbols, Asad insisted that religion is no more distinct from common sense than secular Western beliefs. ∎

Religion is dynamic

Western scholars have often cast Islam as monolithic, or slow to change. However, research into the multiple-yet-shared meanings of Islam to its diverse practitioners offers a compelling account of the power dynamics at play in everyday life. In *Recognizing Islam: An Anthropologist's Introduction* (1983), British social anthropologist Michael Gilsenan's vivid ethnographic portraits – based on his observations from the field – reveal the constant reinvention of tradition that takes place, both in the day-to-day lives of ordinary Muslims, and amongst literate elites competing to establish their authority to define Islam. Looking beyond Western definitions of Islam and seeing the way its daily practices are woven into all aspects of life highlights the role that the Islamic faith plays in the structures of society and the impacts of capitalism and modernization on Muslim spirituality in Southwest Asia and North Africa.

There cannot be a universal definition of religion […] because that definition is itself the historical product of discursive processes.
Talal Asad

INTERPRETATION OCCURS AT THE TROWEL'S EDGE
POST-PROCESSUAL ARCHAEOLOGY

IN CONTEXT

KEY WORK
Ian Hodder, "Burials, Houses, Women, and Men in the European Neolithic", 1984

FIELD
Archaeology

BEFORE
1962 Lewis Binford argues for using scientific principles to study the past, ushering in an era of "new" or "processual" archaeology.

1972 US archaeologist Michael B. Schiffer introduces "behavioural archaeology", which explores how humans engage with the material objects of their time.

AFTER
1990s "Contemporary archaeology" – which looks at the more recent past – expands as a discipline, examining everything from cell phones to toothbrushes from a more subjective point of view.

By the 1960s and 1970s, archaeology had been transformed from a study area pursued by loosely organized groups of antiquarians and looters into an established scientific subject that students could read at university. The formalization of archaeology as a science involved generating universal laws governing human behaviours that could be tested and replicated, a turn towards what is known as "processualist" theory.

In the late 1970s, British archaeologist Ian Hodder founded "post-processual archaeology" to counter and critique processualism. A processualist might argue that

Upright slabs divide the Midhowe cairn at Rousay, Orkney, into stalls. Initially, the dead were buried in a crouched position on a bench, where they could be visited by loved ones.

all pre-industrial settlements are located a certain distance from water because water is necessary for survival. A post-processualist, however, will also consider the social, political, and economic reasons that a group may have for settling in a particular location. Explanations could include building a settlement near where a significant battle had taken place, or where an important elder was buried. Post-processualism, therefore, focuses on determining the cultural reasons for what happened in the past.

Making sense of megaliths

In his 1984 paper "Burials, Houses, Women, and Men in the European Neolithic", Hodder applied post-processualist theories to his analysis of megaliths and tombs in Neolithic Europe. Processualists attribute the emergence and abundance of European megaliths to environmental issues. They claim that megaliths were essentially ancient fences used to mark political and social boundaries that appeared across the world when populations expanded and resources became finite. Hodder found this explanation

See also: Revolutions in prehistory 74–75 ▪ The New Archaeology 110–15
▪ Processual archaeology 136–37

simplistic, arguing that archaeologists must look at a region's history, and explore what type of buildings existed prior to megaliths to better understand their design and purpose. By examining the architectural history of Neolithic Europe, Hodder formed an alternative, post-processualist interpretation: megalithic tombs were inspired by houses.

Hodder found that tombs and houses across Neolithic Europe have remarkable similarities, with comparable widths, lengths, and layouts. They share decorative features and designs, and their entrances often face the same cardinal orientation. In line with the post-processualist tradition of understanding the cultural meaning behind artefacts and architecture, Hodder explored the symbolism and meaning of Neolithic tomb design. According to Hodder, megalithic tombs served as a way of commemorating and connecting with ancestors when communities dispersed as modes of agriculture and production changed.

New inspiration

Post-processualist thought inspired other new ways of interpreting the past. Feminist archaeology emerged at a similar time and began to explore how modern stereotypes regarding women – as home makers, for example – had infiltrated archaeological depictions of women in past societies. Other archaeologists expressed interest in how individuals, not groups, shaped the course of history and took action to alter their material world. And a small group of post-processualist archaeologists adopted a position known as "extreme relativism", arguing that the past is unknowable and that our interpretations of it are merely a reflection of the present. ▪

Without consideration of the cultural context one cannot hope to understand the effects of past social actions.
Ian Hodder

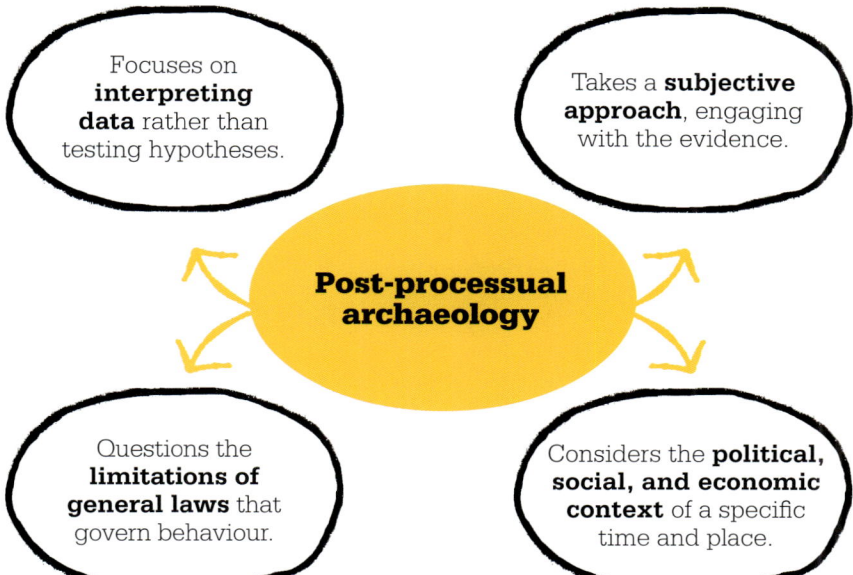

Focuses on **interpreting data** rather than testing hypotheses.

Takes a **subjective approach**, engaging with the evidence.

Post-processual archaeology

Questions the **limitations of general laws** that govern behaviour.

Considers the **political, social, and economic context** of a specific time and place.

Multivocal archaeology at Çatalhöyük

Located in Türkiye, Çatalhöyük is a Neolithic site where up to 8,000 people lived over the course of 4,000 years. It is one of the first large-scale permanent settlements where people turned from a nomadic lifestyle to one that involved living in households. They crafted expressive art, such as animal figurines and paintings featuring residents hunting.

The site's unique design and artworks inspired Hodder to explore how and why the community accomplished its remarkable feats. Working at the site between 1993 and 2018, he recruited hundreds of archaeologists, ethnographers, and artists to work side by side. They analysed artefacts as soon as they were excavated, or at the "trowel's edge", and recorded and published their findings online to allow others to interpret Çatalhöyük's data. This working method is known as "multivocal archaeology", in which numerous people share their opinions on what happened at a site.

THE NOTION OF KINSHIP IS UNDEFINED AND VACUOUS
KINSHIP STUDIES

IN CONTEXT

KEY WORK
David Schneider, *A Critique of the Study of Kinship*, 1984

FIELD
Sociocultural anthropology

BEFORE
1870 Following American Civil War-era debates on interracial relationships, US anthropologist Lewis Henry Morgan theorizes that blood-based kinship represents "one of the earliest acts of human intelligence".

1949 In *The Elementary Structures of Kinship*, which is dedicated to Morgan, Claude Lévi-Strauss states that the prohibition of incest is culturally universal.

AFTER
2004 Janet Carsten's *After Kinship* shows how non-genealogical "relatedness" is created through sharing, eating together, and care.

In 1984, US anthropologist David Schneider indicted his earlier work on the Indigenous people of Yap, Micronesia, for applying his Western understanding of kinship to their cultural practices. Schneider realized that, for this community, effective cooperation in working the land was more important in determining who would inherit that land than patrilineage. Essentially, it was the act of doing that shaped kinship more than being.

Flawed perspective

Schneider identified the way in which kinship studies assumed that Western procreation-based notions of belonging were universal. He found that other anthropologists studying kinship reproduced Lewis Henry Morgan's suggestion that "fictive" adoptive relationships are derived from "real" biological kin. For Schneider, the distinction between the universal idea of kinship, and other economic, political, and religious concepts that are present across cultures, is the assumption that "blood is thicker than water". To abandon the idea that all cultures subscribe to this view, Schneider suggested that it was important to "first establish the units which the particular culture itself marks".

Schneider's concept of relational belonging, rather than a biological given, encouraged the study of formerly overlooked perspectives, particularly in gender studies. ∎

The study of kinship derives directly and practically unaltered from the ethnoepistemology of European culture.
David Schneider

See also: The concept of reciprocity 58–61 ∙ Kinship and social order 68–69

THE JAPANESE PAST AND THE AMERICAN PRESENT
ADAPTING CULTURAL TRADITIONS

IN CONTEXT

KEY WORK
**Sylvia Junko Yanagisako,
Transforming the Past,
1985**

FIELD
Sociocultural anthropology

BEFORE
1968 David Schneider's
American Kinship gives a
symbolic analysis of kinship.

1973 US anthropologist
Clifford Geertz proposes that
culture is formed of symbols
to be interpreted.

AFTER
1987 Jane Fishburne Collier
and Yanagisako's collection
of essays, *Gender and Kinship*,
brings a feminist perspective
to debates around kinship
theory in anthropology.

1995 *Naturalizing Power*,
edited by Yanagisako and
US anthropologist Carol
Delaney, discusses power
and inequality in feminist
anthropology.

S tudies of immigrants to
the US have often assumed
that families continue
to observe traditions from their
homeland. However, Sylvia Junko
Yanagisako's analysis of two
generations of Japanese Americans
revealed the transformational
aspects of immigration on families
and kinship.

Yanagisako conducted
interviews with first generation
US immigrants from Japan – who
were known as *Issei* – and their
US-born children, called *Nisei*. Her
interviews focused on marriages,
filial relations, and siblinghood.
Issei, she found, prioritized
arranged marriages, male
dominance, and family duty. By
contrast, *Nisei* appeared to opt for
marriages based on love – with
parental approval – and expected
the couple to live separately from
the family. Yanagisako found that
Nisei relationships retained male
leadership but valued women more.
These shifts reflected a negotiation
between the past and the present,
and between the two cultures.

Japanese American marriage
has been transformed
as one generation's cultural
reasoning has been
succeeded by another's.
Sylvia Junko Yanagisako

Yanagisako showed how both
generations saw in their kinship a
symbolic opposition between their
Japanese and American identities.

Reinventing cultural norms
Yanagisako's study speaks to the
ways in which ethnic groups in the
US seldom replicate the ideas and
norms of their parents. Rather, new
generations reinterpret these norms
as they negotiate US society. ∎

See also: Origins of culture 32–33 ▪ Culture shapes behaviour 62–67 ▪ Kinship
ideologies 218–19

HYBRIDS OF MACHINE AND ORGANISM
MULTISPECIES ETHNOGRAPHY

IN CONTEXT

KEY WORK
Donna Haraway, *A Manifesto for Cyborgs*, 1985

FIELD
Sociocultural anthropology

BEFORE
1974 Luce Irigaray analyzes male-centric biases in Western philosophy and psychology.

1985 Anne Fausto-Sterling scrutinizes biological theories about sex differences.

AFTER
1995 *Patchwork Girl* by Shelley Jackson addresses themes of subjectivity, posthumanism, and reproduction.

1995 Sharona Ben-Tov claims that Haraway's cyborg myth is not cross-culturally applicable.

2006 Viewing the cyborg as an inaccurate metaphor for the contemporary digital era, N. Katherine Hayles proposes the interconnected "cognisphere."

In today's technologically driven societies, artificial intelligence writes poetry; robots assist with surgery; and cars drive themselves, blurring the boundary between what is human and what is machine. This is not, however, an entirely novel concept. Decades ago, in the 1980s, feminist scholar Donna Haraway was contemplating the social and philosophical effects of new technologies on human bodies and our cultures.

Rather than demonize new technology as antihuman, Haraway sees it as freeing us from long-standing assumptions about

A world ... in which people are not afraid of their joint kinship with animals and machines ...
Donna Haraway

ourselves. In her famous essay, *A Manifesto for Cyborgs: Science, Technology, and Socialist Feminism in the 1980s*, Haraway considers how three binary oppositions that characterize Western thought have been undermined. First, the juxtaposition of humans and animals is challenged by Charles Darwin's theory of evolution, which described a common origin for all living things. Second, the divide between animals (including humans) and machines is eroded by newly engineered forms, such as the cyborg. Third, the separation of the physical world from the nonphysical world is blurred by new technology.

A multispecies world

For Haraway, the fusion of formerly distinct phenomena should not be rejected, but should be embraced for liberating us from rigid ways of being. A good example is the cyborg itself—an entity that combines human and machine, that restructures the very nature of our bodies. Haraway sees the cyborg as part of an emergent "chimeric" world. The term "chimera" derives from Greek mythology, where it refers to a

See also: Gender, sexuality, and power 158–159 ▪ Gender equality 266 ▪ Challenging systemic oppression 294–295

> I would rather be
> a cyborg than
> a goddess.
> **Donna Haraway**

fantastic creature composed of several animals: the head of a goat, the body of a lion, and a snake for the tail. By merging different species, the chimera extends the possibility of what is real, freeing us from traditional ontological categories (defined categories of existence).

Becoming fluid

Haraway suggests that the liberating potential of the chimera can be applied to the gender binary, which had assumed that people are universally either female or male

due to their innate biological constitution. However, just as the cyborg blends human and machine, so can modern bodies conflate the differences between the sexes. According to Haraway, bodies have a chimeric quality as neither male nor female but as a fluid combination of both. In this way, the cyborg becomes a useful metaphor for her feminist critique of gender and patriarchy. Some critics felt that Haraway's cyborg metaphor could not be applied across various cultures and omitted the intangible aspects of humanism.

Ultimately, Haraway proposes a "socialist feminism" in which modern technology is harnessed, not rejected, and used to resist traditional dichotomies in ways that foster real social change. ▪

Innovations in robotics have created artificial limbs that can be controlled with impulses from the muscles and with sensors that can provide users with touch information.

Donna Haraway

Donna Haraway is a Professor Emerita in the Departments of History of Consciousness and Feminist Studies at the University of California, Santa Cruz. After studying zoology and philosophy in college, Haraway earned a PhD in biology from Yale University. Her publications, which tend to be interdisciplinary and theoretical, explore the human–machine relationship, animal–human interface, and technoscience. Recognizing the limitations of scientific objectivity, Haraway uses the term "situated knowledge" to emphasize that ways of knowing are shaped by social contexts. From her feminist perspective, she endorses the liberating effects of technology and champions the increased participation of women in the practice and study of technoscientific innovations.

Other key works

1989 *Primate Visions: Gender, Race, and Nature in the World of Modern Science*
1991 *Simians, Cyborgs, and Women: The Reinvention of Nature*
2003 *The Companion Species Manifesto*

CULTURE IS HISTORICALLY ALTERED IN ACTION

STRUCTURE AND AGENCY

IN CONTEXT

KEY WORK
Marshall Sahlins, *Islands of History*, 1985

FIELD
Sociocultural anthropology

BEFORE
1948 US anthropologist Leslie White argues that the environment determines culture. Humans are powerless to shape their development.

1973 According to US anthropologist Clifford Geertz, shared symbols and the ways people interpret them lie at the heart of cultural practices.

AFTER
1993 US anthropologist Michael Taussig explores how Indigenous myth and ritual sustain cultural identity, even as global influences bring about dramatic change.

Anthropology sometimes inspires feelings of powerlessness. Scholars as varied as Émile Durkheim and Ruth Benedict have argued that an individual's aspirations, dreams, and desires are shaped by overwhelmingly powerful social forces. Yet this raises a dilemma: if culture so profoundly moulds individuals, how can they escape its grip to enact change? Are people bound to their cultural programming, or is there room for "agency" – the capacity to act independently and make their own choices? These were the questions that confronted US anthropologist Marshall Sahlins when he set

See also: The social roots of religion 42–43 ▪ Culture and personality 70–73
▪ Structuralism 108 ▪ Feminist anthropology 140–45 ▪ Global capitalism 186–87

out to understand the world around him and discover how the actions of a single individual can make a difference in the grand scheme of things.

Activism versus theory

When people ask these questions today, they might be hoping to end poverty or reverse climate change – but when Sahlins posed these questions in the 1960s and 1970s, he was thinking about the Vietnam War. In the classroom, Sahlins taught the theory of unilinear evolution, which argued that history followed its own course and that individual action was largely ineffective. Outside the classroom, however, Sahlins was campaigning against US imperialism in Southeast Asia. This raised a contradiction – how could you be an activist and at the same time believe that you had no agency? Sahlins realized his political commitments were at odds with his intellectual position.

Sahlins believed that individuals possessed agency, but understanding how and why they acquired it was difficult. While kings, queens, and presidents could change history, the Vietnam War demonstrated the limits of their power – even the most powerful military in the world could not conquer peasants who longed for freedom. Additionally, figures such as Napoleon and Martin Luther King could emerge from relative obscurity and still change the world. How had that happened?

Sahlins was not satisfied with anthropology's existing theories of agency. Followers of Franz Boas argued that it was impossible to make generalizations about history because each moment was unique. »

Millions of young Americans opposed the Vietnam War in the 1960s and 1970s, providing Sahlins with a clear example of individual activism confronting larger societal forces.

Marshall Sahlins

Born to Jewish immigrants in Chicago, US, in 1930, Marshal Sahlins studied anthropology at the University of Michigan, where his mentor was Leslie White, a proponent of theories of cultural evolution.

Sahlins earned his PhD from Columbia University and then conducted fieldwork in Fiji. He returned to Michigan as a professor and was an exponent of evolutionary theory and an activist against the Vietnam War.

Between 1967 to 1969 Sahlins taught in Paris, where he was exposed to continental philosophy and became a member of Claude Lévi-Strauss's seminar. Following this he carried out research in Hawaii and took a position at the University of Chicago.

After his retirement from Chicago, he started his own publishing house, Prickly Paradigm, which published short polemical pamphlets. Marshall Sahlins died in 2021.

Other key works

1973 *Stone Age Economics*
1976 *Culture and Practical Reason*
2000 *Culture in Practice*

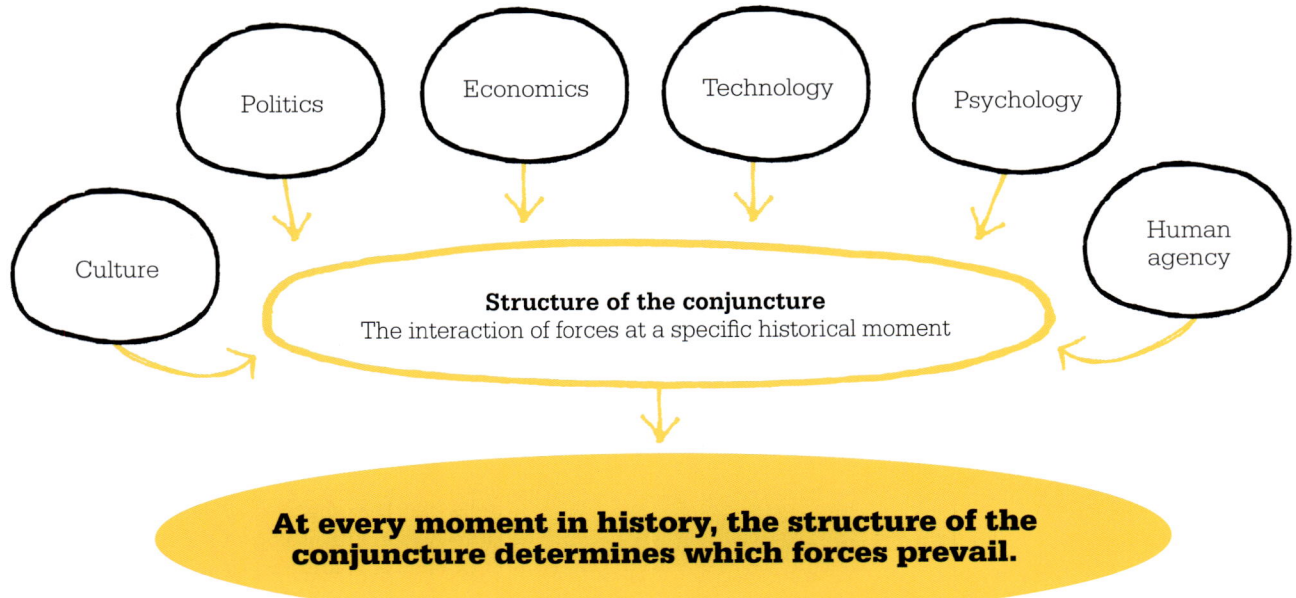

At every moment in history, the structure of the conjuncture determines which forces prevail.

Most other schools of thought believed that one single force determined behavior: for instance, structuralists thought it was shaped by cultural structures; materialists thought lives were shaped by the environment; and Marxists thought the mode of production determined everything.

Forces shaping history
During his time studying Pacific Island cultures in Fiji and Hawaii, Sahlins realized that all these schools of thought were right—but only sometimes. What anthropology needed, he argued, was a theory that explained why certain forces—including human choice and freedom—were decisive at some moments of history, but not others. His solution was the theory of the "structure of the conjuncture."

For Sahlins, "structure" referred to the recurring patterns of culture—the beliefs, traditions, and power relations that shape how people act. At any moment in

history, he argued, a "conjuncture" occurs—the coming together of multiple forces, such as psychology, geography, technology, politics, and free will. The outcome depends on the "structure" of the conjuncture, or how these forces interact. Structure acts like a blueprint: it does not determine every move, but it defines what is possible.

The strength of Sahlins's model was its versatility. It could be used to analyze specific historical conjunctures to explain why certain forces prevailed. It could also offer broader insights into the different types of conjunctures and how they worked.

Sahlins believed that different cultures shape history in different ways. In Fijian and Hawaiian cultures, nobility, such as kings and queens—sometimes called "chiefs" in English—are very important. When a king decides to go to war or convert to Christianity, it can make history. By contrast, Amazonian societies prioritize

equality—no one can make decisions for the whole group. In these cultures, history is made by consensus, not decree.

Culture can even influence what is perceived as chance. For example, when British explorer Captain Cook arrived in Hawaii in January 1778 during Makahiki, an agricultural festival, he was seen as a *kinolau* (Hawaiian for "avatar" or "version") of the Hawaiian divinity Lono, who was central to the festival. Had Cook arrived a month earlier or later, history might have unfolded differently.

Sahlins argued that even seemingly European-driven changes often hinged on Indigenous cultural rules. For instance, in the 1800s a European castaway, named Charles Savage, introduced guns to Fiji. This revolutionized warfare—not because guns were superior, because clubs were more effective in close combat. The real difference was Savage's willingness to target the nobility, something no Fijian commoner would do. Ironically, Sahlins noted, it was Fijian culture that empowered a white person.

Rules and the game

Sahlins's theory highlighted that many apparent opposites are actually parts of a single process. In English-speaking Protestant countries, agency and structure are often treated as opposing forces—prompting philosophers such as John Stuart Mill to reflect on how to balance individual rights and government control. Sahlins, however, saw agency as a *result* of structure, not something opposing it. In a game of tennis, he argued, a player's ability to make choices and win—their agency—is only possible because of the game's rules—its structure. The rules of a game define how to score points. If there were no rules, there would be no game, and therefore no agency. In fact, for Sahlins structure and agency are two different ways of looking at a single process of action.

Sahlins argued that structure not only enables agency—it is the result of it. The world is influenced by past actions of our own, as well as those of other people. Today, women can vote. That legal structure is a part of our lives. It exists because of the agency of suffragists such as Emmeline Pankhurst and Ida Wells-Barnett who fought successfully to pass laws giving women the right to vote. Sahlins believed that history is a process: agency creates structure, which then empowers agency that in turn alters the structure, in an ongoing cycle.

Sahlins is remembered today primarily as a theorist, and his ideas have influenced many other scholars. Tongan anthropologist Epeli Hauʻofa, for instance, was heavily influenced by Sahlins in his essay "Our Sea of Islands." Hauʻofa saw the Pacific as a single cultural region connected by the ocean, rather than a group of small isolated islands with distinct cultures. Each island is a unique transformation or version of the broader regional culture. Pacific Islanders should not be ashamed to embrace modern conveniences—being true to your culture is, Hauʻofa believed, more about finding what is authentic in the present than slavishly adhering to the past.

US anthropologist David Graeber, an anarchist and academic, wrote compellingly about the Occupy Wall Street movement of 2011 using Sahlins's ideas to show how transforming deeper cultural structures and beliefs is itself a political act because it allows us to imagine new forms of politics and novel ways of life.

Sahlins's theories offer scholars a framework for understanding how individuals and societies interact to create change. His insights also provide tools for those seeking to transform the world, bridging the gap between theoretical understanding and practical action. ■

In action, meanings are always at risk.
Marshall Sahlins

How different are other cultures?

In the 1990s, a debate took place between Marshall Sahlins and Sri Lankan anthropologist Gananath Obeyesekere over cultural difference. In an unusual twist Sahlins—a white American—argued that Westerners could not fully understand non-Western cultures, while Obeyesekere claimed they could.

Sahlins maintained that when Captain Cook first visited Hawaii in the 18th century, Hawaiians believed he was the god Lono. Obeyesekere disagreed, arguing that all human beings are much the same—and too rational to make such a mistake. Myths about Cook's divinity were merely yarns told by Europeans. Sahlins, taking his lead from Hawaiian activists, insisted that Hawaiians were radically different from their colonizers.

While Sahlins's account of Cook is widely considered the more accurate, some critics have accused him of failing to fully engage with the Indigenous people he sought to represent.

Captain James Cook was killed during a confrontation with Hawaiians in 1779 after he attempted to capture the Hawaiian ruling chief.

SUGAR
SHAPED THE
MODERN WORLD

THE ANTHROPOLOGY OF FOOD

IN CONTEXT

KEY WORK
Sidney Mintz, *Sweetness and Power: The Place of Sugar in Modern History*, 1985

FIELD
Sociocultural anthropology

BEFORE
1934 In *Patterns of Culture*, Mintz's mentor Ruth Benedict examines the relationship between cultures and individual personalities.

1944 Trinidadian historian Eric Williams describes in *Capitalism and Slavery* how the slave trade across the Caribbean enabled Britain to develop industrial capitalism.

AFTER
2000 US religious historian Daniel Sack publishes *Whitebread Protestants*, which looks at the significance of food in solidifying bonds in American church communities.

For most people, sugar is an integral part of their diet. Its presence is often obvious—in candies, cakes, or desserts—but sugar may also be a subtle component of savory foods, such as crackers or bread. We seldom think about where this ingredient originated or why it has become so ubiquitous, but these tiny white grains have exerted an outsize impact not just on global eating habits but on the modern world order itself, something examined in the 1980s by US anthropologist Sidney Mintz.

Transformed diet

Anthropologists have studied how the human "sweet tooth" first emerged and how it has changed since the days of our hunter-gathering ancestors. For them, sweet foods such as berries, fruits, and raw honey were most likely scarce or seasonal, so these tasty, high-calorie treats, which helped to fuel the early human search for sustenance, could be consumed only occasionally.

By contrast, in many countries today, there is almost unlimited access to heavily sweetened foods

Slave and proletarian together powered the imperial economic system that kept the one supplied with manacles and the other with sugar and rum.
Sidney Mintz

and drinks. Coca-Cola, for example, is the world's most popular fizzy drink, with 1.9 billion servings consumed every day. The recipe contains around 0.37 oz (10.6 g) of sugar per 3.4 fl oz (100 ml) of liquid—about seven teaspoons of sugar per 12 fl oz (330-ml) can. Given that this is just one of many sugary beverages among countless sweet snacks, the volume of sugar consumed is hard to imagine.

In *Sweetness and Power*, Mintz investigates how, with the introduction of sugar, "the

---

Sidney Mintz

Born in New Jersey in 1922, Sidney Mintz studied psychology at Brooklyn College in New York City, then enlisted in the US Army Air Corps in 1943. After World War II, he studied for a PhD at New York's Columbia University. His first fieldwork—in 1948–1949, under Ruth Benedict—was in Puerto Rico, where he focused on the life history of a sugarcane worker.

After receiving his doctorate in 1951, Mintz became a lecturer in anthropology at Yale University before founding the Anthropology Department at Johns Hopkins University in 1974. He used both archival and ethnographic research to examine slavery, globalization, and the impact of capitalism.

Mintz became known as the "father of food anthropology" for his work on sugar, food habits, and global food systems. He died in 2015.

Other key works

1960 *Worker in the Cane*
1996 *Tasting Food, Tasting Freedom*

See also: Culture and personality 70–73 ▪ Social and cultural dimensions of nutrition 80–83 ▪ Food and modernity 267 ▪ Nutrition and human evolution 280

diet of a whole species was gradually … remade." Drawing on archival research and ethnographic fieldwork, as well as Marxist theory, he traced the social impact of an industry that was born out of the colonial encounter and expanded into a massive capitalist enterprise.

The spread of sugar

Mintz explained that sugar was a valued commodity even before it became a major industry. Researchers believe that people on the island of New Guinea domesticated sugarcane and enjoyed chewing it as a sweet treat as far back as 10,000 years ago. Cultivation of the crop spread to Asia, and about 3,000 years ago people in India began processing the cane to produce "free sugar"—a form that allowed it to be added to food or drink. Traders carried this free sugar across Southwest Asia, the Mediterranean, and into Europe, where people used it as a spice, a sweetener, an ingredient in medicines, and a preservative.

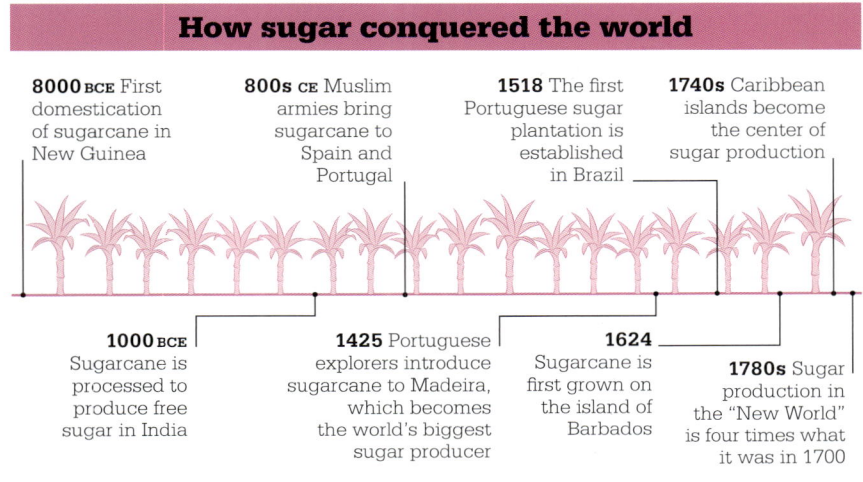

How sugar conquered the world

8000 BCE First domestication of sugarcane in New Guinea

800s CE Muslim armies bring sugarcane to Spain and Portugal

1518 The first Portuguese sugar plantation is established in Brazil

1740s Caribbean islands become the center of sugar production

1000 BCE Sugarcane is processed to produce free sugar in India

1425 Portuguese explorers introduce sugarcane to Madeira, which becomes the world's biggest sugar producer

1624 Sugarcane is first grown on the island of Barbados

1780s Sugar production in the "New World" is four times what it was in 1700

Initially in Europe, sugar was a luxury that only the wealthy could afford. As the elites craved more sugar, they faced the dilemma of how to increase its supply. Sugarcane thrives in warm, tropical climates, but it does not grow well in the more temperate seasonal conditions found in Europe. Furthermore, sugar production required a large labor force. Workers were needed on the plantations to grow and harvest the sugarcane. More labor still was needed in factories to grind the cane into a liquid that could be heated to expose the crystals that are further refined to make table sugar.

As European colonizers explored the Americas during the 17th century, they discovered land that was ideal for growing sugarcane in Barbados, Jamaica, and other Caribbean islands. However, the Caribbean islands could not provide a sufficiently large pool of local workers for the labor-intensive sugar-growing and refining processes. As a consequence, millions of people from Africa were enslaved and forcibly transported across the Atlantic Ocean to work on the newly established plantations. After the abolition of the slave »

Sugar production had a huge social impact on islands such as Antigua. Vast numbers of enslaved people and indentured laborers were put to work to ensure the colonizers turned a profit.

trade in 1807, several thousand indentured labourers were brought over from India and China to supplement the workforce.

Consumption boost

While the increase in sugar production was made possible by colonialism and the ruthless exploitation of land and resources, the consumption of sugar in Europe, Mintz suggested, was boosted by the continent's emergent capitalist system. Nineteenth-century German-born philosopher Karl Marx viewed the economy as a major influence on all aspects of society. He explained that, under capitalism, the owners of the means of production – the bourgeoisie – seek only to enrich themselves and, in an endless pursuit of profit, exploit their workers by paying them less than they are worth. Importantly, Marx suggested that the sway of the bourgeoisie extends far beyond the economy, shaping politics, the family, religion, and all other areas of cultural life.

According to Mintz, as sugar was incorporated into the capitalist economy, it led to the development of new cultural practices and food

preferences. By the late 18th century, sugar had become more affordable and was widely enjoyed: between 1710 and 1770, Britain's sugar consumption increased fivefold.

No longer a luxury item or the preserve of the rich, sugar was introduced to the British working class as an additive for tea. The newly acquired preference for sweetened tea had an additional side effect: both sugar and tea are stimulants that enabled the workers to toil harder for more hours. These longer work patterns aligned with capitalist goals to increase the productivity of the workforce. Mintz argued that as labourers worked more, the family meal at home was gradually replaced with high-energy, often sugar-filled foods that could be eaten at work. The introduction of these new foods into their diet augmented the demands for increased sugar production.

Sugar and capitalism

The role of sugar in a capitalist economy remains relevant today, as people eat prepackaged or fast food that saves them time, which enables them to remain in their

> The history of sugar is a history of power, influence, and decision-making, as well as of pleasure, desire, and satisfaction.
> **Sidney Mintz**

workplaces longer and contribute more to the larger economy. The sugar in these foods is believed to make them more palatable. However, Mintz claimed that people do not choose to consume more sugar simply because it tastes good. Rather, he wrote, what someone wants or needs to eat makes sense "only in terms of one's preferences and aspirations – in terms, that is, of the social context of consumption".

Over time, people acquired an insatiable taste for sugar, and it became a major commodity deemed

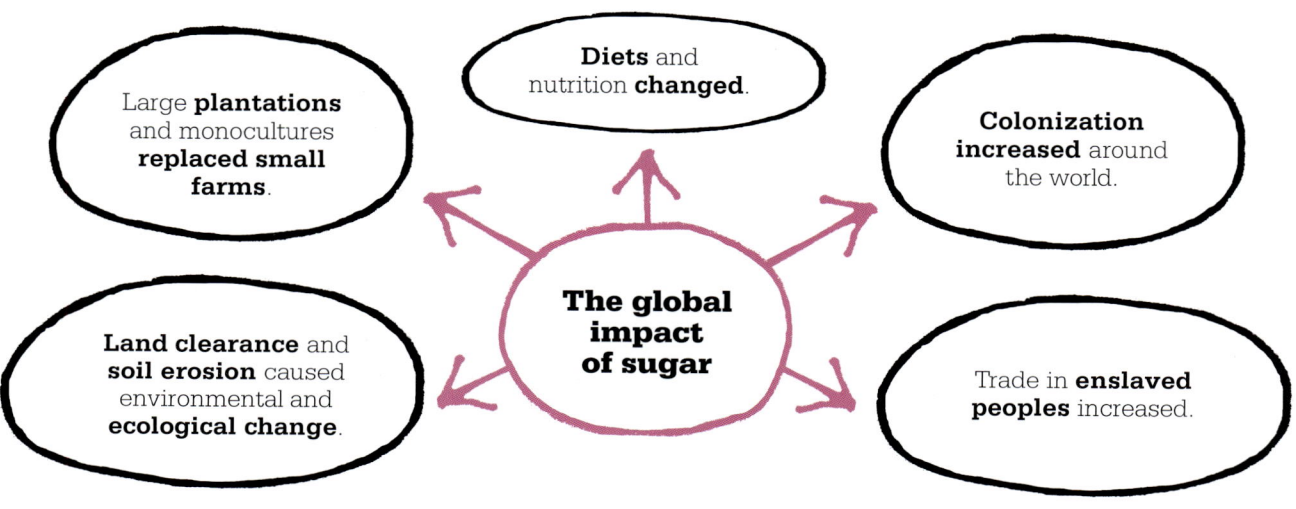

Large **plantations** and monocultures **replaced small farms**.

Diets and nutrition **changed**.

Colonization increased around the world.

Land clearance and **soil erosion** caused environmental and **ecological change**.

The global impact of sugar

Trade in **enslaved peoples** increased.

to be necessary in every kitchen. This preference for sweetness was partly engineered by outside forces – namely capitalism – and partly by "inside meanings" related to class, identity, and status.

Ultimately, Mintz revealed that sugar not only changed people's diets but also affected their social relationships. Even as people consume more sugar, he argued, they rarely think about how its production was made possible by the enslavement of human beings, or how its consumption is enabled by capitalist labour demands that rely on the exploitation of workers.

Cultural impact

With *Sweetness and Power*, Mintz became recognized as a pioneer of the anthropology of food. This field of study begins with the assumption that food is more than fuel for our body, more than just a universal biological necessity. Rather, food production and consumption occur within sociopolitical contexts that have far-reaching cultural implications.

Mintz, however, was not the first academic to study food in this way. British anthropologist Mary Douglas's 1972 essay "Deciphering

Sugar appears almost inescapable in modern diets. Since the late 20th century, hidden sugars in processed and prepackaged foods have helped to drive an increase in overall consumption.

a Meal" used a symbolic approach to decode the social meanings of food categories and rules, such as Jewish food taboos.

Later, Indian-American anthropologist Arjun Appadurai's 1988 article "How to Make a National Cuisine: Cookbooks in Contemporary India" analysed how Indian cookery books have created a "national cuisine" that draws upon the country's diversity. Through preparing the recipes recommended in these volumes, one experiences the different caste-based and regional foodways that are present throughout India.

These and other studies show that what we eat and how we eat are never as simple as they may appear. It is only by asking questions about where a food comes from, who makes it, who consumes it, who benefits, and who loses out that we are led to consider the array of cultural meanings, political implications, and global ramifications inherent in our food. ∎

Deciphering a meal

In 1972, Mary Douglas applied a structuralist approach to understanding food categories and food sharing. In effect, she constructed the "semiotics of a meal" by examining the rules, symbols, and rituals that shape mealtimes across various settings – including her own family – and religious contexts. Meals are, she argued, an expression of shared social identity and relationships.

Douglas also considered Jewish dietary laws. Through a series of diagrams, she used Jewish rules to classify animals based on their degree of holiness. These rules determine whether animals are fit or unfit to be eaten. Moreover, among edible animals, meat must be separated from blood, and milk must be separated from meat. Douglas's larger argument was that cultural beliefs influence what people can and cannot eat, how food is processed, and the overall experience of mealtimes.

Sugar has been the most powerful, the most pervasive, and the most durable of the commodities that have changed the world.
Sidney Mintz

COMMODITIES HAVE SOCIAL LIVES

THE VALUE OF OBJECTS

IN CONTEXT

KEY WORK
Arjun Appadurai, *The Social Life of Things*, 1986

FIELD
Sociocultural anthropology

BEFORE
1922 Bronisław Malinowski describes the ceremonial exchange of shell necklaces, and the role of objects in maintaining relationships.

1925 Marcel Mauss writes about gifts, explaining that they are never truly free and that they come with obligations.

AFTER
1998 In *A Theory of Shopping*, British anthropologist Daniel Miller argues that shopping serves as a ritualistic practice, especially in families.

2014 US anthropologist Rebecca Bryant explores how objects have trajectories that sometimes overlap and sometimes diverge from people's own trajectories.

The objects people own and use—whether utensils, furniture, jewelery, or even weapons—play a significant role in shaping their lives. Anthropologists have long studied how people interact with these objects, which they call "material culture." During the 1980s, Indian-American anthropologist Arjun Appadurai developed a new way of thinking about material culture. He showed how everyday items carry cultural and economic value that reflects the complexities of the societies in which they are created.

Appadurai argued that objects do not have meaning in themselves. Their significance comes from how people interact with them—how they are used, exchanged, or thought about within social and cultural contexts. His work shifted anthropological discussions from studying material culture as static artifacts to exploring the dynamic way in which objects are shaped by history, economics, and culture.

Value and alienation
Appadurai built on German philosopher Karl Marx's theory of commodification. Marx argued that an object becomes a "commodity" when it is sold, gaining value based on what people are willing to pay for it—its "exchange value." This differs from its "use value," based on how it is used in daily life. Marx also believed that workers become disconnected or "alienated" from the objects they make. Instead of being defined by their creators, objects are shaped by the demands of the marketplace.

However, Appadurai argued that the value and meaning of an object varies across cultures. In a global marketplace, where the producer and the consumer are not only geographically distant but also live in different cultural, political, and social contexts, assigning a single meaning to

Objects on sale at a flea market may acquire a new significance or meaning in the context of their new owner's life.

See also: Biopsychological functionalism 50–55 ▪ The concept of reciprocity 58–61 ▪ The anthropology of food 200–205 ▪ Anthropologies of the future 308–309

```
┌─────────────────────────┐   ┌─────────────────────────┐
│   Object creation       │   │   Cultural context      │
│   Objects emerge from   │   │   Objects are embedded  │
│   human creativity      │   │   with cultural meanings│
│   and labor.            │   │   from the outside world.│
└─────────────────────────┘   └─────────────────────────┘
              │                            │
              ▼                            ▼
┌─────────────────────────────────────────────────────────┐
│                   Commodity phase                        │
│   When objects enter markets they become commodities.    │
└─────────────────────────────────────────────────────────┘
                            │
                            ▼
┌─────────────────────────────────────────────────────────┐
│                  Trajectories of use                     │
│   Objects travel, and gain new meanings in different contexts.│
└─────────────────────────────────────────────────────────┘
                            │
                            ▼
┌─────────────────────────────────────────────────────────┐
│             Consumption and transformation               │
│   Objects are integrated into lives, and acquire personal significance.│
└─────────────────────────────────────────────────────────┘
                            │
                            ▼
┌─────────────────────────────────────────────────────────┐
│              Circulation or redistribution               │
│   Objects often find new lives, restarting the cycle.    │
└─────────────────────────────────────────────────────────┘
```

an object becomes problematic. Instead, Appadurai emphasized that an object's meaning depends on the perspectives and experiences of those who interact with it.

Shifting values

Use-value and exchange-value, Appadurai argued, are unstable, and subject to many influences in the globalized world. He emphasized the cultural distinctiveness and the ingenuity that different societies bring to processes of exchange. Appadurai offered a new perspective on globalization—he described it as a process that creates new connections but also introduces disconnections and fragmentation.

A focus on the social life of things, Appadurai suggested, provides a powerful way to trace historical connections and identify diverse, localized cultural meanings. By analyzing how objects are used and given meaning, anthropologists can study both large-scale economic trends, and the local ways in which communities responded to such policies.

Drawing on Appadurai, other anthropologists have documented the complex creativity underlying processes of exchange. US anthropologist Annette Weiner proposed a model of "keeping-while-giving" as a cultural practice of exchange that challenges

The cultural biography of things

Igor Kopytoff, a US cultural anthropologist, introduced the concept of the "biography of things" to challenge three key assumptions in economic anthropology: that objects are exchangeable, but people are not; that commodities remain commodities after exchange; and that markets and gift economies are distinct systems. Kopytoff argues that these distinctions are ideological rather than real, highlighting how slavery commodified humans within capitalism.

Kopytoff contends that objects shift between commoditization—when they are exchangeable—and singularization—when they are rendered uniquely valuable or worthless. These dynamics reflect broad cultural and personal tensions, as individuals navigate the pressures of commoditization while attributing personal and cultural meaning to objects.

Western assumptions of ownership grounded in exclusive ties. In her 1988 study of the Trobriand Islanders of Papua New Guinea, Weiner used the term "inalienable possessions" to describe objects—such as dresses, food, or carvings—that retain ties to specific owners, even when exchanged. These items map social relations and embody identities tied to particular lineages or groups, challenging Western notions of exclusive ownership. Weiner emphasized that these objects can simultaneously foster new networks while maintaining the original owners' power and influence, even beyond their direct possession. ▪

POETRY IS A DISCOURSE OF DEFIANCE

ORAL POETRY

IN CONTEXT

KEY WORK
Lila Abu-Lughod, *Veiled Sentiments: Honor and Poetry in a Bedouin Society*, 1986

FIELD
Sociocultural anthropology

BEFORE
1977 French sociologist Pierre Bourdieu coins the term "habitus" to refer to the habits, skills, and dispositions acquired through socialization.

1978 Palestinian-American academic Edward Said critiques the way in which the West typically portrays the East as exotic and inferior. He argues that these views perpetuate colonial dominance through cultural stereotypes.

AFTER
2024 French athletes are banned from wearing hijabs at the Paris Olympics. This is widely viewed as an insulting and discriminatory policy.

Exploring the intricate social dynamics of the Awlad Ali Bedouin community in Egypt, Lila Abu-Lughod argues that women within this culture challenge Western stereotypes through expressive cultural practices such as emotive poetry. Abu-Lughod observes that Bedouin society is highly structured with distinct roles for men and women, and individuals are closely tied to their family networks. These networks shape social affiliations and status, and there is a strong emphasis within Bedouin society on maintaining family honour.

Indirect expression

An important part of Abu-Lughod's argument is her concept of "veiled sentiments" – the practice in which women express their true emotions indirectly, often through poetry, and particularly in Ginnawa poems. These short, evocative, and lyrical poems often reflect themes of love, loss, and longing. They allow women to express themselves while also conforming to the external expectations of modesty, decorum, and honour. In a society where direct expression of emotions, especially love and desire, is considered inappropriate and can lead to social sanctions, Ginnawa poetry becomes an important, socially acceptable outlet for women to convey their innermost feelings.

Abu-Lughod explores how Bedouin poetry serves multiple functions beyond artistic and emotional expression. It is also a means of social critique, allowing

The poems of Hissa Hilal, a Bedouin poet from Saudi Arabia, continue the tradition of self-expression, storytelling, and political debate.

See also: Culture and personality 70–73 ▪ Feminist anthropology 140–45 ▪ Gender, sexuality, and power 158–59 ▪ Cultural intimacy 230–33

> The stoic acceptance of emotional pain is another aspect of self-mastery.
> **Lila Abu-Lughod**

women to make subtle comments on societal norms, which plays a role in negotiating power dynamics. Abu-Lughod discusses how, in a society where they have limited public roles, women use poetry to discreetly assert their desires and emotions, challenging assumptions about their passivity and subordination.

A point of honour

Abu-Lughod also examines the role of emotions in shaping social relationships and hierarchies within the community. She argues that emotions – far from being private experiences – are deeply intertwined with broader social structures. For instance, socially unacceptable expressions of emotions of love and desire can negatively affect family alliances, and the family's reputation within the community.

Abu-Lughod explores the importance of honour in regulating behaviour and maintaining social order. Since honour is closely tied to perceptions of respectability, women feel pressure to manage their emotions and uphold these ideals. Abu-Lughod reveals how individuals handle the tension between their personal desires and societal expectations, and how they often turn to the use of poetry to navigate these complex emotional landscapes.

Abu-Lughod's work critiques Western stereotypes that often depict Middle Eastern women as oppressed and voiceless – and in doing so, demonstrates their agency and resilience. ▪

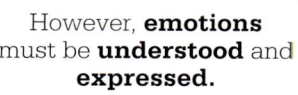

Outward expressions of intense emotions are not **socially acceptable.**

However, **emotions** must be **understood** and **expressed.**

Emotions can be **expressed privately** and indirectly through **poetry.**

A vibrant inner world can exist in parallel with the outer world.

Protesters, including many Muslim women, marched against a ban on modest clothing on beaches in France in 2004.

Do Muslim women need saving?

In her wider work, Lila Abu-Lughod critiques Western narratives that portray Muslim women as universally oppressed and in need of rescue. She argues against the simplistic dichotomy of Western liberation versus Eastern oppression and notes that Western intervention in the lives of Muslim women often perpetuates colonial attitudes of superiority and overlooks the agency that women have in their social worlds. Challenging the idea that Muslim women are passive victims of their cultures, Abu-Lughod highlights how Western discourse often ignores that Muslim women actively participate in shaping their own lives and societies. She argues that interventions framed as "saving" are not liberating, but patronize and culturally oppress Muslim women. Instead, Abu-Lughod advocates solidarity and respectful engagement that recognizes the agency and diversity of Muslim women's experiences.

COMMON CULTURAL ELEMENTS EARLY FARMERS BROUGHT

THE AGRICULTURAL THEORY OF LANGUAGE DIFFUSION

IN CONTEXT

KEY WORK
**Colin Renfrew,
Archaeology and Language,
1987**

FIELD
Archaeology

BEFORE
1813 British scientist Thomas Young coins the term "Indo-European" to describe the related languages that span Europe and Asia.

1956 Lithuanian archaeologist Marija Gimbutas explores the Kurgan hypothesis – the theory that Indo-European languages stem from an ancestor in the steppe region of Eastern Europe.

AFTER
2012 Researchers at the University of Auckland, New Zealand, test the Anatolian and Kurgan hypotheses with tracing techniques used for viruses. Their findings support the Anatolian hypothesis.

During the 1980s, British archaeologist Colin Renfrew transformed perceptions of how languages developed with his work on the origins of Indo-European languages – a collection of more than 400 different languages spoken across Europe and South Asia, that includes Latin, Greek, and Sanskrit. Based on his analysis of both archaeological and linguistic data, Renfrew argued that the peaceful spread of agriculture explained the relationship between different languages. Renfrew's

Pottery and raw materials such as bronze found at locations where Indo-European languages are spoken helped to inform Renfrew's theory of how language spread through agricultural expansion.

groundbreaking work generated a huge amount of interest, as it represented a multidisciplinary approach – using linguistics, anthropology, and archaeology to investigate the origins of language.

New methodology
The correlation of linguistic data to archaeological finds made Renfrew's work unique. His primary proposal was that Indo-European languages spread through the peaceful migration of farming communities, whose languages spread as agricultural practices expanded geographically. Renfrew's theory was controversial and contradicted the popular hypothesis that languages spread through invasion and colonization. Known as the Anatolian hypothesis, Renfrew stated that Indo-European languages would have had their first speakers in Anatolia around 7000 BCE, and then spread from this region to Europe. Archaeological evidence showed that during this time – the Neolithic period – agriculture began to spread from central Asia across Europe. Farming was therefore believed to have propelled populations to migrate during the

See also: Origins of culture 32–33 ▪ Language and cognition 88–89 ▪ The rules of language 109 ▪ The significance of early trade 307

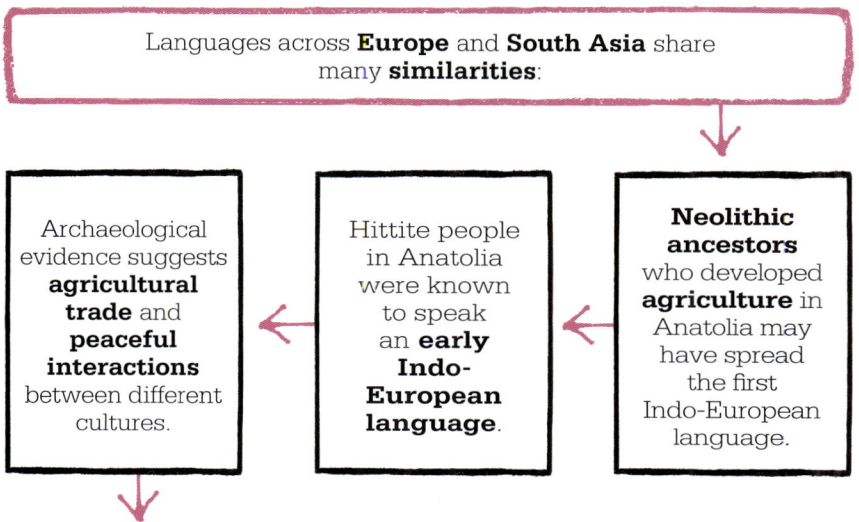

Languages across **Europe** and **South Asia** share many **similarities**:

Archaeological evidence suggests **agricultural trade** and **peaceful interactions** between different cultures.

Hittite people in Anatolia were known to speak an **early Indo-European language**.

Neolithic ancestors who developed **agriculture** in Anatolia may have spread the first Indo-European language.

Indo-European languages developed from the spread of agriculture.

Neolithic period, which led to the spread of an early form of Indo-European language.

Simplified approach
Renfrew proposed a relatively straightforward, linear model of language transmission. However, linguists responding to his work argued that the spread of language was far more complex and involved multiple waves of migration, cultural interactions, trade networks, and conquests. Similarly, linguistic anthropologists emphasized that sociocultural and political factors dramatically influenced how dialects and languages became dominant and were propagated. Renfrew's colleagues claimed that the Anatolian hypothesis lacked substantial archaeological evidence to support large-scale peaceful migrations, and the evidence did not consistently support a direct correlation between agricultural expansion and linguistic spread. Genetic studies also revealed more complex Neolithic movements than Renfrew's model suggested.

Innovative thought
While Renfrew's model was critiqued for its simplistic view of what was likely an intricate process of language transmission and evolution, it was respected for its great innovation. Renfrew later revised his thinking to state that only a precursor to Indo-European language was present in 7000 BCE. Regardless, from a broader anthropological standpoint, Renfrew's work has encouraged the use of multidisciplinary anthropology and has inspired new research methods. ▪

Radiocarbon dating and linguistics

Radiocarbon dating is the method of measuring the carbon atoms inside dead organic material, such as human remains or plant matter, to understand how long ago it lived. When an organism dies, its carbon atoms begin to change into other atoms. As this transformation happens over time, scientists can determine how old the remains are by counting the number of carbon atoms it has left. Renfrew used radiocarbon data to correlate the spread of agriculture with potential language dispersal. Today, the study of ancient languages relies on radiocarbon-dated archaeological sites, alongside glottochronology – the use of data to establish when languages diverged from a common ancestor – to establish the timeline of when inscriptions, tablets, and other written materials were made. This interdisciplinary data can be used to explain when certain languages were likely to have been in use.

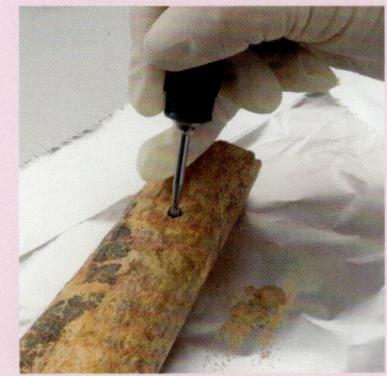

The age of organic material from an ancient human bone can be established as up to 50,000 years old using radiocarbon dating.

A POWERFUL, EVEN ALL-CONSUMING BEAST

NATIONALIST THOUGHT

IN CONTEXT

KEY WORK
Bruce Kapferer, *Legends of People, Myths of State*, 1988

FIELD
Sociocultural anthropology

BEFORE
1969 In *Homo Hierarchicus* Louis Dumont explores the idea that Western egalitarianism is a natural successor to hierarchical systems.

1983 Benedict Anderson's work *Imagined Communities* examines how nationalist identities emerged in Europe from the 15th century onwards.

1983 Anti-Tamil pogroms during "Black July" lead to civil war in Sri Lanka.

AFTER
2013 Essays by scholars David Rampton, Roshan de Silva Wijeyeratne, Rohan Bastin, and Barry Morris in a new edition of *Legends of the People* show that nationalism keeps evolving.

Following the outbreak of riots across Sri Lanka in 1983, Australian anthropologist Bruce Kapferer examined why nationalism can lead to violence. In *Legends of People, Myths of State,* he ambitiously juxtaposes Sri Lankan nationalism with that of Australia to shed light on both.

Shaping nationalism

For Kapferer, "nationalism makes culture into an object and thing of worship", often by depicting a primordial past. People draw from this past when crafting their sense of nation in the present. Examining what culture means is therefore central to understanding how people construct nationalist ideas. Kapferer suggests that culture is dictated by the cosmology of a particular group and their understanding of fundamental units, including the nation, the state, and the person.

In a Sri Lankan cosmology, the state and nation form a whole. That whole is made up of individuals

---

In a **hierarchical model** of nationalism, the **state** and its **nation** form a **single entity**.

Threats to the **nation** threaten the **individual**.

In **egalitarian models** of nationalism, **individuals** are the **building blocks** of the **nation**.

State defends the nation by protecting the rights of the individual.

Nationalism shapes the present and the future.

See also: Caste systems 122–23 ▪ Structure and agency 196–97 ▪ The aftermath of violence 272–77 ▪ Political violence and conflict 316

In the *Mahavamsa*, Sanghamitt, the daughter of Emperor Ashoka, and her brother Mahinda spread the teachings of the Buddha in Sri Lanka.

whose intrinsic differences are expressed through a hierarchical system of status. As people are fundamentally part of the whole, anything that threatens the nation also threatens each person.

In Australian egalitarianism, the state and nation are not equivalent; instead individuals are the building blocks of the nation. Individuals are intrinsically of equal status, expressing difference through their autonomy. The state defends the nation by protecting individual rights to autonomy.

Kapferer argues that myths of the past reify these cosmologies. In the Sri Lankan *Mahavamsa*, the Sri Lankan state is invaded by outsiders, who affect the unity of the whole. By contrast, in Australian Anzac stories, individual acts of heroism are used to construct an Australian sense of the nation. Kapferer shows that both of these nationalist representations of the past contribute to their present-day

social imaginaries – and that both hierarchical and egalitarian cosmologies can shape violence. For example, in Sri Lanka, populations affected by ethnic violence fled to areas dominated by their own ethnic group, which reinforced the narrative that groups are "naturally opposed". According to Kapferer, nationalism perpetuates a "logic which has become the only truth".

Day-to-day nationalism

Kapferer highlights that nationalism is not external, but woven into daily life. In everyday rituals people reflect on their culture, and in doing so, they reimagine the nation and therefore constantly reconstitute their worlds. He argues that nationalism "conditions what it reflects": this means that nationalism is shaped by context, which in turn shapes the future in ways that exceed this context.

Critical reactions

Kapferer's decision to compare nationalism in countries as distinct as Sri Lanka and Australia provoked

Nationalism… throws into relief some of the ways in which human beings comprehend their realities.
Bruce Kapferer

criticism. However, he later argued that his objective in juxtaposing two such different states was to illuminate different aspects of nationalism, and to challenge nationalist thinking. By placing nationalism at the centre of everyday life, Kapferer sought to dispel deep-seated assumptions that researchers sometimes make when explaining human action and demonstrated the value of a cultural approach to understanding modern societies. ▪

The crisis of violence in Sri Lanka

In 1984, social anthropologist Stanley Tambiah explored what had caused the Sri Lankan riots a year earlier. He probed "under the surface" of tensions to reveal a history of nationalism before and after independence. Tambiah suggests that in the pre-colonial period before *c.*1600, "galactic polities" across Sri Lanka featured centralized governments with satellites that easily incorporated minorities. During the British period (1815–1948), both the census and elective representation hardened ethnic distinctions. Ethnic polarization accelerated after independence, and violence exacerbated the rifts between groups. Casting minorities as an enemy rendered them abstract and more easily de-humanized. As groups began to define themselves in opposition to others, they became increasingly homogeneous. The polarization of Tamils and Sinhalese resulted in violence, and also caused resistance to change.

THE MYTH OF MERITOCRACY
WHITE PRIVILEGE

IN CONTEXT

KEY WORK
Peggy McIntosh, "White Privilege and Male Privilege", 1988

FIELD
Sociocultural anthropology

BEFORE
1910 W.E.B. Du Bois publishes "The Souls of White Folk", in which he argues that whiteness provides white Americans with racialized self-esteem and a sense of entitlement. He also posits that white supremacy is the foundation of racism, capitalism, and colonialism, and exacerbates sexism.

AFTER
1995 In his article "History and Black Consciousness: The Political Culture of Black America", US academic Manning Marable argues that white privilege is intentionally created and upheld through detailed political planning.

In the late 1980s, Peggy McIntosh, a US feminist and anti-racist scholar, explored the concepts of privilege and how it intersects with different identities, such as gender, race, class, and sexuality. Social inequality had often been studied from the perspective of the disempowered. However, as she examined the ways in which being white was viewed as the default in society, McIntosh exposed the pernicious ways that white privilege functions – by normalizing white experiences and perspectives.

McIntosh acknowledged her own resistance to studying privilege: she much preferred to focus on gender. However, her work on gender inequality caused her to recognize that just as men enjoy the unearned advantages in society of male privilege, white people also benefit from social attitudes that often go unnoticed or unchallenged, known as white privilege. She uses the metaphor of an invisible backpack filled with privileges that white people carry around, often unconsciously, and contrasts this with the burdens and barriers that non-white and non-male individuals face on a regular basis.

McIntosh emphasizes the importance of recognizing that these privileges do not come as a result of personal achievements, but a system of advantages that contributes to inequality. She encourages readers to use their privilege to dismantle systems of oppression rather than to perpetuate them. ∎

Whites are carefully taught not to recognize white privilege, as males are taught not to recognize male privilege.
Peggy McIntosh

See also: Fighting racial segregation 30–31 ▪ Development and colonial attitudes 226–29 ▪ The role of African American Vernacular English 254–55

AN IDENTITY TENUOUSLY CONSTITUTED THROUGH A STYLIZED REPETITION OF ACTS
GENDER PERFORMATIVITY

IN CONTEXT

KEY WORK
Judith Butler, *Gender Trouble*, 1990

FIELD
Sociocultural anthropology

BEFORE
1949 Simone de Beauvoir's *The Second Sex*, critiques the oppression of women. It becomes a foundational text for contemporary feminists, and influences critiques of gender essentialism – the idea that genders have distinct, intrinsic attributes.

1972 *Mother Camp* by Esther Newton explores drag queen culture in Chicago. It examines how drag artists challenge conventions of gender identity and sexuality.

AFTER
2010 Melissa Tyler and Laurie Cohen publish *Spaces that Matter*, a study on organizational space and gender performativity.

K nown for their work in gender and queer studies – and especially for coining the term gender performativity – US scholar Judith Butler argues that gender is not a fixed, innate trait but something that is dynamically constructed through repeated performance. They suggest that gender is therefore a contingent identity that is enacted through repeated behaviours and actions.

According to Butler, societal norms shape how individuals understand and express their gender. These norms are created and enforced through institutions and discourse. This way of understanding gender differs from the binary, where only males and females, or men and women, exist. Instead, Butler states that appreciating the performative quality of gender better represents its diversity and fluidity.

Intersecting identities

Butler's theory of gender performativity also recognizes that gender intersects with other social

Stage shows by drag artists that involved playing with gender norms helped to inform Butler's analysis of gender performativity.

identities including sexuality, race, and class. They emphasize that different people's experience of gender varies greatly due to multiple intersecting factors. As a result, Butler's work shows that individuals can and do negotiate multiple identities and forms of expression. ∎

See also: Gender, sexuality, and power 158–59 ∎ Gender equality 266 ∎ Challenging systemic oppression 294–95

EMOTION HAS BEEN GIVEN A GENDER

EMOTIONAL CONTROL

IN CONTEXT

KEY WORK
Catherine E. Lutz,
***Engendered Emotion*, 1990**

FIELD
Sociocultural anthropology

BEFORE
1976 Researchers J. Condry and S. Condry publish "Sex differences: A study of the eye of the beholder". The study finds that the expression of a baby is perceived as a different emotion based on whether the baby is a boy or a girl.

AFTER
1998 US communications professor Dana Cloud examines the discourse on psychotherapy that emerged after the Vietnam War, connecting it to political and economic agendas.

2015 Psychologist Tara M. Chaplin explores when in child development a gender difference in emotional expression occurs.

When you begin to look and listen, it becomes relatively easy to identify the different ways in which the emotions of men and women are discussed and understood in society. These narratives can be seen almost everywhere – for instance, in the marketing and packaging of products, or new employee manuals at the workplace. During the 1980s, US anthropologist Catherine Lutz began to explore the intersection of emotional expression and gendered power dynamics within the context of US culture and discourse. Lutz

Gendered socialization begins at a young age, with girls often encouraged to play with toys that develop caring skills, such as dolls and dolls' houses.

argued that emotions are not just personal experiences but reactions that are shaped by social norms and power structures, particularly in how they are perceived and controlled in gendered discourse.

Differences in socialization

Central to Lutz's analysis is the concept of emotional control as a form of social regulation that varies significantly between genders. She describes how traditional gender roles in US society prescribe different emotional norms for men and women. Men are often socialized to control most of their emotions, except for anger and assertiveness, which are associated with power, control, and rationality. On the other hand, women are typically encouraged to express emotions such as warmth and empathy, reinforcing stereotypical roles of nurturing and caretaking.

Lutz examines how these gendered emotional norms are perpetuated and reinforced through language and discourse. She highlights how cultural narratives and societal expectations shape the emotional expressions and responses of different individuals.

See also: Comparative ethnography 84–85 ▪ Feminist anthropology 140–45
▪ Gender, sexuality, and power 158–59

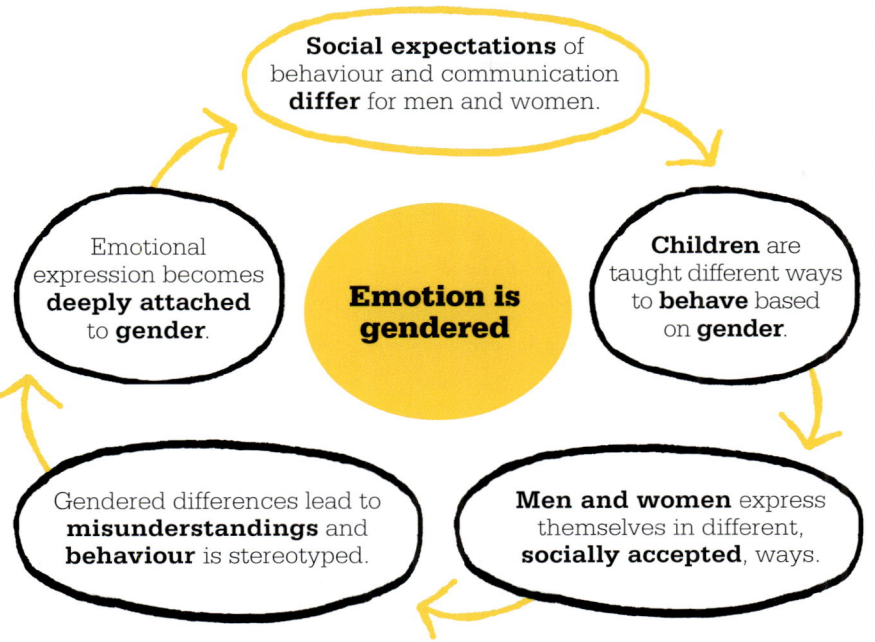

Social expectations of behaviour and communication **differ** for men and women.

Emotional expression becomes **deeply attached** to **gender**.

Emotion is gendered

Children are taught different ways to **behave** based on **gender**.

Gendered differences lead to **misunderstandings** and **behaviour** is stereotyped.

Men and women express themselves in different, **socially accepted**, ways.

For example, women who display assertiveness or anger may be labelled as aggressive, emotional, or irrational, whereas men exhibiting vulnerability or sadness may be viewed as less masculine, weak, or lacking control.

Double standards

Lutz also explores the discourse of emotional control in various societal domains, including in politics, workplaces, and interpersonal relationships. She analyses how emotional displays and responses are strategically used to assert authority, maintain dominance, or challenge power structures. Importantly, she critiques the double standards that often penalize women and minorities for emotional expression while validating similar behaviours in men. Lutz argues that restrictive emotional expectations based on gender limit authentic expression and perpetuate inequalities by reinforcing gender stereotypes and marginalizing those who deviate from traditional norms.

Reconsidering expression

Lutz's work offers a critical examination of how gender influences emotional expression and control within US society. Her analysis underscores the complex interplay between gender, power dynamics, and cultural expectations in shaping emotional norms and behaviours. By unpacking these dynamics, Lutz encourages readers to reconsider the ways in which emotional expression is understood, valued, and regulated based on gender. Ultimately, Lutz advocates for more inclusive and equitable approaches to emotional diversity and expression in society. ▪

Communication differences

US linguist Deborah Tannen explored differences in communication styles between men and women – how they can lead to conflict and affect power relations in the workplace. Tannen argues that men and women often have different priorities in communication, which are shaped by cultural norms.

By analysing the linguistic patterns of each gender, she identified that men use "report talk", which focuses on conveying information, asserting status, and solving problems. In contrast, women use "rapport talk", to build connections, express feelings, and seek empathy. These differences can lead to misinterpretations. For instance, women may feel dismissed when men respond to their problems with solutions rather than emotional support. Conversely, men may perceive women's conversational styles as indirect or unclear, leading to frustration or confusion.

By association with the female, [emotion] vindicates the distinction between and hierarchy of men and women.
Catherine E. Lutz

OUR KIND OF FAMILY
KINSHIP IDEOLOGIES

During the late 1980s, US anthropologist Kath Weston was focused on "discovering the stuff of everyday life". Weston – a lesbian resident of San Francisco – conducted ethnographic fieldwork among her local gay and lesbian community. The resulting study – *Families We Choose: Gays, Lesbians, and Kinship* – drew on her status as an "insider" in innovative ways, and her methodologies remain relevant today.

Rather than scouring gay organizations and community spaces for participants, Weston relied on her own personal

Gay or chosen families might incorporate friends, lovers, or children, in any combination.
Kath Weston

connections and on "snowball sampling" – a technique in which the subjects themselves recruit and suggest additional participants – to create a diverse sample that included people of colour and individuals from working-class backgrounds.

Weston followed the anthropological tradition of using pseudonyms for participants, but she also opted to assign a surname to each person to give them more dignity, and as a mark of respect.

Choosing kinship
Weston used the participants' coming-out stories as a point of departure for exploring issues of identity and relationships with both blood and adoptive relatives. She found that when gay men and lesbians disclosed their sexuality, they discovered the truth and durability of their kinship relations. If their coming-out story received a positive response, that could reaffirm kinship, but a negative response threatened to shatter these bonds. However, Weston also pointed out that claiming a "gay family" did not necessarily require a

See also: Gender, sexuality, and power 158–59 ▪ Anthropology at home 170–71 ▪ Kinship studies 192
▪ Adapting cultural traditions 193

break from one's family of origin. In other words, chosen families are not merely surrogates or replacements for lost kinship.

At a time in the early 1990s when many gay men and lesbians feared that coming out would mean giving up or renouncing their families, Weston showed that they could actually construct families of their own choosing. For Weston, "families we choose" must be understood alongside biological families, or – as some lesbians and gay men described them – "blood families" or "straight families".

Legal implications

The families we choose are created on foundations of love to provide mutual sustenance and safety. They can integrate relationships across households,

LGBTQIA+ individuals may choose their own community as family to counteract shared experiences of isolation and rejection, and to secure a sense of acceptance without judgment.

and they can encompass financial exchange, emotional assistance, care-giving responsibilities, and co-parenting arrangements.

Weston's concept of chosen families has powerful implications. For example, domestic partner legislation in the US requires shared residence of cohabitation. However, if one follows the logic of chosen families, it should be possible for a person to pick as a partner a good friend who does not live with them to be the recipient of their employment benefits, such as health insurance.

Weston's gay kinship ideologies challenged the assumption that "procreation alone constitutes kinship". She claimed that the act of choosing one's own family "presents a kind of collective coming-out story: a tale of lesbians and gay men moving out of isolation and into kinship". ▪

Kath Weston

Born in Illinois, US, in 1958, Kath Weston grew up in a working-class family. She earned a BA and MA from the University of Chicago and an MA and PhD from Stanford University. The author of six books, she has conducted fieldwork in North America, India, Japan, the UK, and the Andaman and Nicobar islands on topics such as gender and sexuality, kinship, and the political economy.

Weston has taught at several universities in the US and around the world, including Cambridge, UK, and Tokyo, Japan. Additionally, she has held professorships at the universities of Virginia and Edinburgh, and she has fellowships from the National Science Foundation, the Guggenheim Foundation, and the Rockefeller Foundation.

In 2022, the Association of Queer Anthropology awarded Weston the Distinguished Achievement Award for her pioneering work.

Other key works

1996 *Render Me, Gender Me*
2002 *Gender in Real Time*

WINDOWS ON CULTURES
MUSEUM ANTHROPOLOGY

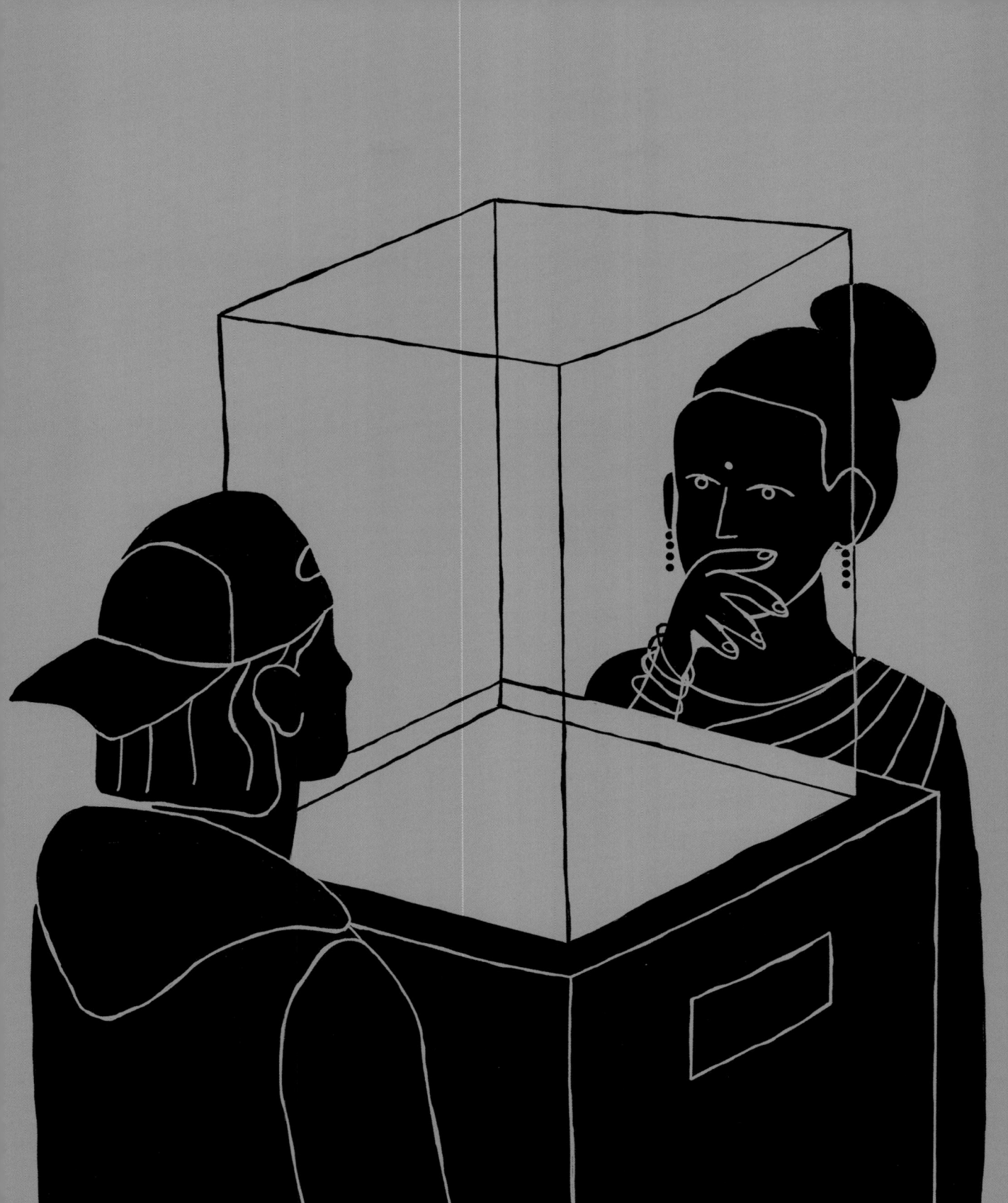

IN CONTEXT

KEY WORK
Michael Ames, *Cannibal Tours and Glass Boxes*, 1992

FIELD
Sociocultural anthropology

BEFORE
1894 US anthropologist Franz Boas plays a key role in establishing the Field Museum in Chicago, US.

1982 The Michael Rockefeller Wing opens at the Metropolitan Museum of Art in New York, displaying works of what the museum describes as "primitive art".

AFTER
2006 In an act of reconciliation, the Swedish government returns a totem pole – taken in 1929 – to the Haisla Nation in Canada.

2022 Cynthia Chavez Lamar becomes the first Indigenous American woman to head a Smithsonian Museum.

Museums are a kind of cannibalism made safe for polite society.
Jane Tompkins
"At the Buffalo Bill Museum", *South Atlantic Quarterly*, June 1988

Museums of anthropology are not only places where objects are displayed – they are also sites that shape how people understand cultures, histories, and identities. In recent decades, questions about ownership, representation, and ethical responsibility have challenged traditional museum practices.

One scholar who actively confronted these issues was Canadian anthropologist Michael Ames. As director of the Museum of Anthropology at the University of British Columbia, Vancouver, from 1974 to 1997, he oversaw one of the richest collections of Indigenous art from the Pacific Northwest. Ames not only witnessed ethical debates surrounding museum collections first-hand, but also played a central role in shaping discussions about the relationship between objects and their source communities.

In *Cannibal Tours and Glass Boxes*, first published in 1986 and expanded in 1992, Ames reflected on these debates and changing relationships, such as the growing

The Pitt Rivers Museum in Oxford, UK, holds colonial-era collections that were shaped by imperial histories, and are now a focus of intense debate.

calls for the repatriation of artefacts, and the contested celebrations of 1992 in North and South America and Spain, marking the 500th anniversary of Columbus's arrival in the Americas.

Curiosity to control

By their nature, museums are places that collect and classify the material culture of others. While the practice of collecting art or objects of interest dates back to antiquity, from the 15th century it was European expansion that popularized the "curiosity cabinet" – a collection of rare or exotic objects displayed in private chambers or royal courts. By the 18th century, the emphasis on curiosity and wonder had been replaced by attempts to organize objects into stable classifications. Divisions were used to draw clear boundaries between the "savage"

See also: Reflexive ethnography 162–65 ▪ The value of objects 206–07
▪ The ethics of anthropology 248–49 ▪ DNA politics 282–83

and the "civilized" and demonstrate the stages in humanity's technological and moral progress. The anthropology museum as we know it today – laid out with displays of objects arranged by culture area – was developed in Chicago by Franz Boas during the 1890s. By the mid-20th century, however, many collections were gradually being redefined as art, with important consequences for their monetary, symbolic, and political value.

Although museum collections have evolved over time, some of the assumptions that guide their formation and display have remained unchanged. Anthropology emerged at the height of European imperialism, and was used by colonial administrations as a tool to demonstrate the control they had over people, nature, and resources. By the time Ames was writing in the 1980s and 1990s, many museum specialists had begun to challenge the more racist legacies of anthropological collections and the discipline as a whole. Museum collections, however, continued to rely on strict divisions: between scientists and the people whose objects were displayed under glass; and between expert curators and lay spectators. For the most part, museum specialists decided what was worth collecting and preserving, and how objects would be displayed to the public.

Museum ideology

Ames argued that far from being neutral arrangements, museum collections were ideologically active environments. Rather than representing people from other cultures, the anthropology collection

> Museums put nature and culture under glass, in display cases, and, therefore, under control.
> **Michael Ames**

was a historically situated institution that depicted the expectations, desires, and ambitions of the societies in which it was located. Seeking to uncover the social, political, and economic systems that shaped the anthropology museum, Ames made the museum itself an object of ethnographic study.

Ames posed a series of questions that shaped many debates about anthropological collections in the 1980s. Who gets a say about what is collected and exhibited in the museum? Who can claim access to Indigenous knowledge? Who has the right to control the narrative of representation? Should non-Indigenous outsiders continue to interpret Indigenous creativity? Should members of Indigenous communities and descendants of source communities have a say in the answers to these questions – and should the public at large? Ultimately, Ames asked whether the anthropology museum was worth preserving, and whether museums could become spaces for fostering conversation between people with many different perspectives. »

Repatriating objects

In October 2022, the Smithsonian National Museum of African Art in Washington, DC, US, transferred ownership of its Benin bronzes to Nigeria. These artefacts, looted by the British in 1897, had long been at the centre of calls for repatriation. Other contested items include the 16th-century Aztec emperor Moctezuma II's headdress in the Weltmuseum in Vienna, Austria, and the Parthenon Sculptures known as the Elgin Marbles at the British Museum in London.

Institutions justify retaining such objects by arguing that they were acquired via a sale or a gift, or that the countries reclaiming objects do not have specialists to care for them. They also claim that the objects belong to all humanity, and that Western museums can offer the best access.

Those seeking repatriation contend that the objects are not merely collectables, but have cultural, spiritual, or practical significance, and that museums in the West are inaccessible to the source communities. Recently, public opinion has shifted in favour of re-examining the ethical relationships linking museums and source communities.

Moctezuma's headdress is over 500 years old. The brilliant green quetzal feathers are in a fragile state due to age and insect infestations.

The Acropolis Museum in Athens displays replicas of the Parthenon sculptures. The originals, held in London, provoke intense debate, as Greece calls for their return.

At a 1988 conference on heritage in Ottawa, Canada, Georges Erasmus, National Chief of the Assembly of First Nations, acknowledged the efforts of those who had dedicated their careers to presenting what they believed was an accurate portrayal of Indigenous peoples. But, he insisted, "it was time to turn the page". Erasmus demanded control of the narrative of representation by members of First Nations. For Ames, this constituted a new stage in the development of anthropology museums – one which incorporated the insider's view.

Heritage at a cost

A common defence of anthropology collections was that they preserved objects that might otherwise have been lost to history. Proponents argued that museums safeguarded, documented, and conserved these artefacts. However, this came at a cost: conquest, displacement, and plunder, as well as the rigid codification of Indigenous material cultures and traditions. Indigenous peoples were often reduced to stereotypes, distanced from their own heritage.

Even as exhibition styles changed, museums continued to impose classifications, "freezing" Indigenous peoples into fixed anthropological categories. As a Haida artist from north of Vancouver put it to Ames, "You haven't done a damn thing for Indians. We don't feel at home in your museums because they don't tell us our story."

In much the same way, contemporary Indigenous artists have been kept out of galleries when their art was not deemed "Indigenous" or "authentic" enough, reinforcing the notion that artistic evolution and the freedom to move beyond tradition are privileges reserved for white artists.

The line between tradition and modernity is not a natural one – it is shaped by politics. The decision to place Indigenous objects in anthropology museums rather than galleries reflects externally imposed aesthetic norms and economic factors. In fact, Ames insisted that such a choice made little sense for Indigenous material culture. Instead of debating their proper place, the focus should be on the impact of these decisions.

Ames suggested anthropologists ask themselves how objects express power relations. What are the consequences of stereotyping on the people portrayed as others? Is the art of others trivialized by being exposed in museums? What happens when museums "museumify" living traditions? Increased participation of Indigenous curators in exhibits has created new possibilities to break free from rigid classifications and allow Indigenous people to reclaim control of their history.

However, incorporating insider perspectives in museum displays does not guarantee consensus – insiders also have many views. In his work as a museum director, Ames observed that some Indigenous people took pride in displaying their heritage in museums, while others opposed it. Some believed totem poles should be left to decay in their villages,

Since those who control history are the ones who benefit from it, people should have the right to the facts of their own lives.
Michael Ames

while others felt a spiritual connection to those preserved in museums. Similarly, while some approved of museum conservation methods, others rejected them for disregarding traditional ways of caring for objects.

Museums for all

Since the late 20th century, questions have emerged about the relationship between museums – especially those that are publicly funded – and the broader public. Traditionally, museums were seen as tools for educating ordinary citizens, operating under a model that divided specialists from lay audiences. By the time Ames published *Cannibal Tours and Glass Boxes*, the fact that museums received public money led to debates about their responsibility to be accountable to all

stakeholders. Museums, it was increasingly argued, should serve everyone, and work to attract people from all classes.

Ames likened the modern model of public institutions in a consumer society to a fast-food restaurant, where success is defined by numbers; perfectibility as profitability; and happiness as the consumption of mass-produced commodities. This approach highlighted a tension between the goal of entertaining the many, and the need to accommodate the rights, demands, and tastes of minority groups. Ames called on anthropologists to reflect on the potential of their field to serve as a space for meaningful dialogue between people quite different from one another in interest, outlook, wealth, and power. ∎

They can embrace **multiculturalism**, engage with **local communities**, and serve as **social hubs**.

They can address **repatriation issues** and ensure **ethical acquisition** practices.

How museums can be relevant in the modern world:

They can encourage greater participation of **Indigenous curators** and **source communities**.

They can foster **dialogue and debate**, and serve as platforms for **cross-cultural understanding**.

Protecting Indigenous American heritage

Enacted in the US in 1990, the Native American Graves Protection and Repatriation Act (NAGPRA) supports the protection and return of Native American human remains, funerary objects, and objects of cultural heritage to their lineal descendants. Federal agencies and institutions receiving federal funds must consult with descendants, evaluate requests for repatriation, and give notice before transferring remains and objects.

The Act's objectives are clear, but its interpretation and enforcement have proved to be complicated. It can be difficult to prove relationships between Indigenous people and objects when lineal descendants cannot be identified. Decisions about displaying Indigenous American material culture also remain contentious. In 2024, New York's American Museum of Natural History closed two halls citing concerns over the display of human remains and sacred objects, and acknowledging that many items had been acquired unethically.

NAGPRA has also sparked fierce debates between Native American rights activists and scientists. A notable case involved the 9,000-year-old skeleton known as Kennewick Man, discovered in 1996. Scientists initially argued that the remains were not linked to modern tribes, but after years of dispute, the bones were returned to the Confederated Tribes of the Umatilla Indian Reservation for burial.

AN APPARATUS FOR THE EXERCISE OF POWER

DEVELOPMENT AND COLONIAL ATTITUDES

IN CONTEXT

KEY WORK
**Arturo Escobar,
Encountering Development,
1995**

FIELD
Sociocultural anthropology

BEFORE
1949 A paper by Argentine
economist Raúl Prebisch
categorizes the world into a
core of wealthy, industrialized
nations and a periphery of less
developed states.

1973 Saudi anthropologist Talal
Asad asserts that anthropology
is "rooted in an unequal power
encounter between the West
and the 'Third World'".

AFTER
2010 Argentine philosopher
Maria Lugones suggests
that colonial constructions
of gender facilitate the
subjugation of Indigenous
people and their lands.

During the 1960s, as the
pre-war colonial order
disintegrated, the "First
World" – the capitalist powers of the
West – found itself in competition
with the "Second World" – the
communist states – to influence
political outcomes in the "Third
World" – poorer countries, including
the non-aligned former colonies.

In *Encountering Development*,
Colombian-American anthropologist
Arturo Escobar suggests that
discourses about development echo
colonialism by subordinating "Third
World" countries to capitalist powers
of the "First World". In his opinion,
development replaced the West's
direct colonial rule and military

See also: Local belief systems 78–79 ▪ Gender, sexuality, and power 158–59 ▪ Religion and secular power 188–89 ▪ Structure and agency 196–99

The discourse and strategy of development produced … massive underdevelopment and impoverishment, untold exploitation and oppression.
Arturo Escobar

occupation of the "Third World" with a system of meaning-making that promoted the growth of capital markets, facilitated international investment, indebted "Third World" nations, and followed the patriarchal values of modern Europe.

Development discourse

Escobar argues that discussions around development generally portray the "Third World" as a space full of problems that can only be resolved using the expertise of professionals, such as economists

and planners. Professional "experts" come with cultural values, norms, and ideals that they believe to be grounded in rational analysis and universally valid, rather than specific to the culture of European modernity. Their expert opinions are not necessarily shared by a project's "beneficiaries", but because they are backed by institutions and systems of knowledge-making that do share the same values, they feed into development agendas, importing European ideas into "Third World" nations in processes that are often hidden from view. According to Escobar, this development discourse reinforces colonial relations between the West and the rest of the world.

Escobar draws on French philosopher Michel Foucault's method of discourse analysis to trace the relationship between the knowledge produced about the "Third World" and the power over people and policies within it. He claims that discourse analysis makes it possible to see "how certain representations become dominant and shape indelibly the ways in which reality is imagined and acted upon". In other words, »

The Modernity/Coloniality Group

Set up in the late 1990s by Argentine philosopher Walter Mignolo, the Modernity/Coloniality Group (MCG) explores how European modernity has always been based on the subjugation of non-Western people. The panel includes eminent scholars such as Arturo Escobar.

MCG investigates the role that systems of knowledge production and dissemination play in sustaining colonial relations of power. For this, it draws on the analysis of post-colonial societies carried out by the scholar-led Subaltern Studies Group of South Asia.

The relationship between the flows of capital and knowledge between Europe and the rest of the world also comes under scrutiny. MCG links the capacity to produce knowledge to political and economic power. Ultimately, the group calls for the decolonization of knowledge production, and the recognition of the value of knowledge produced by non-Western, Indigenous, and other people.

Culturally **European economic theories** inform development discourse.

Institutions develop plans based on these representations.

This impoverishes the beneficiaries, enriches the institutions and nations promoting development, and maintains colonial power relations.

Development discourse represents its beneficiaries according to **capitalist values**.

Implementing these **plans** forces **beneficiaries** to behave according to **capitalist norms**.

what we are able to recognize, speak about, and even think is made possible by the language and imagery available to us. Specifically, creating client categories – such as peasants, workers, or the environment – lays the groundwork for programmes that manage these client categories in ways that serve the interests of global capital.

Establishing "truth"

Discourses that are framed as universally valid and supported by powerful institutions – such as universities, the World Bank, and the US Agency for International Development (USAID) – become recognized as "true". In Escobar's words, "much of an institution's effectiveness in producing power relations is the result of practices that are … seen as rational" – and therefore never challenged or even scrutinized. By tracing the historical roots of a discourse, it is possible to uncover the process by which it has come to be accepted as truth. Escobar shows that

development discourse draws heavily on the thinking of European economists; for instance, interventions designed to alleviate hunger and poverty reflect the capitalist values of the experts who create the programmes.

Escobar is fiercely critical of Eurocentric development economics for an unwavering focus on growth; blindness to other forms of economic thought; and an inability to recognize the biases of the scholars who produce that knowledge. He claims that by treating non-capitalist forms of economics as "backwards", development economists present "Third World" people as belonging to a bygone era – which allows them to avoid taking their "beneficiaries" seriously.

Defining peasantry

Between 1975 and 1990, the World Bank sponsored a series of programmes intended to alleviate hunger in Colombia, Escobar's home country. The most important

> Peasant resistance reflects more than the struggle for land and living conditions; it is above all …
> a cultural struggle.
> **Arturo Escobar**

of these programmes was the Integrated Rural Development Program. Escobar argues that while these programmes largely failed to meet their stated objectives, they had – and continue to have – other effects that "contribute to producing and formalizing social relations, divisions of labour, and cultural forms". According to Escobar, these "instrument effects" significantly rearranged Colombian society in ways that did little to alleviate poverty or hunger; instead, they facilitated market expansion and capital accumulation.

Escobar claims that the plans defined "peasants" in purely economic terms as people labouring on land rather than as people trying to live a full and fulfilling life. "Modernizing" these peasants involved providing them with the technologies, credit, and markets necessary to increase the economic value of their production. Anything that fell outside of this

Farmers harvest coca leaves, Colombia's main black-market cash crop. A government programme aiming to replace this illicit cultivation has met with mixed reactions.

modernizing agenda was cast as a backwards tradition that would impede growth and development.

A fully modernized peasantry would consist of market-oriented entrepreneurs – rational economic actors unencumbered by social relations. Implementing this vision spurred a shift to cash crops – that is, crops grown with a view to sell on – and away from traditional food crops, which reduced the amount of food available to sustain the poorest people.

Women and sustainability

Escobar also accuses development discourse of ignoring or hiding the contribution that women make to the rural community and its economy. Instead, women are seen as having a role only in the unpaid, reproductive labour of the household. Since most integrated rural development interventions are intended to improve the economic output of agricultural activities – which are thought of as being the realm of men – women are largely left off the agenda.

Interventions that do target women are framed as "home economics". However – according to Escobar – efforts to include the female population aim "to make

Development anthropology

Anthropologists have a complex relationship with the development industry. During the 1950s and 1960s, they worked alongside development professionals to understand the needs and perspectives of the beneficiaries of development projects. At that time, anthropologists expected development to bring "backwards" or "traditional" people into the modern age. As they began to realize that the recipients did not always see the projects as beneficial to their communities, anthropologists came to criticize development. They began to view non-Western, Indigenous, and "other" people as active subjects in the present world. Now most anthropologists consider "other" ways of understanding and enacting the world not as backwards, traditional, or destined to disappear, but rather as viable alternatives in the face of climate change and human impact on the planet.

women produce and reproduce more efficiently", rather than support their lives as autonomous human beings, and they ignore the ways in which women understand and make meaning in their own lives.

Finally, Escobar criticizes development discourse for seeing the environment as a collection of natural resources to be managed for capitalist expansion through "sustainable development". Ideas about sustainable development, however, presuppose economic growth as a desirable outcome. He argues that this casts poor farmers

as abusers of valuable natural resources, ignoring the inequities produced by global capitalism.

Reframing the present

Escobar's work contributes to an understanding of dependency theory, which sees the relationship between a core of wealthy nations and a periphery of less developed states – and specifically the way in which knowledge, resources, capital, and power flow between them – as the main reason for global inequality. In this context, Escobar argues, European "modernity" is and always has been tied to colonialism: European wealth depends on the impoverishment of the colonial world; European ideas of modernity are based on ideas of the colonized world as backwards; and European ideas of development frame the rest of the world as part of the past.

According to Escobar, the economic and political power of Europe and the West still depends on the ongoing exploitation and subjugation of nations on the periphery – and development discourse is an effective tool for normalizing that subjugation. ∎

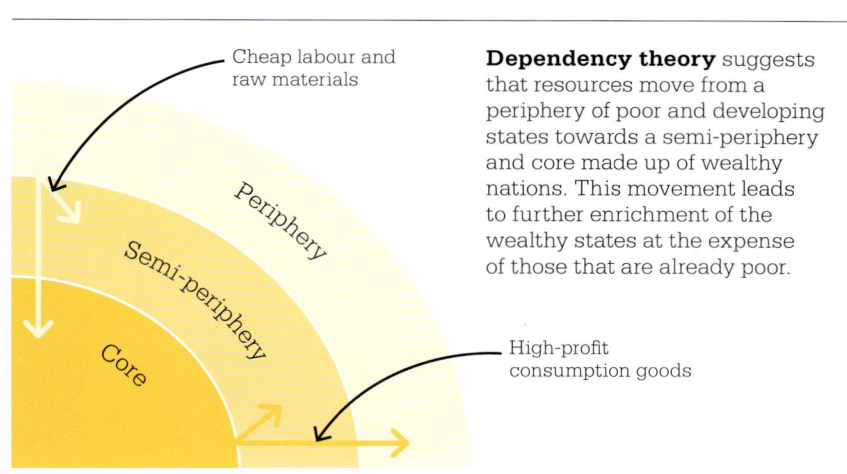

Cheap labour and raw materials

Periphery

Semi-periphery

Core

Dependency theory suggests that resources move from a periphery of poor and developing states towards a semi-periphery and core made up of wealthy nations. This movement leads to further enrichment of the wealthy states at the expense of those that are already poor.

High-profit consumption goods

TRAITS THAT PROVIDE A COMMON SOCIAL IDENTITY

CULTURAL INTIMACY

IN CONTEXT

KEY WORK
Michael Herzfeld, *Cultural Intimacy*, 1996

FIELD
Sociocultural anthropology

BEFORE
1964 British anthropologist John Campbell's writings about nomadic shepherds in the Greek mountains inspire a new generation to study social groups in Europe.

1983 Anglo-Irish anthropologist Benedict Anderson argues that the emergence of mass print culture shaped modern national identities.

AFTER
2020 Herzfeld expands his concept of cultural intimacy to professional communities, including anthropologists. He highlights the responsibilities they hold to those they study.

The concept of "cultural intimacy", proposed by British anthropologist Michael Herzfeld in 1996, rests on the recognition that within a nation there are customs and everyday behaviours that may be a source of embarrassment or derision for outsiders, even as they provide insiders with feelings of social belonging, comfort, and pride. As Herzfeld illustrates, in Italy, the practice of tax evasion is often criticized by outsiders as a sign of a dysfunctional state. Yet for many Italians, it is seen as a form of resistance to an impersonal bureaucracy or even a clever way to "beat the system".

See also: Purity and society 120 ▪ Defining ethnicity 130–31 ▪ Thick description 146–53 ▪ Global capitalism 186–87

State
The governing entity uses stereotypes to create a sense of unity.

People
Citizens reinterpret national stereotypes to assert identity, authenticity, or resistance.

Cultural intimacy is a shared common ground that encompasses potentially embarrassing but unifying traits.

Recognizable stereotypes
Widely understood generalizations about the nation.

Structural nostalgia
A shared longing for an idealized past.

Social poetics
The creative use of shared cultural traits to negotiate identity.

Michael Herzfeld

Born in London, UK, in 1947, Michael Herzfeld studied languages and ancient history at secondary school, and taught himself Italian and Modern Greek. After graduating from Cambridge, he spent a year in Greece researching Greek folklore. He completed his DPhil in Social Anthropology at Oxford based on his ethnographic work in rural Greece.

Herzfeld moved to the US in 1978. He taught at Vassar College, Indiana University, and from 1991–2018 at Harvard University. He held honorary and visiting posts around the world.

Herzfeld's prolific field research in Greece, Italy, and Thailand has resulted in numerous publications that contribute to the honing of anthropological theory and ethnographic methodology, as well as to the anthropology of Europe; masculinity studies; heritage studies; and the anthropology of the contemporary nation-state.

Other key works

1985 *The Poetics of Manhood*
1987 *Anthropology Through the Looking-Glass*

Before the 1990s, few anthropologists chose to study communities in Europe, and most did not engage with the nation-state, regarding it as a disruptive force that could be dismissed from their studies of everyday life. In questioning this approach, Herzfeld identified a broader problem – the Western logic that portrays states and nations as stable and impenetrable entities that are categorically different from their constituents.

According to Herzfeld, this way of thinking stemmed from a human tendency to see the world in binary terms. This was reinforced by "essentialization" – reducing diversity to a few core traits – and

"reification" – turning fluid concepts into fixed, permanent realities. Constant repetition of this combination of logic and rhetoric in forms such as architecture, laws, literature, popular entertainment, and everyday conversations, created the perception of a unified and timeless people, bound together by customs, language, and traditions that define the nation-state.

The state and the people

Herzfeld set out to study nation-states and nationalism as integral aspects of social life. He studied the phrases used to refer to "the state" and "the people" – two distinct kinds of entities often at odds with each »

Members of a Greek-American community in California smash plates during a celebration – a tradition that reinforces cultural identity through a familiar act of symbolic excess.

Identity in motion

Herzfeld argued that cultural intimacy is never rigid. People often use the same familiar stereotypes in different contexts to say different things. Through "social poetics" – the view that social life may be a continual process in which acknowledging a few shared traits can work in various ways – cultural intimacy can be expressed to mock pretentiousness or assert authenticity; to demonstrate social unity or signal distinction and resistance.

According to Herzfeld, elites, politicians, and bureaucrats often use unflattering stereotypes to advance the state's agendas, even as they mock or scorn the very citizens that they represent. Ordinary people, however, may turn the same stereotype on its head in their social poetics – to demonstrate, for example, that officials in the supposedly just state undermine national unity by accepting bribes and favouring certain groups over others.

National stereotypes, although often embarrassing, are powerful because they resonate across social levels. Herzfeld's concept of cultural

other. Surprisingly, he found that representatives of each group use the same essentializing rhetoric and reifying worldview to describe who they are and to distinguish themselves from others.

Herzfeld discovered that even as citizens and states affirm that they are two different kinds of entities, they easily communicate, intersect, and overlap with each other. These interactions are possible because they share common ground. It is this common ground of established but potentially embarrassing customs and behaviours that Herzfeld calls "cultural intimacy".

Rural chapels, where villagers can invoke saints as witnesses to binding agreements, are often chosen as venues for oath-swearing rituals.

Oath-taking ceremonies

Traits highlighted as the essence of "national character" often derive from communities in remote areas. Herzfeld's fieldwork among shepherds in mountainous regions of Crete revealed the complex social dynamics behind animal theft. Often fuelled by a desire to gain recognition, or to take revenge, the process involves many acts of social poetics, which may or may not involve the state.

Shepherds resolve disputes with other shepherds and the state through oath-taking – a form of social poetics where they swear their innocence before a priest, religious icon, or even in secular courts. Such public rituals not only serve as moral and legal statements but also reaffirm bonds of kinship and faith.

These practices echo Greek ideals of masculinity – protecting the family, providing livelihoods, and avenging wrongs – while asserting honour, divine authority, and communal freedom.

> Nation-state ideologies tend to divide the world into Manichaean pairs… But people's actual use of that rhetoric may be subversive.
> **Michael Herzfeld**

intimacy provides anthropologists with a valuable framework for understanding how social identities are constructed, contested, and reinforced within the nation-state.

Structural nostalgia

Herzfeld's concept of "structural nostalgia" refers to the use of myths and collective memories to contrast the present with an idealized past – it often expresses a desire to restore certain aspects of that past. As with national stereotypes, structural nostalgia is a versatile rhetorical tool. It can affirm unity, sharpen divisions, or create a complex mix of both.

Herzfeld traces the roots of this concept to the biblical story of the Fall in the *Book of Genesis*, where the expulsion of Adam and Eve from the Garden of Eden explains why humanity is fated to toil in an imperfect world. However, at the same time, the Bible offers a message of hope through the possibility of redemption.

States often use structural nostalgia to justify their authority, claiming they prevent chaos and create order. However, citizens, especially those in marginalized communities, may reinterpret

this narrative. They might idealize a time before state-imposed restrictions, taxes, and bureaucracy, framing their actions as resistance to unjust demands.

The shared rhetoric of structural nostalgia creates the cultural intimacy that enables government officials and citizens to engage in a dynamic exchange. As Herzfeld observes, everyone recognizes that greedy officials take bribes to favour powerful patrons, just as tales of virtuous tax evaders who claim their illegal acts are responses to unjust state demands resonate widely. Through these arguments, both the state and its citizens are revealed as fluid and contested, rather than solid or homogeneous entities.

The middle ground

According to Herzfeld, an effective study of nationalism and a nation-state requires anthropologists to avoid "static truths" and examine how the state works from every angle. This means creating a broad ethnography that is neither strictly top-down nor bottom-up. Anthropologists should delve into how stereotypes are used and manipulated by all segments of

the population – from the declarations, policies, and rituals of state elites to the everyday actions of ordinary citizens and marginal groups. They must explore the middle ground of ambiguity in these interactions and rhetoric.

The concept of cultural intimacy recognizes "that essentialism and agency are two sides of the same coin, as are state and people". By mapping the common ground of cultural intimacy, examining the complex relationships between a government and its people, and demonstrating how state authorities and citizens interpret the social poetics that they perform and witness, Herzfeld's concept of cultural intimacy delivers both a theory and a method. These tools allow anthropologists to penetrate, engage with, and disrupt ideas about seemingly opaque nation-states that once kept anthropologists beyond the pale. ∎

A stained-glass window shows Adam and Eve's expulsion from Eden – a founding myth of loss and redemption. Herzfeld suggests the myth underpins structural nostalgia in the Western imagination.

EVERYTHING WE KNOW IS UP FOR GRABS

TRANSITOLOGY

IN CONTEXT

KEY WORK
Katherine Verdery,
What was Socialism, and
***What Comes Next?*, 1996**

FIELD
Sociocultural anthropology

BEFORE
1980 János Kornai concludes that socialist economies are inherently prone to chronic shortages.

1989 The Berlin Wall falls, marking the beginning of the end of socialism in Eastern Europe.

AFTER
2004–13 The European Union expands eastwards, incorporating many former socialist countries.

2006 Alexei Yurchak publishes *Everything Was Forever, Until It Was No More*, a book that explores the nature of Soviet socialism and its collapse.

When I use the word "transition", then, I put it in quotes so as to mock the naivete of so much fashionable transitology.
Katherine Verdery

The collapse of socialism in Central and Eastern Europe and the Soviet Union was a dramatic process that transformed the political and economic landscape of the region and, indeed, the world. For many observers at the time, the fall of the Berlin Wall in 1989 and end of the Soviet Union in 1991 signified not just the disintegration of an empire and its ideology, but also the global reordering of Cold War geopolitics. US political scientist Francis Fukuyama described this period as "the end of history"; he suggested that with the disappearance of its main competitor, liberalism had emerged as the only viable ideology, and capitalism the only possible economic structure.

In the early 1990s, the term "transition" became the most common way to describe the political, economic, and cultural changes that were sweeping across the region. "Transitology" was a concept developed by policymakers, with guidance

The fall of the Berlin Wall in 1989 became a dramatic symbol of the end of socialism. The period after offered opportunities to some but devastating social consequences for others.

from economists and political scientists, that suggested countries had no choice other than to adopt Western-style democracy and capitalism. Chief among the policies advocated by transitology were democratization, marketization, and privatization – all of which, it was assumed, would lead to the same "textbook capitalism", regardless of the local contexts and histories. At its most dramatic, transition took the form of "shock therapy" – a swift and aggressive dismantling of key socialist institutions, especially economic ones, that exacted a heavy social price.

Criticizing transition
Anthropologists were sharply critical the concept of transitology. During the Cold War, their research typically focused on the cultures and societies

What is the definition of socialism? The longest and most painful route from capitalism to capitalism.
Katherine Verdery

of post-colonial regions. However, with the end of socialism, scholars – such as US anthropologist Katherine Verdery and Russian-American Soviet specialist Alexei Yurchak – began to study the former socialist countries. They found that the dominant narratives surrounding these nations' transitions were heavily shaped by economists and political scientists promoting rapid Westernization. To remain relevant, anthropologists had to demonstrate the importance of their discipline – with its emphasis on culture and society – to understanding how these societies were changing.

From the start, anthropologists challenged the assumptions of transition models, arguing that they presented a simplistic view of history. These models, they claimed, assumed a predetermined path with a clear beginning (socialism), a definitive end (capitalism), and a sharp break between the two. That socialism should inescapably give way to capitalism was by no means a certainty. For anthropology, the end of history was not yet written.

Moreover, anthropologists argued that the simplified portrayal of socialism within transition models was also flawed: socialism had many forms and local variations. It was not to be summarily dismissed as unsalvageable "communism" or "totalitarianism", they insisted.

The idea that socialism could be eradicated through "shock therapy" struck anthropologists as overly simplistic and naive at best. They believed this approach ignored the complexities of historical change, which is always shaped by the legacies of the past.

Understanding the past

One of the most articulate critics of the transition model was the Katherine Verdery. In the early 1990s, she influenced academic discussion, arguing that "transformation", rather than "transition", was the better way to understand the changes unfolding in former socialist countries. Transformation, Verdery argued, was an open-ended process that embraced uncertainty and focused on local contexts and everyday lives, instead of grand, overarching theories. Her approach recognized the potential for diverse, hybrid systems to emerge, rather than a uniform, "textbook" version of capitalism.

Verdery's concept of transformation was bolstered by her ambitious theory of socialism, which drew inspiration from both Western Marxist thought and the work of Eastern European intellectuals such as economist János Kornai and sociologist Iván Szelényi – both from Hungary – and the Romanian sociologist Pavel Câmpeanu. In *What was Socialism, and What Comes Next?* Verdery offered a nuanced and detailed account of the region's recent past through her discussion of socialism and its demise.

Verdery's work focused on "actually existing socialism" – the system of socialism implemented in Eastern Europe and the Soviet Union during the Cold War. Rather than analysing the era through Marxist ideals, Verdery »

Hypernormalization

Russian-American anthropologist Alexei Yurchak introduced the term "hypernormalization" in the early 2000s to describe a key paradox of late socialism. Although the Soviet system was widely seen as dysfunctional, its rituals and official language continued to be strictly observed.

People took part in official life not because they believed in it, but because there seemed to be no other option. In this way, the system was so normal that it had become "hypernormal". Yurchak's idea helps to explain how the collapse of socialism felt both sudden and inevitable.

Like Verdery, Yurchak rejected overly simplistic models of transition. He demonstrated that even as regimes crumbled, people navigated their lives through continuity, improvization, and quiet forms of adaptation that carried on into the postsocialist period. Both scholars emphasised the messiness of lived experience and the persistence of habits in times of upheaval.

Economic change
Privatization, marketization, deindustrialization, informal economies

Migration and mobility
Labour migration, depopulation of rural areas, transnational networks

Postsocialism is an ongoing transformation shaped by local histories and uncertain futures.

Political change
Rise of nationalism, populism, new authoritarianism, "civil society"

Social stratification
Emergence of new elites, precarity, working-class dispossession

Memory and nostalgia
Socialist-era values, objects, and spaces reinterpreted in the present

examined the lived realities of these socialist systems. She highlighted the emphasis on production over consumption, the role of redistribution and social welfare programs, and the pervasive influence of centralized planning and bureaucracy. Most significantly, Verdery identified chronic shortages as a defining feature of these economies, which fundamentally shaped daily life and forced citizens to develop informal survival strategies. While acknowledging the influence of socialist ideology, Verdery emphasized the gap between official rhetoric and lived experience, highlighting the diverse, often contradictory ways in which individuals navigated these systems.

The postsocialist approach

Verdery's critique of the "transition" model paved the way for a new understanding of the post-communist era, often referred to as "postsocialism." Although it came to be widely used as a way to define a specific historical period, Verdery saw postsocialism as more than just a chronological label. She used it as a "critical standpoint" from which to assess past, present, and future of the region but also to deconstruct

Crowds gather in Moscow for the opening of the USSR's first McDonald's fast-food restaurant in 1990. Capitalism offered choice and abundance – but only for those who could afford it.

Western assumptions that dominated Cold War thinking. Postsocialism, therefore, provided an opportunity for anthropologists to question the meaning and validity of key terms such as "market" or "private property", and, ultimately, "capitalism" and "democracy". For Verdery, it represented a global phenomenon relevant not only to Eastern Europe but also to the socialist experiments in Africa and Asia, and even the potential for a socialist politics in the West.

A defining feature of postsocialist anthropology was its attention to both ethnographic detail and the broader context of regional and global transformations. At first, research concentrated on how the rules and structures of socialism played out in people's everyday lives. For example, studying what people bought and consumed became a key way to understand the long-term effects of socialist economies that had been marked by shortage. By the early 2000s, studying consumption also became a way to understand people's memories of socialism, and even their nostalgia for it.

Social costs of transition

In the early 1990s, sweeping privatization and decollectivization – the dismantling of state farms and redistribution of land – completely reshaped how people worked and owned property across Eastern Europe. These transitional policies produced devastating social consequences: poverty, hunger, and the erosion of social networks. Such deprivation fundamentally reshaped political consciousness, making people increasingly receptive to authoritarian solutions.

Class divisions re-emerged with intensity. On one side stood those chasing the dream of middle-class stability. On the other was the dispossessed working class who found expression in populist movements and nationalist rhetoric that prefigured the rise of the far right in the 2010s and 2020s.

Women bore some of the heaviest costs of transition. Under socialism, they had achieved formal workplace equality and were promoted to prominent public roles, even as they faced persistent sexism. After 1989, the elimination of social protections, such as free childcare and

A 1960s poster glorifies Soviet cosmonaut Valentina Tereshkova, the first woman in space. Three decades later, women once celebrated for their role as workers were being told that their place was back in the home.

guaranteed employment, pushed many women into informal work, or caused them to retreat into domestic life. As Verdery noted, the "reprivatization" of women's labour – framed as a return to "natural" gender roles – became a tool for legitimizing capitalist transition.

The social upheaval forced people to repurpose old survival strategies for new crises, "making-do" and "getting-by" as they had under socialism – but now without its guarantees. As US anthropologist Melissa Caldwell's research showed in 1990s Moscow, the same informal networks that once navigated shortages now patched holes in the collapsing welfare state. What began as temporary adaptations became permanent fixtures of life after socialism, revealing transition not as a bridge to prosperity, but as a long reckoning with loss. ∎

Post-socialist migration

The collapse of state socialism triggered a wave of migration across Europe and Eurasia. Soaring unemployment and economic instability drove millions to seek work abroad – Polish labourers to the UK, Romanian caregivers to Italy, and Uzbek workers to Moscow's markets.

Scholars such as British anthropologist Caroline Humphrey studied how migrants navigated cultural dislocation, as Soviet-era collectivist identities clashed with capitalist individualism. British sociologist Michael Burawoy analysed their role in global capitalism, noting how low-wage postsocialist labour sustained Western Europe's service sectors.

These flows reshaped societies: remittances became lifelines for households, while rural regions depopulated. Migration remains a defining legacy of socialism's fall – a story of survival amid systemic rupture.

Romanian workers harvest grapes at an English vineyard. Since the fall of state socialism, the movement of labour from Eastern to Western Europe has reshaped economies.

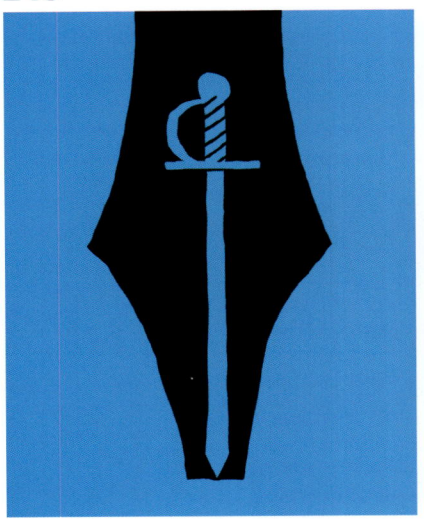

THE PEN IS A DOUBLE-EDGED SWORD
ACADEMIC DISIDENTIFICATION

IN CONTEXT

KEY WORK
**Signithia Fordham,
Blacked Out, 1996**

FIELD
Sociocultural anthropology

BEFORE
1924 W.E.B. Du Bois compiles
the contributions of Black
people to the US. He argues
that Black people are as
capable as any other people,
but are hindered by society.

1974 Nigerian-American
anthropologist John Ogbu
publishes *The Next
Generation*, in which he
explores the reasons why some
children from minority ethnic
groups struggle to succeed
in academic systems.

AFTER
2000 Signithia Fordham
publishes "Why Can't Sonya
(and Kwame) Fail Math?",
which looks at how race
and gender can affect
academic performance.

Drawing on research interests in race, gender, and identity politics, US anthropologist Signithia Fordham conducted a ground-breaking ethnography exploring the social dynamics of race, achievement, and identity among African American high school students – looking in particular at how race affected educational performance.

Fordham places the identity struggles of Black students in the context of the US Civil Rights movement of the 1950s and 1960s, which resulted in the racial desegregation of schools.

Based on extensive ethnographic research at a predominantly Black urban high school in Washington, D.C., US – referred to in the research as Capital High – Fordham provided a nuanced exploration of how race, identity, and educational success intersect in complex ways. Fordham's concept of academic disidentification – the separation of identity from academic value or success – emerged from her observations of African American students who deliberately underperformed or resisted their own academic success to avoid being seen as "acting white".

Protecting racial identity
Fordham observed that such disidentification served as a survival strategy for the students to maintain racial authenticity and group solidarity as they navigated the pressures between academic achievement and maintaining a sense of their own identity.

Large-scale structural racism, Fordham argues, was behind the operating ideology of schools. She noted that curricula and school programmes had been set without factoring in the existing culture of students from African American

See also: Fighting racial segregation 30–31 ▪ Cultural intimacy 230–33 ▪ Accents, dialects, and code-switching 244–45 ▪ Critical ethnography 270–71

or other marginalized backgrounds. The result of this was that the educational system of Capital High was organized in ways that many Black students found alienating and hostile.

In her detailed interviews with students, Fordham found that some presented resistance to educational achievement, which Fordham rationalized as "their fear of being consumed by both the norms and values of (an) Other and by (an) Other that historically appropriated Black humanness". Fordham argued that by resisting the norms of educational systems and academic success, the students show agency, and push against the dominant culture of an education system that was created to serve white students.

In this way, academic achievement could be viewed as a form of cultural betrayal. Fordham suggested that because of this sense of disloyalty, existing peer dynamics and social expectations within the Black student community may have discouraged

Academic success is associated with **whiteness.**

Black students may feel **"other"** in academic spaces because of its **perceived whiteness.**

Participating and succeeding in such a white space can be seen as **"acting white"**.

academic achievement and affected how these students formed their academic identities.

Multifaceted identity

Although Fordham's work predates the widespread use of the term "intersectionality", she examined how identities of race, gender, and class interacted and influenced each other within an educational setting. Her ethnographic work provided evidence for the systemic barriers to academic success for students from Black and ethnic minority backgrounds in the US, and gave an explanation for why academic disidentification persists. Fordham also advocated for researchers to focus on the conscious and complex strategies that students develop in order to deal with institutional and community pressures. ▪

Intersectionality

The concept of intersectionality – the understanding that different identities meet to produce an individual lived experience – has brought attention to the nuances of personal identities and encouraged anthropologists to move beyond reductive descriptions of social dynamics. By acknowledging intersectionality in research, anthropologists gain a dynamic understanding of complex identities and reveal how power, privilege, and marginalization operate across different social contexts. Intersectionality also offers a theoretical framework for understanding human experience, requiring ethnographic research to be holistic and comprehensive. Expecting identities to have intersectional qualities promotes the understanding of how identities are constructed and experienced, while highlighting how power structures shape experiences. In this way, anthropologists can prevent an oversimplification of cultural practices and social interactions.

The Pride flag, which represents LGBTQ+ identities, was updated in 2018 to acknowledge intersectional identities such as race and gender.

THE MIND AS A CATHEDRAL

COGNITIVE FLUIDITY

IN CONTEXT

KEY WORK
Steven Mithen, *The Prehistory of the Mind*, 1996

FIELD
Biological anthropology

BEFORE
1970 Austrian-American neurobiologist Eric Kandel establishes that higher brain functions, such as memory and learning, are associated with physical processes in the brain.

1983 In *The Modularity of Mind*, US philosopher Jerry Fodor suggests that the brain is composed of neural structures with distinct functions.

AFTER
2023 A European initiative known as the "10-year Human Brain Project" publishes a comprehensive atlas of the brain that defines the shape and location of brain regions.

By the 1970s, much was understood about the physiology of the human brain, but questions remained about how it had evolved to be so advanced. It was generally accepted that the brain is made up of different neural structures, each with a distinct function. These had evolved by natural selection to guide a variety of behaviours, such as competing, cooperating, or remembering a route to search for food. In 1983, US cognitive psychologist Howard Gardner used the analogy of a Swiss army knife to describe the brain as a single unit that contains several different tools to perform different functions. For British archaeologist Steven Mithen, the critical step in the evolution of the modern human brain was the switch from a mind "designed like a Swiss army knife to one with cognitive fluidity".

Cathedral of many parts

In his 1996 book *The Prehistory of the Mind*, Mithen uses the analogy of a cathedral to describe the development of the human brain. The foundations are general

Mithen argues that early human minds would have been unable to put natural and social intelligence together to make a joke about an animal going to a bar to order a drink.

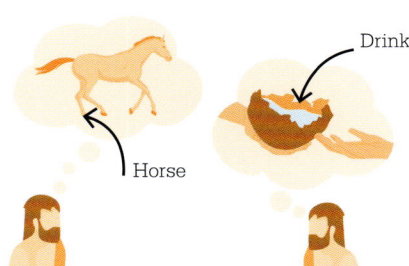

Horse buys a drink

Drink

Horse

Natural history intelligence
allowed early humans to think about an animal.

Social intelligence
enabled early humans to understand social transactions.

Cognitive fluidity
means modern humans can put ideas together for a purpose, such as being funny.

See also: The rules of language 109 ▪ The New Archaeology 110–15 ▪ The agricultural theory of language diffusion 210–11

Creative collaboration

In his 2017 book *The Creative Spark*, US anthropologist Agustín Fuentes describes collaboration and creativity as being central to the evolution of human culture – and there is much evidence to support this view. A team of Spanish archaeologists investigated Upper Palaeozoic cave art in Europe and found that 56 caves contained a total of 769 hand motifs. By comparing the hand motifs from five of the caves with a modern reference population, they were able to assign the Palaeolithic hand motifs to specific age groups, and found that all age ranges were represented. At Fuente del Salín, Cantabria, for example, 27 per cent of the motifs had been made by children under the age of 7, and a further 9 per cent by those aged 7 to 12 years. These findings, and the wide range of footprints that cover the cave floor, clearly indicate that art was a collaborative activity 35,000 to 40,000 years ago.

The cave art in Cueva de las Manos, Argentina, shows clear expressions of culture, depicting hunting scenes and abstract art as well as hand motifs.

intelligence, something all apes have to a high degree, with the facility to learn and solve problems. Built upon these foundations are cognitive specializations, with different domains responsible for social, natural, technical, and – later – linguistic intelligence. In early human minds, each domain acted independently and could be likened to chapels built around the sides of a cathedral. Mithen explains the mind's evolution as an increasing level of interaction between these domains. He argues that language was restricted initially to the social domain, and used to regulate social interactions. However, gradually, snippets of language began to flow into the other domains, which enabled humans to talk about other things. Individuals who learned from this new information had an advantage, because they became better at making informed decisions about toolmaking, hunting, and providing care for offspring, for example.

Cultural explosion

Natural selection accelerated neurological changes within the brain, and increasing interaction between the domains meant that people began to bring different types of information together into a single idea. According to Mithen, it was this cognitive fluidity that produced a creative and cultural explosion between 60,000 and 30,000 years ago, that enabled people to build boats that crossed the Pacific, create cave art, design complex tools, and believe in religious ideologies.

Although Mithen's idea – that an understanding of cultural advances may provide insights into the brain's evolution – gained much publicity, critics argued that it is hard to draw neurological conclusions from the available archaeological evidence: archaeologists have, for example, shown that Neanderthals also created cave art. ▪

Studying how the stone tools produced by prehistoric humans evolved helps anthropologists and archaeologists to understand the development of technical intelligence.

There was a cultural explosion in the fourth and final act of our past.
Steven Mithen

CONSTRUCTS THAT CLASSIFY PEOPLE
ACCENTS, DIALECTS, AND CODE-SWITCHING

IN CONTEXT

KEY WORK
Bonnie Urciuoli, *Exposing Prejudice*, 1997

FIELD
Linguistic anthropology

BEFORE
1956 US linguist Einar Haugen coins the term "code-switching" to describe the "language alternation" process.

1980 US linguist Shana Poplack writes about code-switching in her influential paper "Sometimes I'll Start a Sentence in Spanish y Termino en Español".

AFTER
2015 US comedians Keegan-Michael Key and Jordan Peele create the character Luther, President Obama's anger translator, who reinterprets the president's placid statements.

2019 US professor Myles Durkee's research explores the costs of code-switching for cultural minorities.

The way in which people speak can influence communication and social status just as much as what people actually say. In her book *Exposing Prejudice*, US linguistic anthropologist Bonnie Urciuoli explores this subject and the concept of code-switching in the context of Puerto Rican communities in New York.

Protesters taking part in New York's annual Puerto Rican Day Parade carry signs that make their point in both English and Spanish.

Code-switching refers to the practice of alternating between different language varieties or dialects, often within the same conversation or interaction. Urciuoli focuses on how the language varieties used by her research participants intersect with larger social identities, including race and social class.

High and low language
Most languages are subject to a phenomenon known as diglossia, which means that there are "high" and "low" varieties. The high

See also: The structure of language 44–45 ▪ Language and cognition 88–89 ▪ English vernacular 116–19 ▪ Ritual and language 166 ▪ The role of African American Vernacular English 254–55

Code-switching is dancing between vocal styles and rhythms. This dance is part celebration – of the richness, intricacies, and blurry borders of our cultures.
Bonnie Urciuoli

variety refers to the register that is spoken in formal settings, such as a courtroom, or a classroom, or written in books. Low varieties include the vernacular that is used in day-to-day speech patterns and to communicate informally with family and friends. People choose the high or low variety depending on who they are speaking with, and what they are attempting to convey about themselves.

In addition, entire languages are valued in different ways in different cultural contexts. Although most Puerto Ricans speak some English, many rate their English abilities as "poor" or "bad". When Puerto Ricans move to New York, they frequently become linguistically and economically segregated, and they find that the employment opportunities available to them are few and poorly rewarded.

Urciuoli notes that within this context, Puerto Ricans in New York strategically use both English and Spanish. Her research indicates that code-switching is not simply a linguistic phenomenon, but

something that reflects the complex social and cultural practices that shape people's identities. Central to Urciuoli's analysis is the idea that language serves as a symbolic resource that Puerto Ricans use to negotiate their social positioning and assert their cultural identities. She suggests that code-switching is not a random or arbitrary linguistic behaviour, but something that people deliberately choose to do in order to navigate social hierarchies, express identity or affiliations, or assert belonging in social groups.

Dynamic identities

Urciuoli describes how, depending on the context, audience, or situation, people might code-switch between Spanish and

English. In the inner sphere of New York's Puerto Rican community, an individual's use of Spanish often expresses solidarity with their ethnic and cultural roots, and it reinforces a sense of belonging and identity within the community. Conversely, outside of their own community, Puerto Rican people might choose to switch to English, rather than speaking Spanish, to navigate what may otherwise be an unbalanced relationship between the speakers.

This alternation between languages allows individuals to dynamically express their identities and assert their Puerto Rican heritage while also adapting to the linguistic demands of diverse social contexts. ▪

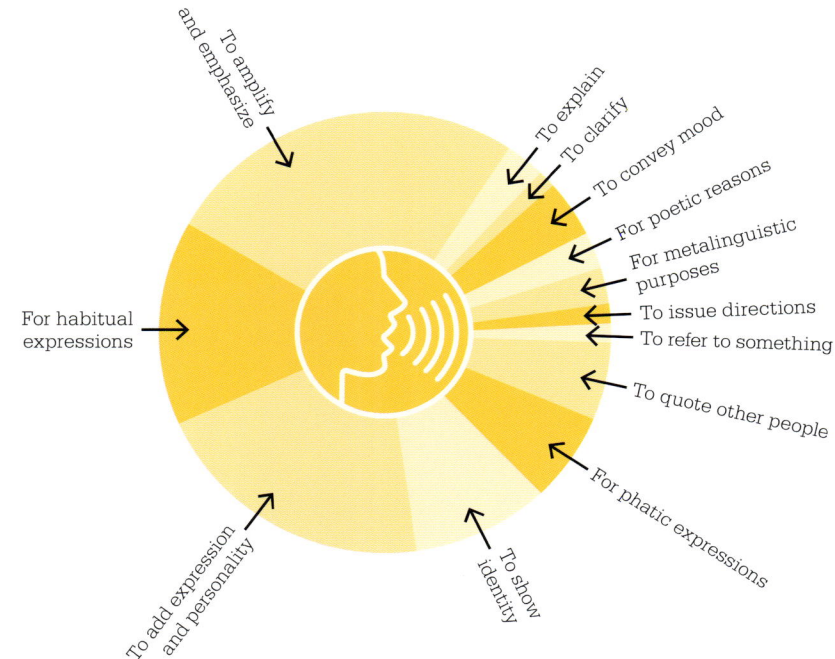

There are many reasons for code-switching – from the desire to indicate solidarity with an interlocutor, to the need to cultivate social relationships via simple interactions (phatic expressions), such as polite greetings and small talk.

YOUR WORLD HAS A CENTRE YOU CARRY WITH YOU
TRANSCULTURAL PREDICAMENTS

IN CONTEXT

KEY WORK
James Clifford, *Routes*, 1997

FIELD
Sociocultural anthropology

BEFORE
1922 Bronisław Malinowski and A.R. Radcliffe-Brown publish key works that set precedents for social anthropological analysis and ethnographic writing.

1988 James Clifford's *The Predicament of Culture* examines the power dynamics and interpretative challenges faced by anthropologists and cultural critics in a postcolonial world.

AFTER
2004 *The Cultural Politics of Emotion* by Sara Ahmed examines how emotions shape cultural politics. It builds on Clifford's insights into the interplay between translation, travel, and cultural experience.

As world cultures became increasingly interconnected at the end of the 20th century, US sociocultural anthropologist and theorist James Clifford examined the relationship between ethnography and cultural representation by exploring the concepts of travel and translating, particularly in the context of displaying cultures in museums.

Bustling markets are dynamic spaces where different cultures meet and interact. Spaces like these make travellers and translators of everyone who visits them.

His text is intended to encourage both ethnographers and travellers alike to appreciate how the movements of people, ideas, and commodities contribute to cultural hybridity and fluid identities.

Moveable roots

The central orienting idea in *Routes: Travel and Translation in the Late 20th Century* is the metaphor of routes versus roots. Clifford looks at how, in traditional ethnography, the anthropologist is rooted in the location. The anthropologist arrives at the far-flung, relatively isolated community

See also: Anthropology at home 170–71 ▪ Museum anthropology 220–25
▪ The ethics of anthropology 248–49 ▪ Citizenship and belonging 278–79

The meaning of hand signals and gestures can vary greatly between cultures. Travellers are often warned that some innocuous hand gesture may have a negative meaning and cause offence when used in other countries. Even if the gesture is inoffensive, it might not convey the intended information.

Italy
What exactly do you mean?

Greece
That's just perfect

Egypt
Be patient

and embeds themself in day-to-day life to understand how the "native" people view their worlds.

However, Clifford suggests that anthropologists should also look at "routes" as sites of cultural contact as well. He encourages anthropologists to consider cultural contact in dynamic spaces where the local and global intersect, and view cultural insiders as a "traveller and translator" of cultural difference. Clifford also states that anthropologists ought to look at travelling cultures as well as settled ones, for instance in contexts such as tourism, war, and trade. He

When borders gain a paradoxical centrality, margins, edges, and lines of communication emerge as complex maps and histories.
James Clifford

argues that anthropologists should not just seek to understand people who belong to cultures that travel: they should also look at traveller cultures, and the lives of people who define themselves as being on the move and mediate their identity in relation to others.

Importance of translation

Clifford also examines the way in which different cultures are depicted and translated – or interpreted – by museums. He critiques the traditional Western model that presents cultural groups as static or having existed in a pristine form only in the past. Displays in these museums are often problematic: typically, they view cultures from a single – usually colonial – perspective that tends to highlight the ways in which that culture was irrevocably changed as a result of colonial contact. Clifford contrasts this with museum models that successfully portray change itself as "authentic" culture, as well as those that give a degree of agency to the people who are depicted in the exhibit.

Clifford's use of the concept of translation extends beyond the linguistic definition and

Flexible citizenship

The concept of citizenship usually evokes the idea of legal belonging to a single geographically bound country. However, in *Flexible Citizenship: The Cultural Logics of Transnationality* (1999) Aihwa Ong explores citizenship in the context of globalization. Ong argues that traditional understandings of citizenship are inadequate when people, goods, and capital travel across borders frequently and with ease.

Ong's central idea is "flexible citizenship", which refers to the distinctive ways in which individuals navigate their increasingly globalized world and capitalize on the economic opportunities it offers by maintaining ties to multiple countries. Ong argues that "in the era of globalization, individuals as well as governments develop a flexible notion of citizenship and sovereignty as strategies to accumulate power and capital". In this way, Ong describes how individuals have agency in navigating their lives and play a direct role in reshaping the meanings and practices of citizenship.

encompasses cultural translation – defined as the process by which meanings and practices are interpreted and adapted across cultural boundaries.

Importantly Clifford's analysis demonstrates how travel and translation are intertwined with globalization and diaspora. This in turn, he argues, challenges conventional notions of fixed cultural boundaries and identities of modernity. ■

DO NO HARM
THE ETHICS OF ANTHROPOLOGY

Franz Boas, the father of American anthropology, sought to establish a distinct school of anthropology that diverged from European traditions. Alongside notable students such as Margaret Mead, Ruth Benedict, Zora Neale Hurston, Alfred Kroeber, and Edward Sapir, Boas prioritized cultural relativism – understanding others' beliefs and practices within their cultural context without judgment – and rigorous research methodologies. In particular, his own research worked to counter the scientific racism prevalent in the early 20th century and reject the hierarchical categorization of societies based on evolutionary stages. However, the work of early anthropologists was not immune to ethical and moral problems.

Early history

In its early stages, anthropology was intertwined with colonialism and imperialism. Research was often conducted among Indigenous people without meaningful collaboration or consent. Some early anthropological studies contributed to the stigmatization

Cultural bias and kinship

In the second half of the 20th century, anthropologists began to critique the way in which they studied and interpreted ideas around families and kinship. They were concerned that Western anthropologists often projected their own cultural biases onto the societies they studied, and used Western-derived frameworks to categorize non-Western groups from around the world in their attempts to understand them.

Anthropologist David Schneider's work was particularly persuasive in arguing against the use of Western cultural norms and categories as universal standards for understanding societies. His influential book, *American Kinship: A Cultural Account* (1968), examined the extent to which anthropological theories had been shaped by Western ideologies. Coining the concept "kinship as a cultural system", he emphasized that kinship practices and meanings are socially constructed and vary enormously across cultures.

See also: "The noble savage" 23 ▪ Origins of culture 32–33 ▪ Cultural relativism 34–41 ▪ Autoethnography 76–77

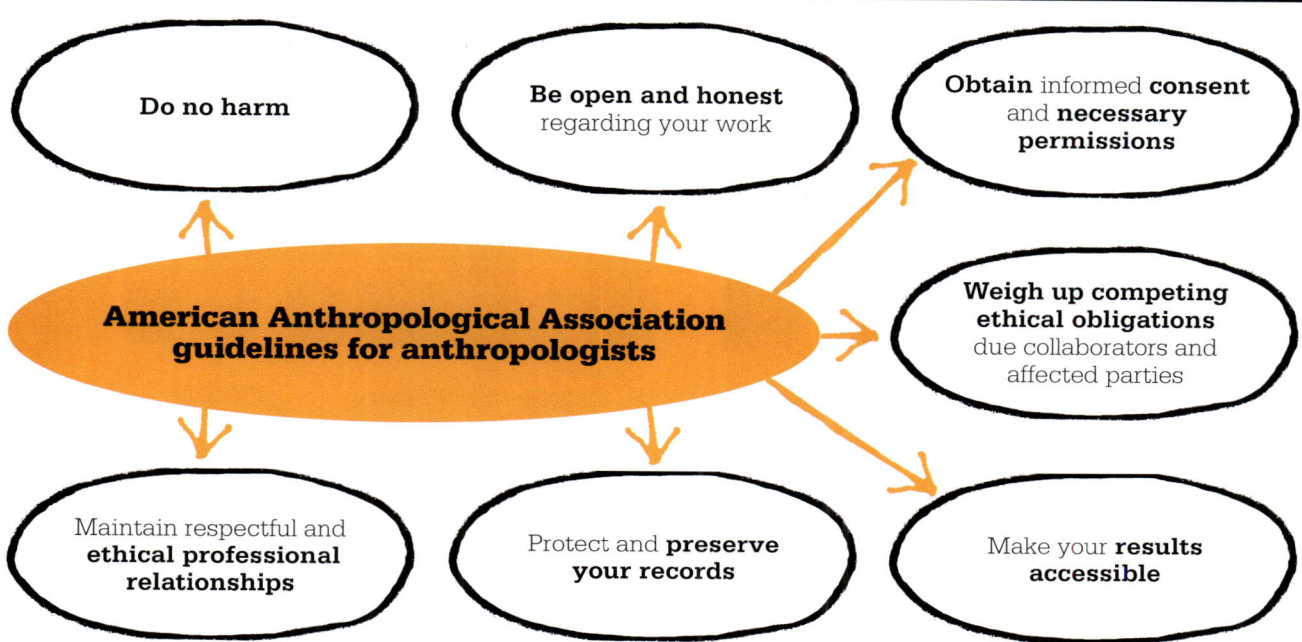

and exploitation of studied communities – and in some instances, research findings were used to justify discriminatory policies, perpetuate stereotypes, and even to inform government military operations.

As anthropology evolved and changed, the nature of ethical problems also shifted, but did not disappear. Towards the end of the 20th century, a series of ethical scandals rocked US anthropology. The most well known scandal involved anthropologist Napoleon Chagnon and his work among the Yanomama (or Yanomami) in South America from the 1960s to the 1980s. Chagnon's work depicted the Yanomama as a violent and aggressive society. Critics at the time argued that Chagnon intentionally shaped and exaggerated his findings to sensationalize his results. The

scandal reignited in 2000 with the publication of investigative journalist Patrick Tierney's book *Darkness in El Dorado*, which accused Chagnon and his team of a number of ethical and human rights violations, including exacerbating violence, sexual exploitation, and spreading disease among the Yanomama.

Code of conduct

The intense pressure created by the Chagnon and other ethics scandals led the American Anthropological Association (AAA) – the preeminent association for professional anthropologists in the US – to develop a set of ethical standards. The code of ethics, which was published in 1998 as the *Principles of Professional Responsibility*, required all anthropologists practising in the US to abide by its standards. By adhering to these

principles, anthropologists strive to contribute to the ethical practice of anthropology and to develop positive relationships with their research participants, the communities that they study, and the broader public. ▪

The behavior of an individual is determined not by his racial affiliation, but by the character of his ancestry and his cultural environment
Franz Boas
Race and Democratic Society, 1945

CONTEMP
ANTHROP
2000 ONWARDS

ORARY
OLOGY

John and Russell Rickford explore the rules and attitudes to **African American Vernacular English**.

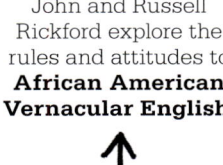

2000

2002

Faye Ginsburg shows how **marginalized communities "talk back"** using different forms of **media**.

David Lewis Williams suggests that **cave art** may have a **ritual** and **symbolic significance**.

2002

2005

Soyini Maddison encourages the use of critical ethnography to address **inequality** and **injustice**.

Veena Das examines how **victims** of **trauma** use the patterns of everyday life to **rebuild their lives**.

2006

2008

Ruth Mandel debates whether **citizenship** gives **migrants** a sense of **belonging**.

T he 21st century has brought unprecedented global challenges – from the social costs of climate change and growing inequality to the politics of identity and the digital revolution. As a result, anthropology has grown more interdisciplinary, experimental, and globally engaged than ever before, as scholars explore new methods to confront some of the most urgent issues of our time. Alongside this, archaeological discoveries and new technologies have reshaped understandings of early human societies and the ways in which the past continues to inform the present.

New frontiers
Advances in science have transformed how scholars study human origins and identity.

Evolutionary geneticist Svante Pääbo's sequencing of Neanderthal DNA revealed unexpected interbreeding with modern humans, rewriting the evolutionary story. Sequencing DNA has revealed the movements, diets, and relationships of long-dead populations.

Anthropologists such as Kim TallBear have responded critically to the use of DNA to reveal ancestry, drawing attention to how such work intersects with colonial histories, Indigenous sovereignty, and the politics of identity. Anthropologist Jason De León combines forensics and ethnography to document migrant journeys across deserts, exposing the violence embedded in border policies.

Anthropology has continued to focus on the marginalized and the disposessed. Veena Das examines

how marginalized communities endure trauma, from war to poverty, while Soyini Madison's critical ethnography brings the voices of activists fighting oppression to the fore. Gender remains central, whether in Saba Mahmood's analysis of Muslim women's piety or Shanshan Du's work on matrilineal societies challenging Western feminist assumptions.

Changing methods
Contemporary anthropology has also seen methodological innovation. Long-term deep interviewing has become a powerful tool in capturing personal experience over time, while the ethnography of media opens new perspectives on how identity, power, and belonging are shaped

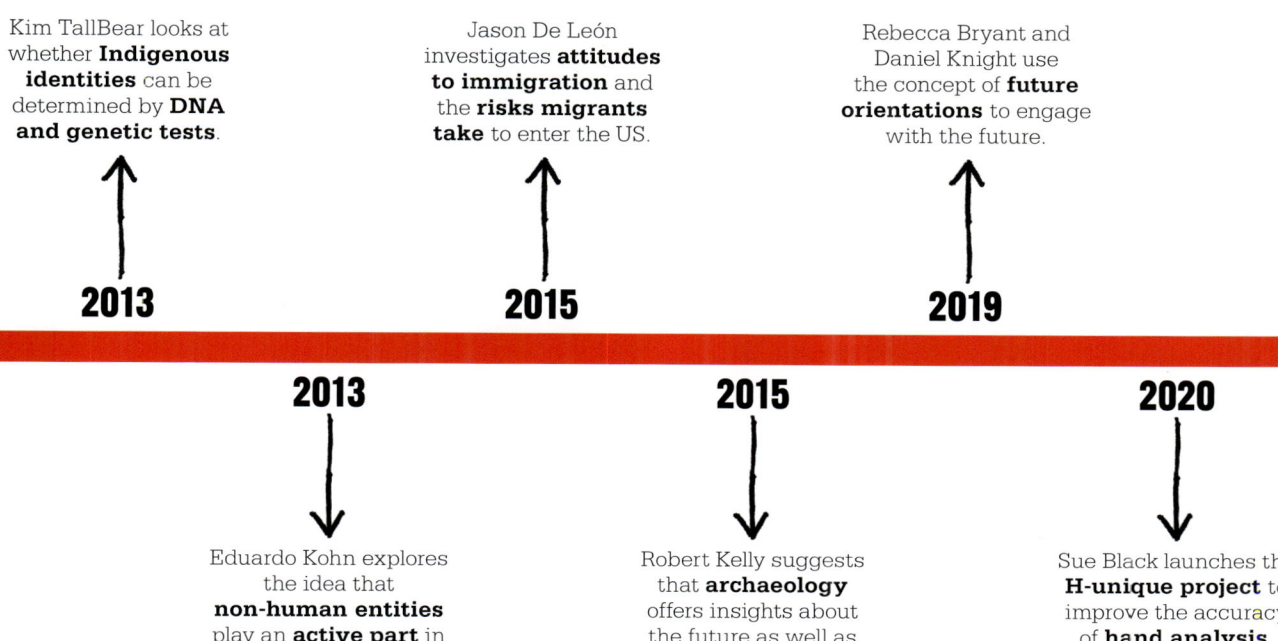

Kim TallBear looks at whether **Indigenous identities** can be determined by **DNA and genetic tests**.

2013

Jason De León investigates **attitudes to immigration** and the **risks migrants take** to enter the US.

2015

Rebecca Bryant and Daniel Knight use the concept of **future orientations** to engage with the future.

2019

2013

Eduardo Kohn explores the idea that **non-human entities** play an **active part** in **shaping our world**.

2015

Robert Kelly suggests that **archaeology** offers insights about the future as well as the past.

2020

Sue Black launches the **H-unique project** to improve the accuracy of **hand analysis**.

---

through film, television, and digital communication. Scholars such as Faye Ginsburg, Lila Abu-Lughod, and Brian Larkin have examined how media forms reflect and remake cultural worlds. At the same time, visual and material anthropology remain important. Anthropologists such as Jane Lydon explore how photography can both document and influence social relations.

Reimagining the past

Archaeologists continue to uncover new understandings of early human societies. David Lewis-Williams' work on symbolic cave art points to the importance of ritual, memory, and representation in the lives of early humans. Robert L. Kelly has examined the technological transformations

that shaped early human societies, from stone tools to shifting patterns of mobility and settlement.

Mary Stiner's work on early human burials highlights the emotional and symbolic dimensions of prehistoric life. Rick Potts has explored how environmental instability influenced human evolution, emphasising adaptability as a key feature of our species. Together with discoveries of wooden tools and early evidence of long-distance exchange networks, such research challenges the idea that prehistory was simple or static.

Uncertain future

Anthropology today grapples with how people imagine and respond to future uncertainty. The effects of climate change, pandemics, and

political instability have made visible the ways in which crises are endured unevenly across the globe. Anthropologists are studying loneliness, displacement, and belonging – what it means to be part of a community in a rapidly changing world. Work by scholars such as Ruth Mandel and Yael Navaro explores how migration and conflict transform identities and reshape citizenship.

Across all its subfields, contemporary anthropology continues to question assumptions, amplify diverse voices, and seek out the connections between past and present, the self and other, the human and non-human. It remains a vital discipline for understanding how people live, suffer, adapt, and hope in a time of profound global transformation. ∎

AN IDENTITY MARKER
THE ROLE OF AFRICAN AMERICAN VERNACULAR ENGLISH

IN CONTEXT

KEY WORK
John and Russell Rickford,
Spoken Soul, **2000**

FIELD
**Linguistic anthropology;
sociocultural anthropology**

BEFORE
1938 Jazz singer Cab Calloway
publishes *Hepster's Dictionary,*
which explains the lexicon of
"jive talk".

1972 *Language in the Inner
City* by US linguist William
Labov helps to establish AAVE
as an acceptable dialect.

1975 US social psychologist
Robert Williams's *Ebonics*
defines the social dialects
of Black people in the US.

AFTER
2015 A Stanford University
report finds that young Black
Americans speak less AAVE
and more Standard English
when they move to wealthier
neighbourhoods.

African American Vernacular English (AAVE), also known as Black American, or Ebonics – a portmanteau of "ebony" and "phonics" – is the dialect spoken by most Black Americans in the home, on the street, at school, and in church. It features many words not in the Standard English lexicon –

AAVE features in the lyrics of many rap artists, including those of Kendrick Lamar who won the 2018 Pulitzer Prize for Music for his album, *Damn.*

"chillin", "dis", "hood", "peeps", for example – and constructions such as "ain't" for "hasn't", "isn't", or "didn't", and "Kendrick very cool" for "Kendrick's very cool". Linguists still debate the origins of AAVE, but most believe that the dialect has three roots: Standard English; creole English languages that emerged in the 17th and 18th centuries among enslaved people who spoke mutually unintelligible, mostly West African languages; and elements of African languages themselves.

Love it or hate it
In their 2000 book *Spoken Soul: The Story of Black English,* US linguist John Rickford and his journalist son Russell explore the love-hate relationship between US society and AAVE. Describing the importance of the vernacular as not just a variant dialect but the "soul of Black identity through the generations", they bemoan the fact that AAVE is often scorned by white society. They cite evidence from a 1999 survey of Black American undergraduates at Stanford University, California, who described themselves as bidialectal: code-switching

See also: Language and cognition 88–89 ▪ English vernacular 116–19 ▪ Accents, dialects, and code-switching 244–45

Rules of African American Vernacular English		
AAVE		**Standard English**
She be dancing	**Tense variation**	She is always dancing
Can't nobody tell me nothing	**Negation**	Nobody can tell me anything
He alright	**Absence of copula**	He is alright
Look at the **po**-lice	**Front-stressing**	Look at the po-**lice**
She hear you	**Letter dropping**	She hears you

between "spoken soul" and Standard English as the audience and situation demanded. Even more sinister, the Rickfords argue that negative attitudes to Black language are born of racism.

Described by US linguist Geneva Smitherman as "truly da bomb", *Spoken Soul* has proved to be a game-changer because it explores and analyses every aspect of the Black American dialect. As well as covering vocabulary, grammar, pronunciation, and AAVE in education and history, the book contrasts the negativity directed towards the dialect with the acclaim received by AAVE writers such as James Baldwin, June Jordan, and Claude Brown.

Popular culture

AAVE has long been accepted as part of popular culture in the US. For example, in the late 1930s, jazz lyrics – including "jive talk" – were widely sung in AAVE, and also became popular among white audiences in the following decade.

In her 1937 novel *Their Eyes Were Watching God,* US writer Zora Neale Hurston crafted characters who expressed the richness of Black language, despite fierce resistance from critics who derided AAVE as deficient English or worse. Nobel-prize winning author Toni Morrison, who was strongly influenced by Hurston, told an interviewer in 1981 that the language she used was the most distinctive ingredient of her writing: "The worst thing that could happen would be to lose that language". AAVE is commonly used in film and theatre script writing, and ubiquitous in funk, hip-hop, and rap lyrics. Due to the widespread popularity of US culture, the dialect has now spread globally. ▪

Ebonics in schools

In 1973, US psychologist Robert Williams introduced the term "Ebonics" at a conference discussing the language of Black children. His aim in naming the dialect was to counter criticisms of it as nothing more than slang. The name stayed below the radar until 1996, when a furore erupted over the curriculum policy of the Oakland, California, school board. In light of acute educational problems facing Black American pupils, the board concluded that taking account of the students' vernacular might help their education. However, the policy was misrepresented in the media, giving the impression that Standard English had been abandoned in favour of Ebonics. The controversy spawned an outpouring of racism, and the school board dropped the word "Ebonics" from its curriculum statement. Later, the Linguistic Society of America, not known for its radicalism, backed a resolution supporting the school board's policy as "linguistically and pedagogically sound".

A DYNAMIC AND COLLABORATIVE PROCESS
LONG-TERM DEEP INTERVIEWING TECHNIQUES

IN CONTEXT

KEY WORK
Mimi Nichter, *Fat Talk*, 2000

FIELD
Sociocultural anthropology

BEFORE
1990s Research areas including gender, youth culture, body image, and "girl studies" emerge as anthropologists question the colonial roots of traditional anthropology and begin to study groups within their own societies in a more ethical and reflective way.

1997 US social historian Joan Jacobs Brumberg publishes *The Body Project*, which explores how the relationship that American girls have with their bodies has evolved over the last two centuries.

AFTER
2004 "Fat studies", a growing interdisciplinary field, challenges societal norms about body size and beauty.

In recent decades, many anthropologists have shifted the focus of their research to studying everyday life in familiar settings. The practice of "anthropology at home" allows them to conduct long-term qualitative research in communities within their own country, and prioritize the voices of their participants.

Since the 1990s, anthropologist Mimi Nichter has researched the life stages of women, revealing with nuance the complexity of individual stories. Her studies intersect with fields such as "girl studies" and "fat studies", as she examines how societal pressures, media portrayals, and family dynamics shape young women's views of themselves and their bodies.

In *Fat Talk: What Girls and Their Parents Say about Dieting*, Nichter demonstrates how qualitative research can amplify participant voices and provide deep insights into social phenomena. Based on a three-year study of American teenage girls, her book explores the nuances of female teenagehood as a life stage shaped by personal, family, peer group, societal, and global influences.

A deeper understanding

Nichter based her book around a series of in-depth encounters with her participants. She dedicated time to understanding both individual stories and shared experiences, demonstrating her commitment to long-term ethnography. Her research was part of a broader "Teen Lifestyle Project", conducted by a team of cultural and nutritional

Young women experience weight and perceive body image in different ways, shaped by factors such as family dynamics, friendships, culture, and personal perceptions.

See also: Culture shapes behaviour 62–67 ▪ Social and cultural dimensions of nutrition 80–83 ▪ Feminist anthropology 140–45 ▪ Thick description 146–53 ▪ Gender performativity 215 ▪ Food and modernity 267

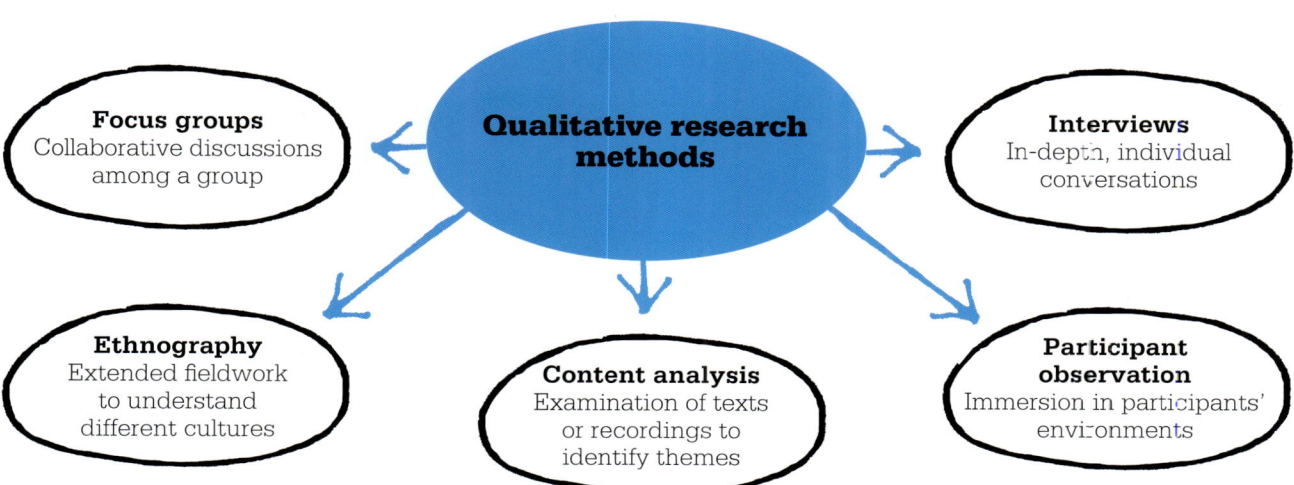

Focus groups
Collaborative discussions among a group

Qualitative research methods

Interviews
In-depth, individual conversations

Ethnography
Extended fieldwork to understand different cultures

Content analysis
Examination of texts or recordings to identify themes

Participant observation
Immersion in participants' environments

anthropologists. The ethnography was based in four urban schools in Tucson, Arizona, and included 240 girls aged between 13 and 15. The participants reflected local and national ethnic diversity: 70 per cent were white, 10 per cent Latina, and 5 per cent African American.

Nichter's book challenges the often negative portrayal of girl teenagehood by engaging with it as a period of social, emotional, and physiological development. *Fat Talk* highlights individual voices, and captures the girls' resilience and critical intelligence. It reveals that girl teenagehood is shaped by cultural context – it is not a universal experience, but rather one that is influenced by different expectations, norms, and values across communities.

Creating solidarity
Nichter uses the phrase "fat talk" to describe how teenage girls habitually express concerns about their weight. It acts as part of a social ritual among friends that creates solidarity, but Nichter notes

that "talking the talk doesn't necessarily reflect actual behaviour; rather, it indexes important personal and cultural concerns". In her analysis, white girls talked about dieting more than they actually followed diets, while black girls expressed greater body satisfaction, and placed more importance on "attitude". Nichter also investigates the influence of family dynamics on girls' body image, noting how mothers tend to engage in "fat talk", while fathers tease daughters about their body shape.

Through semi-structured interviews and focus groups, Nichter's study brings the voices of the teenage girls to the fore, expanding understanding of how the girls experience their own bodies. It reveals the interactive process of female socialization, as well as the struggles that girls face to achieve a cultural ideal of beauty within a framework of "fat talk", dieting rhetoric, societal pressures, media influence, gendered identities, and the objectified nature of girl- and womanhood. ▪

The power of voice

Voice is a key aspect of human expression, associated with individuality, power, and authority. Recognizing voice as a form of self-representation is an essential tenet of an ethically informed discipline, especially as anthropologists seek to address the politics of representation. Listening to others and ensuring that their voices shape research is central to ethnography.

The realization that people can speak for themselves has encouraged anthropologists to study power struggles, injustices, and aspirations across cultures. The strong connection between voice, authority, and narrative reminds scholars that the perspectives and expressions shared by their research collaborators are also shaped by historical and cultural influences.

GENDER IDENTITY STARTS BEFORE BIRTH
SOCIALIZATION OF GENDER ROLES

IN CONTEXT

KEY WORK
Leela Dube,
Anthropological
Explorations in Gender:
Intersecting Fields, 2001

FIELD
Sociocultural anthropology

BEFORE
1953 Indian sociologist Irawati Karve notes a link between a woman's status and the structure of her family.

1955 British anthropologist Kathleen Gough writes about female initiation rites and how they reinforce gender roles.

1980s Leela Dube's writing helps to bring attention to the issue of sex-selective abortion and its impact on gender inequality in India.

1997 Indian sociologist Kamala Ganesh builds on Dube's work, exploring how traditional family structures are changing in modern India.

Everyday customs, language, and stories play a crucial role in shaping the lives of girls and women. Through her work on gender and kinship in South Asia, Indian anthropologist Leela Dube examined how these elements influence gender roles.

Dube's writings revealed how women are socialized into gendered roles through everyday practices and relationships from birth. Drawing on her own experiences, she highlighted the deep connection between gender and kinship – the ways in which people are related through blood, marriage, and adoption – showing how these systems produce and reinforce gender norms.

Kinship and gender roles
Dube's work focused on different types of kinship: she studied both "patrilineal" systems – where inheritance follows the male line – and "matrilineal" systems, where

The historic practice of sati, when a widow sacrificed herself on her husband's pyre, is an extreme example of female self-sacrifice and devotion.

See also: Culture shapes behaviour 62–67 ▪ Kinship and social order 68–69 ▪ Feminist anthropology 140–45 ▪ Thick description 146–53 ▪ Religion and secular power 188–89 ▪ Adapting cultural traditions 193 ▪ Oral poetry 208–09

Kinship in families can follow different paths: matrilineal systems trace through mothers, while patrilineal systems trace through fathers.

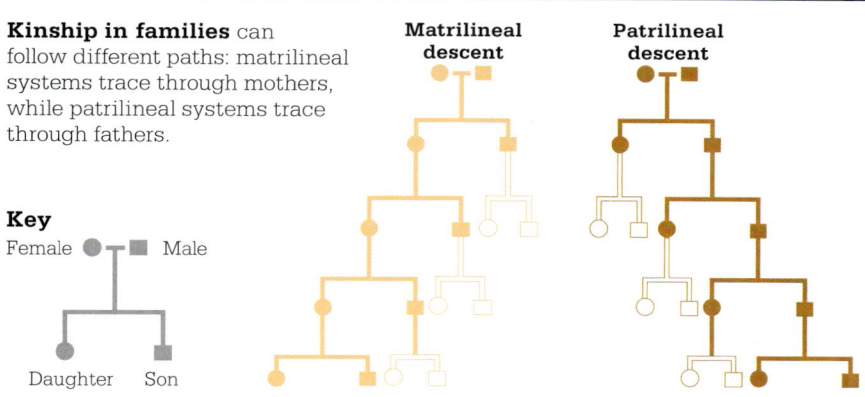

Matrilineal descent

Patrilineal descent

Key

Female ● ⊤ ■ Male

Daughter Son

Over the years I became acutely aware of the derivative nature of women's status in rituals and rules of kinship and everyday life.
Leela Dube

inheritance follows the female line. Her findings revealed that while women faced inequality in both systems, their position in patrilineal societies was worse. Patrilineal systems, she observed, socialize girls to see their stay in their birth home as temporary, using stories and rituals to reinforce this. These cultural practices made it seem natural for girls to feel less entitled, and prepared them for subordinate roles in their marital homes.

Tales of inequality

In patrilineal societies, Dube argued, proverbs, myths, and tales shape gendered identities. Sayings, such as one from northeastern India comparing daughters to clarified butter that spoils if not "used" in time, stigmatized unmarried or widowed women, and encouraged early marriage. Sons, by contrast, were presented as permanent family members, with cultural practices emphasizing their stable, privileged position in the family. Dube's studies showed how these symbolic gender differences translated into material inequalities, especially with regard to property rights.

Dube, using examples from her own life and those of her informants, highlighted the diverse and recurring themes in proverbs, myths, and practices across India that reinforced women's secondary roles to men. Mythical tales promoted self-sacrifice, while ritual observances and other religious practices taught girls to aspire to a good husband and prepare themselves for subordination in their marital homes.

Leela Dube's work highlighted the gendered nature of fieldwork, and she critically examined her own position as an upper-caste Hindu woman working in diverse contexts. This self-awareness helped her to work with diverse communities – ranging from Kamar and Gond tribal women in central India to Muslim communities in the south of the country. Drawing on her own upbringing, Dube used her personal experiences to engage deeply with the language, metaphors, and stories of the communities she studied. ▪

The Story of Seed and Earth

Leela Dube's essay on the "Seed and Earth" metaphor examined how this concept, widely used in Indian oral and written traditions, reflects perceptions of reproduction. The metaphor portrays the man as the seed-giver and the woman as the nourishing earth, while the child is a product of the seed. This positions the woman as secondary in the process, emphasizing asymmetrical relations between men and women in reproduction.

Dube argued that this metaphor is used to justify ownership and material inequality. The seed (man) owns the product (child) and the field (woman), leaving women without claims over their offspring or labour. Sons are valued as they carry the father's name and bloodline, while daughters are seen as transient, ritually given away to other families. Dube links these beliefs to broader systems of gendered labour and resource ownership in patrilineal societies.

TELEVISION HAS LED US TO SEE OUR OWN DAILY LIVES AS DRAMAS
ETHNOGRAPHY OF MEDIA

IN CONTEXT

KEY WORK
Faye Ginsburg, Lila Abu Lughod, and Brian Larkin, *Media Worlds*, 2002

FIELD
Sociocultural anthropology

BEFORE
1975 Academic John Culkin establishes the first media studies MA course in the US at Antioch College.

AFTER
2004 *Anthropology and Mass Communication* is published by US anthropologist Mark Allen Peterson. The book examines the ways in which the anthropological study of media and mass communication is shaped by sociology.

2005 Eric W. Rothenbuhler and Mihai Coman publish *Media Anthropology*, with essays highlighting some of the issues surrounding the use of media in anthropology.

The 1980s and 1990s saw the introduction of new technology – personal computers, the internet, and mobile phones – support the influence of media such as film, television, radio, and online articles across the world. In the years that followed, these media and their constantly evolving technology infiltrated previously isolated communities. This prompted anthropologists to study how people from all walks of life were affected by technological change, and the ways in which media and technology had been harnessed to advance cultural needs and aspirations.

Advances in technology and the **accessibility** of **new media** can shape anthropological studies:

Groups can document their **own culture**, which creates more **source material** to study.

The globalization of media means that groups have **easy access** to the **cultures** and **ideas** of others.

The use of new technology as a **research tool** can influence how non-anthropologists use **different media**.

Technological innovations in media allow anthropologists to push the boundaries of ethnography.

See also: The anthropology of sound 184–85 ▪ The power of photography 292–93

Social media influencers use this new format to share their lives or information, shape opinion, build community, and market products.

The power of social media

In the 21st century, increased public access to the internet, the rise of smartphones, and the advancement of social media have had an unparalleled impact on contemporary life in almost every culture across the world. Social media in particular augments a critically important part of human existence – social lives. It has shaped how users share and receive information and opinions, influenced the ways in which people perceive themselves and form their identity, and affects how users understand the wider world. The ubiquitous nature of social media has led anthropologists to consider what consequences it may have on different communities and the implications for social practices around the world. As the first generation for whom social media has always been a part of life reaches adulthood, anthropologists debate how social media affects culture, kinship, and the ways in which people relate to one another.

Global power

In *Media Worlds*, anthropologists Faye Ginsburg, Lila Abu Lughod, and Brian Larkin explored the production, circulation, and consumption of media across cultures. They observed its political dimensions, and showed how many cultures used media in creative ways to tell their stories and resist dominant powers. Drawing on case studies from Indigenous peoples of Australia, Brazil, and North America, Ginsburg and her colleagues showed that media and technology were global phenomena that allowed unique expressions.

One of their core discussions revolved around what Ginsburg referred to as "screen memories" – the stories and histories told by Indigenous peoples through new media. She stated that these screen memories were used to circulate

The award-winning 2002 film
Rabbit-Proof Fence, had a powerful impact by sharing the experiences of First Nations peoples at the hands of the Australian government.

ideas and experiences beyond the community and had been influential in establishing claims to land and cultural rights. The ability of Indigenous peoples to access and control media contributed to their increased empowerment.

Talking back

In examining the use of media and technology by marginalized communities, Ginsburg and her colleagues demonstrated how technology that had traditionally been associated with Western capitalist countries was taken up and adapted in nuanced ways to suit the needs of different cultures. In this manner, media and technology enabled previously isolated Indigenous communities, to "talk back" to the power structures that had historically controlled their interests. ▪

"ARGUABLY THE MOST IMPORTANT AUSTRALIAN FILM IN 20 YEARS."

Michael Hutak - Australian Style

RABBIT-PROOF FENCE

PG PARENTAL GUIDANCE RECOMMENDED FOR PERSONS UNDER 15 YEARS ADULT THEMES

DIRECTED BY PHILLIP NOYCE

A LANGUAGE OF THE MIND

SYMBOLISM IN CAVE ART

IN CONTEXT

KEY WORK
David Lewis-Williams,
The Mind in the Cave, **2002**

FIELD
Archaeology

BEFORE
1879 Marcelino Sanz de
Sautuola discovers rock art
in the Cave of Altamira, on
his estate in northern Spain.

1984 In *The Dawn of
European Art*, André Leroi-
Gourhan analyses the various
techniques, forms, and
meanings of cave art.

AFTER
2018 A study using Uranium-
Thorium dating concludes that
cave art at La Pasiega, Spain,
was made by Neanderthals.

2023 Palaeolithic clay
paintings of horses and
deer are discovered at Cova
Dones, Valencia, Spain.

In 1880, Marcelino Sanz de
Sautuola suggested that the
complex mural of bison found
in Spain's Altamira Caves dated
back to prehistoric times. Experts
in the field quickly discredited
him, dubbing Palaeolithic humans
"too savage" to create such
sophisticated art. Subsequent
discoveries made the authenticity
of cave art impossible to deny and
forced scientists to re-examine
their prejudices against the early
human mind.

South African cognitive
archaeologist David Lewis-
Williams challenged the simplistic
interpretation of cave art as a
narrative piece; he suggested

See also: The New Archaeology 110–15 ▪ Processual archaeology 136–37
▪ Cognitive fluidity 242–43 ▪ Human burials 306

The Altamira bison is a colourful portrayal of a now-extinct species created about 14,000 years ago. The animal also appears in Indonesian cave paintings that date back 44,000 years.

instead that it might have had a ritual and symbolic purpose. His book, *The Mind in the Cave,* is a collection of articles exploring cave art and the academic controversies that surround it, as well as its connection to human consciousness.

Decoration or symbolism?

Palaeolithic cave art features an impressive diversity of locations, subjects, and methods. The caves in which art has been found vary enormously in size and shape – from dark, narrow passages, to huge caverns. However, the artworks – depictions of animals, humans, anthropomorphic beings, and geometric patterns – consistently interact with the contours of the rock. This makes the caves themselves an integral part of each image, whether it

has been painted onto the surface, engraved or etched into the rock, or created from the impressions left by early human hands trailing through mud and clay.

At first, anthropologists interpreted cave scenes as simple observations of the outside world. In the 1860s, French archaeologist Édouard Piette suggested that the natural abundance of environmental resources during the Palaeolithic Period granted humans the leisure to create art for art's sake. However, the secluded and often inaccessible nature of many cave sites encouraged others to question these theories.

A form of totemism

Some researchers believed that humans created these images to invoke sympathetic magic that would encourage animals to breed, or hunting magic to make prey more vulnerable in a chase. However, in his 1945 paper *Prehistoric Cave Paintings,* German-American art historian Max Raphael argued that the »

A feminist approach

Specializing in the Late Ice Age, or Palaeolithic Period, US archaeologist Margaret Conkey challenges the male-dominated perspectives that have historically shaped her field of study. She proves that by adopting a feminist approach, researchers can reach more nuanced and accurate conclusions about the past.

Conkey criticizes the assumption that men were the primary creators of cave paintings, emphasizing that it is impossible to know definitively who made them. She also challenges the widely held belief that male hunting activities were the driving force behind human evolution, arguing that this view overlooks the significant contributions that women made to the development and survival of *Homo sapiens*.

Conkey's work highlights essential roles that women played in prehistoric societies and advocates a more balanced and inclusive understanding of human history.

The very idea of Palaeolithic art was deeply disturbing. Was not art one of the great achievements of high civilizations?
David Lewis-Williams

portrayals are less about invoking the occult and, instead, are likely to be metaphorical examples of Palaeolithic totemism – kinship between a social group and a spirit-being such as an animal.

Raphael claimed that each clan represented itself as an animal or figure, and the way these symbols interacted on cave walls reflected the group's social relationships. For example, two partially overlapping animal depictions with their heads turned away might indicate warring communities. By contrast, if one figure was contained within another, it portrayed an alliance. This hypothesis encouraged a more sophisticated view of the work of Palaeolithic cave artists because it suggested that each cave contained a single complex composition rather than a series of unconnected individual "spells".

Evolving ideas

In the 1960s, French archaeologist André Leroi-Gourhan expounded on Raphael's metaphorical interpretation by applying the framework of binary opposition to the symbols and animals most often

Understanding cave art

Hand markings, made by pressing or dragging a painted hand on the wall, are the simplest form of self-expression.

Animals do not necessarily have a literal meaning. A bison, for example, may indicate abundance.

Human figures are a representation of the self, but also family, companionship, and community.

Hunting imagery can indicate the desire for success in the hunt – almost like a modern-day vision board.

seen in cave art. Leroi-Gourhan theorized that small herbivores – such as horses – and narrow signs like strokes represented masculinity, while large herbivores – such as bison – and broad signs like ovals implied femininity.

The theories of Raphael and Leroi-Gourhan were at the forefront of the movement to redefine "savage" Palaeolithic beings as humans with consciousness, creativity, and complex social dynamics – a perspective that ties

in closely with Lewis-Williams's interpretation of cave art as evidence of human evolution.

Lewis-Williams suggested that the figures depicted in cave art are early examples of symbolism. He argued that the image of an animal cannot exist without intrinsic associations. For instance, the bison was essential to the survival of early humans: they used its meat for food, its hide for warmth and protection, and its bones for tools. Logically, then, Lewis-Williams

Aboriginal rock art

Researchers estimate that there are more than 100,000 significant ancient rock-art locations around Australia, many of which are sacred to Aboriginal (First Nations) peoples. Australian Aboriginal art represents the world's oldest continuous art-making tradition. Some of this rock art has been dated to around 30,000 years ago, but the discovery of art-making tools dating from about 50,000 years ago suggests that this was a long-established custom.

Ancient Aboriginal rock art often depicts geometric shapes, or animal or human silhouettes. The most common forms found in Australia are petroglyphs (engravings) and pictographs (paintings). While petroglyphs involve removing rock to leave a negative impression, pictographs are made by applying wet pigments – such as charcoal, clay, chalk, and ochre – to the rock by hand or with brushes made from chewed sticks or hair. Sometimes the artist would use an object – such as a hand – as a stencil and blow colour over it.

Depictions of Wandjina rain spirits at a site in Western Australia may have been a way to communicate a bond to the land and its resources.

The human hands in Argentina's Cueva de las Manos were created at least 9,500 years ago by blowing pigment over the body part. Each print may have marked a person's presence.

believed, humans would associate an image of bison with ideas of prosperity and abundance.

Levels of awareness

Much of Lewis-Williams's research focused on the brain, particularly the evolutionary differences between Neanderthals and *Homo sapiens*. He drew upon the spectrum of consciousness that modern humans experience.

At one end of the spectrum is alertness, the state during which humans engage with the environment. This progresses into daydreaming, in which we are awake but lost in our thoughts. Minor hallucinations can occur during hypnagogia, the state in which we are half-asleep; this shifts to rapid eye movement (REM) sleep, during which most dreams take place.

Hypnagogic hallucinations can be far more intense than REM-phase dreams, with vivid visual and auditory sensations. When humans undergo these extreme hallucinatory experiences, they might feel weightless or constricted, as if they are flying through the air or suffocating underground. Lewis-Williams believed that the contrasting nature of the visions experienced in this hypnagogic stage may have played a crucial part in the development of religion, because it provides a plausible explanation for the duality of heaven and hell that is present in many faiths.

Early humans were moved to record their visions on the walls, ceiling, and floor of caves.

Lewis-Williams argued that the consciousness required to make these complex, symbolic images did not exist within Neanderthals. In his opinion, only *Homo sapiens* developed both the sense of self and the long-term memory that were necessary in order to communicate their dreams and create a belief system. He also suggested that *Homo sapiens* must have had clearly defined "zoomorphic mental images" in order to reproduce them on cave walls.

Once human beings had developed higher-order consciousness, they had the ability to see mental images projected onto surfaces and to experience afterimages.
David Lewis-Williams

Spirituality and religion

The transition from mental image to physical depiction, in turn, led to the development of a religious hierarchy. Artists were lauded for their connection to the spiritual realm, which elevated their social standing. Seers may have strengthened this division by restricting access to the caves. In some parts of the cave, large groups performed rituals to create collective artworks, but in other sections, only specific individuals could experience full hallucinatory immersion and commune with the spirit animals, which granted them religious power.

Lewis-Williams's research redefined Palaeolithic cave art as a reflection of early human consciousness and symbolic thinking. He argued that this art was integral to the development of religion, social hierarchy, and human identity, and set *Homo sapiens* apart from other species. He highlighted cave art as crucial evidence of our cognitive and cultural evolution by exploring the connection between altered states of consciousness and the creation of symbolic imagery. ∎

EVERYTHING COMES IN PAIRS
GENDER EQUALITY

IN CONTEXT

KEY WORK
Shanshan Du, *Chopsticks Only Work in Pairs*, 2002

FIELD
Sociocultural anthropology

BEFORE
1928 Margaret Mead studies the cultural traits of men and women in Papua New Guinea. She argues that culture conditions gender expression.

1982 Karen Sacks's research into production and power examines the role of women in societies throughout history. Her work challenges earlier studies that characterized women's roles as inherently tied to their gender.

AFTER
2015 Research by anthropologist Mark Dyble shows that modern hunter-gatherer societies are egalitarian. This suggests that prehistoric societies may also have had gender equality.

Feminist anthropologists have long searched for societies that exhibit genuine gender equity. Although this work has provided a wealth of valuable insights into global gender dynamics, it has not yielded the results that anthropologists had hoped for. According to anthropologist Shanshan Du, the search has been largely unsuccessful because these studies look for utopian societies.

Rejecting utopian ideals
Based on her ethnographic fieldwork on Lahu culture in Southwest China, Du suggests that gender-egalitarian societies do exist if we shift our attention away from the utopian ideals embedded in mainstream Western feminism. Du states that one particularly problematic aspect is the emphasis on the woman as an individual actor in society. Du argues that in the context of Lahu society, gender equity exists in the form of the husband and wife as a unit. Once a woman and man

marry, they form a pair that rises in the social hierarchy. Together, the couple hold a social status in which their responsibilities, authority, and prestige are intertwined. When raising a family, the wife-husband pair work in conjunction with each other, with very little gendered division of labour. Du's provocative exploration of alternative ideas about equality offers new avenues to explore gender equity. ∎

Typically, little children from two to six years old are socialized without gender distinction to play both domestic and outdoor roles through games.
Shanshan Du

See also: The concept of reciprocity 58–61 ▪ Processual archaeology 136–37 ▪ Women and the political economy 156–57

THEIR CUISINE CONVEYED THEIR IDENTITY
FOOD AND MODERNITY

IN CONTEXT

KEY WORK
Carole Counihan, *Around the Tuscan Table*, 2004

FIELD
Sociocultural anthropology

BEFORE
1932 Audrey Richards establishes the field of nutritional anthropology while researching the diets of Bantu peoples in Southern Africa.

1986 Sidney Mintz explores how sugar affects labour migration, power relations, and has symbolic meanings.

AFTER
2005 US anthropologist William Roseberry tracks how changing coffee-drinking choices reflect class and aspirations in the US.

2021 Anthropologist Nir Avieli studies the complex personal and political reasons behind the rapid growth of vegetarianism in a small town in Vietnam.

Until the mid-20th century, Italy endured centuries of food insecurity, and, as a result, working people developed a distinct diet. In the 1980s, however, when US anthropologist Carole Counihan was studying food habits in the city of Florence, she found that a rapid transformation in food production, distribution, and consumption had taken place. Food had become an integral part of a changing value system and evolving social relationships.

New habits

Although the roots of traditional peasant foods were still evident, Counihan discovered that there had been major changes in diet, as well as how people ate. Eating alone, once a sign of social isolation, had become normal, and workplace routines had disrupted the practice of families sharing meals twice a day. More women were working outside of the home, which limited their time to prepare traditional foods. Attitudes towards food became contradictory:

Artworks depicting peasant foods and the joy of eating – such as this fresco by Giandomenico Tiepolo – have contributed to the romanticization of humble traditional dishes.

although the old foods were highly prized, their preparation was undervalued. A longing for the old ways was accompanied by concerns about excess, processed food, and nutrition. Counihan notes that responses to food recorded in her early studies of "only a little, but let it be good", had by the 1990s become "a lot, but is it good?". ∎

See also: Social and cultural dimensions of nutrition 80–83 ∎ The anthropology of food 200–05 ∎ Nutrition and human evolution 280

THE VEIL AS A FORM OF AGENCY
THE GENDER POLITICS OF PIETY

IN CONTEXT

KEY WORK
Saba Mahmood, *Politics of Piety*, 2005

FIELD
Sociocultural anthropology

BEFORE
1967 E.E. Evans-Pritchard publishes *Theories of Primitive Religion* in which he notes that when studying religious observance, anthropologists often fail to understand the minds of their subjects.

1993 Talal Asad argues in *Genealogies of Religion* that the politicization of religion is a European construct.

AFTER
2015 Jeanette S. Jouili publishes *Pious Practices and Secular Constraints*, arguing that women in conservative Islamic groups have an ethical struggle between their desire for piety and the will to counter negative representations of Islam.

Studying the religious observance of Muslim women in Egypt in the 1990s, Pakistani anthropologist Saba Mahmood developed an intricate critique of assumptions in feminist theory about autonomy and agency. Mahmood saw the participation of Muslim women in Islamic norms not as obedience to the patriarchy, but as a project to cultivate themselves as pious subjects. She argued that this practice of self-formation in the Islamic tradition required a new definition of what constitutes human agency.

Women wear niqabs in an expression of piety in Cairo, Egypt, in 1999, following a ruling by the Egyptian supreme court that banned the wearing of niqabs in schools.

Ethical self-cultivation

To understand practices like veiling and praying, Mahmood used the idea of positive ethics in which external actions create corresponding inward dispositions. In this model, an individual acquires moral virtues by repeatedly performing the actions associated with those virtues.

Mahmood argued that religious observances such as praying and wearing a veil are necessary to achieving inward dispositions like modesty and faith. The women she studied, for instance, had no assumption that the desire to pray was natural; rather, Mahmood stated, it was "created through a set of disciplinary acts" that caused the individual to eventually want to pray. Likewise, wearing a veil did not express an already pious self, but through this bodily practice the individual came to embody piety. The repeated practice of veiling created an inward disposition for modesty because desire was the product of action.

Mahmood's theory of self-cultivation transformed thinking about ritual practice. In contrast to many scholars who interpreted veiling as part of an already formed

See also: The universal nature of religion 28–29 ▪ Religion and secular power 188–89 ▪ Oral poetry 208–09 ▪ The evangelical experience 281

Conservative dress codes **associated with religion** can be **interpreted** in different ways:

Religious doctrine can be used as a form of **social control**.	**Religious beliefs** can be deepened by **observances** such as practising prayer.
Religion teaches that women are **valued** for their piety.	Piety is built through **disciplined observance** of religious practices.
Women must **act** or **dress** in a certain way to be seen as **pious**.	Wearing **religious dress** helps women to **embody** pious ways of being.
Women can be controlled and sometimes oppressed by religion.	**Women are active participants in their religion and piety.**

Saba Mahmood

Born in Lahore, Pakistan in 1962, Saba Mahmood was an anthropologist of Islam and secularism. She moved to the US to study, first at the University of Washington from 1981 and later at Stanford University, where she gained her PhD in 1998. She taught at the University of Chicago before becoming professor of anthropology at UC Berkeley from 2004 to 2017. Mahmood is best known for her ground-breaking ethnography of the 1990s women's mosque movement in Egypt, for which she won an award from the American Political Science Association. She was a fellow of the Center for Advanced Study in the Behavioral Sciences at Stanford University and a fellow of the Humanities Research Institute at the University of California. Mahmood died in 2018.

Other key works

2012 *Religious Freedom, Minority Rights, and Geopolitics*
2015 *Religious Difference in a Secular Age*
2015 *Politics of Religious Freedom*

---

identity, Mahmood insisted that veiling and other practices brought a self into being.

Rethinking agency

Mahmood's theory challenged existing assumptions about agency being the capacity to realize one's interests against the weight of customs and traditions. By using their agency to uphold the norms of their religion, the women were countering liberal expectations that agency can only be achieved by contesting social norms.

Mahmood found that this research destabilized her own certainties and political ideas as a progressive feminist, but she then recognized the importance of decentring and rethinking the normative frameworks about individual agency. This was particularly important, Mahmood emphasized, in the context of a global "War on Terror" that took place in the early 2000s, when these liberal frameworks were being co-opted to justify violence against Muslim people on a massive scale. ▪

AIM TO ILLUMINATE, BUILD UNDERSTANDING, OR CHALLENGE ASSUMPTIONS
CRITICAL ETHNOGRAPHY

IN CONTEXT

KEY WORK
D. Soyini Madison,
Critical Ethnography:
Method, Ethics, and
Performance, 2005

FIELD
Sociocultural anthropology

BEFORE
1970s Feminist insights,
such as those made by US
anthropologist Sherry Ortner,
encourage anthropologists
to explore personal biases
and historical contexts.

1986 *Writing Culture*, edited
by US anthropologists James
Clifford and George Marcus,
highlights how ethnography
is shaped by the researcher's
political context.

AFTER
2019 US anthropologist
Anand Pandian explores
in *A Possible Anthropology*
how anthropology can
creatively address moral
and political issues.

Ethnography has been an indispensable tool at the heart of anthropology for generations. It allows scholars to learn about cultures and communities by living alongside the people they are studying. Their participation in daily life provides anthropologists with insights into how societies solve common human problems, and allows them to engage directly with the unpredictability of everyday life.

US anthropologist Soyini Madison has been central in developing critical ethnography, an approach that urges anthropologists to examine the emotional, practical, and structural dynamics of their fieldwork. This method encourages researchers to address issues of inequality and injustice. Madison calls on scholars to approach their work with a focus on relationships, ethical responsibility, and the performative aspects of culture. These elements, she argues, are crucial for shaping and legitimizing anthropology in the modern world.

E. Patrick Johnson, a US performance scholar, adapts his fieldwork with Black gay men in the American South into staged readings that blur boundaries between research and activism.

See also: Studying up 138–39 ▪ Feminist anthropology 140–45 ▪ Thick description 146–53 ▪ Women and the political economy 156–57 ▪ Anthropology at home 170–71 ▪ Long-term deep interviewing techniques 256–57

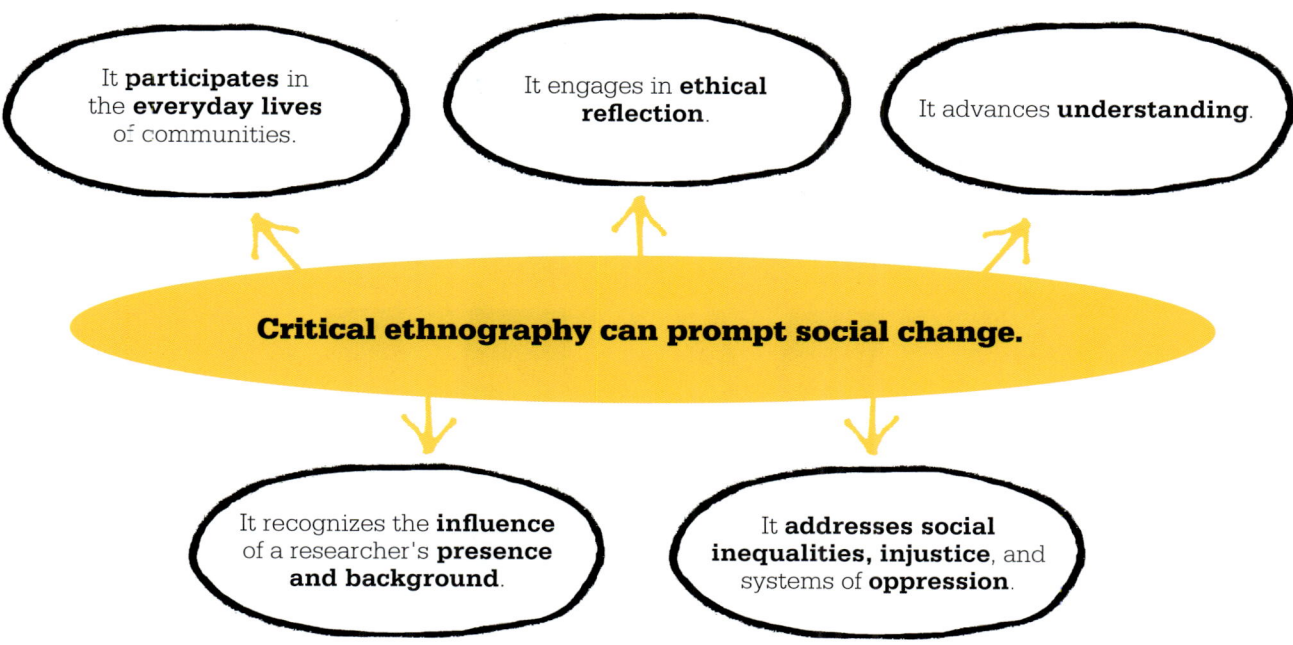

It **participates** in the **everyday lives** of communities.

It engages in **ethical reflection**.

It advances **understanding**.

Critical ethnography can prompt social change.

It recognizes the **influence** of a researcher's **presence and background**.

It **addresses social inequalities, injustice**, and systems of **oppression**.

Critical ethnography uses a range of methods and builds trust by engaging deeply with the daily lives of community members. It focuses on how human actions shape and are shaped by social worlds, and requires ethnographers to be acutely aware of their own role and the power dynamics that influence their research.

Fieldwork's ethical heart

Madison recognizes that even the most carefully planned fieldwork brings challenges and occasional misunderstandings. However, it also provides opportunities for joy and friendship. She calls for a meticulous research design and preparation, rejecting stereotypes that dismiss ethnography as a "soft skill". Madison contrasts the supposed objectivity often claimed by other disciplines with the nuance that ethnology offers.

For her, ethics and morality transform ethnology into a rigorous and respectful mode of inquiry.

Ethnography is built around the intersection of lives and the performative aspects of fieldwork and writing. Recounting these relationships involves exploring creative forms. Writing is a performance in which the anthropologist takes on the role of reporter, storyteller, friend, or outsider, and crafts a drama that defines the anthropological narrative. Madison is particularly concerned with how these stories can be transformed into public events and theatre, examining questions of perspective, ownership, and audience reception.

Critical ethnography highlights the discipline's limitations but also advocates a commitment to ethical purposes. It provides a tool that helps make anthropology relevant today. ▪

Public anthropology

Some anthropologists choose to engage with a broad, general audience to address social issues in ways that are accessible and impactful. Involving the public can bring attention to topics like climate change or social inequality, and encourage dialogue and action. Soyini Madison's work provides many examples of this type of outreach. They include performances based on her fieldwork, such as *Is it a Human Being or a Girl?* staged at the University of Ghana in 2000. The performance explored the intersection of traditional religious practices, women's rights, and poverty. This reimagining of anthropology highlights its potential to drive social change.

SURVIVORS REMAKE THEIR WORLDS

THE AFTERMATH OF VIOLENCE

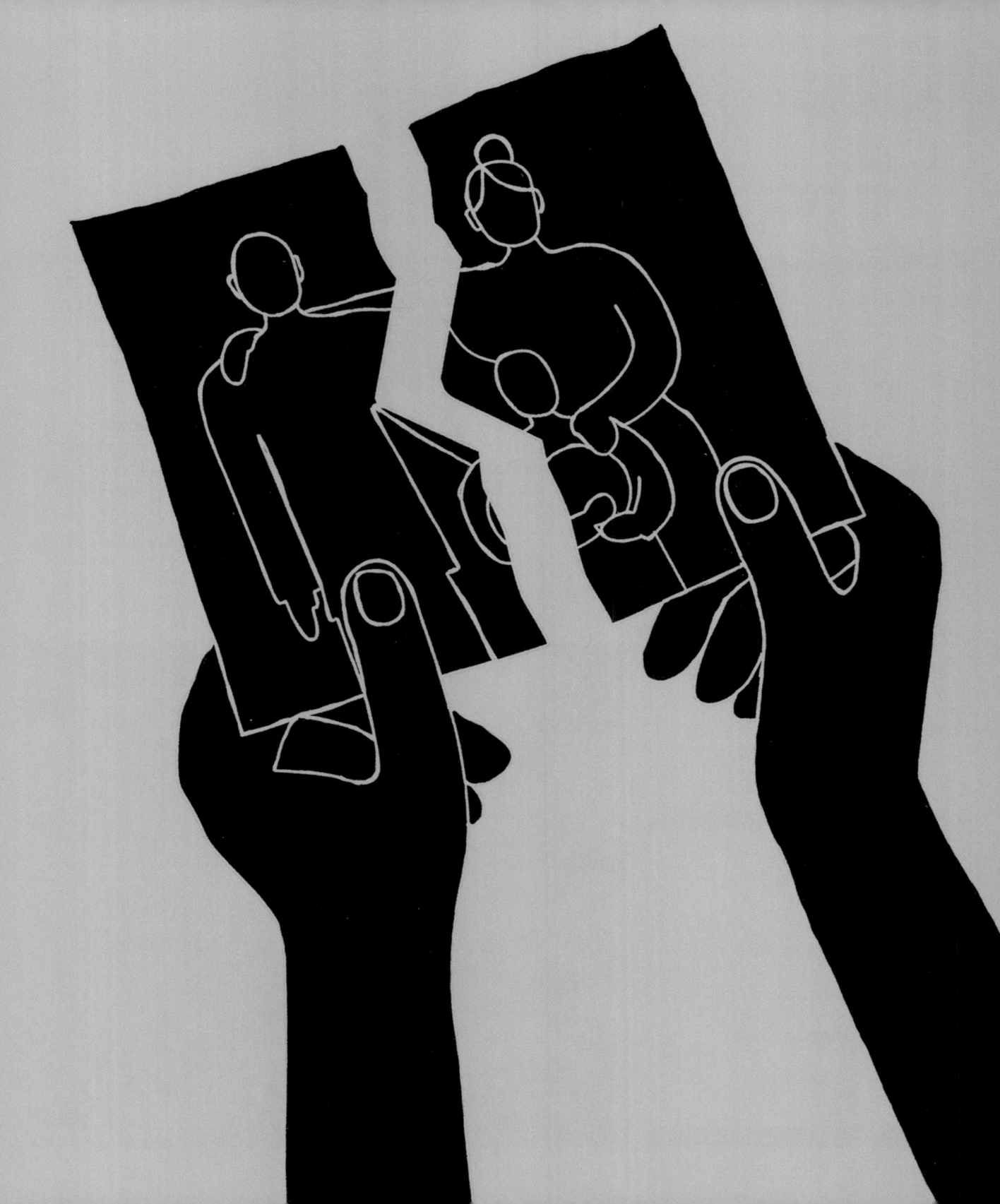

IN CONTEXT

KEY WORK
Veena Das, *Life and Words: Violence and the Descent into the Ordinary*, 2006

FIELD
Sociocultural anthropology

BEFORE
1953 In *Philosophical Investigations*, Austrian philosopher Ludwig Wittgenstein argues that language conveys meaning and shapes reality – but sometimes actions are needed to express the unpeakable.

AFTER
2010 French anthropologist Didier Fassin publishes "Ethics of Survival", which studies the ethics of reflection and action in sustaining life.

2015 In *Spectral Wound* anthropologist Nayanika Mookherjee explores public memories of violence and practices of repair following the Bangladesh war of 1971.

Violence… calls into question the very idea of life – we reach not the end of some intellectual agreement but the end of criteria.
Veena Das

Exploring how extraordinary acts of violence transcend the bounds of time and language, Indian anthropologist Veena Das reasons that violence is processed by victims in the tasks of everyday life. In particular, Das demonstrates how the most extreme acts of violence are often marked by thick silences, with the horror of events rarely expressed in language. She shows how violent incidents and the suffering they cause continue to affect victims as they return to an "ordinary" life.

In *Life and Words*, Das focuses on the lives of survivors of the violence that occurred during the Partition of India in 1947, and the anti-Sikh riots that followed the assassination of Indira Gandhi in 1984. Using extensive ethnographic research in informal settlements called bastis in Delhi, India, and archival research techniques to support her argument, Das takes a distinctive approach to ethnography. She looks at the detail of individual lives, tracing how her subject's relationships and experiences develop in the context of their family and community networks over months and years. Das explores how the violence that shatters the norms of everyday life might be best understood – not through the exceptional nature of the event, but through the necessary work of rebuilding as people return to the routines of ordinary life.

Creating social norms
Das argues that acts of violence can disrupt the usual dynamics that reinforce the connection

Hundreds of Muslim people in India wait for protected transportation to a refugee camp in Pakistan during the period of violence that surrounded the partition of India and Pakistan in 1947.

See also: Language and cognition 88–89 ▪ The fluidity of social systems 102–03 ▪ Oral poetry 208–09 ▪ Anthropologies of the future 308–09 ▪ Political violence and conflict 316

between family, community, and state. Following Partition, the new nations of India and Pakistan enforced the repatriation of women deemed to have settled on the "wrong side" of the new borders. Das observes that this policy occurred because the narrative of women willingly marrying into a family from a different group was not compatible with the justifications behind Partition – that Muslim and Hindu communities must be separate – or the idea of the new nations as guardians of their citizens. Instead, these women's individual narratives were rewritten by the nations as abduction or forced marriage.

The logic of the state and the family usually reinforce one another, but because these pre-Partition marriages were deemed illegitimate by the newly formed nations, children resulting from them also became collateral in repatriations – perceived as belonging neither to their repatriated mother nor their father's family. Children were generally sent with their mother leaving fathers and paternal families to grieve the child's absence. Despite this apparent cruelty in separating families and regardless of many women's resistance to repatriation, Das considers that the enforcement of Partition at the family level was required to uphold the legitimacy of state institutions, and the boundaries between Hindu and Muslim communities.

According to Das, despite public discourses that repatriations were made for the sake of the individual women and children, what was truly at stake was the legitimacy

An **extraordinary event** occurs, **violently disrupting** a person's life.

This **disrupts** how people **relate** to **themselves** and **others**.

The **after-effects** of violence **alter the experience** of what is **ordinary**.

To rebuild an ordinary life, survivors of violence must engage with everyday life.

of the new nations. However, this disrupted the usual priority order of family, community, and state. The firm boundaries required between partitioned communities and nations could not easily be integrated into the institution of the family. This made it even harder for repatriated women attempting to rebuild their lives to articulate their experiences. The narratives for repatriation provided by the new nations led to what Das describes as a "zone of silence" around Partition for these women.

Unspoken damage

Das observes that the after-effects of extraordinary violence are rarely articulated verbally and she draws heavily on the sociolinguistic insights of Austrian philosopher Ludwig Wittgenstein. She takes on his core ideas about language:

firstly that speaking is viewed as an activity and a form of life; secondly, that meaning is derived from the context in which language is spoken; and finally that all forms of communication are viewed in their cultural framework. Das uses these theories to interpret the social relationships and ways of living that survivors of violence choose, and views them as forms of cultural communication that are filled with meaning. For example, a young widow may willingly undertake all of the most tedious chores in her father-in-law's house rather than live a quieter life in the home of her parents, to show herself honourable according to the social norms that dictate a woman's place after marriage is with her husband's family, and to avoid becoming a burden to her natal family. »

> When faced with the kind of trauma that violence visits on us, we have to be engaged in decisions that shape the way that we come to understand our place in the world.
> **Veena Das**

In a process that Das describes as a descent into the ordinary, life is sustained by survivors through engaging in the production of an everyday life again. But this can only be achieved by avoiding laments on the violence they have experienced. Attempts to articulate the incident or its implications in the forms made available by language and social norms are either too exaggerated to be authentic, or entirely inadequate at expressing the events and the feelings attached them. Silence reigns because continuing with the ordinary banalities of life, when violence is actively remembered and communicated, would be unbearable for the survivor.

Becoming ordinary

One of Das's case studies concerns Asha, a 55-year-old woman who had been widowed in 1941 at the age of 20 when her husband had been infected with typhoid. After her husband's death, Asha lived in the house of her late husband's elder brother in Lahore, Pakistan, where she took close care of a nephew and came to informally adopt him. During Partition, Asha's affluent conjugal family lost everything and escaped to India amidst the violence. The family scattered to various other relatives in locations across the new nation. Asha initially stayed at her father's home, but she realized that her presence would ultimately become a burden to the household. Asha was able to perceive this not through direct communication from her family members but through what Das terms an "aesthetic of gestures", including implied words, performative gestures, and social context that Das describes as a "repertoire of culturally dense notions". Eventually, Asha decided to leave her father's house and marry again.

Das uses Asha's culturally laden utterances expressing the Punjabi idea of a woman's destiny being in her husband's house to explain this new marriage. As a widow, Asha became a burden both to her conjugal and natal families after their fortunes declined following Partition. By remarrying, Asha's relationship with her first husband's family became tense, but she continued to nurture her connection with them over a number of years through letter-writing and performances of service for them. Her aim was to retain her relationship with her nephew and maintain a sense of the ordinary through their connection. Das places the choices Asha makes regarding where to live, remarriage, and her effortlessly sustained relationship with her first husband's family as the work of everyday life – a descent into the ordinary that must negotiate cultural and social challenges to produce a "normal" and liveable life.

Rejecting the ordinary

The life trajectory of Asha may be compared with another case study Das uses, focusing on Shanti, a Punjabi Sikh woman living in Delhi. Shanti's husband and four sons were burned alive in the anti-Sikh violence following the assassination of Indian Prime Minister Indira Gandhi by her Sikh bodyguards in 1984. Shanti, who also had two daughters, never recovered from the death of her husband and sons, instead spending her days disconsolately in her room, and either refused or was incapable of interacting with her surviving daughters. She was cared for by female relatives, and never left alone as she frequently expressed a desire to end her life. In Das's view, Shanti's refusal or inability to engage with ordinary life suspended the horror of the violence and loss she experienced.

Sikh families and communities in India begin to regroup and rebuild their lives following three days of riots and violence against the community in November 1984.

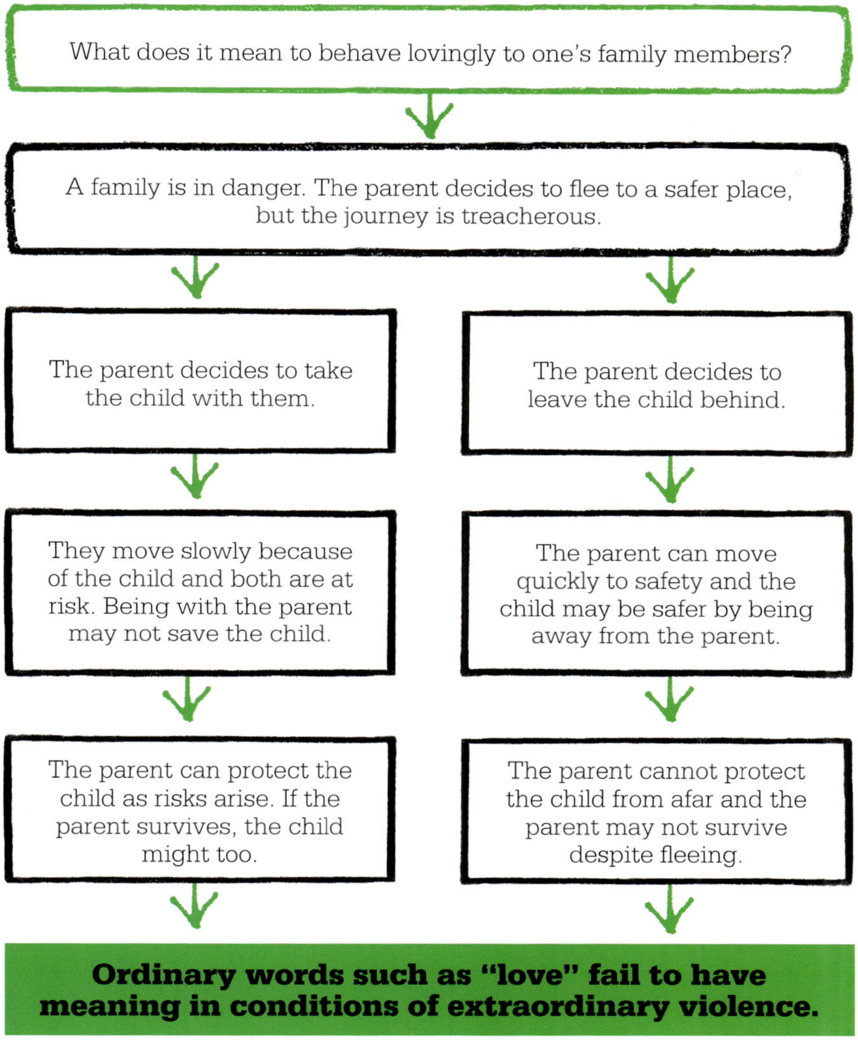

What does it mean to behave lovingly to one's family members?

⬇

A family is in danger. The parent decides to flee to a safer place, but the journey is treacherous.

⬇

The parent decides to take the child with them.

⬇

They move slowly because of the child and both are at risk. Being with the parent may not save the child.

⬇

The parent can protect the child as risks arise. If the parent survives, the child might too.

⬇

The parent decides to leave the child behind.

⬇

The parent can move quickly to safety and the child may be safer by being away from the parent.

⬇

The parent cannot protect the child from afar and the parent may not survive despite fleeing.

⬇

Ordinary words such as "love" fail to have meaning in conditions of extraordinary violence.

Veena Das

Born in India in 1945, Das studied at Indraprastha College for Women and later at the Delhi School of Economics, where she taught anthropology and sociology from 1967, and also received her PhD in 1970. In 1995, she received a gold medal from the Swedish Society for Anthropology and Geography for her work. From 1997 – in addition to her teaching at the Delhi School of Economics – she became professor of anthropology at the New School for Social Research in New York. In 2000, Das joined Johns Hopkins University in the US as a research professor. She was awarded the Nessim Habif Prize from the University of Geneva in 2014, and became a Fellow of the British Academy in 2019. In 2021 Das became the chair of the Department of Anthropology at Johns Hopkins University.

Other key works

1990 *Mirrors of Violence*
1996 *Critical Events*
2020 *Textures of the Ordinary*
2022 *Slum Acts*

However, it also meant that the violence she experienced was carried through every aspect of her lived existence, and continued into the lives of those around her. Das contemplates, however, that a descent into an ordinary life would be difficult for Shanti to achieve, in the context of losing her husband and sons in a society where a woman's role in the family and in her wider community is primarily structured around her interactions with her male relatives.

Making the everyday
By exploring the aftermath of violence as it is experienced in everyday lives, and the noticeable absence of discussion about it, Das offers a distinctive anthropology of violence, intimacy, and the creation of the ordinary. From her detailed study of women negotiating the effects of loss and displacement, she notes that after acts of extraordinary violence, the most notable expression in survivors is conspicuous silence. ∎

HOME AND NOT-HOME
CITIZENSHIP AND BELONGING

IN CONTEXT

KEY WORK
Ruth Mandel,
Cosmopolitan Anxieties,
2008

FIELD
Sociocultural anthropology

BEFORE
1986 Caroline Brettell,
a Canadian cultural
anthropologist, examines
the survival strategies of
immigrants and those left
behind in *Men Who Migrate,
Women Who Wait.*

1994 In *Nations Unbound,*
Linda Basch and colleagues
explore how immigrants build
social networks across national
boundaries, challenging
concepts of citizenship.

AFTER
2024 In *Foreign in Two
Homelands,* US historian
Michelle Lynn Kahn looks
at the dual estrangement of
Turkish migrants, felt in both
their home and host countries.

For the Turkish migrant communities living in Germany, citizenship and belonging do not necessarily go hand in hand. After experiencing huge population losses during World War II, Germany began to invite workers to migrate there in the 1950s and 1960s. The loss of East German labour after the building of the Berlin Wall saw an increase in recruitment, largely from Türkiye, and by 1968 1 million "guest workers" lived in Germany.

In the 1980s and 1990s, US anthropologist Ruth Mandel carried out fieldwork in Berlin and found that many Germans saw themselves as cosmopolitan people, distancing themselves from the Nazi regime. In reality, they were struggling to accept the "cosmopolitans next door": Turkish-German immigrants.

Kreuzberg
During the 1970s and 1980s, Berlin's Kreuzberg district was stigmatized as the largest Turkish ghetto in

Migrants who arrive in a host country to **fill skills shortages** are regarded as **"guests"**.

Migrant families that **retain their language** and cultural traditions while **living in a host country** are seen as **"outsiders"**.

Descendants of migrants who are born in a host country are deemed **"nationals with foreign heritage"** and may struggle to feel accepted.

Nationality and citizenship do not automatically instil a sense of belonging.

See also: Adapting cultural traditions 193 ▪ The value of objects 206–07 ▪ Transcultural predicaments 246–47

Young Turkish protesters march in 1981 against stricter child and youth migration laws specifically aimed at the Turkish community, with a banner that reads: "We do not want to be the Jews of tomorrow".

Europe. Although Turks made up only 19 per cent of the population, Germans perceived the area to be dangerous. They saw the Turkish lifestyle – particularly Turkish women wearing headscarves – as conflicting with their own moral beliefs, and held concerns about non-German foods, mosques, and the Turkish they heard being spoken in the streets. Migrants from Türkiye felt fairly comfortable in Kreuzberg, as they could go about their day speaking Turkish in local shops and schools. However, there was still an underlying fear of the Germans. The migrants also worried about what they saw as immoral behaviour among Germans, such as eating pork and dressing immodestly.

Echoes of history

In her 2008 book *Cosmopolitan Anxieties*, Mandel looks at how assumptions about what it means to be a "real" German perpetuate notions of "us and them". She explains how Nazi-era citizenship law influenced beliefs about authentic inherited "Germanness". Even once this law was liberalized

in 2000, having a passport afforded German nationality but not social or cultural Germanness.

Mandel compares the experiences of Turkish immigrants, ethnic Germans (Russian-Germans), and Jews to comprehend why a German citizen with a Turkish background may not be popularly understood to be a "real" German. In the 1990s, 2 million ethnic Germans were invited from the former Soviet Union. Most spoke no German, but their racial heritage

automatically qualified them for German passports. This distinction gave them a superior status to Turkish Germans who had lived in Germany for decades. Similarly, the post-World War II Jewish community continually heard that they were "Jewish co-citizens" – never simply Germans.

The European diaspora context has, however, presented fresh opportunities for groups that faced ongoing discrimination in Türkiye to find new expression. Germany has seen a flowering of expressive culture among migrant musicians, poets, playwrights, and filmmakers. Their cultural production is often perceived as "ethnic art" – not of equal status to the work of their German colleagues – but with passing decades, intermarriage, and evolving global attitudes, changes are beginning to appear. ▪

The headscarf debate

Many Germans believe that Turkish women cannot fully integrate into German society as long as they wear headscarves. It is assumed that men force their wives and daughters to wear them, but Mandel's analysis shows the situation is far more complex. Ethnographic research reveals that women and girls have their own ideas about why they wear headscarves. Some see it as a moral issue; others as a matter of identity. The latter

believe that Germans think that all Turkish women wear scarves and choose to cover their head to display their Turkishness.

Mandel's work shows that large segments of the Turkish population object to wearing headscarves, including those who identify as secular and anti-religious. Additionally, Alevis, who make up Türkiye's largest religious minority, are not required to wear headscarves. As "uncovered Turks", Alevis have sometimes been seen by Germans to be the "better integrated" migrants.

WE NEED COOKED FOOD

NUTRITION AND HUMAN EVOLUTION

IN CONTEXT

KEY WORK
**Richard Wrangham,
*Catching Fire: How
Cooking Made Us Human*,
2009**

FIELD
Biological anthropology

BEFORE
2002 The raw food "paleo diet"
becomes popular following the
publication of *The Paleo Diet*
by Loren Cordain.

AFTER
2019 Researchers studying the
effects of a raw food diet learn
that eating raw foods disrupts
gut bacterial physiology and
changes digestive processes.

2022 Archaeologists at a
site in Gesher Benot Ya'aqov,
Israel, discover evidence of fish
cookery that dates to about
780,000 years ago. This predates
the arrival of modern humans,
and suggests that early human
species cooked food before
Homo sapiens evolved.

Anthropologist Richard Wrangham spurred public and academic interest with his exploration of the role that cooking has played in human evolution. He argued that cooking made food easier to digest and unlocked more nutrients. According to Wrangham, this meant that early humans consuming cooked food began to obtain more energy from their diet for less effort, which led to changes in the human physique.

The transformative moment that gave rise to the genus *Homo* ... stemmed from the control of fire and the advent of cooked meals.
Richard Wrangham

Large, thickly enamelled teeth became smaller, and humans evolved less powerful jaws as food became easier to chew. Wrangham also noted that when compared with other primates, the human gut is about 60 per cent smaller than would be expected. This was likely the result of cooked food requiring a less complex digestive system as the cooking process partially breaks down the food.

Developing a bigger brain

The shift to cooked food may also have caused the size of the human brain to increase. Calorically, the brain is an expensive organ; Wrangham suggested that the metabolic energy saved in the digestive process was reallocated to the development of the brain. This in turn caused a series of cognitive and behavioural changes in humans. Wrangham also reasoned that communal acts of cooking and sharing food facilitated social bonding and cooperation, and may have contributed to the development of human societies. ■

See also: Social and cultural dimensions of nutrition 80–83 ■ The anthropology of food 200–05 ■ Food and modernity 267

GOD SPEAKS TO THE HUMAN MIND
THE EVANGELICAL EXPERIENCE

IN CONTEXT

KEY WORK
T.M. Luhrmann, *When God Talks Back*, 2012

FIELD
Sociocultural anthropology

BEFORE
1937 British anthropologist
E.E. Evans-Pritchard publishes
Witchcraft, Oracles, and Magic Among the Azande, arguing
that magic is logical in a
cultural context.

1966 Clifford Geertz publishes
"Religion as a Cultural
System", claiming that religion
can be understood as a system
of symbols that shape belief.

AFTER
2020 Luhrmann publishes
How God Becomes Real. She
posits that the effort of making
God real for believers explains
the power of their faith.

2022 A Pew Research Center
study finds an increase in
people who are not affiliated
with any religion.

Amid an increase in secularism in the US, new forms of Christianity have emerged that encourage profound relationships with God. In particular, evangelical churches have replaced formal attire and sombre sermons with casual wear, rock music, and interactive faith. Notably, these churches are not fringe groups, and they attract a wide variety of people.

Close to God
To learn more about US evangelicalism, Tanya Luhrmann joined the Vineyard Christian Fellowship, where congregants told her that to really understand their faith, she should have a cup of coffee with God. For these evangelicals, God is "a deeply human, even vulnerable God who loves us unconditionally and wants nothing more than to be our friend". In this context, God is not a distant spirit but a constant companion who cares about everything from one's daily concerns to one's existential doubts.

Worshippers at Vineyard churches in the US engaging in music-based prayer were observed by Luhrmann to feel a closeness to God.

Luhrmann examines how believers engage in a learning process to experience God in this way. They train their mind to attend to thoughts, sensations, and emotions that suggest evidence of God, re-interpreting everyday things as signs of God. In so doing, evangelicals use their mind to experience a real God who speaks to the human need to feel heard and loved. ■

See also: The universal nature of religion 28–29 ▪ The social roots of religion 42–43 ▪ The fluidity of social systems 102–03

MOLECULAR ORIGINS

DNA POLITICS

The question of who is Native American and who has the power to decide has become a feature of debates about Indigenous identity. In *Native American DNA*, US anthropologist Kim TallBear examines how genetic science intersects with identities, sovereignty, and cultural belonging. A member of the Sisseton-Wahpeton Oyate, TallBear challenges the simplistic narratives about ancestry and identity that often result from genetic research.

Identity can be based on biological ancestry

⬇

Consumer DNA tests provide **clear and simple results**.

⬇

Laboratories determine group **membership** based on **genetics**.

⬇

This **simplistic** approach overlooks the effects of kinship and **cultural practices**.

Identity can be based on kinship and cultural belonging

⬇

Oral history and cultural knowledge underpin **shared heritage** and **social ties**.

⬇

Indigenous leaders and communities uphold membership **through culture**.

⬇

This approach **values** cultural continuity and **complex identities**.

TallBear's work addresses DNA testing in the context of historical and ongoing exploitation of Indigenous communities. She questions the deterministic view of genetic science, which attempts to define Indigenous identities through genetic markers, and disregards the complexities of affiliations, kinship systems, and the cultural practices that define Indigenous peoples.

Science and identity

TallBear points out that membership to a Native American nation is a legal category developed within a historical context. The use of DNA testing to determine membership into a nation is problematic because the genetic "markers" selected by researchers are not defined by Indigenous communities, but rather by what is assumed to be a neutral scientific process. However, like any other

Traditional clothing, as worn by a member of the Onion Lake Cree Nation performing a Chicken Dance, enables Indigenous peoples to acknowledge and express their cultural identity.

> The power inequalities are real in this world in which DNA narratives increasingly grab centre stage in the telling of human history and the construction of human identities.
> **Kim TallBear**

human activity, science is shaped by particular social, economic, historical, and political processes.

Central to TallBear's critique is the concept of "settler colonial science". She argues that much of Western science was developed to justify the dispossession and marginalization of Indigenous peoples. Even today, it informs Western outlooks that prioritize genetics over Indigenous ways of knowing and being. While TallBear recognizes that genetic science can be appealing – and that some Indigenous people have adopted it as part of how they articulate their identity – she ultimately rejects the notion that genetic data alone can determine Indigenous ancestry.

TallBear challenges the harmful narratives that can arise from genetic analysis, arguing that they revive elements of racist colonial ideas. She asserts that, in the context of establishing heritage, Indigenous perspectives should be placed at the heart of discussions about the use of genetic research. ▪

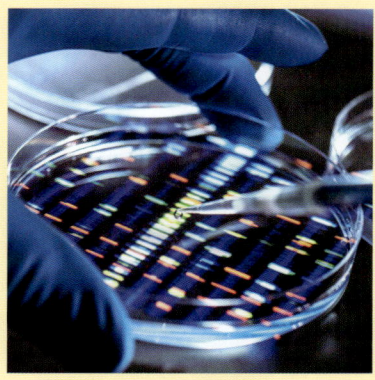

DNA testing

Anthropologists argue that DNA testing oversimplifies complex social identities and cultural affiliations by reducing identity to genetic markers or ancestry percentages. This approach disregards the fluid and contextual nature of human identity: it reinforces stereotypes and overlooks the experiences and cultural practices that shape a person's sense of self.

DNA testing also raises ethical concerns around consent and privacy. Many companies collect and store vast amounts of genetic data without transparent policies on how this information is used, shared, or protected. This raises questions about the ownership of genetic information and the potential misuse of data for profit, discrimination, or other exploitative purposes.

In addition, the way in which ancestry tests use genetic markers to categorize individuals into fixed racial groups can perpetuate false notions that race is a biological fact, rather than a social construct – and this can serve to reinforce racial stereotypes and inequalities.

THE FOREST HAS ITS OWN LIFE

RELATING TO NON-HUMAN BEINGS

IN CONTEXT

KEY WORK
Eduardo Kohn, *How Forests Think*, **2013**

FIELD
Sociocultural anthropology

BEFORE
1972 British anthropologist Gregory Bateson proposes that the concept of "mind" emerges not just in humans but in the relationships between living beings and their environments.

1991 Bruno Latour critiques Western science for artificially dividing "nature" and "society", and ignoring their interconnectedness.

AFTER
2015 Anna Tsing publishes *The Mushroom at the End of the World*, illustrating how non-human species survive in contemporary landscapes.

2017 New Zealand grants legal personhood to the Whanganui River, recognizing Māori beliefs that view the river as a sacred ancestor.

How other kinds of beings see us matters. That other kinds of beings see us changes things.
Eduardo Kohn

Anthropologists have long grappled with theorizing the role of non-humans – such as animals, plants, landscapes, and objects – in shaping human societies. They have also struggled to include non humans as active participants in shaping the world in ethnographic studies. By the mid-20th century, sociocultural anthropology had largely accepted the distinction between culture and nature, with culture regarded as a socially constructed system that anthropologists could interpret. This approach, exemplified by Clifford Geertz's work, treated culture as something that could be read like text.

However, global challenges have prompted a reassessment of these categories. Climate change, the exploitation of non-human life in industries such as factory farming and industrial agriculture, and the ethical concerns surrounding how anthropologists represent other cultures have all contributed to this shift. These issues have

Ecuador's Amazonian rainforest is central to Eduardo Kohn's work on interspecies communication. Kohn argues humans, animals, and plants engage in shared meaning-making.

encouraged scholars to rethink the boundaries between human and non-human worlds, reconsider the role of non-humans in social life, and question what constitutes society itself.

The ontological turn

One approach to address this anthropological crisis is called the ontological turn – a movement that challenges the idea that humans alone define reality. Ontology, a branch of philosophy, explores the nature of reality, and the ontological turn asks: how do different communities – human and non-human – understand and shape reality itself?

This approach is associated with scholars such as French philosopher and sociologist Bruno Latour, French anthropologist Philippe Descola, Brazilian

See also: The structure of language 44–45 ▪ Language and cognition 88–89 ▪ Structuralism 108
▪ Chimpanzee behaviours 132–35 ▪ The capacity for communication 182 ▪ Multispecies ethnography 194–95

anthropologist Eduardo Viveiros de Castro, and US anthropologist Anna Tsing. Although their ideas differ, they share a common argument: reality is not solely constructed through human culture or language. Instead, it is shaped by animals, plants, landscapes, and even objects. For example, Latour's Actor-Network Theory (ANT) suggests that everything – from smartphones to forests – has "agency", or the ability to act and influence outcomes. In rejecting anthropocentrism – the belief that humans are superior to other life forms – these thinkers highlight how entangled human existence is with the rest of the planet.

The forest's voice

Canadian-American anthropologist Eduardo Kohn is among the scholars engaging with these ideas. His book *How Forests Think* – based on four years of fieldwork with the Runa people in the Upper Amazon – explores how non-human life, including animals, plants, and spirits, participates in meaning-

making. His work challenges conventional ideas about what it means to think and who – or what – is capable of doing so.

Kohn expands the ontological turn's focus on non-human life by drawing on the semiotic framework of US scientist Charles Sanders Peirce, and the work of US biological anthropologist Terrence Deacon. Peirce's semiotics explores how signs create meaning, and provides a way to understand how both humans and non-humans use signs to communicate. In *How Forests Think*, Kohn explores how the Runa people communicate with the beings that inhabit the forest and how these beings, in turn, communicate with them. At its core, Kohn's book is an exploration of what it truly means to communicate.

Kohn chose Ecuador's Amazonian rainforest as his field site because its extraordinary biodiversity made it an ideal setting to examine communication across species. As one of the most densely interconnected ecosystems

on the planet, it offers a vivid example of how meaning emerges not only among humans but between humans, animals, and the environment itself.

The meaning of thinking

Traditional anthropology claimed that only humans have the ability to think, and view language as the system through which we make sense of the world. Kohn, however, questions this belief. He argues that the way humans think – shaped by the structure of our language – has influenced how we view other life forms. Specifically, Kohn suggests that the binary thinking present in language – where everything is understood in terms of opposites like human and animal, or nature and culture – leads us to project this same way of thinking onto all living things, and assume that only humans can truly "think".

Kohn critiques this approach for relegating non-humans to the status of mute objects onto which humans project meaning. »

Surviving in the ruins of capitalism

Chinese-American anthropologist Anna Tsing's *The Mushroom at the End of the World* (2015) investigates how life persists in landscapes scarred by capitalism.

Her book is centred on the matsutake mushroom, a delicacy in Japan, which thrives in the disturbed environments and degraded forests of Oregon, US, Yunnan, China, and Finnish Lapland. Tsing traces how marginalized groups – displaced loggers, refugees, and

Indigenous foragers – harvest these mushrooms, and sell them through global supply chains to luxury markets.

Unlike crops that succumb to industrial control, matsutake resist cultivation, and only flourish in capitalist "ruins." This paradox underscores Tsing's argument: survival hinges on collaboration among humans and non-humans. Foragers, traders, and ecosystems form fragile alliances to navigate precarious economic conditions and sustain livelihoods.

Harvesting matsutake mushrooms builds a connection between nature, foragers, traders, and global markets.

A woolly monkey, which is native to the Amazon rainforest, uses vocalizations to communicate with its social group over several acres of forest. In particular, females use clicks and teeth chatters to call to their mates.

Instead, he argues that meaning is embedded in the world, existing outside of human minds. For example, when we walk in a forest and a thought arises, Kohn suggests that this thought may not be just our inner response to external stimuli, but rather something co-produced with the forest itself, composed by the myriad of "thinking" beings that inhabit it.

Including the thoughts of non-human beings in anthropological studies raises important theoretical questions and ethical considerations. Kohn's work challenges us to rethink how we categorize and understand the world, urging scholars to expand their ideas to include the ways non-human creatures think and communicate.

The life of signs

Semiotics – the study of how signs interact and create meaning – provides a framework for understanding communication among humans and non-living things. Kohn identifies three interrelated types of sign – icons, indexes, and symbols. Together these form a dynamic system of communication that works on different levels.

Icons are the simplest type of sign. They create a general, broad image or representation of something, often without providing much detail. Icons work by highlighting certain features that resemble the object or event they represent, while ignoring others. For example, a photograph, a map, or even words that imitate sounds – such as "buzz" or "meow" – are all icons.

Indexes rely on icons for their existence but are more specific. They emerge from the relationships between icons and prompt action by encouraging the interpreter to think about the consequences of their actions. For example, when a monkey hears a crash in the forest, it anticipates danger based on previous experiences. Similarly, a dog learns that the word "sit" signals the promise of a treat.

Symbols rely on both icons and indexes but are more complex than the previous two signs from which they emerge. They are unique to humans and arise from the ability to think through language. One peculiar characteristic of symbolic signification is its tendency to break from the usual chain of meaning. This can create a sense of separation from the rest of life – a divide that humans must overcome.

Kohn suggests that when a person becomes overly absorbed in their own mind, or disengaged from their environment, it may result in panic. This feeling represents a deep disconnection from the broader network of meaning-making, or "semiosis," that exists across life. Kohn's system of signs forms a hierarchical "living system" in

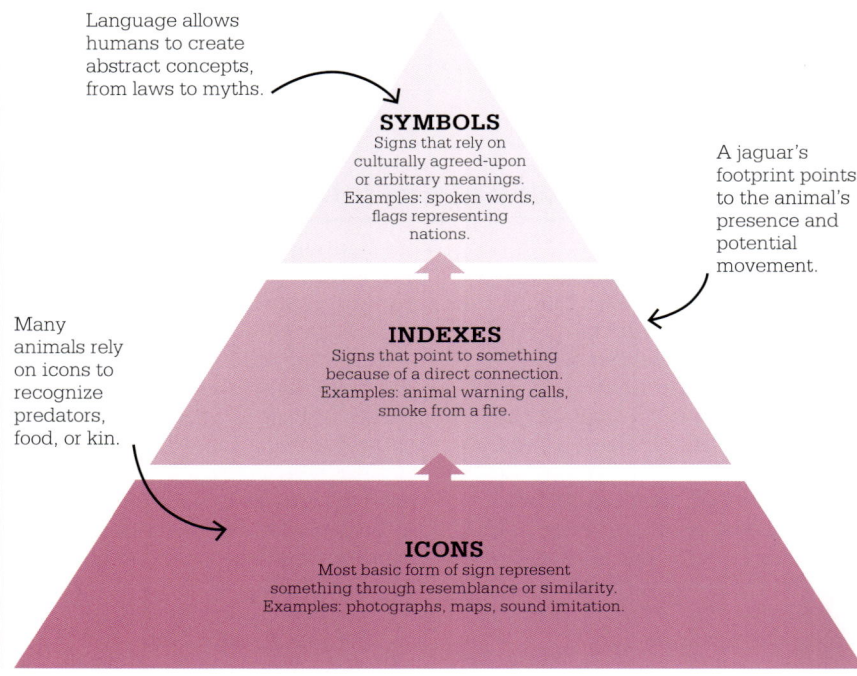

Language allows humans to create abstract concepts, from laws to myths.

A jaguar's footprint points to the animal's presence and potential movement.

Many animals rely on icons to recognize predators, food, or kin.

SYMBOLS
Signs that rely on culturally agreed-upon or arbitrary meanings. Examples: spoken words, flags representing nations.

INDEXES
Signs that point to something because of a direct connection. Examples: animal warning calls, smoke from a fire.

ICONS
Most basic form of sign represent something through resemblance or similarity. Examples: photographs, maps, sound imitation.

which all forms of life participate, communicating and creating a dynamic exchange of meaning across species and environments.

Patterns without design

Kohn also adopted Terrence Deacon's concept of "form" to explain how natural patterns in forests emerge from dynamic interactions within an ecosystem. Unlike signs, which require active interpretation, form arises spontaneously from the interactions within ecosystems – whether between trees, animals, or non-living elements. It is a fundamental property of the world itself, not something imposed on the world by human thought.

To illustrate this concept, Kohn uses the example of the rubber boom in the Amazon to show how distinct elements can come together to constitute a form. In the late 19th century, innovations in the car industry increased the European demand for rubber, which ultimately led to colonial violence and the exploitation of Indigenous people in the region. Kohn argues that this event was not merely the outcome of economic pressures but emerged from the interplay of a variety of factors. Rubber trees, for example, naturally grow far apart – a spacing that, while making them difficult to cultivate, also made the trees resistant to parasites. This spacing was part of a larger configuration that includes the regions's intricate river networks, which enabled the effective transport of rubber but also gave colonizers easy access to otherwise remote regions. The rubber boom's occurrence in the Amazon was not, Kohn argues, coincidental. It was the result of interactions within this form that involved humans, animals, and

> Forests are good to think because they themselves think. Forests think. I want to take this seriously.
> **Eduardo Kohn**

various other participants. The concept of form is important in Kohn's work because it helps anthropologists to theorize large historical events in a way that is not purely human-centred – while still acknowledging the violence used to push people, animals and landscapes into those forms. It reconceptualizes analytical categories and provides tools to avoid repeating past mistakes. Ultimately, it also forces scholars to recognize that human agency is not the only factor in shaping events.

Thinking beyond human

Kohn's innovative framework challenges many of the assumptions of traditional anthropology by revealing that humans are not the only thinking beings. Other creatures, from monkeys to trees, engage with different types of signs alongside us, participating in the construction of meaning in ways that were overlooked by earlier anthropological structures in the past. His framework helps anthropologists to develop a more inclusive understanding of how the world is continuously being co-created by all its participants. ∎

Actor-network theory

Developed in the 1980s by French sociologist Bruno Latour, Actor-Network Theory (ANT) is a framework that examines how both human and non-human actors – technologies, objects, and institutions – collaboratively shape social networks. Rejecting divisions between society and nature, ANT treats all entities as interconnected "actants" with agency. For instance, a scientific discovery relies not just on a researcher but also on lab tools, funding, and peer reviews.

ANT flattens hierarchies, emphasizing that power arises from relationships, not fixed roles. This approach helps anthropologists to analyse how people, animals, and environments co-create meaning. In Eduardo Kohn's studies of Amazonian ecosystems, ANT's ethos aligns with his view of forests as dynamic, "thinking" spaces shaped by multi- species interactions.

Bruno Latour's theories reimagine the world as a complex network where science, society, and nature are inextricably intertwined.

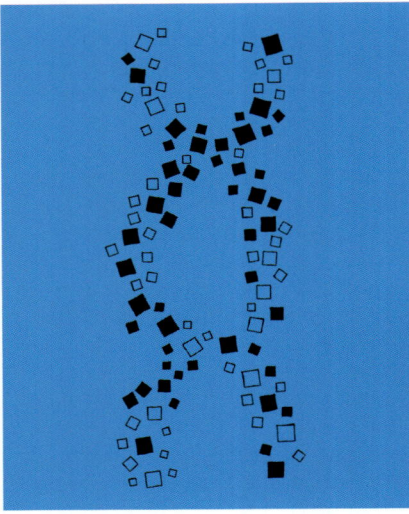

THE MOSAIC THAT IS OUR GENOME

SEQUENCING ANCIENT DNA

The study of ancient DNA has revolutionized the understanding of human evolution, offering unprecedented insights into how *Homo sapiens* is related to extinct hominins. The extraction and sequencing of DNA from ancient remains, once thought impossible due to the degradation of genetic material, became possible thanks to advances in technology. The breakthrough came in 1997, when Swedish evolutionary geneticist Svante Pääbo and his team successfully sequenced a portion of the Neanderthal genome. Their work proved that *Homo sapiens* and Neanderthals are distinct species, and revealed that their lineages diverged about 500,000 years ago.

Ancient connections
By 2010, Pääbo was able to sequence the full Neanderthal genome. His research, published in 2014, revealed that sometime after early modern humans left Africa about 70,000 years ago, they bred with Neanderthals. As a result, between 2 and 4 per cent of the genome of most modern-day Europeans and Asians comes from these Neanderthal ancestors.

Neanderthal genes have been linked to various health conditions in modern humans, including skin disorders, psychiatric issues, and vitamin B1 deficiency, according to researchers at Vanderbilt University, Tennessee, USA.

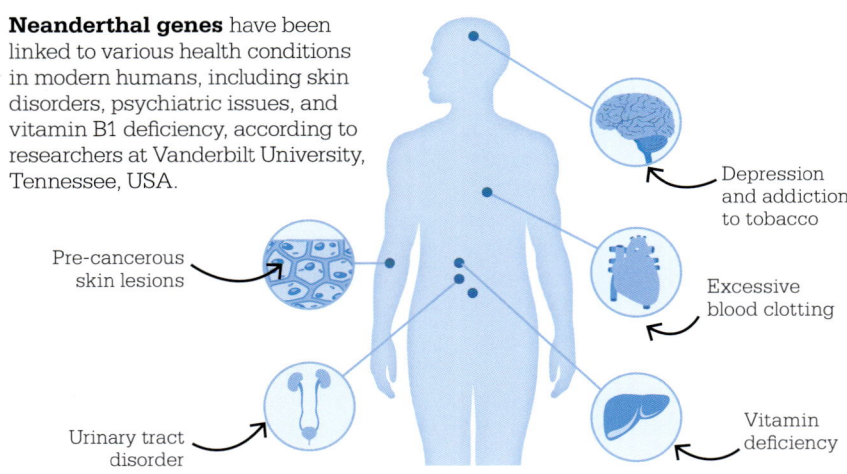

Depression and addiction to tobacco

Excessive blood clotting

Vitamin deficiency

Pre-cancerous skin lesions

Urinary tract disorder

See also: The theory of evolution 24–25 ▪ Unilineal evolution 26–27 ▪ The evolutionary synthesis 86–87 ▪ Origins of humanity 94–101 ▪ Multilinear evolution 104–07 ▪ Human burials 306

Pääbo's team also examined ancient mitochondrial DNA (mtDNA), which is inherited from the mother, and can provide insights into human ancestry. Pääbo made a second surprising discovery in 2010, when he sequenced the mtDNA from a tiny 40,000-year-old finger bone found in Denisova Cave, Siberia. Based on its shape, Pääbo initially thought that the bone had belonged to a Neanderthal. However, the DNA was so distinct that Pääbo concluded it came from a new species of hominin, which he described as Denisovan.

This new species likely lived alongside Neanderthals and humans in Eurasia for tens of thousands of years. Later research showed that like Neanderthals, Denisovans also interbred with early humans. As a result, Southeast Asian and Melanesian peoples today may share up to 6 per cent of their DNA with their Denisovan ancestors.

Genetic legacies

Many Tibetans also carry traces of Denisovan ancestry. In 2010, researchers at the University of California, Berkeley, began to investigate EPAS1, a gene variant found in Tibetan populations. This gene enhances the ability to survive in high-altitude, low-oxygen environments by regulating red blood cell production and preventing the blood from thickening – a danger at high elevations. In 2014, the researchers concluded that the gene variant almost certainly had a Denisovan origin, and that this inherited adaptation enabled Tibetans to survive in hostile conditions.

Pääbo and his team also conducted research into the effects ancient DNA has on human populations today. The findings of a study published in 2020 indicated that Neanderthal genes may influence how the immune system responds to infections. For example, individuals with a specific Neanderthal gene cluster were at higher risk of becoming severely ill with COVID-19. The team discovered that this genetic material is present in around 50 per cent of people in South Asia and 16 per cent of people in Europe.

Nobel recognition

In 2022, Svante Pääbo was awarded the Nobel Prize in Medicine for his discoveries relating to human evolution and the genomes of extinct hominins. His research helped to give rise to the new scientific discipline of paleogenomics. By revealing genetic differences between living humans and extinct hominins, and by identifying how the genetic contributions of ancient hominins affect human health today, paleogenomics opens important new avenues to explore what it means to be human. ▪

> The discovery of the basis of genetic variation has opened inroads to understanding our history as a species.
> **Svante Pääbo**
> *Nature*, 2003

Fossil evaluation
Fossils are selected for DNA analysis according to criteria such as their age or their state of preservation.

Contamination control
The fossil is handled in a sterile room by a researcher wearing protective clothing to avoid contamination.

DNA extraction and sequencing
Chemical processes extract DNA, which is then sequenced to reveal the precise arrangement of its structure.

Data analysis and comparison
The sequenced DNA is compared with that of modern human genomes and other ancient species.

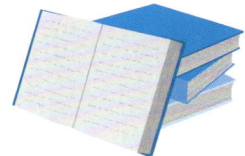

Interpretation and publication
Scientists can identify genes derived from ancient humans in modern populations and assess their effects.

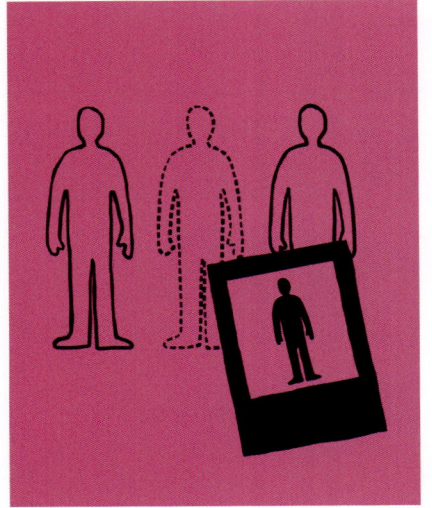

TO PHOTOGRAPH IS TO APPROPRIATE THE THING PHOTOGRAPHED

THE POWER OF PHOTOGRAPHY

IN CONTEXT

KEY WORK
Jane Lydon, *Calling the Shots*, 2014

FIELD
Sociocultural anthropology

BEFORE
1977 US cultural critic Susan Sontag frames photography as an ideological and political act in a series of essays published as *On Photography*.

AFTER
2018 US art historian Tanya Sheehan publishes *Photography and Migration*, which explores the politics and ethics of photography involving migrants.

2020 *National Geographic* reports that COVID-19 travel restrictions caused it to hire more local photojournalists – who were able to secure access to people in their own backyards, and gain their trust – resulting in richer and more nuanced storytelling.

Today, photography is commonplace, but initially the ability to photograph people, places, and things was reserved for the wealthy and those in power. Imperialists and scientists used photography as a weapon, a tool to freeze people of colour in time and place in the service of colonization. During the 19th and early 20th centuries,

Carefully positioned personal items at the centre of this 1880s image suggest that the two women from the Prairie Band Potawatomi Nation influenced the photographer's setup.

Indigenous groups and people of colour were seen to be in need of colonial or scientific intervention and assimilation into the Western world. Photographs depicting people in various states of "evolution" – with white people representing the pinnacle of societal development – appeared to support this idea, and were widely circulated. These images had a lasting impact, and even today may be used to perpetuate racist ideas.

Global archive

Since the 1970s, researchers have written about this global photographic archive, examining how imperialists sought to represent Indigenous groups and people of colour as less advanced or evolved than those in power. These accounts assume that the people who were photographed and depicted in a negative light had no power to counteract or respond to colonizers. Recently, however, new research on the history of photography in Indigenous communities – and the way in which Indigenous people have used historic images in modern times – suggest that this was not always the case.

See also: Local belief systems 78–79 ▪ Commodity fetishism 180–81 ▪ The ethics of anthropology 248–49

Working with photovoice

> **Visual anthropologist** gives each research participant a **camera to document** a particular **issue or experience**.

→

> Participants **take photographs** relating to the area of research and **share them** with the visual anthropologist.

↓

> Anthropologist **interviews participants** about their images to **learn more** about their **experiences**.

←

> **Photovoice research informs the anthropologist's findings.**

In *Calling the Shots*, Australian archaeologist and historian Jane Lydon and her colleagues write that Indigenous people were not always passive victims of colonial photographers. When affordable cameras were introduced in the 20th century, Indigenous groups in Australia began to create their own photographic archives to challenge racist stereotypes. Rather than focusing on a white photographer's interpretation of what they saw, Lydon concentrates on living meanings that photographs have today; for instance, she suggests that an image of an Aboriginal man climbing a tree may be a demonstration of agility.

Photographic agency

In some parts of the world, colonial photographs have been returned – or repatriated – to families and communities. From these images, narratives have emerged that document culture, re-establish family and land connections,

and challenge histories. Many Indigenous groups now safeguard their historic photographs: for example, The Plateau Peoples' Web Portal was created in 2015 to ensure Indigenous people in the US Pacific Northwest have control over their digital archive. It is designed to allow individual groups to determine who can read and view their historic photographs and other material.

Indigenous people have also been able to use photographs to support their claims to land and provide evidence of long-term occupation. The Wurundjeri people in Australia, for example, have drawn upon visual archives to prove their historic connection to land around Melbourne amid attempts by colonizers to deny their presence. Cases like this demonstrate one way in which Indigenous peoples can convert photographs from instruments of discrimination into opportunities to right the wrongs of the past. ▪

Visual anthropology

Encompassing all that is visual in the world – films, photographs, and other media – the field of visual anthropology investigates material created by scholars and anthropologists, as well as that produced by other people they study. In the early days of anthropology, ethnographers created photographs, drawings, and films to document the people and places they encountered. Today, visual anthropologists analyse these materials to make sense of how a place or culture has changed over time.

British visual anthropologist Sabrina Jones photographs that which has been forgotten: unmarked Irish graves known as cillíní. These graves entomb people who were not allowed to be buried in Roman Catholic cemeteries. Jones draws upon photography to give "some sort of permanence to the deaths" in the hope that it will bring peace to those who have been neglected by the Roman Catholic Church.

Irish cillíní often contain sacred objects, brought and arranged by the loved ones who maintain the grave and care for the dead.

BLACK GIRLS SHIFT THE SHAPE OF SPACES

CHALLENGING SYSTEMIC OPPRESSION

Following eight years of fieldwork at a girls' homeless shelter in Detroit, Michigan, Aimee Meredith Cox used the critical perspective of Black girls to analyse the contradictions of US citizenship in the 21st century.

Cox began volunteering at Give Girls a Chance (GGC) – a non-profit, community-based social service

Dance and choreography provide a visual interpretation of Cox's key concept of shapeshifting, showing how young Black women must contort themselves and the world around them.

agency – in 2000, and went on to serve in several different roles, including as a dance teacher and as shelter director. In her book *Shapeshifters*, Cox paints a compelling portrait of a city greatly affected by displacement and urban deindustrialization, and presents "Detroitness" as its own unique identity.

Defining shapeshifting

In a society that often either ignores or maligns young Black women, Cox puts Black girls at the centre of her research, but not as

See also: Fighting racial segregation 30–31 ▪ Academic disidentification 240–41 ▪ The role of African American Vernacular English 254–55 ▪ Long-term deep interviewing techniques 256–57 ▪ Reproductive inequality 310–11

problems to be solved or objects to be worried about. Rather, she affirms their agency, autonomy, and ability to build and create what they need. *Shapeshifters* offers several important theories that advance the fields of Black girlhood studies, anthropology, and even broader Black studies.

Cox defines shapeshifting as something that reveals our collective vulnerabilities. She argues that Black women are "inherently shapeshifters" because circumstances require them to be; they shift the shape of spaces and institutions that attempt to restrict and punish them.

New terminology

Drawing on her background as a dancer, Cox presents a theory of "choreography" to describe how young Black women interact with institutions and state practices. A physical take on shapeshifting, choreography can disrupt the dominant discourse that views young Black women as undesirable, dangerous, and out of place.

> Our failures to articulate and witness Black girlhood as a dynamic, creative space continually being remade in the future tense have grave consequences.
> **Aimee Meredith Cox**

In addition, Cox's theory of "critical entitlement" puts a positive spin on a word that is usually thought of as negative by asserting that young Black women are entitled to protection and care. They have a right to live free from harm – whether physical, emotional, or mental. For instance, some of the young women in the homeless shelter ended up there because they lived in overcrowded, multigenerational family homes in which women performed most of the care-giving, while the men failed to contribute financially or otherwise. Young Black women may decide to flee that kind of scenario because they feel entitled to more than merely surviving.

Reshaping preconceptions

Cox analyses how young Black women are often described in terms of redemption narratives that involve a shift from tragedy to uplift. These stories are often considered necessary for the women to be seen as worthy of concern. Similarly, narratives of exception are used to describe Black girls who achieve a remarkable measure of normative success. Cox asks why young Black women must "beat the odds" in order to be considered worthy.

The young Black women at the heart of Cox's work do not allow themselves to be viewed as statistics; they demand the right to be seen as full human beings who are entitled to all the benefits of citizenship. ∎

Aimee Meredith Cox

Born in 1971, Aimee Meredith Cox grew up in Cincinnati, Ohio. She is a critical ethnographer, writer, and movement artist with a BA in anthropology from Vassar College, New York, and a PhD in cultural anthropology from the University of Michigan. She is currently associate professor of anthropology at New York University.

Cox trained for most of her young adult life in ballet and contemporary dance and toured with the Alvin Ailey repertory ensemble Ailey II and the Dance Theatre of Harlem. She is also a yoga teacher. This background informs her other research interests, which include performance ethnography, youth cultural production, critical race theory, and dance studies.

Other key works

2009 "Thugs, Black Divas, and Gendered Aspirations"
2014 "The Body and the City Project: Young Black Women Making Space, Community, and Love in Newark, New Jersey"

STORIES
TOLD FROM
OBJECTS

DOCUMENTING THE UNDOCUMENTED

The desert is a tool of boundary enforcement and a strategic slayer of border crossers.
Jason De León

Increased **border surveillance** intended to deter migration into the US **funnels migrants** towards less controlled, **riskier entry points**.

US immigration policy uses the desert as a **political weapon**, intentionally causing **migrants' deaths**.

Migrants are so desperate to reach the US that crossing the desert is **not an effective deterrent**.

Policymakers are urged to reconsider the implications of border enforcement on human lives.

US anthropologist Jason De León's interest in the lives of migrants who cross the deserts along the US–Mexico border has resulted in an influential body of work that demonstrates the holistic dimensions of anthropology – and their potential power.

In his book *The Land of Open Graves: Living and Dying on the Migrant Trail*, De León uses research methods from archaeology and forensic anthropology to understand the lives of the undocumented Latino migrants who seek to reach the US. This involves an analysis of items that migrants leave behind during their desert crossing – from backpacks to treasured mementos, and the bodies of fellow travellers.

Anti-immigrant rhetoric portrays those fleeing persecution or war in their countries of origin as a faceless horde, but De León seeks the humanity behind their perilous journeys.

He also employs ethnographic research to explore the real costs of government policies on the lives of migrants and their families. De León's work challenges the "often sterile anthropological discussion about Latino migration" in favour of a more informal approach. He recounts stories, uses humour, and

See also: Fighting racial segregation 30–31 ▪ Biopsychological functionalism 50–55 ▪ Studying up 138–39 ▪ Gender, sexuality, and power 158–59 ▪ The ethics of anthropology 248–49 ▪ Critical ethnography 270–71

gives details of interactions he has had with undocumented migrants and their families, as well as with Mexican and US authorities.

Necroviolent policies

The Land of Open Graves centres on the effects of the Prevention Through Deterrence policy, which has been implemented by the US government since 1994. This policy aims to reduce the numbers of undocumented Latin American immigrants entering the US through Mexico without inspection by increasing border security in areas where it is easiest and safest to cross. The creators of the policy assumed that funnelling migrants into the most dangerous places to cross the border would deter people from attempting to enter the US. However, in practice, the motivations to migrate have proven so strong and dire that people continue to make this journey despite the increased risks.

Prevention Through Deterrence has resulted in thousands of deaths since its implementation,

Common motivations for migration
Organized crime and violence
Political violence and persecution
Climate-related disasters including flooding, droughts and crop failures, lack of potable water, landslides, wildfires
Domestic abuse and lack of social support
Violence and discrimination related to gender and sexuality
Fragile or failed states, and societal collapse

mainly because migrants cross searingly hot, desolate desert landscapes that the US government knows are treacherous and deadly.

De León believes that the government's use of the desert as a political weapon is an example of "necroviolence" – a form of governmental control over the life and death of certain groups. He then illustrates the concept of necropolitics – that is, the ways in which governments politicize necroviolence. The US government uses necropolitical devices such as

the unforgiving Sonoran Desert as a mechanism to distance itself from the act of killing. If the government is not directly responsible for taking a migrant's life, it "cleverly increases the degrees of separation between victim and perpetrator".

According to De León, the US Border Patrol disguises its true intentions by using neutral terminology that redirects blame from the policy itself to the desert. By identifying the natural environment as the main threat to »

A history of US immigration policy

Movement into the US was initially largely unregulated, and the open borders attracted large numbers of settlers. Rising immigration prompted the 1882 Chinese Exclusion Act, the first law to limit immigration based on nationality. The Immigration Act of 1924 introduced quotas that reduced immigration from southern Europe, Asia, and Africa.

In 1965, the Immigration and Nationality Act prioritized family reunification and skilled labour,

and it led to more immigration from Latin America and Asia. The 1986 Immigration Reform and Control Act granted amnesties to undocumented immigrants who had been in the US since before 1982 but imposed penalties on employers hiring illegal aliens.

Debates over border security have shaped 21st-century immigration policy. The Homeland Security Act of 2002 consolidated immigration enforcement under the Department of Homeland Security after the 9/11 attacks.

Immigrants wait to be processed at Ellis Island, New York, in 1907. Issues of security and human rights make migration a contentious topic.

the migrants who choose to cross there, the government hopes to be exonerated in the public eye.

However, the violence that migrants experience on the border is neither random nor unexpected; instead, it is an intentional element of a US federal plan that is rarely seen for what it is: a killing machine that "simultaneously uses and hides behind the viciousness of the Sonoran Desert".

Brutal reality

De León's work exploring migration and government policy highlights the importance of taking a holistic, multidisciplinary approach. Traditionally, anthropologists conduct research employing the particular methods designed for their sub-field. Archaeologists unearth artefacts in a prescribed manner; forensic anthropologists examine specific bone markers; and cultural anthropologists use ethnographic approaches to reveal the cultural framework that guides people's lives. By bringing together these different disciplines, De León is able to offer a comprehensive critique of the consequences of US immigration policy.

> Necropolitics, or killing in the name of sovereignty, is not about abstract notions of reason, truth, or freedom. It's about the tangibles of life and death.
> **Jason De León**

Immigration is a highly sensitive political issue, but the additional dimension of studying human remains introduces another layer of ethical complexity. De León takes photographs of deceased individuals, which helps him to identify them and connect with their families. He argues that the disturbing nature of the photos of dead bodies helps him drive home the point that there is nothing dignified or soothing about the deaths that migrants experience in the desert. Their deaths are shocking and should be alarming to people. They represent stark visual reminders of what the Prevention Through Deterrence policy looks like in reality.

Because many of these migrants die alone and far from population centres, they are unlikely ever to be found. Witnesses of migrant deaths are reluctant to come forward for fear of legal repercussions, and bodies left behind are ravaged by extreme temperatures and scavenging animals. De León points out that this invisibility and desolate suffering are part of necroviolence, and he encourages his readers to recognize the importance of shedding light on this brutal situation.

Dehumanizing deaths

Desert crossings are cruel and brutal experiences during which many people die slow and painful deaths as a result of ailments such as hyperthermia, dehydration, and heatstroke. De León says that to describe these deaths as anything other than horrific does a disservice to those who experienced them, as well as being a denial of the harsh desert reality.

A poignant section of the book expands on the research techniques De León adopted in the desert, including experiments with pigs' carcasses – dressed in clothes a migrant might wear – to study how bodies decompose in such severe conditions.

De León notes that the desert environment severely dehumanizes the remains. In one experiment, he places a note with a name in the

A cross left by border activists marks the spot where a migrant died while trying to cross into the US. More than 220 deaths were reported in this section of the Sonoran Desert in 2020.

pocket of a pig's clothing, mirroring a practice many migrants use in hopes of being identified if they fail to survive. He discovers that the note is entirely lost or destroyed during the decomposition process. Additionally, he describes how vultures, insects, and other animals contribute to the rapid and violent breakdown of the remains.

These observations support De León's argument in two key ways: they highlight the brutal effects of necroviolence on human lives, and they demonstrate the futility of deterrence strategies, showing that people will risk their lives to migrate, often feeling that they have no other choice.

Personal stories

During one of these experiments in the desert, De León and his team stumbled upon the body of a woman. He describes it in vivid detail, noting that her face was "unrecognizable as human". De León contacted the authorities and, with the assistance of a specialized organization, identified the deceased as Maricela, a young woman from Ecuador who had hoped to join her husband's family in New York.

Migrant deaths are mainly due to dehydration: it is physically impossible for travellers to carry the amount of water needed to survive the desert crossing. Charitable organizations are setting up water stations to save people from dehydration.

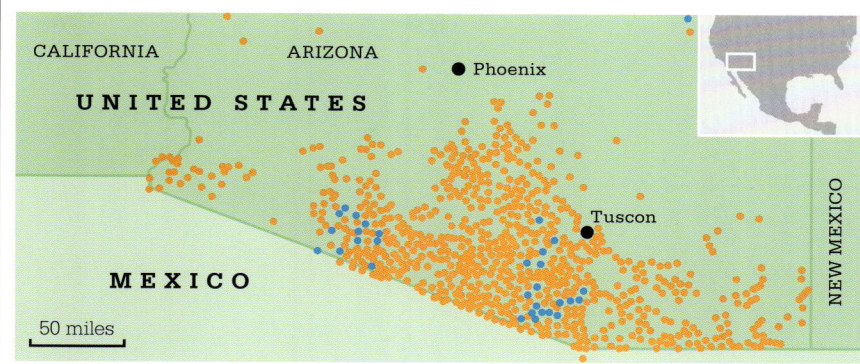

Key
- 🟠 Locations of migrant deaths
- 🔵 Water stations

After discovering her identity, De León reached out to her relatives in both Ecuador and New York. He found out that Maricela had grown up in severe poverty and was seeking a better life in the US but intended to return to Ecuador eventually, with savings to improve her family's living conditions. Fully aware of the risks, Maricela felt compelled to take her chances and make the journey, in the belief that she had no other option for finding a better future.

Maricela, like many others looking to cross, had to pay someone to guide her on her journey towards the border. Her story enforces the rhetoric that Prevention Through Deterrence has professionalized migration. The journey is now much more difficult and dangerous than before, so migrants seek help from other organizations; this gives those groups – including cartels – dangerous political power over already-marginalized migrants. These groups are »

An Israeli guard watches over the wall separating a West Bank village from Jerusalem. The fence is a major impediment to a two-state solution.

Power over life and death

In his 2003 essay "Necropolitics", Cameroonian historian Achille Mbembe explores several ways in which nation-states create and enforce sovereignty through the power to dictate who lives and who must die.

In one powerful example, Mbembe explores the plight of Palestinians and the colonial occupation of Gaza and the West Bank. He argues that the state of Israel employs necropower to establish and enforce its sovereignty. It accomplishes this by fragmenting Palestinian territory and land, and sealing off and expanding Israeli settlements. Its objective is to make the movement of Palestinians and goods impossible "and to implement separation along the model of the apartheid state".

Research has revealed cases throughout the world where governments have devised ways to enact maximum destruction upon certain groups and subject them to a status of living dead.

A teddy bear left behind by migrants planning to wade across the Rio Grande into Texas indicates that people of all ages attempt the cross-border journey.

The geographical location of these discarded artefacts is largely linked to specific stages in the migrants' journey. Early into their clandestine trip, travellers tend to discard only food wrappers and water bottles; as they get closer to the US border, they might drop their backpacks. This may in part be due to bags becoming unbearably heavy after days of walking in unforgiving desert conditions; another possible factor is that migrants need to be unencumbered and able to move swiftly to elude border patrol agents, or to be picked up by a truck for the final stretch. In order to blend in across the border, they will change into a clean outfit and discard the dusty clothes worn in the desert.

known not to follow through on their promises, as well as being guilty of other atrocities, such as physically harming and sexually assaulting their clients.

Archaeological methods

De León catalogues and examines the physical items that migrants discard in the desert to gain insights into their social conditions. He believes that these objects reveal significant details about migrant life.

For example, De León finds that black-painted plastic water bottles are commonly used along migration routes. Scientifically, this choice seems to make little sense, because black bottles absorb more heat from the sun, causing water – a precious resource during the crossing – to evaporate faster in extreme temperatures. However, through interviews with migrants, De León learned that black bottles are the preferred option because white or clear bottles reflect sunlight and make travellers more visible to US border patrol agents.

This discovery led De León to chart the progression of the desert-crossing water bottle – from a regular plastic container rudimentarily wrapped in a black bin liner or painted with shoe polish, to an industrially manufactured black-plastic bottle. This development points to an emerging industry that caters for the specific needs of the migrants.

A migration-related economy has also altered the commercial make-up of border towns, where enterprising individuals have set up stalls selling backpacks, camouflage clothing, hiking boots, and first-aid kits.

Compassionate perspective

The archaeological analysis of material objects leads to a deeper understanding of the social conditions that migrants endure. De León adds a further dimension to his work by shifting the narrative on migration from something statistical to something personal.

A typical immigration debate in the US – as in Europe – treats the issue as a political concern, relying heavily on economic and statistical evidence to bolster arguments. However, statistics alone cannot fully convey the brutal reality of the migrant experience. De León's ethnographic work draws on personal stories: by humanizing migrants, their various motives, and their experiences, he is able to obtain a deeper, more nuanced perspective.

> The dead … are the human grist for the sovereignty machine.
> **Jason De León**

De León believes that having an understanding of the various circumstances of undocumented migrants and the impact of border enforcement policies on human lives will change the tone of the debate on clandestine migration and result in different, more compassionate conclusions.

Other theories

The work carried out by De León complements and expands on traditional theories of borders as sites of control and resistance. For instance, philosopher Michel Foucault saw borders primarily as sites of control and surveillance, where state power regulates the flow of people and goods. This perspective emphasized the role of the government in constructing and enforcing borders to maintain order and sovereignty. The Prevention Through Deterrence policy – which De León suggests is "a strategy that largely relies on rugged and desolate terrain to impede the flow of peoples from the south" – is one such example.

Like Foucault, US anthropologist James C. Scott focused on borders as spaces of resistance where marginalized groups challenge government power through various forms of subversion and evasion. This approach highlights the agency of individuals and communities in negotiating and contesting the restrictions imposed by borders.

Looking at the issue through the prism of necroviolence, De León offers a new way of understanding the implications of these forms of surveillance and control. His work reinforces Scott's concepts by demonstrating how, despite the lack of agency afforded to them, migrants persist and adapt to overcome severe obstacles, such as the harsh conditions of the desert along the southern border of the US.

Pressing for change

The Land of Open Graves emphasizes how sociocultural conditions, environmental factors, and government policies have created a border that has unjustly and unnecessarily taken the lives of many migrants seeking refuge in the US. By focusing on the material and environmental dimensions of migration, De León's holistic research yields powerful insights into a profoundly complex issue. He sheds light on the brutal realities faced by migrants, challenges the detached, policy-driven discourse around border enforcement, and exposes the devastating cost of US border policies.

De León reframes the US–Mexico border as a site of state-sanctioned violence, where the environment is weaponized against the most vulnerable. He urges policymakers and the public to engage with the true consequences of border enforcement, and makes an undeniable case for the reconsideration of these policies. ∎

The Undocumented Migration Project

Directed by Jason De León since its inception in 2009, the Undocumented Migration Project (UMP) is a long-term anthropological programme that uses a combination of archaeological, ethnographic, forensic, and visual approaches to illustrate various aspects of clandestine migration.

Powerful exhibits and installations shared by and co-created with migrants – from photos of loved ones and items of clothing, to discarded water bottles and food wrappers – are intended to help visitors gain an empathetic understanding of the challenges that undocumented migrants face when crossing the dangerous US–Mexico border.

De León's project also aims to help families locate and reunite with loved ones who have gone missing while attempting to cross into the US. Examining the material culture of migrants makes an important contribution to a significant and powerful new type of holistic anthropology.

This quilt made from clothing left in the desert displays the names – or, if unknown, the word *desconocido/a* – of those who died crossing the border.

THE LONGER YOU CAN LOOK BACK, THE FARTHER YOU CAN LOOK FORWARD

A NEW SOCIAL ORDER

IN CONTEXT

KEY WORK
Robert L. Kelly, *The Fifth Beginning: What Six Million Years of Human History Can Tell Us about Our Future*, 2015

FIELD
Archaeology

BEFORE
1962 US archaeologist Lewis Binford helps to establish processual archaeology as the dominant approach in its field. He argues that the goal of archaeology should be to explain why changes happen.

2005 US environmental historian Jared Diamond uses archaeological data to explain why societies succeed or fail.

AFTER
2018 US archaeologist Andrew Roddick uses archaeology to explore the history of climate change, and shows how it can assist in understanding the present and future.

At its core, archaeology is the study of the human past through material remains. However, its broader purpose is often questioned. While its goals include reconstructing history and explaining change, US archaeologist Robert Kelly suggests that its ultimate reward is insight into the future. Humanity, he argues, is approaching a "Fifth Beginning", marked by the end of war and nation states, and the rise of new forms of cooperation.

Kelly draws on the concept of "punctuated equilibrium" from evolutionary biology, which describes how species evolve through long periods of stability

Early humans mastered fire during the First Beginning. Cooked food provided more nutrients and energy, which enabled humans to adapt to and thrive in challenging environments.

interrupted by short bursts of rapid change. He uses this framework to explain humanity's "beginnings": points in history when innovations – such as increased cooperation – and pressures – population growth, for example – converge to create transformative shifts. According to Kelly, we are on the brink of one such tipping point. In perhaps as few as 50 years, he predicts, changes will reshape society into something entirely unprecedented.

Four turning points
Kelly's First Beginning is the emergence of technology. It began more than 3 million years ago with the creation of stone tools, and later included the controlled use of fire. Early tools were simple but vital for survival, as they helped early humans to overcome biological limitations such as small teeth. These developments transformed them from tree-dwelling primates into bipedal, tool-using humans.

The Second Beginning, Kelly suggests, is marked by the emergence of culture, between 200,000 and 50,000 years ago. In this period, humans developed symbolic thinking, art, and sophisticated practices such as

See also: Revolutions in prehistory 74–75 ▪ Multilinear evolution 104–07 ▪ The New Archaeology 110–15 ▪ Post-processual archaeology 190–91

Human beginnings

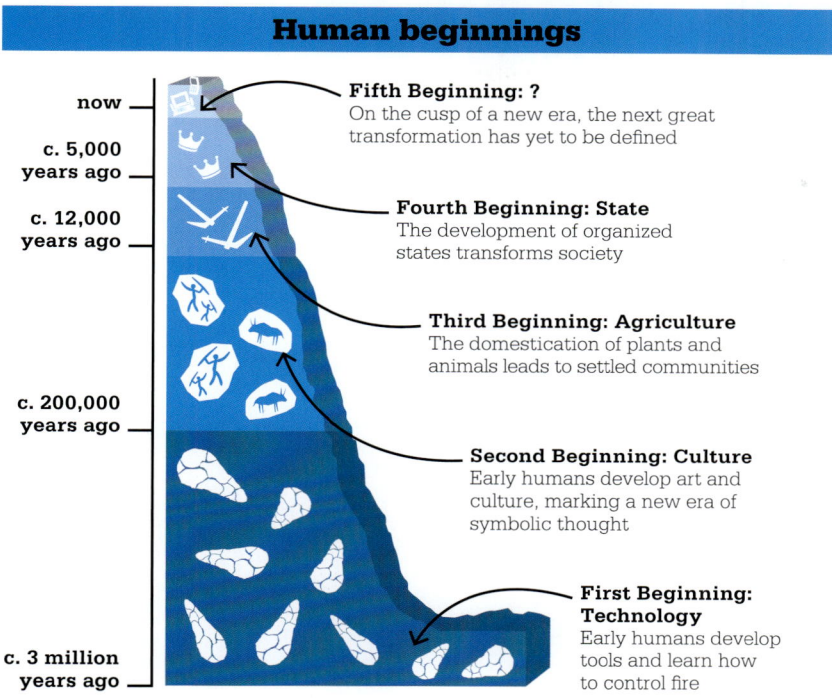

now

c. 5,000 years ago

c. 12,000 years ago

c. 200,000 years ago

c. 3 million years ago

Fifth Beginning: ?
On the cusp of a new era, the next great transformation has yet to be defined

Fourth Beginning: State
The development of organized states transforms society

Third Beginning: Agriculture
The domestication of plants and animals leads to settled communities

Second Beginning: Culture
Early humans develop art and culture, marking a new era of symbolic thought

First Beginning: Technology
Early humans develop tools and learn how to control fire

Robert Kelly

Born in 1955, US archaeologist Robert Kelly is best known for his studies of hunter-gatherer societies. Having earned his PhD from the University of Michigan in 1985, he joined the University of Wyoming in 1997, where he became professor of anthropology.

Kelly's research spans stone-tool technologies, the colonization of the Americas, and the effects of climate change past and present on human behaviour. He has conducted extensive archaeological fieldwork across North and South America, as well as in Micronesia, focusing on how humans have adapted to different environments over time, and how early societies laid the foundations for the development of complex civilizations. Kelly has also carried out fieldwork with modern-day foraging people in Madagascar.

Other key works

1995 *The Foraging Spectrum*
2001 *Prehistory of the Carson Desert and Stillwater Mountains, Nevada*
2007 *Mustang Shelter*
2011 *Doing Archaeology*

---

burying the dead. Kelly highlights the importance of symbolic thought as the foundation of culture, and argues that "supersymbolers" – individuals who used symbols in innovative ways – held a crucial advantage in their communities.

The Third Beginning – the advent of agriculture – started around 12,000 years ago. It was driven by population pressures from successful hunter-gatherer societies rather than a deliberate choice to farm. Environmental changes also favoured agriculture, and led to larger populations, the formation of villages, and social transformations.

The Fourth Beginning – the one that shaped our current era – featured the rapid rise of the state, defined by a hierarchical political structure with rulers, bureaucrats, and labourers. Kelly describes this as a time of "cities, swords, temples, roads, jewellery, chariots, money, and men and women in chains".

A new beginning?

Kelly envisions a Fifth Beginning that is hard to imagine. Unlike the earlier thresholds, which unfolded gradually after major tipping points, the Fifth Beginning will follow soon after the Fourth and occur within hundreds of years, not millennia. Kelly stresses that this change is inevitable, and urges humanity to embrace the challenge, concluding that "human evolution could be, should be, must be up to us".

The tipping point that brings about the Fifth Beginning may also lay the groundwork for a Sixth: if so, the Sixth Beginning may unfold in mere decades. Only archaeologists of the future – and time – will tell. ▪

THE BRIDGE BETWEEN THE LIVING AND THE DECEASED

HUMAN BURIALS

IN CONTEXT

KEY WORK
Mary L. Stiner, "Love and Death in the Stone Age", 2017

FIELD
Archaeology

BEFORE
1960 Welsh anthropologist Glyn Daniel publishes the first comprehensive survey and analysis of prehistoric chamber tombs in France.

2013 In South Africa, Lee Berger and John Hawks discover fossilized skeletons of a new human species – *Homo naledi* – that lived alongside early humans, and appear to have been intentionally buried.

AFTER
2023 Berger and Hawks publish *Cave of Bones* about their discoveries in the South African cave complex where *Homo naledi* was found. They claim that wall markings found in the caves are engravings.

People around the world have cultural practices, rituals, and beliefs surrounding death and burial. It is universal, and humans are the only living species that have sophisticated burial practices. However, it is not known when or why the practice of human burial began. To better answer this, anthropologist Mary Stiner explored skeletal remains and their burial contexts.

Connecting the living and the dead

Stiner's research indicates that immortality had long been a preoccupation among early humans. She determined that humans process death in two primary ways: mourning and commemoration. These behaviours extend beyond immediate grief, with people devising ways to maintain connections with the deceased, such as burying people where they can be visited.

Burial evidence from human species such as Neanderthals and *Homo sapiens* is at least 120,000

The study of early human burial sites can help archaeologists to reconstruct the rituals associated with death, as seen in this artwork.

years old. This suggests that burial may have been a practice of the last common ancestor of modern humans and Neanderthals. As Stiner states, it "implies that both Neanderthals and early anatomically modern humans had already begun to conceive of the individual as unique and irreplaceable". Stiner's research shows how burial and the treatment of the dead is an important element of humanity. ∎

See also: Origins of humanity 94–101 ▪ Burial rituals 183

A NEW BEHAVIOUR IN THE HUMAN REPERTOIRE
THE SIGNIFICANCE OF EARLY TRADE

IN CONTEXT

KEY WORK
Rick Potts, *Long-distance stone transport and pigment use in the earliest Middle Stone Age*, 2018

FIELD
Biological anthropology

BEFORE
1989 While conducting research in southern Kenya, palaeoanthropologist Rick Potts identifies evidence of an increase in environmental variation during ancient human evolution.

2012 Geoscientist Katherine Freeman identifies a series of rapid environmental changes that took place in East Africa roughly 2 million years ago that may be responsible for driving hominin evolution.

AFTER
2020 Rick Potts studies how changing ecological resources in southern Kenya affected hominin adaptations.

Palaeoanthropologists have long known that *Homo sapiens* had behaviours that distinguished them from earlier species. It has, however, been more difficult to determine exactly when different behavioural characteristics emerged. In 2018, a team of researchers led by Rick Potts identified evidence of complex behaviours that had been preserved in the fossil and archaeological record. They included evidence of long-distance trade, the use of colour pigments, and the ability to manufacture sophisticated tools. Significantly, this evidence dated to about 320,000 years ago, around the time that our species began to evolve, which dispels the idea that these behaviours emerged at a later stage of human evolution.

Environmental triggers

These behaviours emerged during a period of tremendous environmental variability and the researchers hypothesized that environmental change itself may have been a selective pressure in human evolution. It is possible that new challenges and opportunities created by climate change resulted in the development of new behaviours, and that the evolutionary advantage that they provided was retained over time. The complex relationship between ancient environmental change and behavioural innovation in early human evolution remains an area of active research. ∎

You can see layers and layers of changes … in this tremendously dynamic setting of Earth that we live on.
Rick Potts
Interview on the "Language of God" podcast, 2019

See also: Origins of humanity 94–101 ▪ Nutrition and human evolution 280 ▪ Early human wood technology 317

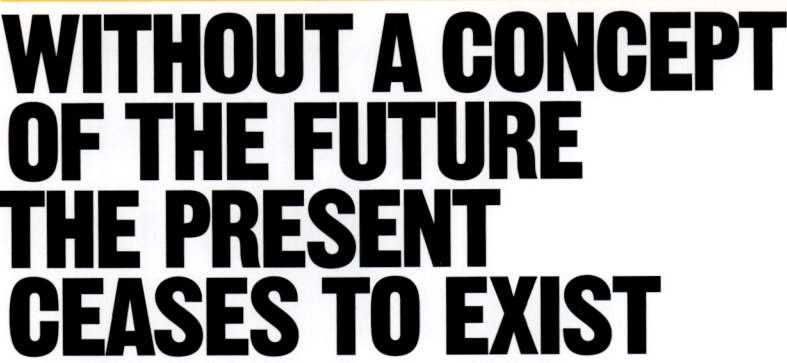

WITHOUT A CONCEPT OF THE FUTURE THE PRESENT CEASES TO EXIST

ANTHROPOLOGIES OF THE FUTURE

IN CONTEXT

KEY WORK
Rebecca Bryant and Daniel M. Knight, *The Anthropology of the Future*, 2019

FIELD
Sociocultural anthropology

BEFORE
1983 German anthropologist Johannes Fabian criticizes the way anthropologists separate their own "here and now" from the "there and then" of the societies they study, and treat those cultures as if they exist in a distant, static past.

2001 British anthropologist Alfred Gell publishes *The Anthropology of Time*, an overview of the most significant theories of time.

AFTER
2021 In *Vertiginous Life*, Daniel Knight examines how individuals navigate and perceive the future in the wake of the 2008 economic crisis.

Ethnologists usually avoid including "the future" in their ethnographies, even as they recognize its importance for understanding life in the present. In their efforts to better understand how people imagine and prepare for the future, cultural anthropologists Rebecca Bryant and Daniel Knight have developed a new approach that explores how overlapping feelings and ideas of time combine with future-orientated perspectives to shape contemporary lives.

In their 2019 book, *The Anthropology of the Future*, Bryant and Knight introduce their ideas by inviting readers to join them

Historically, as they say, the future has gotten short shrift in anthropology.
Rebecca Bryant and Daniel Knight

as they craft a manuscript. While they focus on that future-orientated process, the nearby hum of a washing machine signals that the time will soon come to transfer its contents to the dryer. Outside, bird calls mingle with the noises from a construction site. Bryant and Knight describe these ambient sounds as the things that "embed us in layered and entangled but separate temporalities", adding that they "engage us in temporal orientations of differing depth and urgency". In short, the act of their writing is surrounded by simultaneous processes that hint at the kind of future that might emerge.

Future orientations
The adage "To know where you're going, you need to know where you've been" points to the past as the base of self-knowledge. Bryant and Knight add that some notion of what the future holds is necessary to know the present. To resolve the impossibility of empirically studying a time that has not yet occurred, they propose a concept of "future orientations" to refer to the different ways people think about and engage with the future. Combining approaches from

See also: Thick description 146–53 ▪ Gender, sexuality, and power 158–59 ▪ Mental health and society 172–75 ▪ Structure and agency 196–99 ▪ The value of objects 206–07 ▪ The aftermath of violence 272–77

various academic fields with the feelings and behaviours expressed within each orientation provides anthropologists with the facility to include "the future" as a viable aspect of their research.

Forward perspectives

Drawing on their long-term fieldwork in Cyprus, Greece, and Türkiye, as well as historical and ethnographic cases from the UK and the US, Bryant and Knight outline six future orientations that represent people's emotions, attitudes, coping strategies, and explanations about imagined futures: Anticipation, Expectation, Speculation, Potentiality, Hope, and Destiny.

Future orientations may shift and overlap during fieldwork as people respond to events in the outside world, ranging from natural disasters and political events to provocative artworks or controversial films. They are also affected by the way people react to an immediate change in their circumstances that suggests the predicted outcome may differ from

The six future orientations represent ways in which people perceive and react to potential futures. They illustrate how future possibilities influence current behaviour and attitudes.

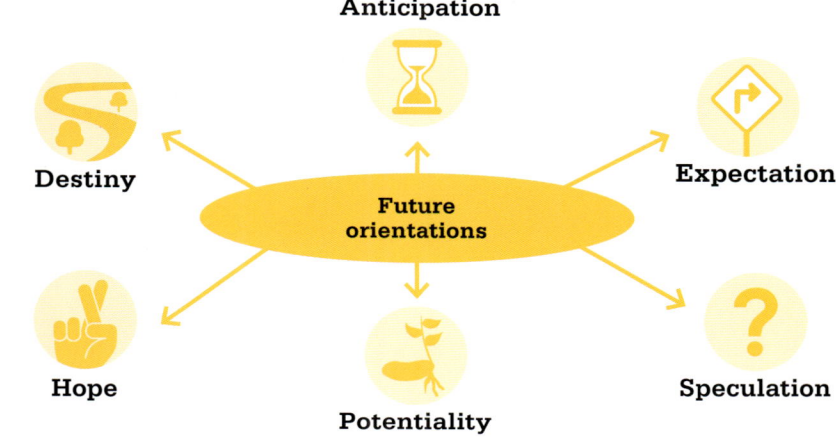

Anticipation

Destiny

Expectation

Future orientations

Hope

Potentiality

Speculation

what was expected. For these reasons, the study of the future in the "shifting present" involves integrating these influences with traditional face-to-face participant observation. Bryant and Knight's orientations present ethnographers with a compelling means to project their work into the future, broadening and deepening

understanding of daily life at particular moments of the present, whether it is war, a crisis, or a time of peace. By providing a gateway towards how people imagine and prepare for "elsetimes" – various possible and unknown futures – *The Anthropology of the Future* adds an important new dynamic to the study of the here and now. ■

Interdisciplinary approaches to time

Time is an inherently interdisciplinary subject – it can be examined through scientific, philosophical, and artistic lenses. Since ancient times, humans have attempted to measure, standardize, save, and even reverse it. Philosophers, artists, and anthropologists have explored its emotional and moral dimensions.

In order to study the future, Bryant and Knight have forged an approach that engages with

philosophers of time, as well as historians and sociologists. They draw on concepts including German philosopher Martin Heidegger's idea of "being-in-the-world", which emphasizes how humans exist within time and space, and US philosopher Theodore Schatzki's exploration of how time and space merge with emotions and actions.

Integrating these perspectives helps Bryant and Knight to explore how people's current thoughts and actions reveal their orientations toward the future.

Water clocks from ancient Egypt measured time by allowing water to drip through a hole in the bowl. Marks inside it served as hour indicators.

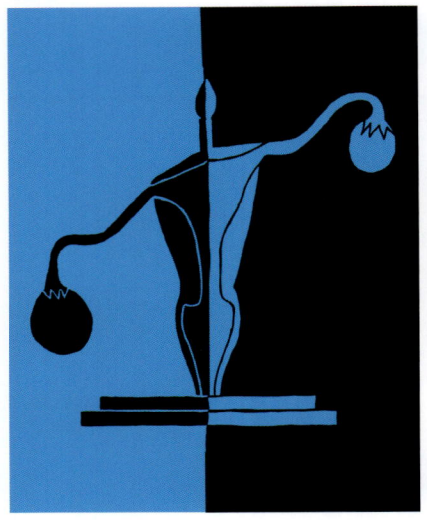

A BIRTH STORY THAT BEARS THE BURDEN OF RACISM
REPRODUCTIVE INEQUALITY

IN CONTEXT

KEY WORK
**Dána-Ain Davis,
Reproductive Injustice,
2019**

FIELD
Medical anthropology

BEFORE
1991 In "The Politics of
Reproduction", Faye Ginsburg
and Rayna Rapp investigate
how local and global politics
intersect with reproduction.

2013 Sociologists Zakiya Luna
and Kristin Luker explore the
relationship between social
movements and the
development of laws around
reproductive justice and rights.

AFTER
2023 Audrey Lyndon and
Dána-Ain Davis publish
"Emotional safety *is* patient
safety", looking at the ways
in which patient safety is
conceptualized and why it
is addressed separately from
patient experience.

While studying the care of premature infants at intensive care units in the US, anthropologist Dána-Ain Davis found that Black women – regardless of their economic status or class – were more likely to give birth prematurely than other women. To understand the causes of this disparity, Davis collected Black women's experiences of prenatal care and childbirth.

From this research, Davis asserts that ideas and practices rooted in racism affect how pregnant Black women are cared for in the US. She argues that ideas about biological race that circulated in medicine and in the sciences while slavery was prevalent in the US have worked their way into present-day perceptions of Black women in the context of reproduction, and that this affects their care. According to Davis, this "underscores the history of Black women's reproductive exploitation and reminds us that Black women have had to endure a medical structure that has historically not really viewed them as worth caring for".

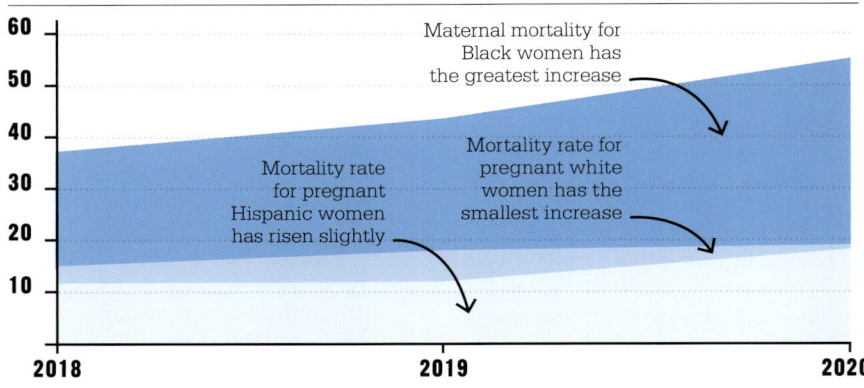

Maternal mortality data in the US shows that Black women are three times more likely to die than other women. Per 100,000 live births, 55.3 Black women died in 2020, compared with 19.1 white women and 18.2 Hispanic women.

See also: The role of African American Vernacular English 254–55 ▪ Critical ethnography 270–71 ▪ Challenging systemic oppression 294–95

Affecting policy

Davis's work on racism in obstetric care contributes to ongoing discussions about Black women's higher likelihood of maternal mortality. The phrase "obstetric racism", which Davis coined in 2018 to define the negative treatment of pregnant people based on their ethnicity, has migrated from the social sciences to the clinical domain. Medical practitioners have consulted with Davis to create a method to capture data about the types of obstetric racism that may be experienced in hospital settings. In this way, Davis's public-facing scholarship wields influence on policymakers, healthcare practitioners – including doctors, nurses, midwives, and doulas – in an effort to improve the experiences and outcomes for an array of pregnant people, and especially pregnant Black women.

Accessible ethnography

One of the most compelling ways Davis has found to make her scholarship accessible to broad

Systemic racism makes it difficult for Black women to **advocate** for their care.

There is little **research** on how to **support** pregnant Black women and mothers.

Racial prejudices lead to reproductive injustices

Fewer **Black doctors** can mean Black women are **misunderstood** or overlooked.

Racial stereotyping leads to a **distrust** of Black women's experiences and needs.

audiences is through compelling visuals. Working with scholar LeConté Dill and designer Cheyenne Varner, Davis has used a graphic format – known as graphic ethnography – to illuminate the burdens of racism during birth. In the resulting graphic *A Birth Story* Davis, Dill, and Varner explain some of the barriers to appropriate care faced by pregnant Black women. By contextualizing her work through stories and in relation to other Black feminist thinkers, Davis ensures that reproductive injustices continue to be an area of focus for medics, policy makers and anthropologists alike. ▪

The graphic novel *Bhimayana*, illustrated by Gond tribal artist Durgabi Vyam, explains experiences of social discrimination in India.

Graphic ethnography

With the boom in popularity of graphic novels during the early 2000s, graphic ethnography – the use of graphics to explain ethnographic studies – has increasingly become a popular medium for circulating anthropological knowledge beyond academic spaces. Taking inspiration from comics and political cartooning, graphic accounts of anthropological research have covered a wide range of topics – from creating an accessible guide to the Native American Graves Protection and Repatriation Act (NAGPRA), to interrogating sex work and tourism in Brazil, and exploring the politics of untouchability in India. Both as stand-alone accounts or by augmenting longer text analysis, these innovations in presenting the findings of studies have made anthropology and ethnography more accessible to a wider audience, bringing academic discourse to the public domain.

EVIDENCE TO IDENTIFY INDIVIDUALS
BIOMETRIC HAND ANATOMY

C hild sexual abuse is a problem that unfortunately vexes law enforcement in all parts of the world. Frequently, abusers share images of their crimes over the internet, which perpetuates the abuse and extends the victimization of survivors. In an attempt to address this problem, forensic anthropologist Sue Black and her team of researchers from Lancaster University and the University of Dundee, launched a multi-year citizen science research programme – H-Unique – with the goal of better understanding hand anatomy. The project arose from Black's ground-breaking research into the forensic identification of hand imagery. Her findings are used by law enforcement to help identify child sexual predators by analysing imagery that includes the hands of abuse suspects.

Defining features

The team recognizes the persistent problem of individuals sharing images of abuse. Although abusers avoid photographing their own faces to conceal their identities, their hands often appear in the images. For more than a decade Black and her team have been using their knowledge of hand anatomy to help identify and convict abusers. However, only a few specialists in the world possess the same level of knowledge of hand anatomy as Black, and her work is in high demand. In addition, her process can be time consuming.

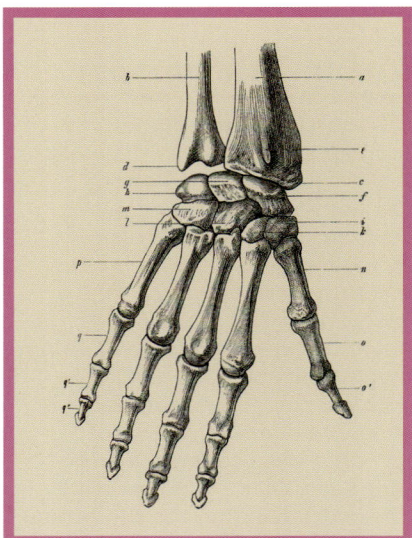

The basic skeletal structure of the human hand is shown in this illustration, but the variations in form and skin markings make each individual's hands unique.

See also: Bioarchaeology 167 ▪ Sequencing ancient DNA 290–91

Believe it or not, our height varies according to the time of day.
Sue Black

Researchers at Lancaster University launched H-Unique in 2020 to find a way to improve the process and accuracy of the photographic analysis of hand anatomy, and allow non-specialists to benefit from the research. The project's aim is to train computer software to automatically scan hand imagery and extract the data required. Unique identifying information that can be used includes both inherent and acquired variation such as vein patterns, freckle patterns, knuckle creases, as well as moles and scars. The project will speed up hand analysis and reduce the exposure of investigators to disturbing images of abuse.

To achieve this goal, the project launched a mobile phone application to enable volunteers to submit photographs of their hands. The researchers then use the data that they collect to train the software to identify how unique a hand is. Black has been able to achieve a high degree of accuracy using this technique, and claims that they can even distinguish between the hands of identical twins. The team suggests that hand anatomy analysis could possibly become more useful in identifying people than DNA.

Volunteers needed

H-Unique is an interdisciplinary project, supported by anatomists, anthropologists, geneticists, bioinformaticians, image analysts, and computer scientists. To achieve its goal, it also requires the participation of 5,000 "citizen scientists" to contribute images to create the world's first searchable database of the anatomy and variations of the human hand. Applied anthropology projects such as this one are important ways that researchers use the knowledge and methods of anthropologists to solve real world problems. ■

Forensic anthropology

Within biological anthropology is a field called forensic anthropology, which analyses human skeletal remains to help solve legal questions regarding the circumstances surrounding a person's death. The primary objective within forensic anthropology is to try to identify the decedent – the person who is deceased – in order to aid in criminal investigations and legal proceedings.

Forensic anthropologists are specialists in osteology (the study of human bones) who are trained to estimate key information about decedents. This typically includes an individual's age at death, skeletal sex, stature, and also possible ancestry. They also look for signs of trauma or disease, as well as unique features such as surgical implants or dental work. They frequently work closely with other specialists, including forensic scientists, forensic pathologists, and law enforcement agencies to provide additional insights into a person's death.

Forensic anthropologists are often responsible for recovering and examining human remains found in clandestine or mass graves.

H-Unique users upload **photos** of their **hands** via **mobile** app.

→

Researchers use **images** to train **AI** to look for and identify **distinguishing features**.

↓

AI can then be used to extract **identifying features** from images of **abuse**.

←

Investigators avoid being exposed to disturbing images.

LONELINESS IS EVERYBODY'S BUSINESS

THE LONELINESS EPIDEMIC

IN CONTEXT

KEY WORK
Chikako Ozawa-de Silva,
The Anatomy of Loneliness,
2021

FIELD
Medical anthropology

BEFORE
1897 Emile Durkheim – often
considered the founder of
modern sociology – publishes
Suicide: A Study in Sociology.

1979 Medical anthropologist
Nancy Scheper-Hughes
explores the link between
social isolation and an increase
in the number of young men
diagnosed with schizophrenia
in rural Ireland.

AFTER
2022 The Center for Countering
Digital Hate reports that TikTok
algorithms encourage young
people to view content on
topics such as eating disorders
and suicide, sometimes within
a few minutes of logging into
the app.

Loneliness refers to a sense of being separate from one's peers, family, and society at large, and severe and chronic loneliness can result in adverse health outcomes, including suicide. It is often assumed that the experience of being lonely is relatively new – for example, loneliness epidemics emerged in the US and Japan during the 1980s. However, people have experienced loneliness across generations, and

Exploring the theme of loneliness
and isolation, Edgar Degas depicts
a couple looking detached, empty,
and sad in his 1875–76 work *In a Café*
(*The Absinthe Drinker*).

practices involving social isolation and casting out individuals from communities are perhaps as old as time. Despite such practices, research has demonstrated that connection and a feeling of belonging have been essential to human evolution. In her 2021 book *The Anatomy of Loneliness,* Japanese anthropologist Chikako Ozawa-de Silva seeks a remedy to what she calls "lonely societies".

Reasons for loneliness
According to Ozawa-de Silva, the causes of loneliness are multilayered. Some people think a lonely person is depressed, and that a depressed person must be lonely, but the two conditions are distinct. Depression is when an individual feels sad, whereas loneliness is when someone feels disconnected. Loneliness can be caused by many factors, including cultural change, economic stress, conflict, and natural disasters.

In Japan, the government and media have framed loneliness and suicide as a problem experienced by young men – one caused by a stagnant economy and high rates of unemployment. Yet Ozawa-de Silva's research suggests that both

See also: The social roots of religion 42–43 ▪ Mental health and society 172–75 ▪ Adapting cultural traditions 193

Societal stressors, such as conflict at work or family problems, may result in an individual **feeling detached** from the world.

→

Lack of support from society can exacerbate **feelings of loneliness** or cause other poor health outcomes.

↓

Loneliness can be addressed by **helping** an individual find their vocation or **achieve a particular goal** in life.

←

It can be helpful to **acknowledge** that loneliness is a shared human experience and that it is **transient in nature**.

↓

It is important to express empathy, care, and compassion for anyone who feels lonely.

---

loneliness and suicide are a much broader problem in Japan, affecting people of all ages and genders. She points to how society itself can exacerbate feelings of loneliness. Many Japanese youth experience "hikikomori" – a withdrawal from society that can last for a short or long period of time. Individuals experiencing this condition live with family members, who provide indefinite care for them. Loneliness is not thought to be the predominant cause of hikikomori, although it can be a by-product.

Fixing "lonely societies"
Loneliness may be a global problem but it can be addressed. It should not be seen as an issue for individuals to tackle, but a public health matter. Some governments and scholars are actively working to help lonely people find a sense of belonging. In Zimbabwe, psychiatrist

Dixon Chibanda has designed the "Friendship Bench" programme to counter social isolation, and community members trained in counselling offer free support to people in need. This programme has also found its way to the US, with schools adding friendship benches for students seeking a connection and a listening ear. ■

Societies do not have to be lonely. People do not have to languish alone.
Chikako Ozawa-de Silva

Socialization and human evolution

The whole world experienced a degree of isolation during the COVID-19 pandemic as governments imposed various measures to contain the virus, but many people found it difficult to follow the restrictions. According to US archaeologist George M. Leader's 2020 article "Why social distancing feels so strange", people have always needed social cohesion and communication to evolve. The human ability to stand upright – known as bipedalism – allowed people to walk, which gave our ancestors the capacity to transport items to share and trade using their hands. Tool-making similarly required new social skills, such as collaboration and cooperation, because the knowledge necessary to make tools had to be shared and passed down from one generation to the next. Socialization is, therefore, crucial to our survival as a species – it has been baked into our genetic makeup for more than a million years.

At a mall in Singapore in 2020, people are separated by safe distancing markers, introduced to curb the spread of COVID-19.

MORE-THAN-HUMAN EFFECTS
POLITICAL VIOLENCE AND CONFLICT

IN CONTEXT

KEY WORK
Yael Navaro et al.,
Reverberations: Violence Across Time and Space,
2021

FIELD
Sociocultural anthropology

BEFORE
1990 US anthropologists Denise Lawrence and Setha Low publish "The Built Environment and Spatial Form", which gathers anthropological theories of space and place.

2010 A new anthropological field – environmental humanities – is conceived by Robert S. Emmett and David E. Nye in *The Environmental Humanities: A Critical Introduction*. The field takes an interdisciplinary approach to examine the relationship between humans and the environment across space and time.

Identifying violence as a crisis of our times, anthropologist Yael Navaro and her colleagues call for a holistic approach to studying its effect on post-war environments. They argue that analysing the relationship between people and non-human entities explains how violence persists.

Legacy of violence
Navaro and her colleagues suggest that violence can be understood through its aftermath. They discuss the effects of violence on non-human entities such as objects, land, and spirits, and note that problems arise with the separation of human life from the ecologies, geographies, and realms in which life is held. People are bonded to these non-human entities and the impact of violence on human life also impacts these entities, which retain the legacy of violence.

This idea is explored across Türkiye, Syria, Lebanon, and South Africa – sites where, the authors claim, violence is anchored in the landscapes, homes, and the

Violence ... permeates people's relations with supernatural beings, with their objects, houses, land, fields, and trees, their built environment, and infrastructures.
Yael Navaro

spiritual world. They note that violence creates enduring suffering – travelling from people to place and non-human entity – and is absorbed into the fabric of life.

By illuminating the pathways that violence takes, we build an understanding of the resonance of violence across space, time, and materials. Violence is not external to society and culture, but a pervasive presence within it. ∎

See also: Nationalist thought 212–13 ▪ The aftermath of violence 272–77

A CAPACITY TO CREATE A BUILT ENVIRONMENT
EARLY HUMAN WOOD TECHNOLOGY

IN CONTEXT

KEY WORK
L. Barham et al., "Evidence for the earliest structural use of wood at least 476,000 years ago", 2023

FIELD
Archaeology

BEFORE
2002 Archaeologists discover evidence of woodworking at Gesher Benot Ya'aqov, Israel. Some pieces of wood from 780,000 years ago show signs of hominin modification.

2020 A 300,000 year-old wooden throwing stick is found in Schöningen, Germany. It shows that Palaeolithic hominins in Northern Europe used wooden weapons.

2022 Scientists in Gantangqing, China discover 35 wooden tools including digging sticks and pointed implements that date from 250,000 to 361,000 years ago.

Wooden artefacts are difficult to find in the archaeological record because they require exceptional conditions for preservation. Freeze and thaw cycles, as well as contact with water, break down wood fibres. As a result, there is limited evidence of when and how early humans used wood.

In 2023, Lawrence Barham and a team of archaeologists at Kalambo Falls, Zambia, discovered two interlocking logs that appeared to be joined with an intentionally cut notch. Scientists dated the wood deposits to around 476,000 years ago, which predates *Homo sapiens*. Microscopic analysis revealed wear consistent with intentional shaping and use of the artefact, leading scientists to conclude that it was early evidence for the structural use of wood.

Notches in the logs excavated at Kalambo Falls in Zambia provide physical evidence of a deliberate intent by early humans in the Pleistocene epoch to create a wooden tool.

Complex behaviours
The find at Kalambo challenges assumptions that early humans primarily used stone tools and had only a limited ability to manipulate materials. It also suggests that species such as *Homo erectus* were capable of advanced planning, foresight, and collaboration, expanding ideas about behavioural complexity in human evolution. Barham's study underscores the adaptive advantages of wooden technology in prehistoric environments, and offers insights into early human lifestyles, tool use, and environmental interactions. ∎

See also: Symbolism in cave art 262–65 ▪ The significance of early trade 307

DIRECTO

RY

DIRECTORY

In addition to the great researchers, practitioners, and thinkers whose work is highlighted in the chapters of this book, many other men and women have made major contributions to the discipline of anthropology. Some are known for the insights that their fieldwork has provided into the culture, kinship, work, and belief systems of people around the world. Others have focused on the development of theory – and many anthropologists have contributed to both theory and practice. Although these people worked in a range of disciplines, all have helped to produce a body of knowledge that makes up our understanding of the evolution, culture, religion, and social relations of humanity.

MAGNUS HUNDT
1449–1519

In 1501, German scholar Magnus Hundt was the first person to use the term "anthropology" in his work *Antropologium de hominis dignitate*. Although his definition of the term was much broader than the current usage, Hundt's text focused on what it means to be human. *Antropologium* was lavishly illustrated with woodcuts, and Hundt used contemporary medical knowledge to describe human anatomy and physiology. It also covered philosophy and religion, arguing that humans represent a microcosm of the world as God created it.
See also: The theory of evolution 24–25

HEINRICH BARTH
1821–1865

German geographer, explorer, and linguist Heinrich Barth was one of the first Europeans to appreciate the importance of Indigenous peoples' oral traditions, many

of which he observed on his travels through north and central Africa. From 1850 to 1855 Barth travelled around the area that now forms Libya, Chad, Cameroon, and Mali, using the name Abd al-Karim Barth al-Inglisi to avoid attracting attention to his foreign identity. Barth's journals of these travels were published in 1857 as *Travels and Discoveries in North and Central Africa*, which described the histories, traditions, and languages of the different peoples he encountered.
See also: The structure of language 44–45

RYUZO TORII
1870–1953

Japanese archaeologist and anthropologist Ryuzo Torii focused on his home country, where he pioneered the use of sound recording in fieldwork and developed the "Torii style" of practice – his research was often followed by exhibits and lectures about his work. A firm believer that research had to take place in the field rather than solely in the

lab, Torii conducted extensive fieldwork among the Ainu people of the Kuril islands. His first expedition away from Japan was in northeast China, where he pioneered the use of photography to record his observations in 1895.
See also: The power of photography 292–93

KUNIO YANAGITA
1875–1962

Often called the father of Japanese folklorism, Kunio Yanagita's regular visits to rural communities in Japan sparked an interest in the lives, customs, and traditions of rural people. He became critical of historical narratives that focused primarily on rulers and high-ranking officials, arguing that the traditions of ordinary people were neglected. He established the study of Japanese folklore – known as "minzokugaku" – publishing *Tono Monogatari* in 1910, which recorded the traditions and legends of the small city of Tono. His last work,

Kaijo no Michi, published in 1961, was a study of the culture, history, and folk traditions of peoples from the Japanese Okinawa islands.

See also: Ritual and language 166

MAURICE LEENHARDT
1878–1954

Working with the Kanak people of New Caledonia from 1902 to 1926, French Christian missionary Maurice Leenhardt fought against the colonial abuses inflicted on Indigenous people during evangelization. His actions were an early example of liberation theology. He maintained that true Christianity should transcend, rather than abolish, the Kanak people's belief in totemism and myth. Leenhardt's close work with rural communities led him to an interest in ethnology, particularly a study of the Kanak people's myths. He maintained that – for the Kanak people – "place" was not a purely geographical concept but the result of their cultural, social, ecological, and cosmological realities.

See also: The universal nature of religion 28–29 ▪ The social roots of religion 42–43

JOSÉ CARLOS MARIÁTEGUI
1894–1930

Strongly influenced by the ideas of Italian Marxism, José Carlos Mariátegui was a Peruvian intellectual and activist. He analysed the evolution of the Peruvian economy, the nature of its capitalist class, and the role of Indigenous peoples within society. He asserted that Peru's workers and Indigenous peoples needed to forge a united front to fight colonialism, racism, and oppression – and create a society free from exploitation.

See also: Global capitalism 186–87 ▪ Development and colonial attitudes 226–29

HORTENSE POWDERMAKER
1896–1970

A pioneer in many respects, US anthropologist Hortense Powdermaker conducted research across continents – North America, Africa, and Oceania. She was the first Western woman to conduct anthropological fieldwork alone in Papua New Guinea in the 1920s. From 1932 to 1934, she conducted comprehensive ethnographic studies of a Black American community in rural Mississippi. She published her research in *After Freedom* in 1939, describing the dynamics of racial exclusion she had observed. Later, Powdermaker studied the Hollywood film community and researched the impact of Western films on gender relations in communities in Zambia.

See also: Fighting racial segregation 30–31 ▪ White privilege 214

JOMO KENYATTA
c.1897–1978

Kenyan activist Jomo Kenyatta's *Facing Mount Kenya: The Tribal Life of the Kikuyu*, published in 1938, was the first anthropological study to be published by an African person about his own people. The book challenged the Eurocentric view – that Africa required "civilizing" by European colonists. Instead, Kenyatta's work emphasized the order and self-sufficiency of Kikuyu society – the largest ethnic group in Kenya. A believer in the unity and solidarity of African peoples, Kenyatta led the campaign for Kenyan independence but was imprisoned by British colonial authorities in 1953. He was released in 1961 and became the first Prime Minister of Kenya in 1963, and the newly independent country's first President in 1964.

See also: White privilege 214 ▪ Development and colonial attitudes 226–29

LESLIE WHITE
1900–1975

In the 1930s, US anthropologist Leslie White conducted ground-breaking fieldwork among the Indigenous Pueblo peoples of the southwest US, revealing new insights into their culture. In *The Science of Culture*, published in 1949, he argued that the study of culture, which he named "culturology", was a science as important as physics and biology. He divided culture into three components – technical, sociological, and ideological. White is also known for developing the theory of cultural evolution – the theory that cultural traits change over time. This brought him into conflict with the supporters of Franz Boas, whose ideas were dominant in US anthropology at the time.

See also: Cultural relativism 34–41

MEYER FORTES
1906–1983

The main research interest of South African-born anthropologist Meyer Fortes was the kinship systems of the Indigenous peoples of West Africa. He was especially interested in the Tallensi people of northern Ghana, who had a strongly patrilineal descent system – each clan consisted of the descendants of a common male ancestor from eight to ten generations ago. He conducted fieldwork among Tallensi people from 1934 to 1938 and published his findings in *The Dynamics of Clanship among the Tallensi* in 1945 and *The Web of Kinship among the Tallensi* in 1949. These texts described the customs, beliefs, and religious values of the Tallensi people. His work set a benchmark for studies of African social organization. Fortes was also strongly opposed to apartheid in South Africa and claimed that it was the duty of anthropologists to investigate the "social qualities of human groups without regard for race privilege".
See also: Kinship and social order 68–69 ▪ Kinship ideologies 218–19

MAX GLUCKMAN
1911–1975

A political activist as well as a renowned social anthropologist, South African-born Max Gluckman conducted fieldwork among the Zulu people of Natal, South Africa, and the Lozi people of Barotseland, Zambia, studying their laws and political systems. One of his biggest contributions was to the understanding of the comparative laws and legal principles of different societies. In 1949, Gluckman became professor of social anthropology at the University of Manchester where he founded the Manchester School of Anthropology.
See also: Comparative ethnography 84–85

ÁNGEL PALERM
1917–80

Spanish-born anthropologist Ángel Palerm was forced to leave his native country for Mexico in 1939 following the defeat of the Republican forces he had fought with in the Spanish Civil War (1936–39). Influenced by these experiences, his primary anthropological interests became the causes of Spain's decline and the impact of the nation's colonialism on the Indigenous peoples of North America. Under the guidance of US anthropologist Isabel Kelly, Palerm carried out comprehensive ethnographic studies of Mexico's Totonac people and he was particularly interested in the pre- and post-Hispanic development of agricultural irrigation.
See also: The Indigenismo movement 56–57 ▪ Development and colonial attitudes 226–29

ERVING GOFFMAN
1922–1982

Canadian-American sociologist and anthropologist Erving Goffman was fascinated by social organization and human interactions. In his 1956 book *The Presentation of Self in Everyday Life*, Goffman proposed the theory of self-presentation – that people adopt a performative or dramatic approach to how they present themselves in social situations – and discussed methods of deference and demeanour in human behaviour. He also wrote about the relationship between ideas of stigma and people living in residential institutions in *Asylums*, published in 1961.
See also: Accents, dialects, and code-switching 244–45

JOHN J. GUMPERZ
1922–2013

A central figure in linguistic anthropology, German-born John J. Gumperz researched the correlation between language and social groups. He studied the Swabian dialect spoken by a community of farmers in Michigan, and revealed that it had evolved from the convergence of two different dialects spoken by two groups of immigrants. Conducting fieldwork in North America, Europe, and Asia, Gumperz argued that linguistic diversity correlates with social stratification: societies that are highly divided into different classes – such as the caste-system in India – have a great diversity of communication styles. In more egalitarian societies, however, this diversity of language is limited. Gumperz also developed theories around the concepts of code-switching and contextualization cues in communication.
See also: Accents, dialects, and code-switching 244–45

CHEIKH ANTA DIOP
1923–1986

Senegalese historian and anthropologist Cheikh Anta Diop

is known for his theory that the Ancient Egyptian civilization, which had long been revered by Western academics, was actually created by Black African people. Although some academics criticized his work, it became central to the development of Afrocentricity – a theory that focuses on the African diaspora. Diop's *Negro Nations and Culture*, published in 1954, and *The African Origin of Civilization*, published in 1974, used archaeological and anthropological evidence to support his view that European historians had understated the extent of Black civilizations. He argued for a shift in attitudes about the place of African people in history.
See also: Origins of humanity 94–101 ▪ Development and colonial attitudes 226–29

DAVID BROKENSHA
1923–2017

The Indigenous Mbeere of eastern Kenya possess an extensive knowledge of their local flora. An understanding of this dynamic relationship formed an important part of South African anthropologist David Brokensha's 18-year research project into social and ecological change in the Siakago area of Kenya. With his partner Bernard Riley, Brokensha created a database of the area's woody plants and charted changes in the incidence of these plants and their use by the Mbeere. The findings of this research were published in 1988 in *The Mbeere in Kenya*, an important work of ecological anthropology.
See also: Medicine and healing practices 168–69 ▪ The anthropology of food 200–05

CHIE NAKANE
1926–2021

Japanese anthropologist Chie Nakane conducted extensive fieldwork in India, China, and Japan focused on comparisons between the social structures of these countries. She is best known for *Japanese Society*, published in 1970, a cross-cultural study of the "vertical principle" – the idea that a society has a vertical hierarchy – in Japanese society and the social relations between individuals, according to their position. An individual's status depends on whether they are "senpai" – a person in a group who has greater experience, wisdom, or age – or "kohai" – a more junior or less experienced person. Nakane claimed that in the vertical principle, senpai offer assistance and advice to kohai, and in return, the social transaction requires that the kohai demonstrate gratitude, respect, or personal loyalty to the senpai.
See also: Caste systems 122–23

ROBERT CARNEIRO
1927–2020

Researching the subsistence economies of the Kuikuro people of Mato Grosso, Brazil, and the Amahuaca people of submontane Peru caused US anthropologist Robert Carneiro to consider how communities come together and eventually form small states. He theorized that environmental or social constraints lead to overpopulation and exerts pressure on a village to expand through conflict at the expense of its neighbours. He posited that

successively larger multi-village units were formed until one of sufficient size and complexity could be described as a state. Carneiro's ideas are articulated in *A Theory of the Origin of the State*, published in 1970.
See also: Origins of culture 32–33 ▪ Stages of social organization 160–61 ▪ The significance of early trade 307

OKOT P'BITEK
1931–1982

A Ugandan social anthropologist and poet, Okot p'Bitek studied the traditions and culture of his own people, the Acholi, and the Lango people of northern Uganda. In the epic poem *Song of Lawino*, published in 1966, he explored the cultural conflict between a rural woman, Lawino, who holds traditional values, and her husband, who has Western beliefs. Another poem from 1970, *Song of Otol*, gives the husband's response, defending Western culture. In 1971, p'Bitek published *African Religions in Western Scholarship*, which asserted that scholarship often focused on Western concerns, and, in 1975, he produced a collection of anthropological essays titled *Africa's Cultural Revolution*. Later, in 1978 he published a compilation of Acholi folktales in *Hare and Hornbill*.
See also: Autoethnography 76–77 ▪ Anthropology at home 170–71

JANE H. HILL
1939–2018

US linguistic anthropologist Jane H. Hill researched the evolution of language between 1972 and

1978. Citing evidence gleaned from teaching sign language to chimpanzees, she argued that language evolved continuously from human's hominid ancestors. Later, she focused her research on the impact of political and economic processes on language structure. In 1986, she and her husband Kenneth Hill published *Speaking Mexicano*, which analysed the way Spanish colonialism fundamentally modified the Nahuatl language spoken by Indigenous people in the Malinche area of what is now Mexico. They explained how the modern version of the language is a syncretic language – a language where a single word can have more than one grammatical function– and incorporates material from Spanish. Later, in the 2008 work *The Everyday Language of White Racism*, Hill revealed how historical racism persists in the everyday language spoken and written by white Americans.
See also: Language and cognition 88–89 ▪ Structuralism 108–09

MARILYN STRATHERN
1941–

British anthropologist Marilyn Strathern studied culture in Papua New Guinea. She examined topics ranging from gender relations to laws and women's scholarship in Indigenous societies. Her doctoral thesis, which was published in 1971 as *Women in Between*, examined the role of women and issues of marriage, divorce, and settlement disputes in the male-dominated Mount Hagen society. Strathern also wrote extensively about reproductive technology

in the UK. In the 1992 title *After Nature: English Kinship in the Late 20th Century*, she argues that the introduction of in vitro fertilization has transformed the natural order, including relationships between the sexes.
See also: Gender, sexuality, and power 158–59

ADAM KUPER
1941–

In 2009, South African-British anthropologist Adam Kuper published *Incest and Influence*, which examined the tendency for the British bourgeois – the wealthy middle-class – to marry first cousins and other close relatives. Citing examples such as businessman Josiah Wedgwood and members of the intellectual Bloomsbury Group, he argued that this behaviour created networks of influence, which consolidated their social position. Kuper also criticized cultural determinism – the theory that human behaviour is shaped by culture. His 1999 book *Culture: the Anthropologists' Account* argued that economic and political forces, biological processes, and social institutions are also important factors determining how people think and behave.
See also: Kinship and social order 68–69

ALFRED GELL
1945–1997

British academic Alfred Gell set out to produce an anthropological theory of visual art, considering the connections between the art itself and the social relations involved in producing, circulating, and receiving

it. He argued that artworks should not be viewed as passive decoration but as the equivalent of individual persons, capable of influencing thoughts and actions. His work was posthumously published in *Art and Agency* in 1998.
See also: The value of objects 206–07

PAUL RICHARDS
1945–

With an interest in citizen science, British-born anthropologist Paul Richards, documented approaches to the Ebola virus in Sierra Leone. He observed that when the virus hit in 2013, the nation's heath systems were ill-prepared to cope, but as patterns of infection became clear to communities, they responded with common sense measures borne of social knowledge. He cited many examples of citizen science rapidly guiding people's behaviour, including the use of bin bags as protective clothing in the absence of Personal Protective Equipment (PPE) and the suspension of traditional burial practices to minimize infections. In his findings, Richards argued that some international aid should be directed towards community education rather than solely to hi-tech health systems.
See also: Medicine and healing practices 168–69 ▪ Development and colonial attitudes 226–29

MICHEL-ROLPH TROUILLOT
1949–2012

Working as a social anthropologist in the US, Haitian-born Michel-Rolph Trouillot focused much of

his research on the Caribbean. His book *Haiti, State Against Nation* was published in 1986, shortly after the fall of the autocratic Duvalier regime that had ruled Haiti from 1957 to 1986. He analysed the regime's origins, how it maintained its brutal stranglehold, and its legacy. In 1988, after studying a banana-producing community in Dominica, Trouillot published *Peasants and Capital*, in which he argued that multinational capitalism prospers from the excess production of Caribbean "peasant" workers – contrary to the idea that peasantry is a relic of pre-industrialization.
See also: Global capitalism 186–87

MICHAEL LAMBEK
1950–

Conducting ethnographic fieldwork on the islands of the western Indian Ocean, Canadian anthropologist Michael Lambek produced new insights into the region's peoples. Studying the seminomadic Sakalava people of western Madagascar, Lambek examined the complex ways in which the island's history shaped the people's daily lives, religion, ritual, and historical consciousness. In another study, recounted in his 2018 work *Islands in the Stream*, Lambok charted the long-term changes in the lives of villagers on the island of Mayotte. Looking at the period between 1975 and 2015, he observed the communities evolve from subsistence farming to industrial benefits such as widespread access to transport, electricity, and running water.
See also: Culture shapes behaviour 62–67

VOLKER SOMMER
1954–

German evolutionary anthropologist Volker Sommer studied primate social and sexual behaviour, rituals, and cognition. His fieldwork has ranged from the study of langurs in India and gibbons in Thailand to chimpanzees in Africa. He observed that cohorts within some species of monkeys and apes have different diets and tool uses, which causes them to develop "us and them" attitudes, leading to violent conflict. In 1999, he founded the Gashaka Primate Project in Nigeria, dedicated to the research of monkeys and chimpanzees. His 2006 work *Homosexual Behaviour in Animals* explored the evolution and role of same-sex sexual interactions between animals.
See also: Chimpanzee behaviours 132–35

JAMES FERGUSON
1959–2025

US academic James Ferguson specialized in the anthropology of international development, particularly as it has affected countries in southern Africa. Much of his work was concerned with how development and modernity impacted the lives of ordinary people. In *The Anti-Politics Machine* published in 1990, he criticized the policies of development agencies in the region, arguing that they had failed to produce any kind of economic stability, depoliticized resource allocation, strengthened bureaucratic power, and perpetuated migrant labour

systems. In the 2015 title *Give a Man a Fish*, he contrasted the rise of social welfare schemes in South Africa – systems that made direct cash payments to large numbers of low-income people – with traditional development programmes such as skill building. He made the case that capitalism and the relationship between production and distribution should be re-examined.
See also: Global capitalism 186–87 ▪ Development and colonial attitudes 226–29

ALPA SHAH
1976–

Concentrating her work on South Asian societies, British social anthropologist Alpa Shah has researched the impact of economic growth on the working poor and migrant labourers in India. She also conducted fieldwork among the revolutionary Naxalite guerillas in their forest encampments in Jharkhand, India, living among them for more than four years. Her observations of their lives and her experiences of learning their language and trekking with them to avoid state security forces were described in *Nightmarch*, published in 2018. In *Ground Down by Growth*, published in the same year, she argued that capitalist economic growth entrenched, rather than erased, social differences in India, leaving members of the Dalit caste and Indigenous peoples, known as Adivasis, at the bottom of social and economic hierarchies.
See also: Caste systems 122–23 ▪ Global capitalism 186–87

GLOSSARY

Acculturation The process that occurs when a culture adopts traditions from another culture.

Autoethnography An ethnographic study that is written by a member of the culture that is being studied.

Biological anthropology The study of non-cultural, or physical, attributes of humans, such as genetic inheritance, biological evolution, or environmental adaptations.

Capitalism An economic system based on the private ownership of property and the means of production, in which firms compete to sell goods at a profit and workers labour for a wage.

Colonialism A phenomenon whereby one country exerts control over another, often exploiting it economically. The term commonly refers to the conquest, settlement, and exploitation of parts of the world by European powers.

Communism An economic system based on collective ownership of property and the means of production.

Construct, social A concept or perception created in society.

Cosmology A people's beliefs and assumptions regarding the world, including how the entities and forces control it, how the Universe is organized, and the place of humans within the world.

Cultural relativism Interpreting the values and behaviours of a culture without making judgments under the bias of one's own culture.

Culture The, customs, knowledge, beliefs, values, and norms that combine to make up the way of life of any society.

Diffusion The adoption by one society of a cultural trait belonging to another as a result of contact between the two.

Discourse In general use, communication in speech or writing; in anthropology, a framework or system of ideas that provides a perspective on life and governs the way in which it can be discussed. Discourse imparts a meaning to events, and varies in different eras, geographical areas, and within social groups.

Ethnicity The shared culture of a social group (such as language or religious belief) that gives its members a common identity and differentiates it from others.

Ethnocentrism The belief that one culture is superior to others.

Ethnography The study of peoples and cultures.

Ethnology The comparative study of the differences between peoples and cultures.

Feminism A social movement that advocates the social, political, and economic equality of the sexes.

Feminism is recognized as having had several "waves", or eras, each with a different agenda of issues.

Functionalism The idea that society is structured like a biological organism, with specialized functions. Every aspect of this society is interdependent and contributes to the overall functioning and stability.

Gender The socially constructed, rather than biological, identity of a person based on norms related to sex. The way that individuals are seen, by themselves and others, in terms of their gender roles and biological sex is described as their gender identity.

Gender role The social behaviours expected of a person based on their gender identity.

Identity The ways that individuals see and define themselves, and how other people define them.

Indigenous A group of people who are native to an area.

Kinship The relationship between individuals within a family system.

Lineage The path of descent that links descendants with a common ancestor.

Linguistic anthropology The study of the function and structure of languages.

Marxism A structural theory of society developed by Karl Marx and

Friedrich Engels, which claims that history consists of epochs and that social change arises out of conflict between social classes – the owners of the means of production and the exploited working masses.

Material culture The history and philosophy of objects; relationships between people and things.

Matriarchy A society controlled by women and mother figures.

Modernity The condition of society from the 17th century onwards, especially the social change created by the Industrial Revolution and urbanization.

Nation A body of people united by culture, history, or language, and usually sharing a particular geographical area.

Nationalism A shared sense of identification that is attached to a nation and stems from a commitment to a common ideology and culture.

Norms Social rules that define what is expected behaviour ("normal") for an individual in a particular society or situation.

Nuclear family A two-generation household of parents and children – a prime agent of socialization.

Participant observation A research technique in which the anthropologist or ethnographer actively participates in the society that they are studying in order to learn more about it, and gain an "insider" perspective.

Patriarchy A society controlled by men or father figures.

Proletariat In Marxist theory (see Marxism), the social class of people who labour for a wage.

Race The social construct of difference between groups of people based on their physical appearance, especially skin tone. Race has been shown to have no biological basis.

Racism A form of prejudice based on negative assumptions about a person that are usually based on physical characteristics, or race.

Rites of passage Formative events that occur at transition points in life.

Roles The patterns of behaviour that are expected from individuals in society. See also *gender role*.

Social class A status hierarchy within the social system, reflecting power, wealth, education, and prestige. Although classes vary by society, Western models generally recognize three broad groups. The upper class is a small social group that has the highest status and owns a disproportionate amount of society's wealth. The term middle class refers to well-educated people who do nonmanual work, often in offices. Working class refers to people with manual jobs, such as factory or agricultural work.

Social mobility The movement of people or categories of people, such as families, from one social class to another.

Social networks The links between individuals, families, and groups with similar interests.

Social structure The social institutions and relationships that form the framework of a society.

Socialism A political doctrine that aims to establish social and economic equality. Socialists argue that if the economy were under the control of the majority of the population, a more equitable social structure would be created.

State An organized authority that has legitimate control over a territory, and a monopoly of the use of force within its territory.

Status The amount of prestige or importance a person has in the eyes of other members of society.

Stereotype A widely held but overly simplified image of a person or social group.

Structuralism The idea that we must understand things – such as a text, human minds, or society – by examining the elements, or pattern of relationships, in its structure.

Subculture A group that is seen as a distinct and separate one within the larger society because while its members may agree with most of a society's values, beliefs, and customs, they differ in others.

Symbolic interactionism The theory that the self is an entity that arises through social interactions.

Values Ideas or beliefs about the worth of a thing, process, or behaviour. A person's values govern the way they behave; a society's values dictate what is important or not important, and what is acceptable or unacceptable.

INDEX

QUOTE ATTRIBUTIONS

ACKNOWLEDGMENTS

Dorling Kindersley would like to thank: Arshti Narang for design assistance; Manpreet Kaur for picture research assistance; Nityanand Kumar, Manish Upreti, and Raman Panwar for technical assistance; Ann Baggaley for proofreading; and Helen Peters for indexing.

PICTURE CREDITS